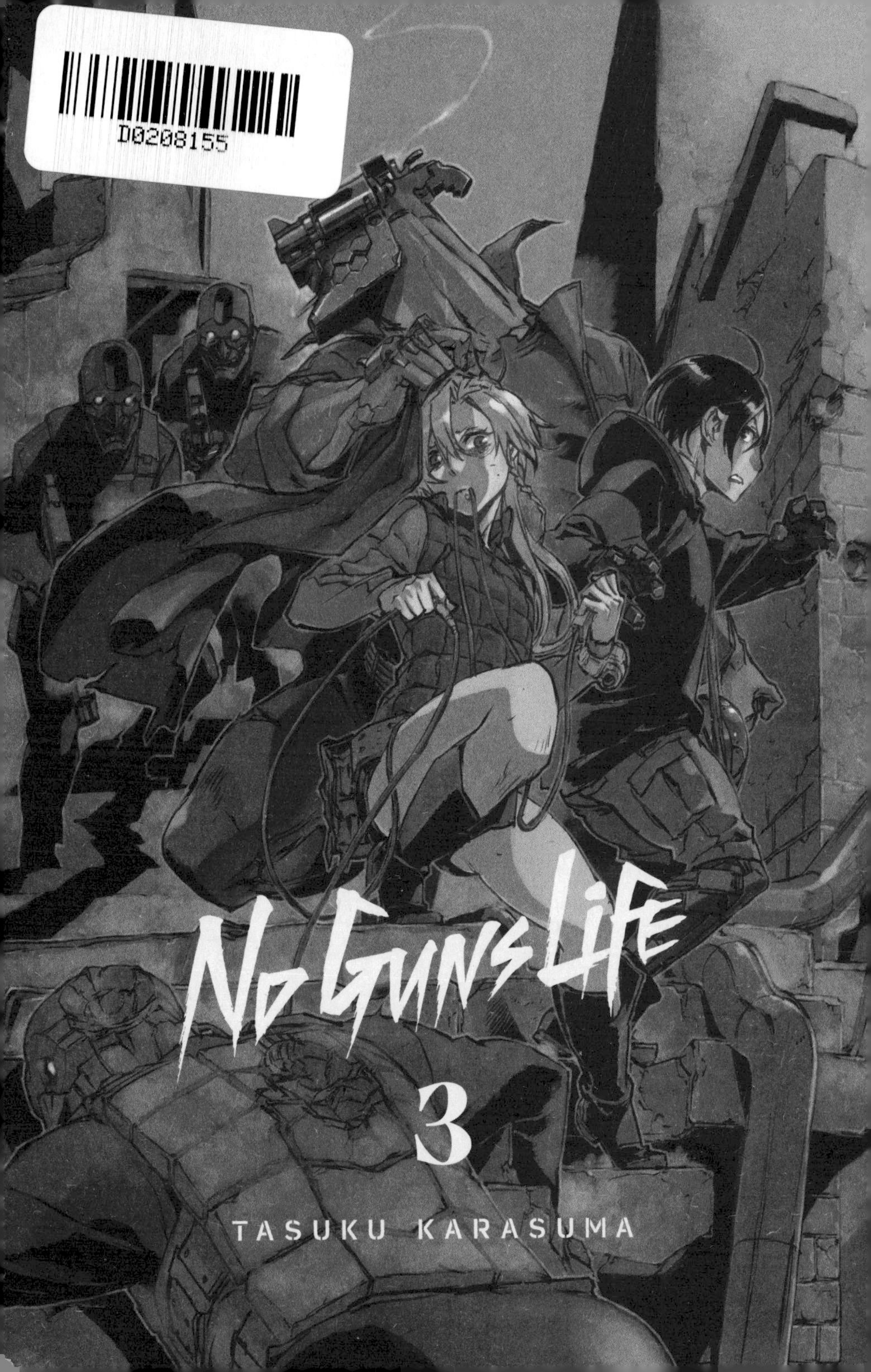
No Guns Life
3
TASUKU KARASUMA

CONTENTS

NO GUNS LIFE

NO GUNS LIFE

The gunsmoke drifts, the muzzle talks

CHARACTERS

JUZO INUI

A veteran of the war who became an over-Extended. His full-body cyborg design is known as a Gun Slave Unit. He makes a living as a Resolver settling issues between Extended and non-Extended.

BERÜHREN CORP.

A giant corporation that basically controls the city. It grew rapidly by developing Extension technology.

EXTENDED MANAGEMENT SQUAD (EMS)

The unit within the Reconstruction Agency that specializes in Extended-related cases.

RECONSTRUCTION AGENC

The government agency for post-war reconstruction.

SPITZBERGEN

An anti-Extension-technology terrorist organization.

TETSURO

A boy with no memory of his past. Implanted with the Harmony device, he can remotely control other Extended.

MARY

An Extension engineer who does black market maintenance work. She's known Juzo for a long time.

OLIVIA

Director of the EMS.

KRONEN

An EMS squad leader. He reports to Olivia and hates Extended.

GONDRY

An Extended suspected in a series of mass murders ten years ago. He wants to kill Mega Armed Sai.

MEGA ARMED SAI TOKISADA

The first ever full-body Extended. During the war he was part of Tindalos, a military unit that Gondry also belonged to.

RELATIONSHIP MAP

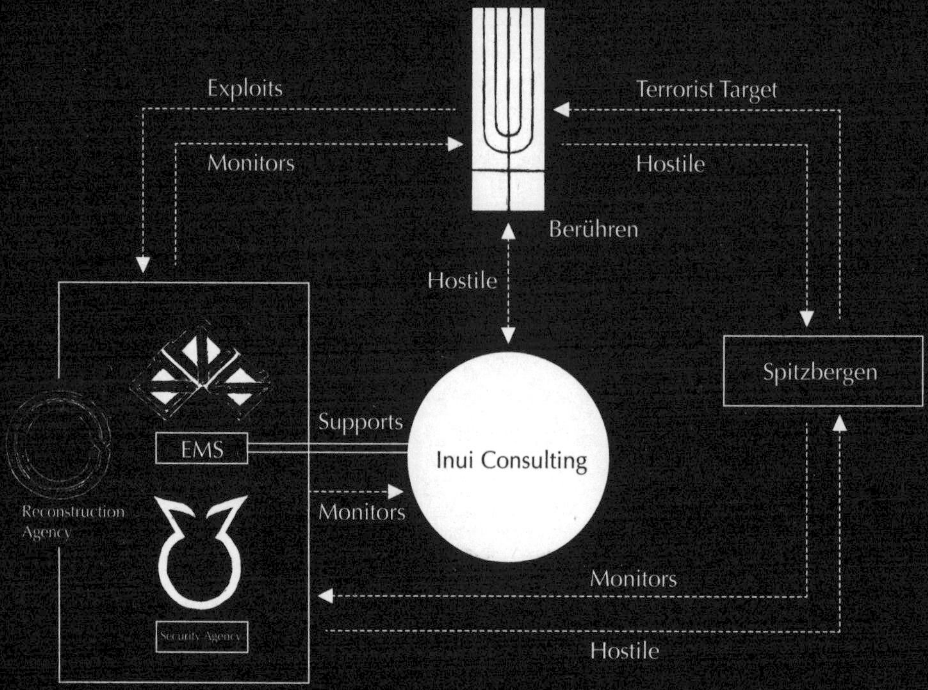

Exploits
Terrorist Target
Monitors
Hostile
Berühren
Hostile
Spitzbergen
Supports
EMS
Inui Consulting
Reconstruction Agency
Monitors
Monitors
Security Agency
Hostile

STORY DIGEST

Juzo Inui is a Resolver who solves problems between the Extended and non-Extended. One day he helps a boy named Testsuro, who turns out to have escaped from the Berühren Corporation, which basically controls the entire city. Juzo refuses to return the boy, putting him in conflict with the company that's bought off most of the city's many corrupt government officials.

Tetsuro was part of a human testing program where he was implanted with an experimental extension called **Harmony**, which allows its user to remotely control other Extended. Berühren sends their top agents after Tetsuro in order to recover the device.

After firing the gun on his head, Juzo is arrested by the Reconstruction Agency, the agency that regulates the Extended. He's released under the condition that he capture a noncompliant Extended named Gondry, who is suspected of committing the Nightmare of Norsescot—a mass murder which took place ten years ago. Gondry comes out of hiding to attack the war hero, and first ever full-body Extended, Mega Armed Sai. Juzo manages to capture Gondry, but another threat remains at large.

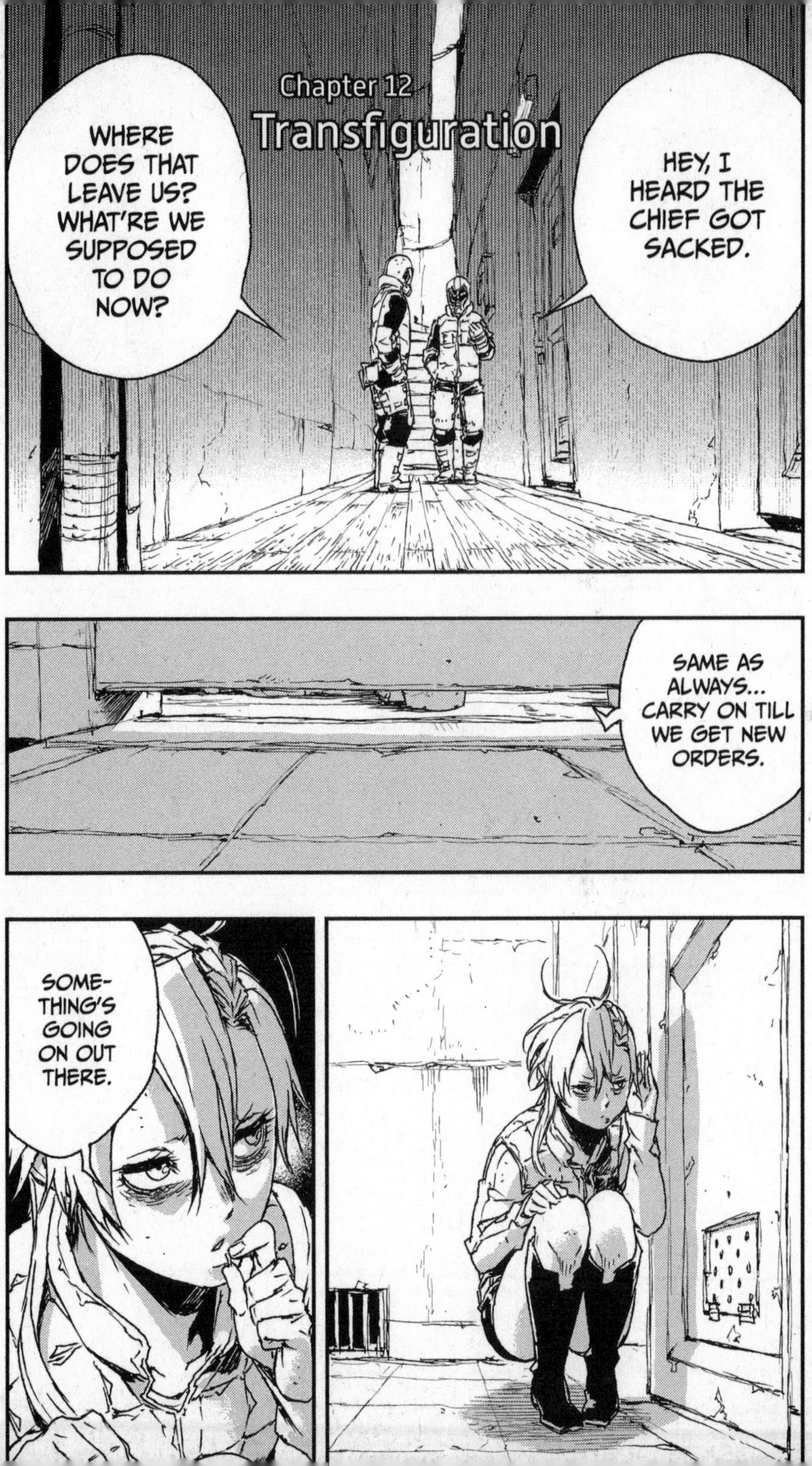
Chapter 12
Transfiguration
HEY, I HEARD THE CHIEF GOT SACKED.
WHERE DOES THAT LEAVE US? WHAT'RE WE SUPPOSED TO DO NOW?
SAME AS ALWAYS... CARRY ON TILL WE GET NEW ORDERS.
SOME-THING'S GOING ON OUT THERE.

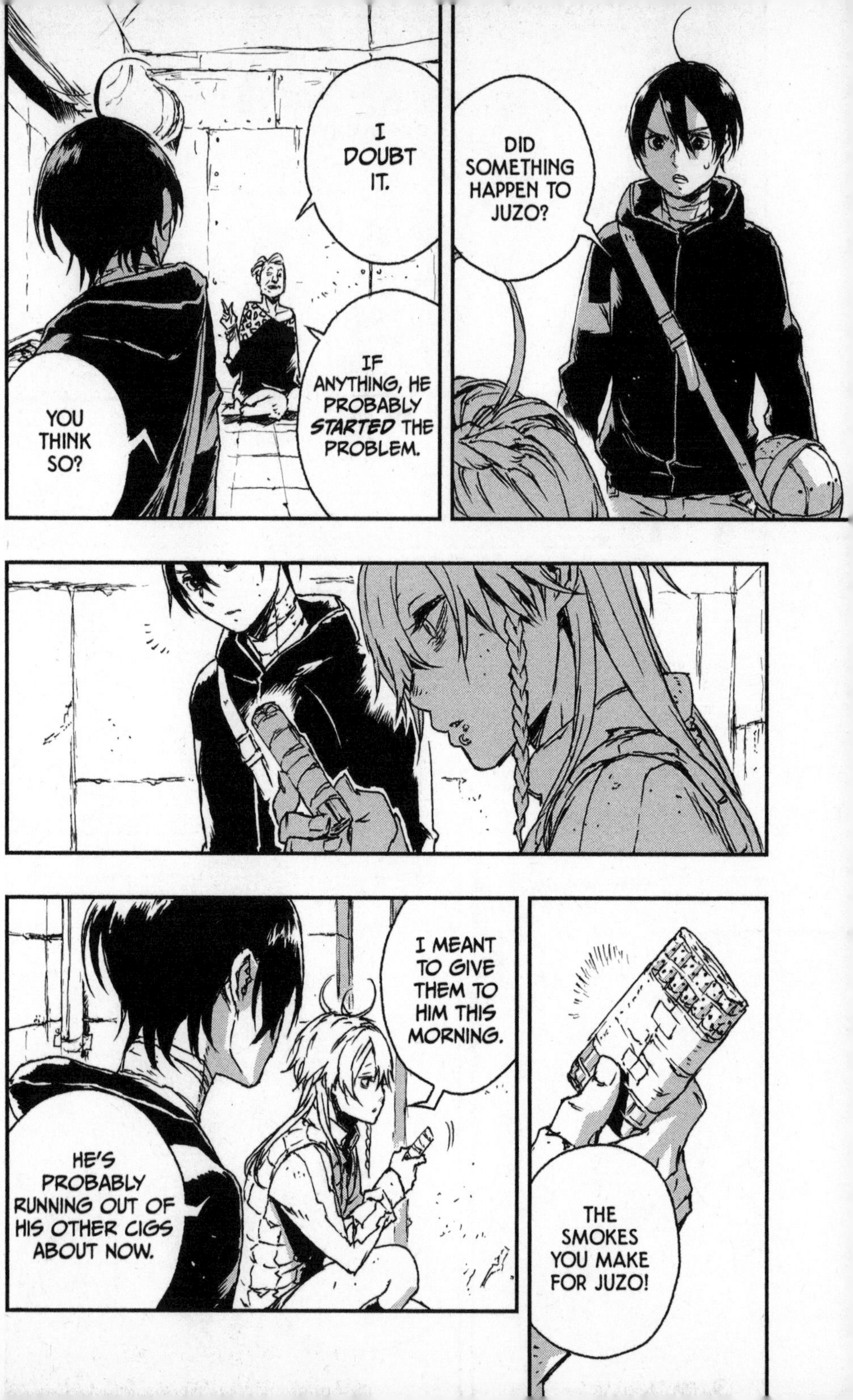
DID SOMETHING HAPPEN TO JUZO?
I DOUBT IT.
IF ANYTHING, HE PROBABLY *STARTED* THE PROBLEM.
YOU THINK SO?
THE SMOKES YOU MAKE FOR JUZO!
I MEANT TO GIVE THEM TO HIM THIS MORNING.
HE'S PROBABLY RUNNING OUT OF HIS OTHER CIGS ABOUT NOW.

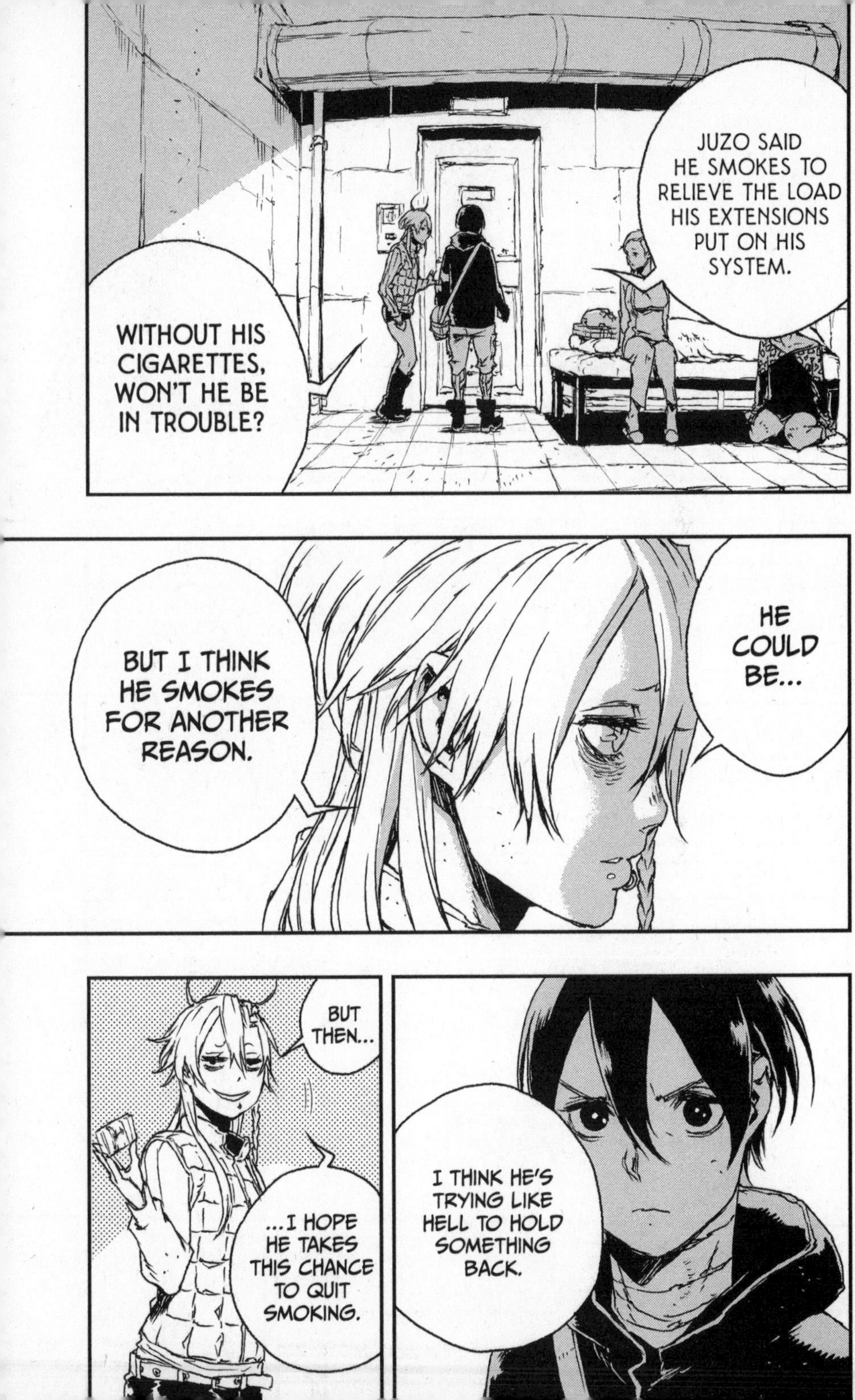
JUZO SAID HE SMOKES TO RELIEVE THE LOAD HIS EXTENSIONS PUT ON HIS SYSTEM.
WITHOUT HIS CIGARETTES, WON'T HE BE IN TROUBLE?
HE COULD BE...
BUT I THINK HE SMOKES FOR ANOTHER REASON.
I THINK HE'S TRYING LIKE HELL TO HOLD SOMETHING BACK.
BUT THEN...
...I HOPE HE TAKES THIS CHANCE TO QUIT SMOKING.

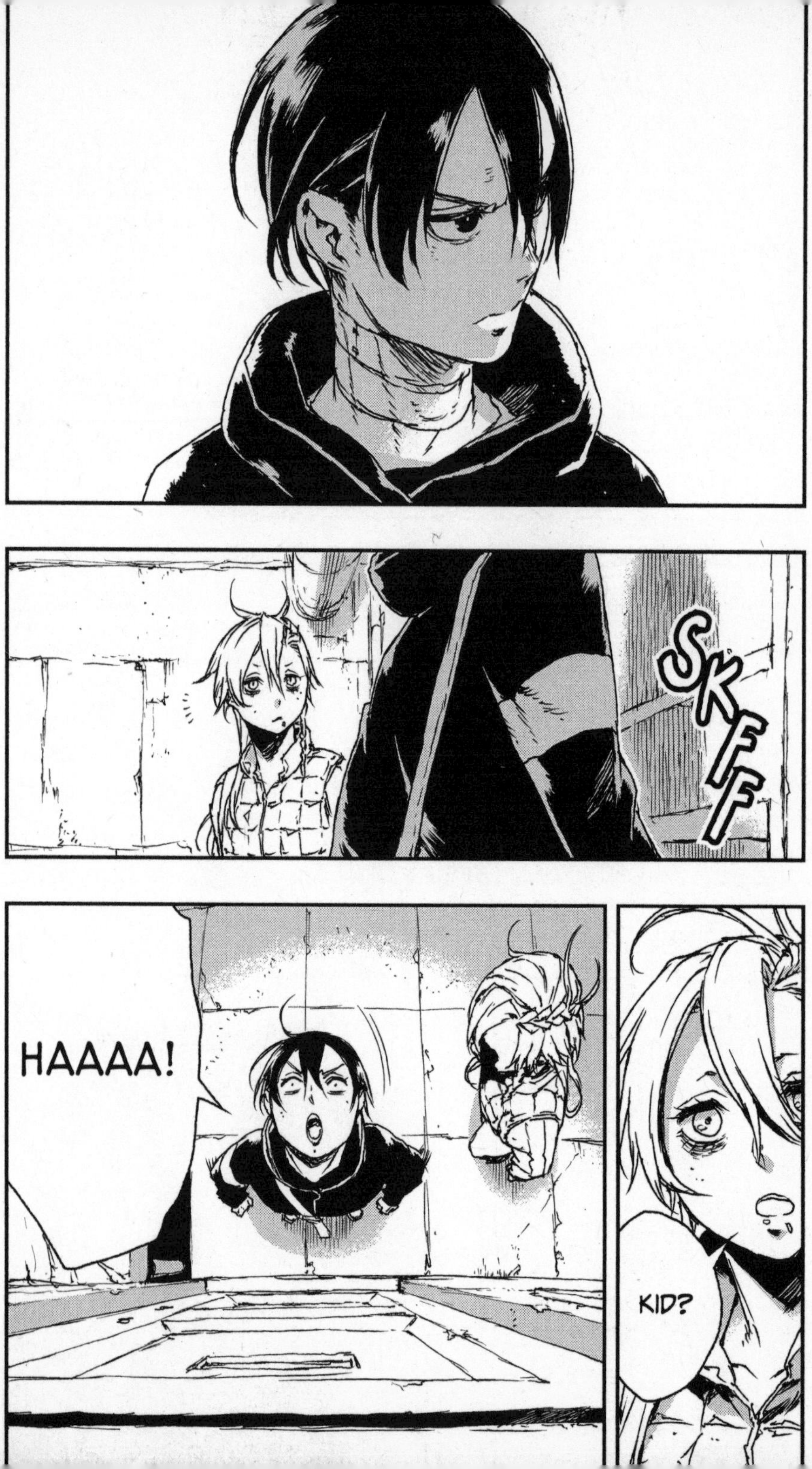
SKFF
KID?
HAAAA!

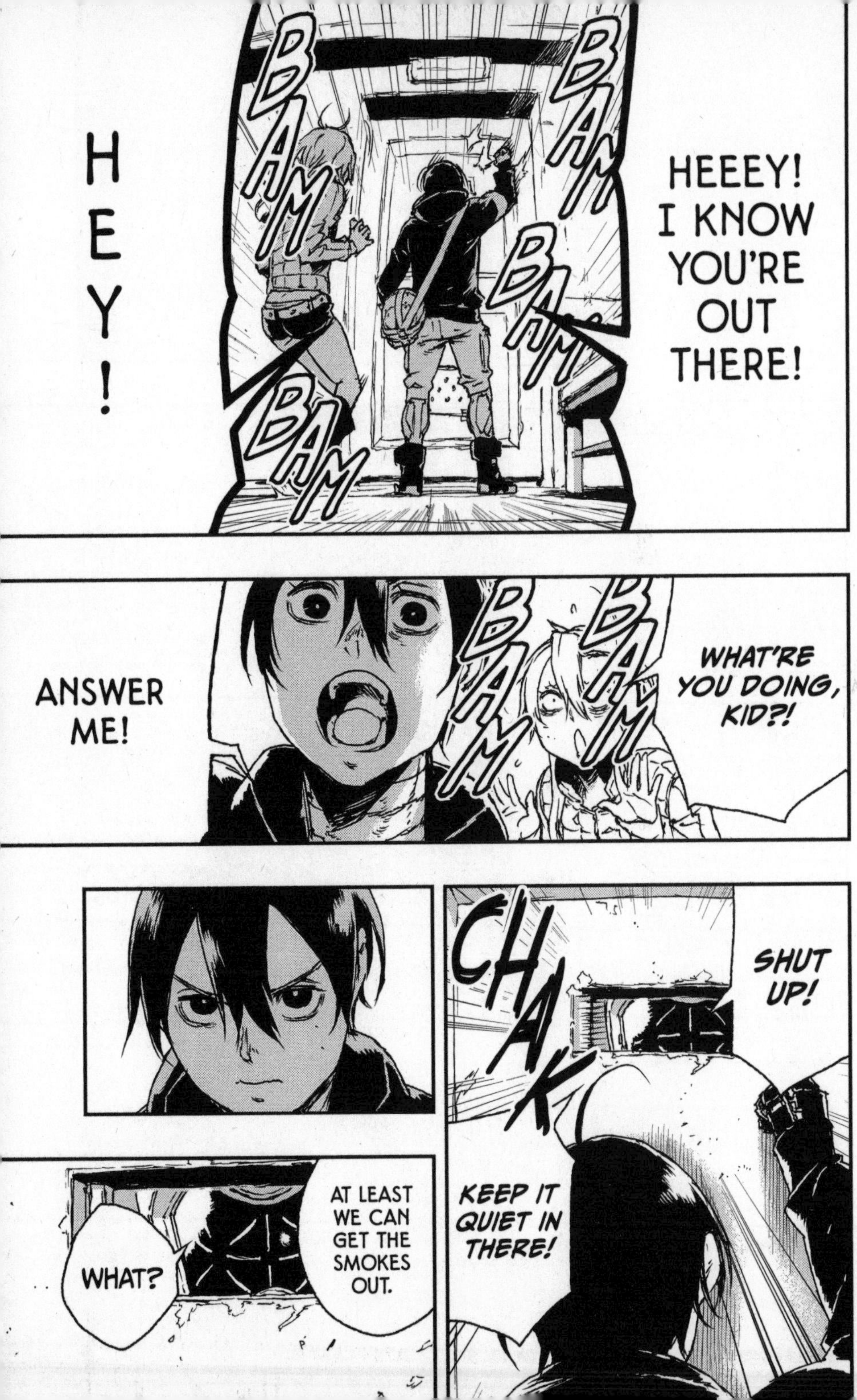
BAM
HEEEY! I KNOW YOU'RE OUT THERE!
BAM
BAM
BAM
HEY!
BAM
WHAT'RE YOU DOING, KID?!
BAM
ANSWER ME!
CHAK
SHUT UP!
KEEP IT QUIET IN THERE!
AT LEAST WE CAN GET THE SMOKES OUT.
WHAT?

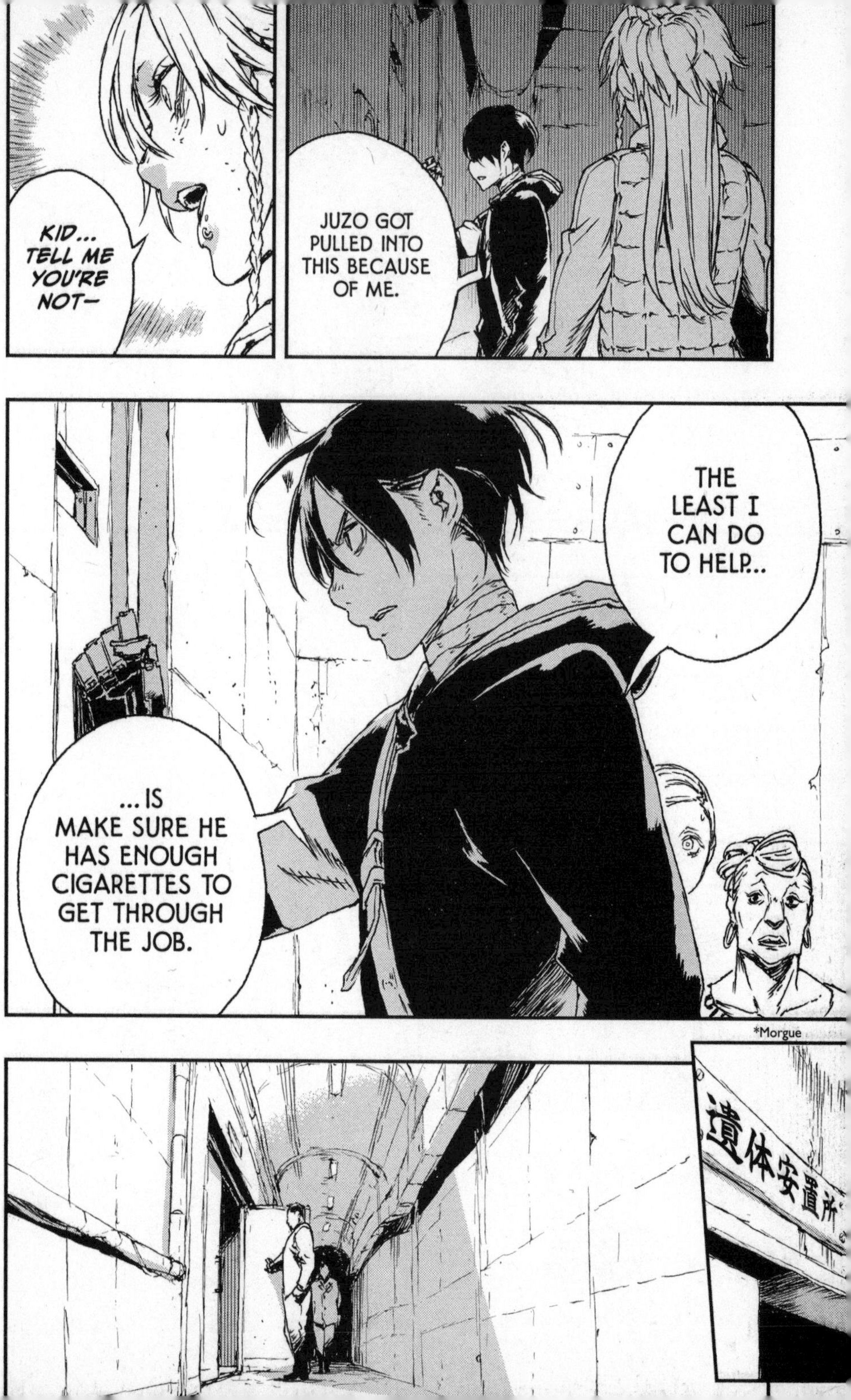
JUZO GOT PULLED INTO THIS BECAUSE OF ME.
KID... TELL ME YOU'RE NOT—
THE LEAST I CAN DO TO HELP...
...IS MAKE SURE HE HAS ENOUGH CIGARETTES TO GET THROUGH THE JOB.
*Morgue
遺体安置所

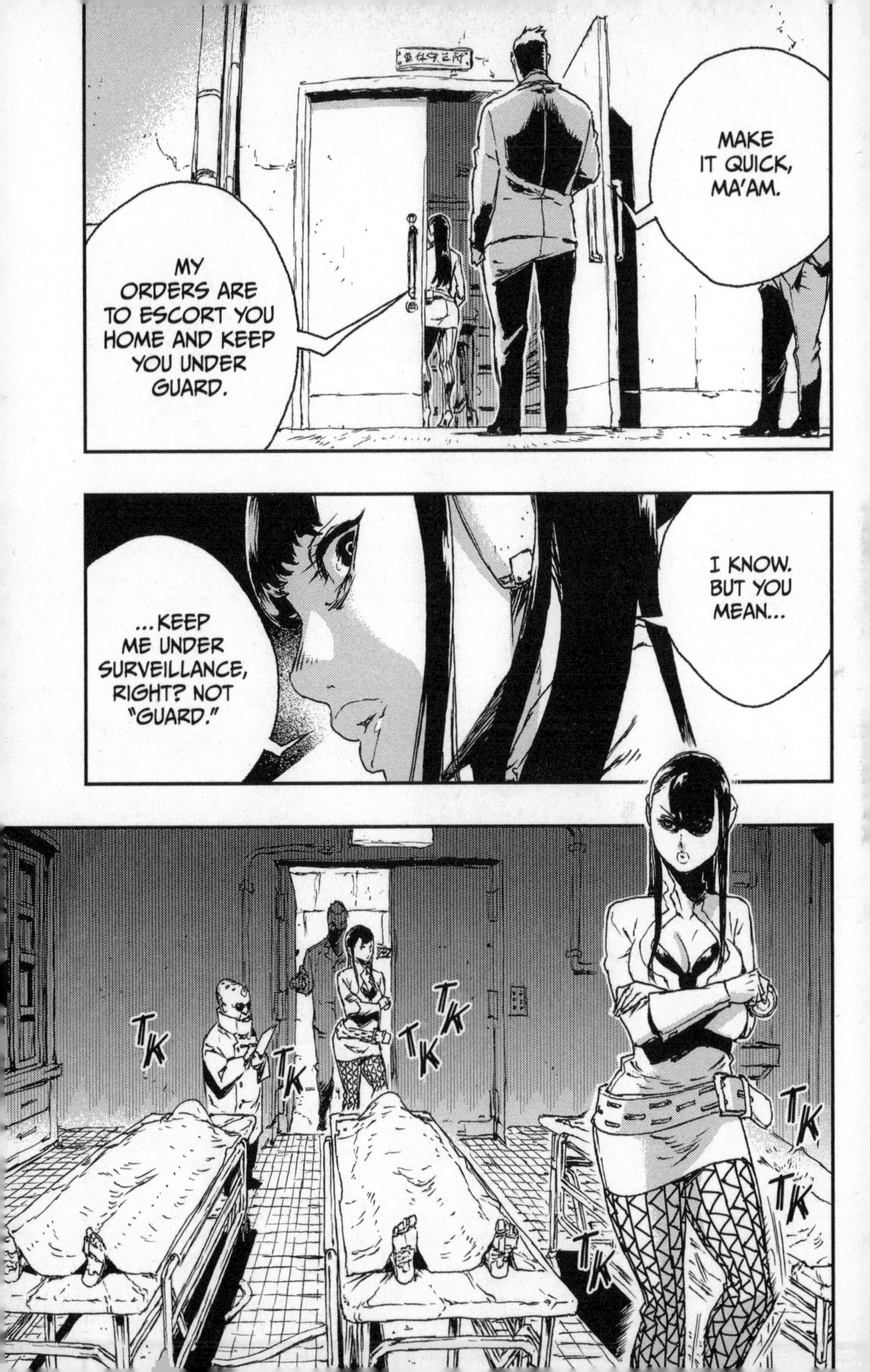
MAKE IT QUICK, MA'AM.
MY ORDERS ARE TO ESCORT YOU HOME AND KEEP YOU UNDER GUARD.
I KNOW. BUT YOU MEAN...
...KEEP ME UNDER SURVEILLANCE, RIGHT? NOT "GUARD."
TK TK
TK TK
TK
TK
TK
TK

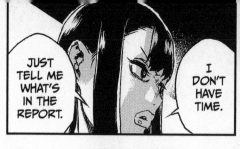

YOU SEEM WORRIED.
YOU MIND NOT OPENING THAT IN HERE?
TK TK TK TK
I DON'T HAVE TIME.
JUST TELL ME WHAT'S IN THE REPORT.
REALLY, PLEASE DON'T.
I'LL BE SMELLING THAT FOR DAYS.
SHFF
I PUT IT ALL IN MY REPORT. WE HAVE THREE VICTIMS...
...BUT THE CAUSE OF DEATH IS DIFFERENT FOR VICTIM ONE.
ALL THREE HAVE LACERATIONS.
THAT'S WHAT KILLED VICTIMS TWO AND THREE.
BUT VICTIM ONE HAS SIGNS OF POSTMORTEM TRAUMA TO THE CHEST.
WITH FULL-BODY EXTENDED, WE CAN'T USE VITAL ORGANS TO FIX THE TIME OF DEATH, SO I CAN'T BE SURE.

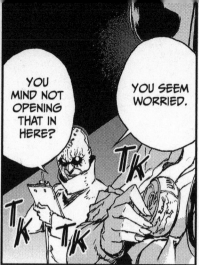

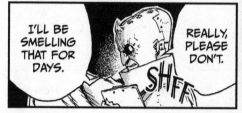

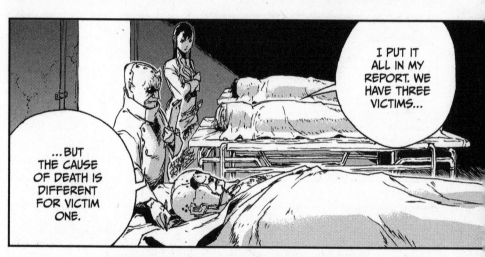

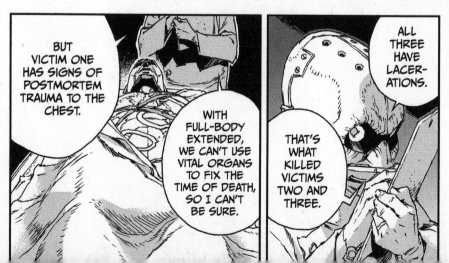

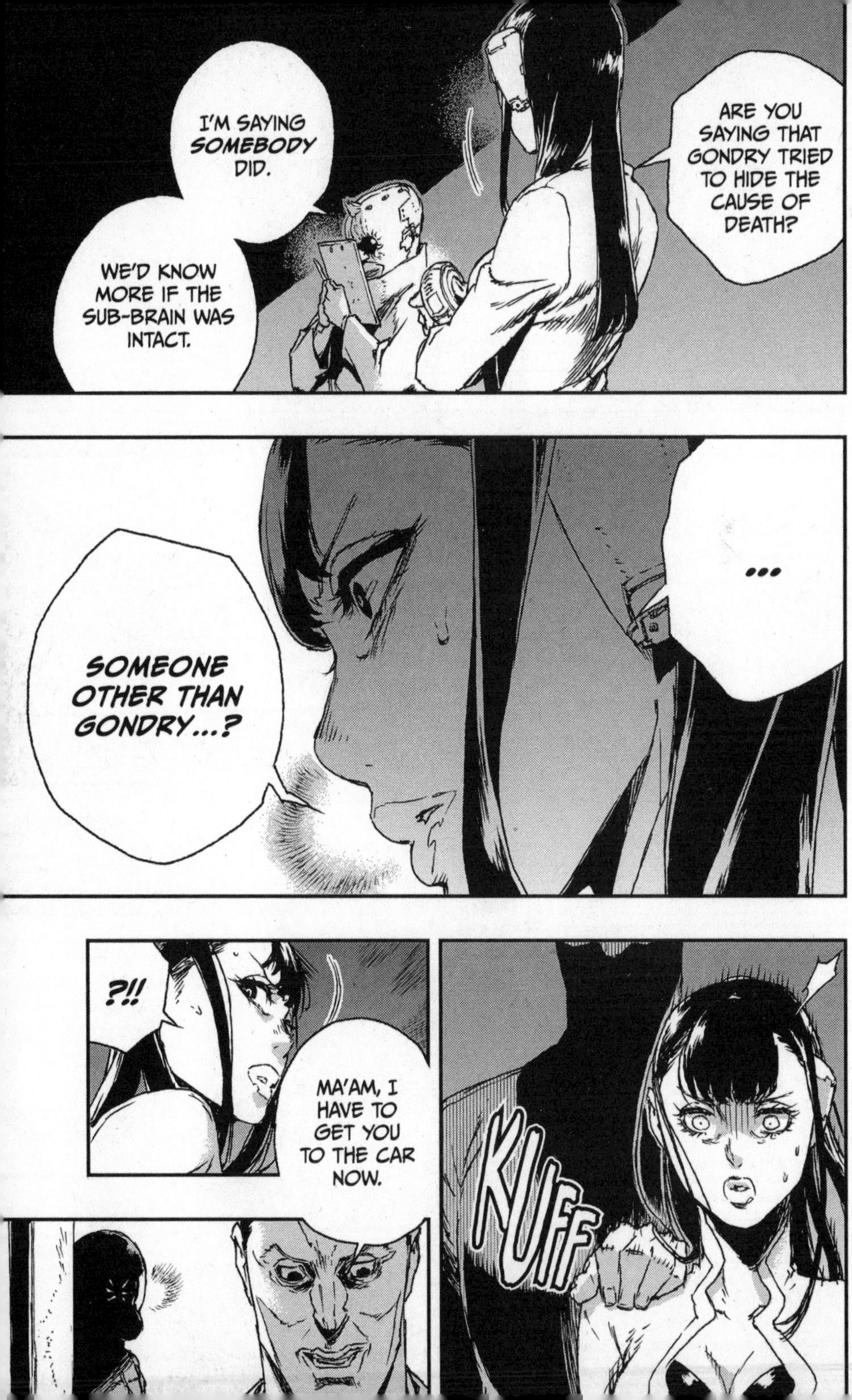
ARE YOU SAYING THAT GONDRY TRIED TO HIDE THE CAUSE OF DEATH?
I'M SAYING *SOMEBODY* DID.
WE'D KNOW MORE IF THE SUB-BRAIN WAS INTACT.
...
SOMEONE OTHER THAN GONDRY...?
KUFF
?!!
MA'AM, I HAVE TO GET YOU TO THE CAR NOW.

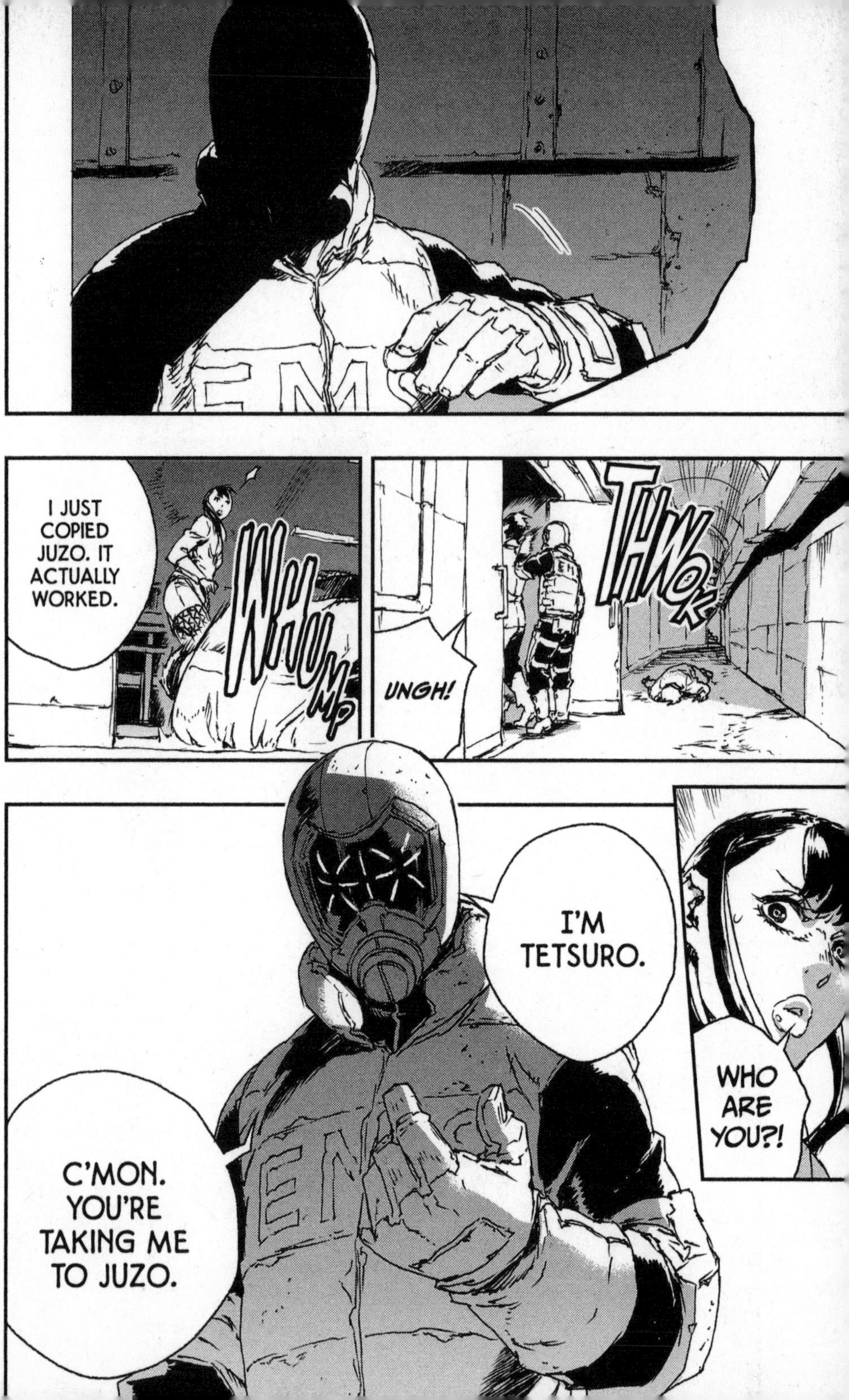
THWOK
UNGH!
WHUMP
I JUST COPIED JUZO. IT ACTUALLY WORKED.
WHO ARE YOU?!
I'M TETSURO.
C'MON. YOU'RE TAKING ME TO JUZO.

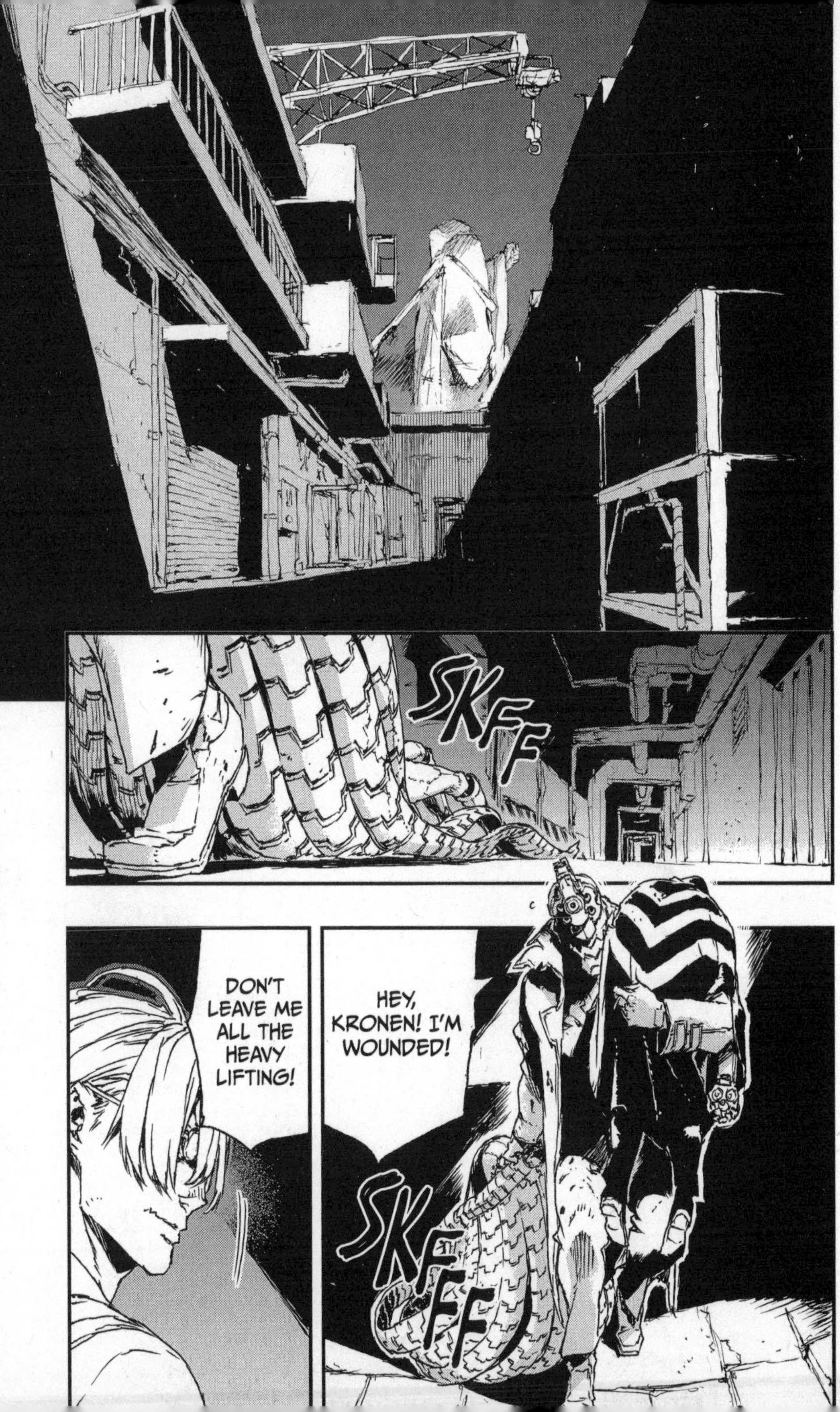
SKFF
HEY, KRONEN! I'M WOUNDED!
SKFFF
DON'T LEAVE ME ALL THE HEAVY LIFTING!

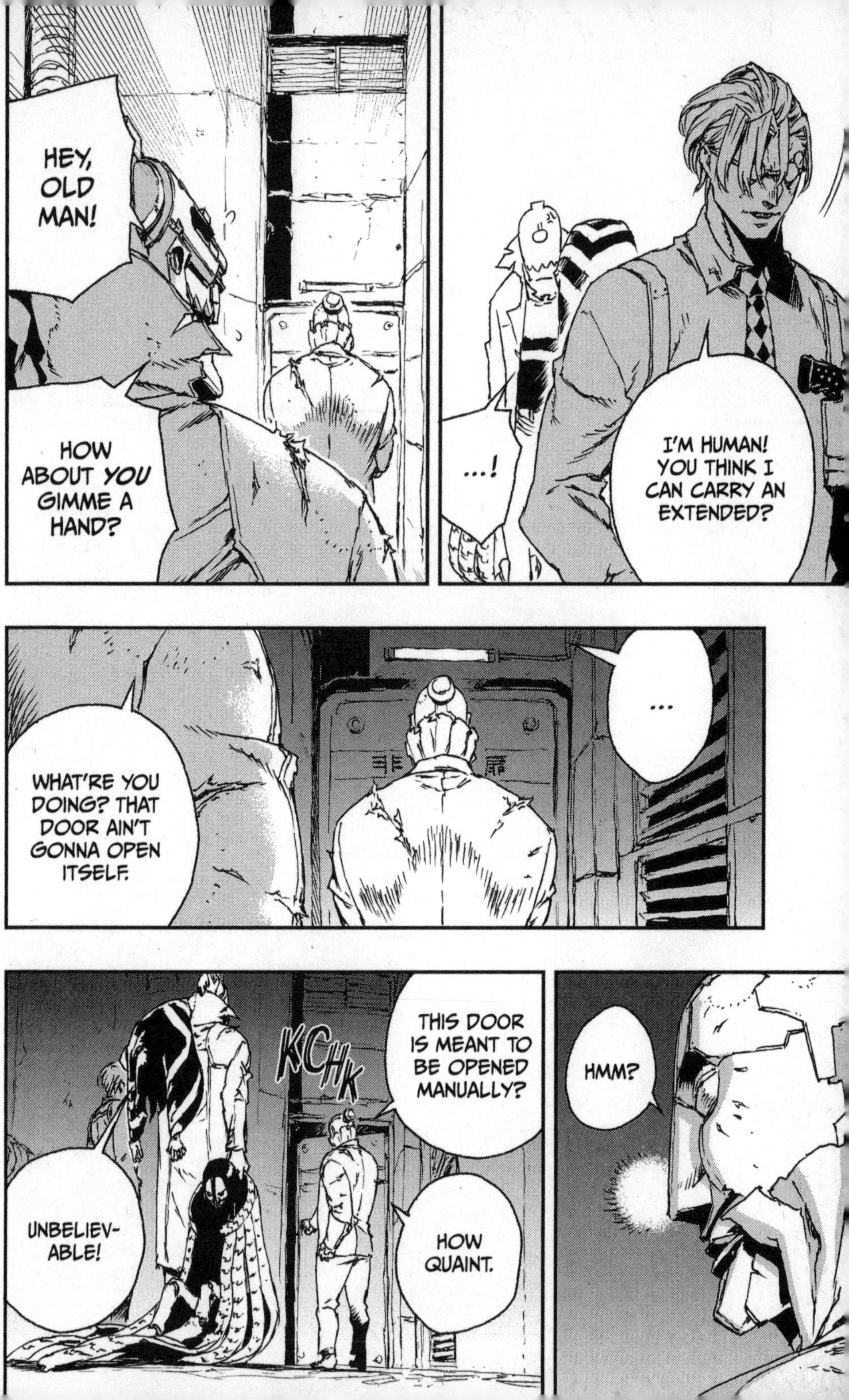
I'M HUMAN! YOU THINK I CAN CARRY AN EXTENDED?
...!
HEY, OLD MAN!
HOW ABOUT YOU GIMME A HAND?
...
WHAT'RE YOU DOING? THAT DOOR AIN'T GONNA OPEN ITSELF.
HMM?
THIS DOOR IS MEANT TO BE OPENED MANUALLY?
KCHK
HOW QUAINT.
UNBELIEV-ABLE!

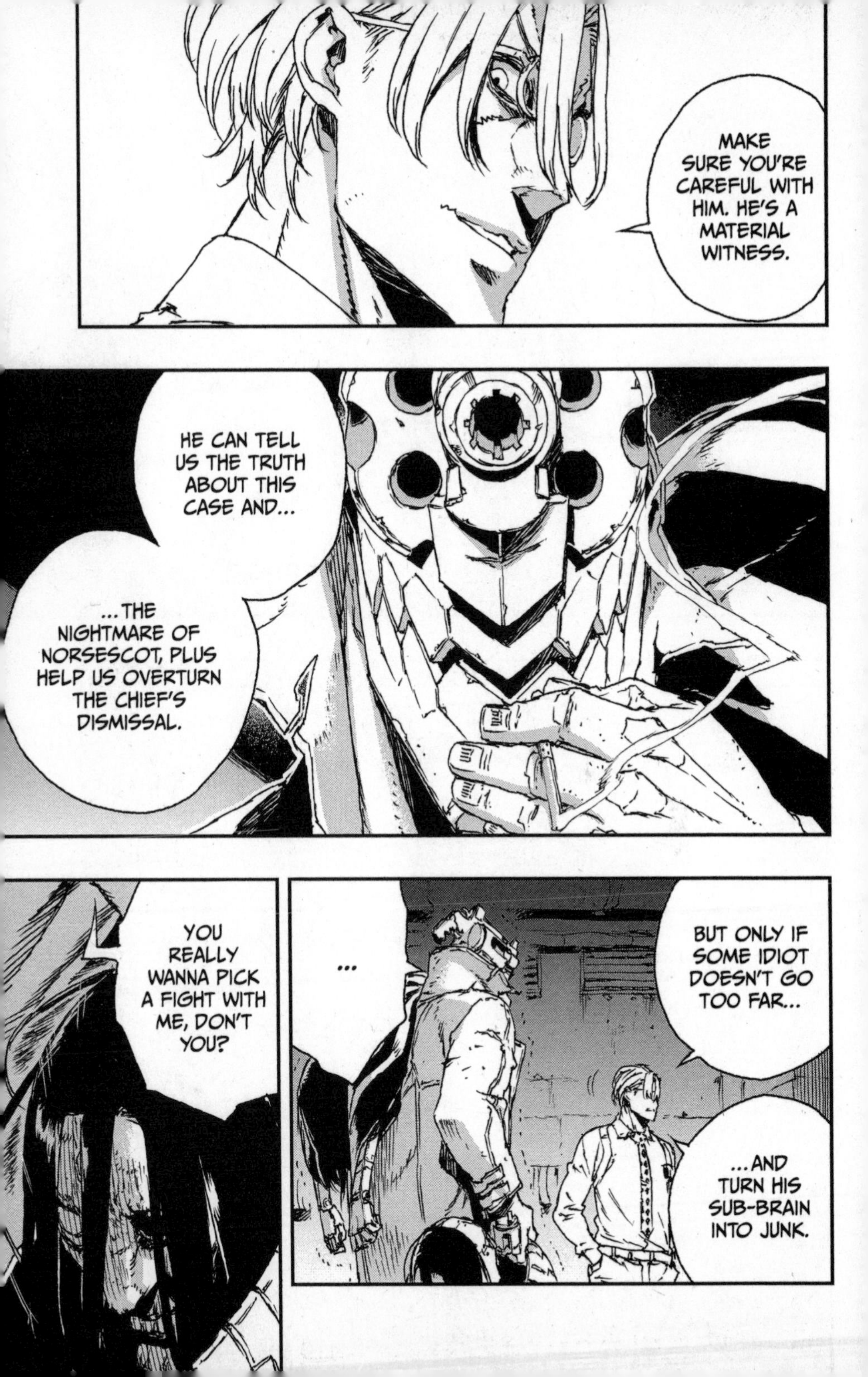
MAKE SURE YOU'RE CAREFUL WITH HIM. HE'S A MATERIAL WITNESS.
HE CAN TELL US THE TRUTH ABOUT THIS CASE AND...
...THE NIGHTMARE OF NORSESCOT, PLUS HELP US OVERTURN THE CHIEF'S DISMISSAL.
BUT ONLY IF SOME IDIOT DOESN'T GO TOO FAR...
...AND TURN HIS SUB-BRAIN INTO JUNK.
...
YOU REALLY WANNA PICK A FIGHT WITH ME, DON'T YOU?

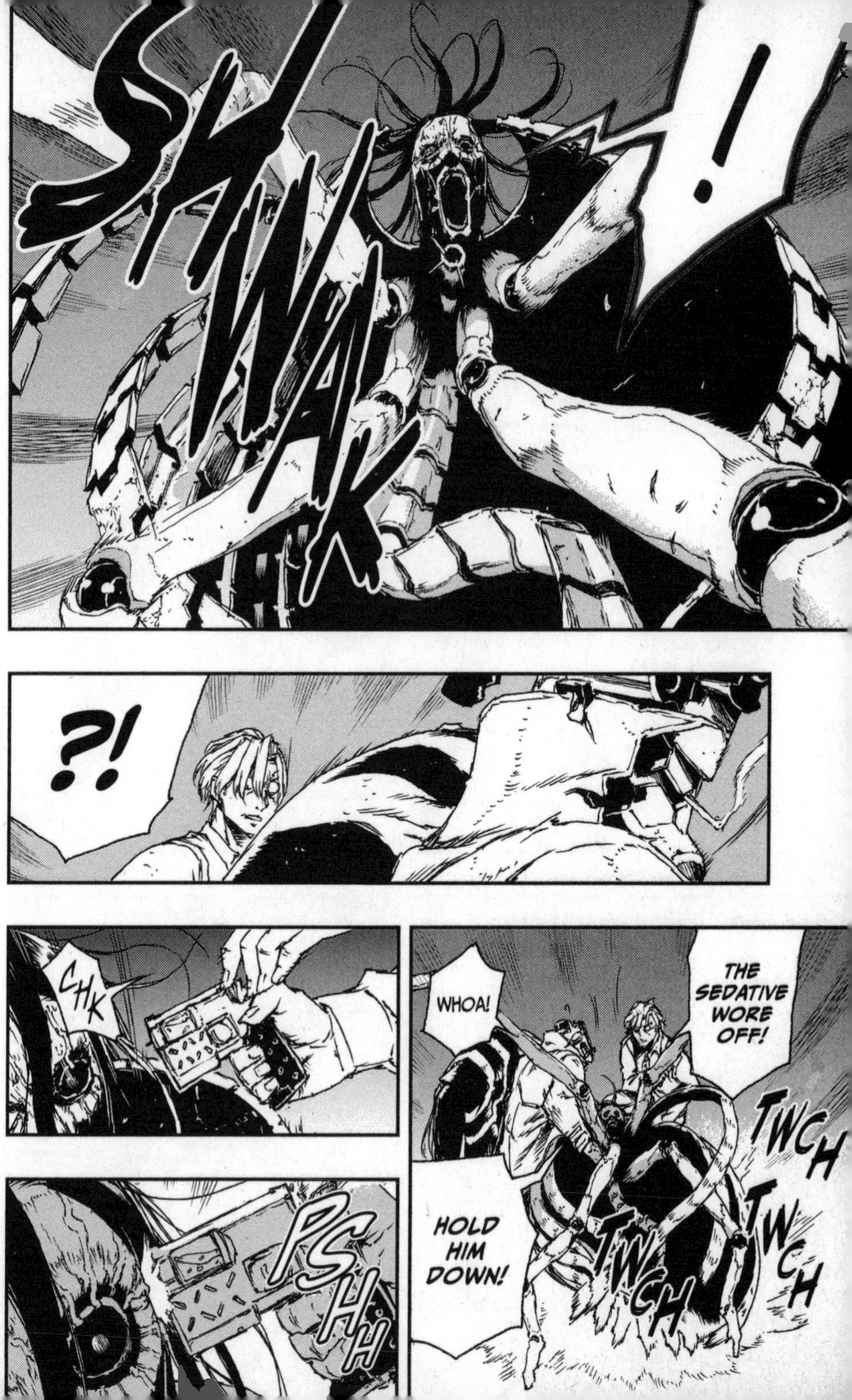

SHWAK
!
?!
THE SEDATIVE WORE OFF!
WHOA!
TWCH
TWCH
TWCH
HOLD HIM DOWN!
TWCH
CHK
PSHH

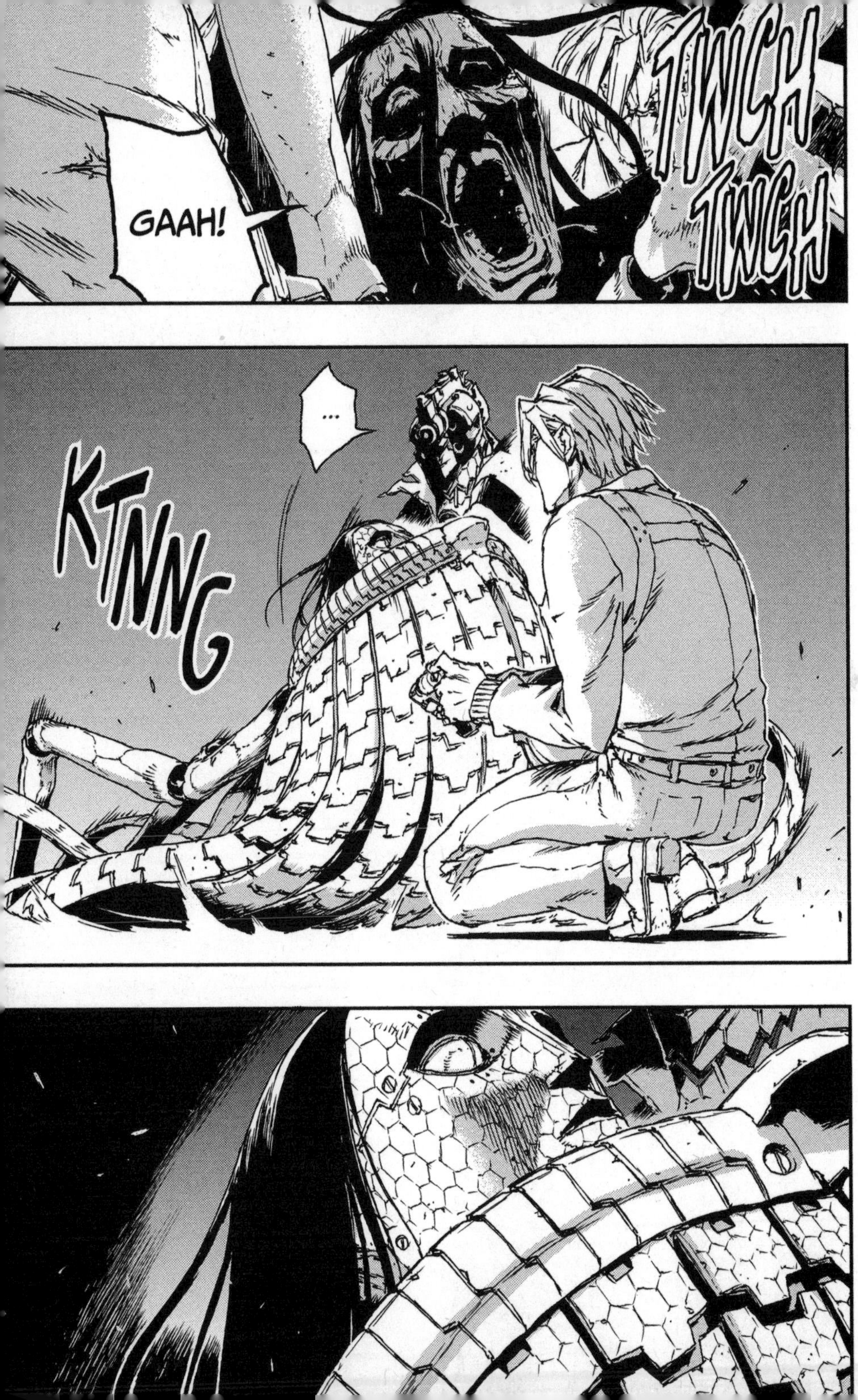
TWCH TWCH
GAAH!
...
KTNNG

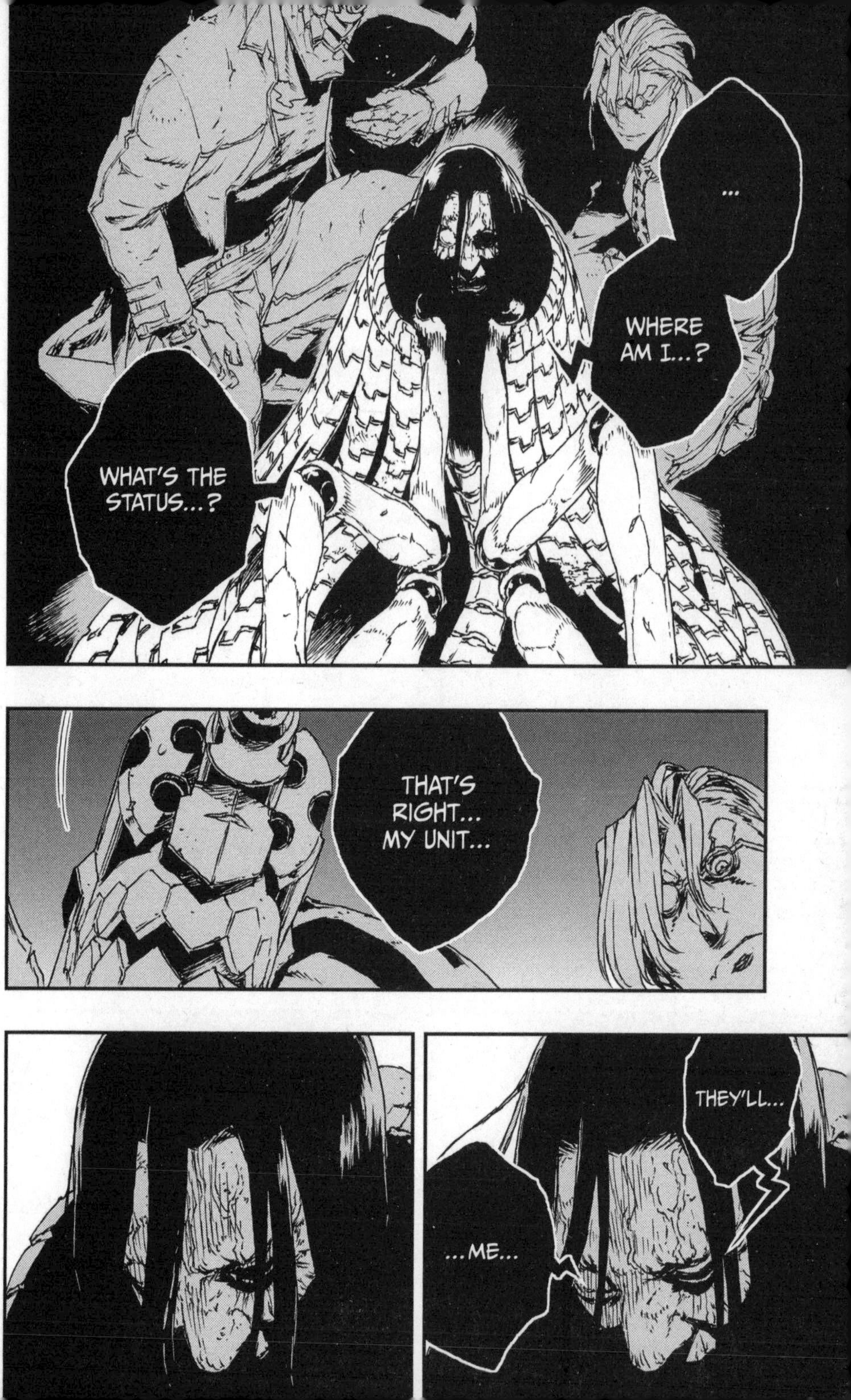
...
WHERE AM I...?
WHAT'S THE STATUS...?
THAT'S RIGHT... MY UNIT...
THEY'LL...
...ME...

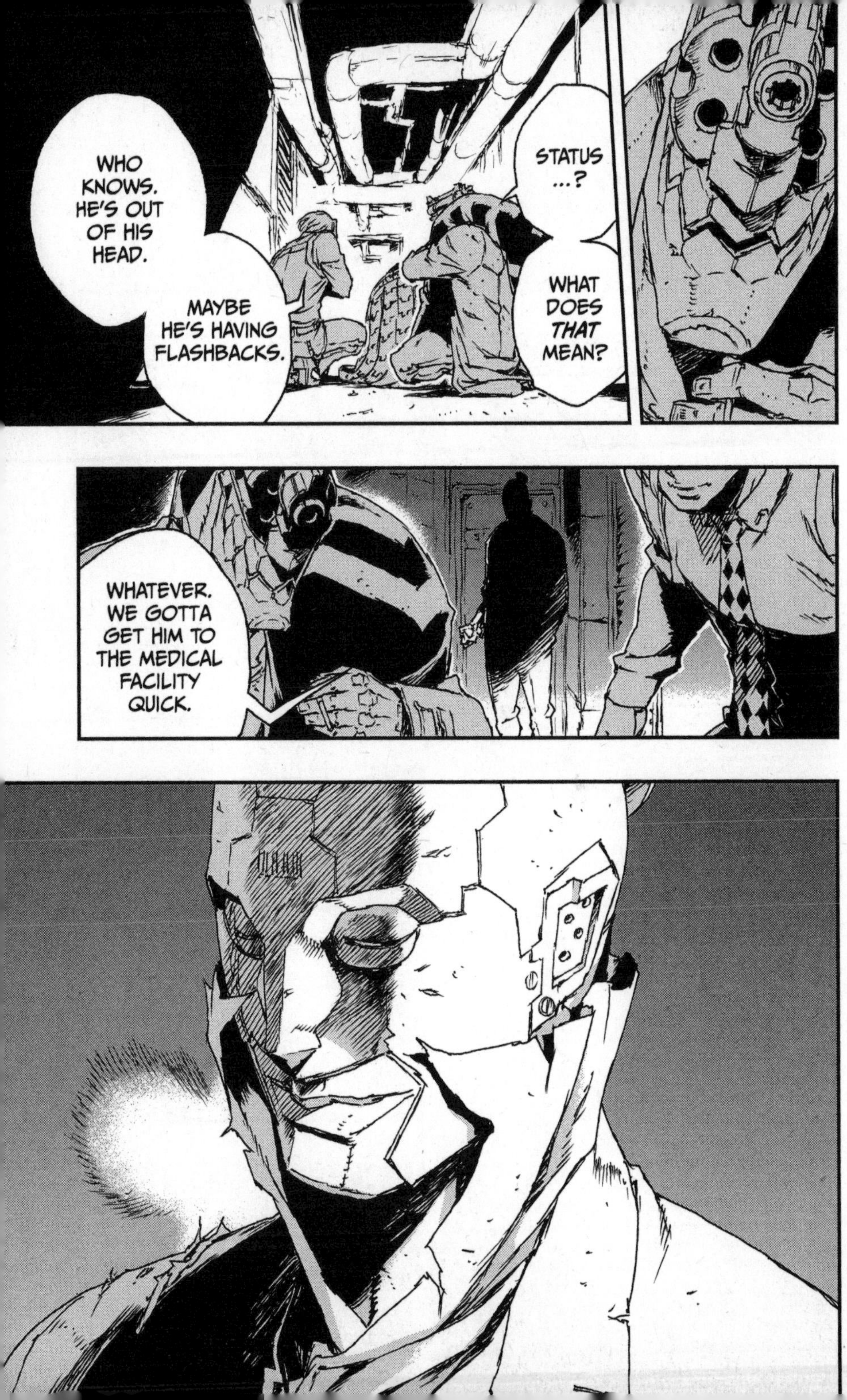
STATUS ...?
WHAT DOES *THAT* MEAN?
WHO KNOWS. HE'S OUT OF HIS HEAD.
MAYBE HE'S HAVING FLASHBACKS.
WHATEVER. WE GOTTA GET HIM TO THE MEDICAL FACILITY QUICK.

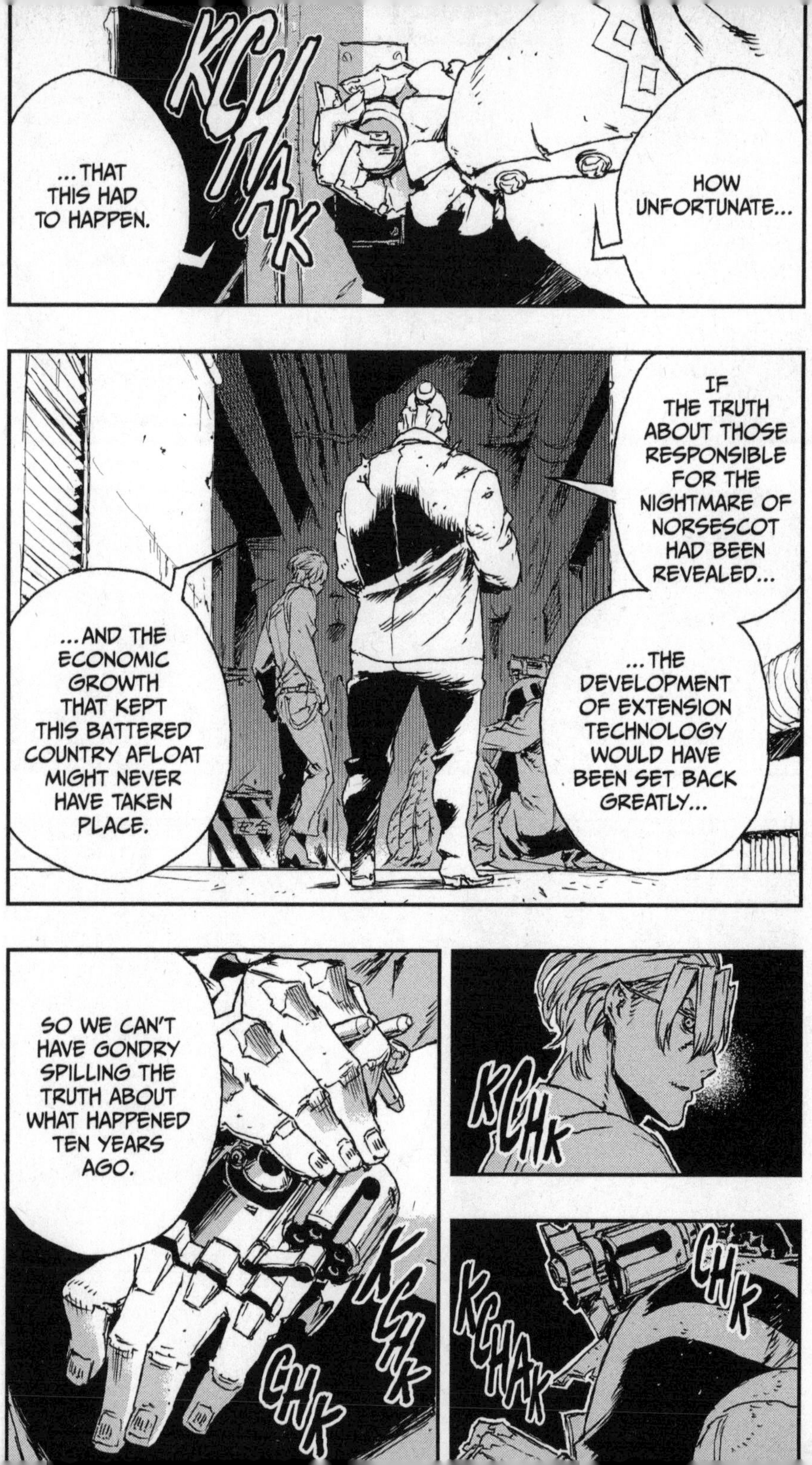
HOW UNFORTUNATE...
KCHAK
...THAT THIS HAD TO HAPPEN.
IF THE TRUTH ABOUT THOSE RESPONSIBLE FOR THE NIGHTMARE OF NORSESCOT HAD BEEN REVEALED...
...THE DEVELOPMENT OF EXTENSION TECHNOLOGY WOULD HAVE BEEN SET BACK GREATLY...
...AND THE ECONOMIC GROWTH THAT KEPT THIS BATTERED COUNTRY AFLOAT MIGHT NEVER HAVE TAKEN PLACE.
KCHK
CHK
KCHAK
SO WE CAN'T HAVE GONDRY SPILLING THE TRUTH ABOUT WHAT HAPPENED TEN YEARS AGO.
KCHK
CHK

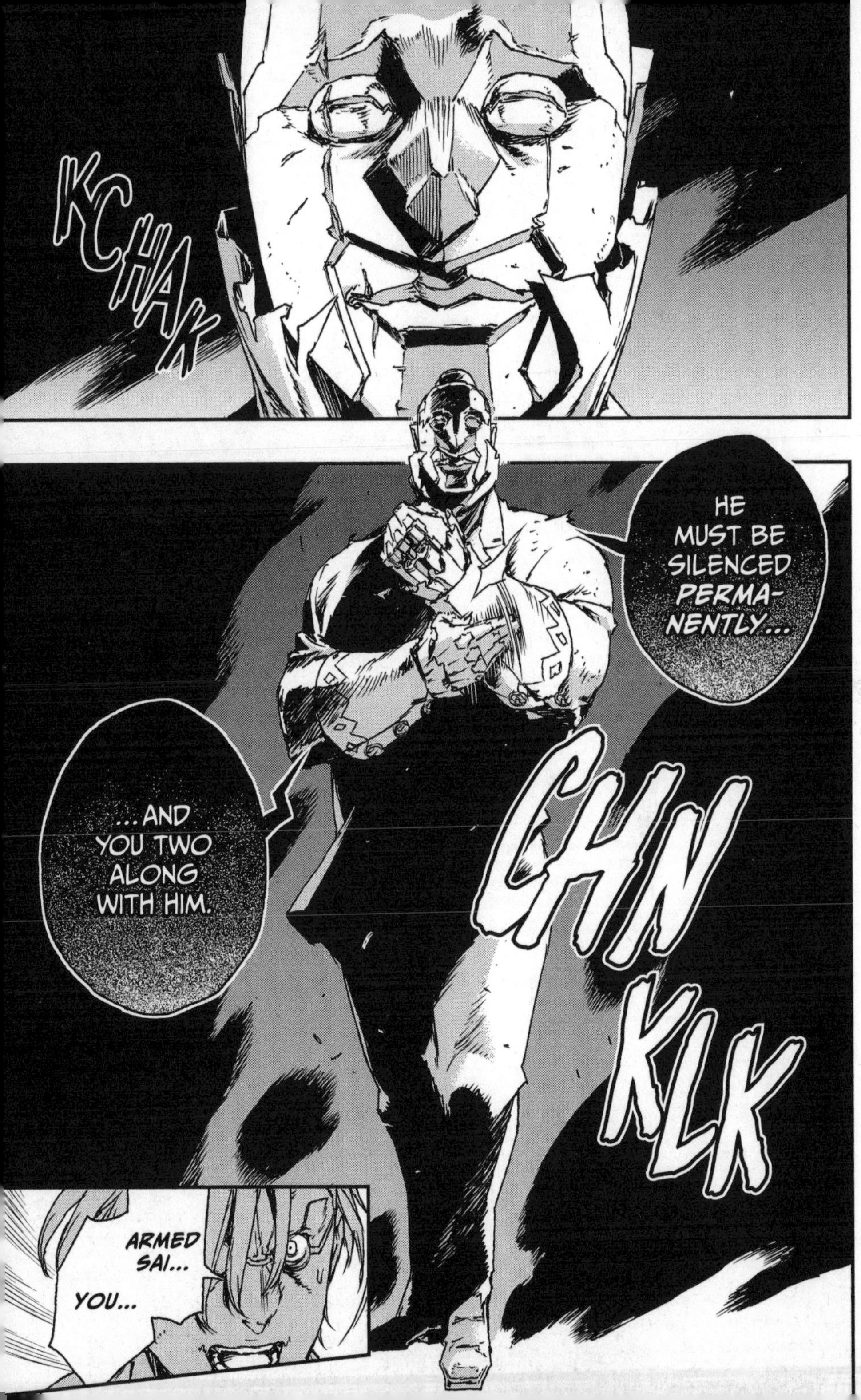
KCHAK
HE MUST BE SILENCED PERMANENTLY...
...AND YOU TWO ALONG WITH HIM.
CHN
KLK
ARMED SAI...
YOU...

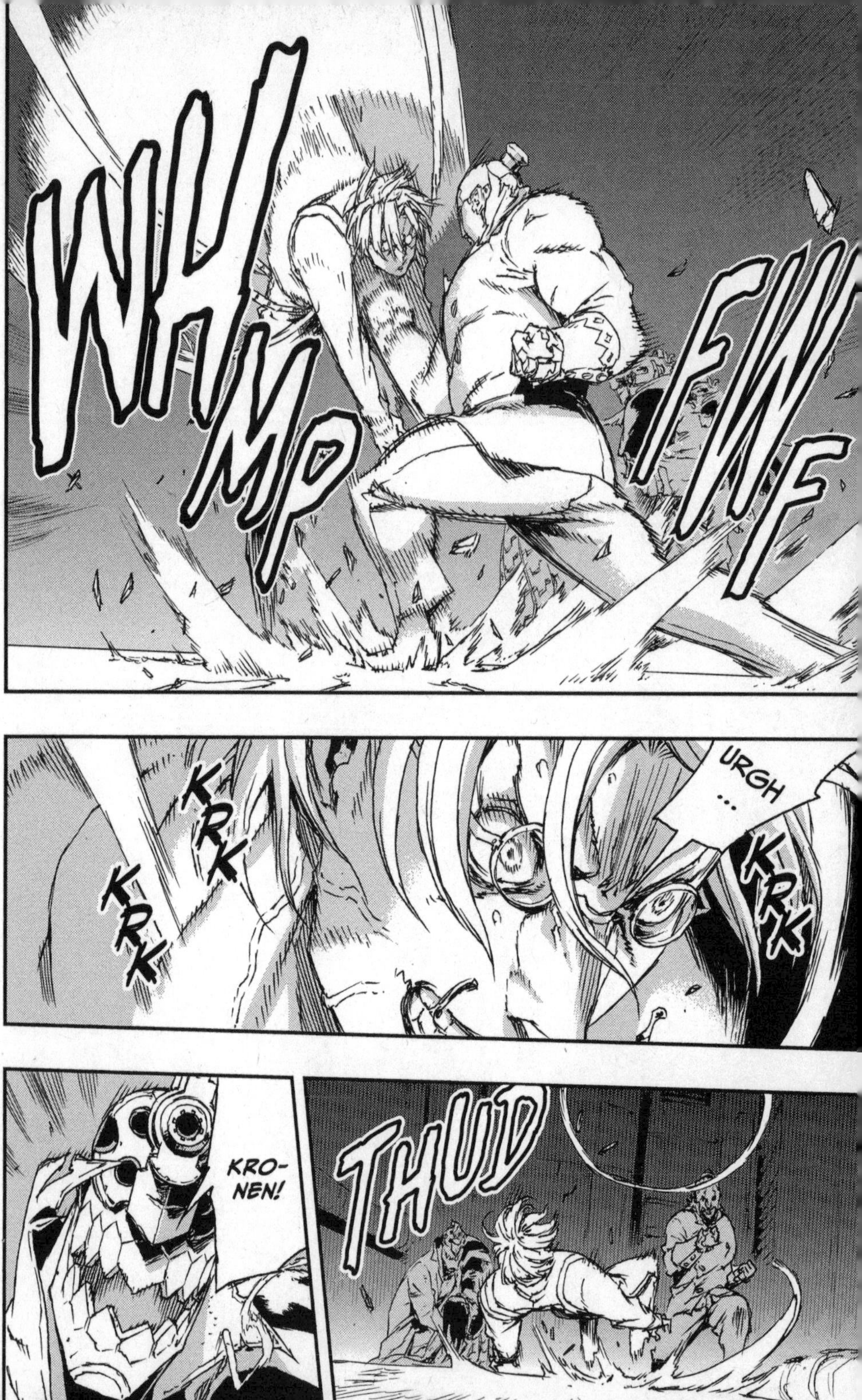
FWF
WHUMP
URGH...
KRK
KRK
KRK
THUD
KRO-
NEN!

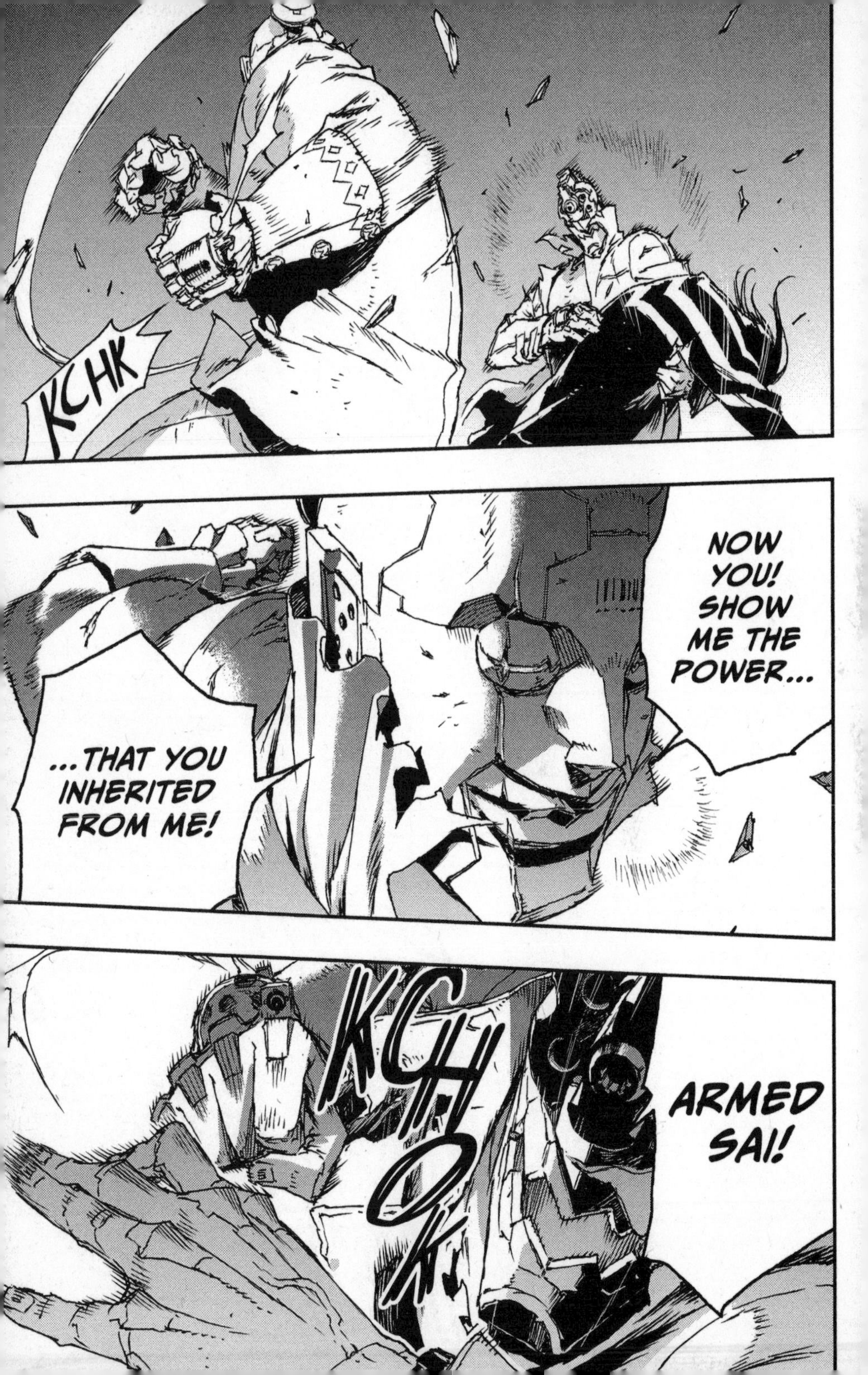
KCHK
NOW YOU! SHOW ME THE POWER...
...THAT YOU INHERITED FROM ME!
ARMED SAI!
KCHOK

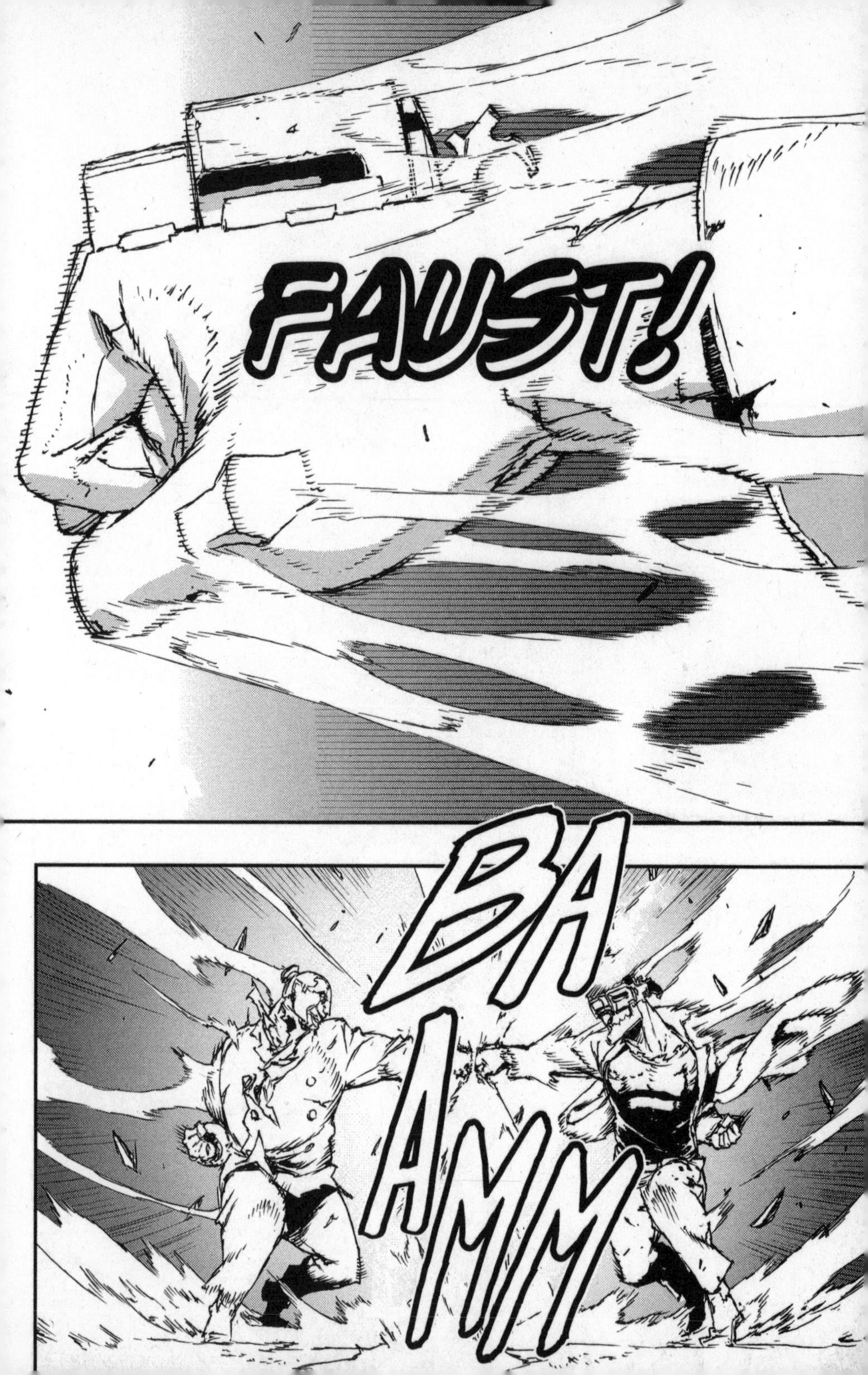
FAUST!
BA
AMM

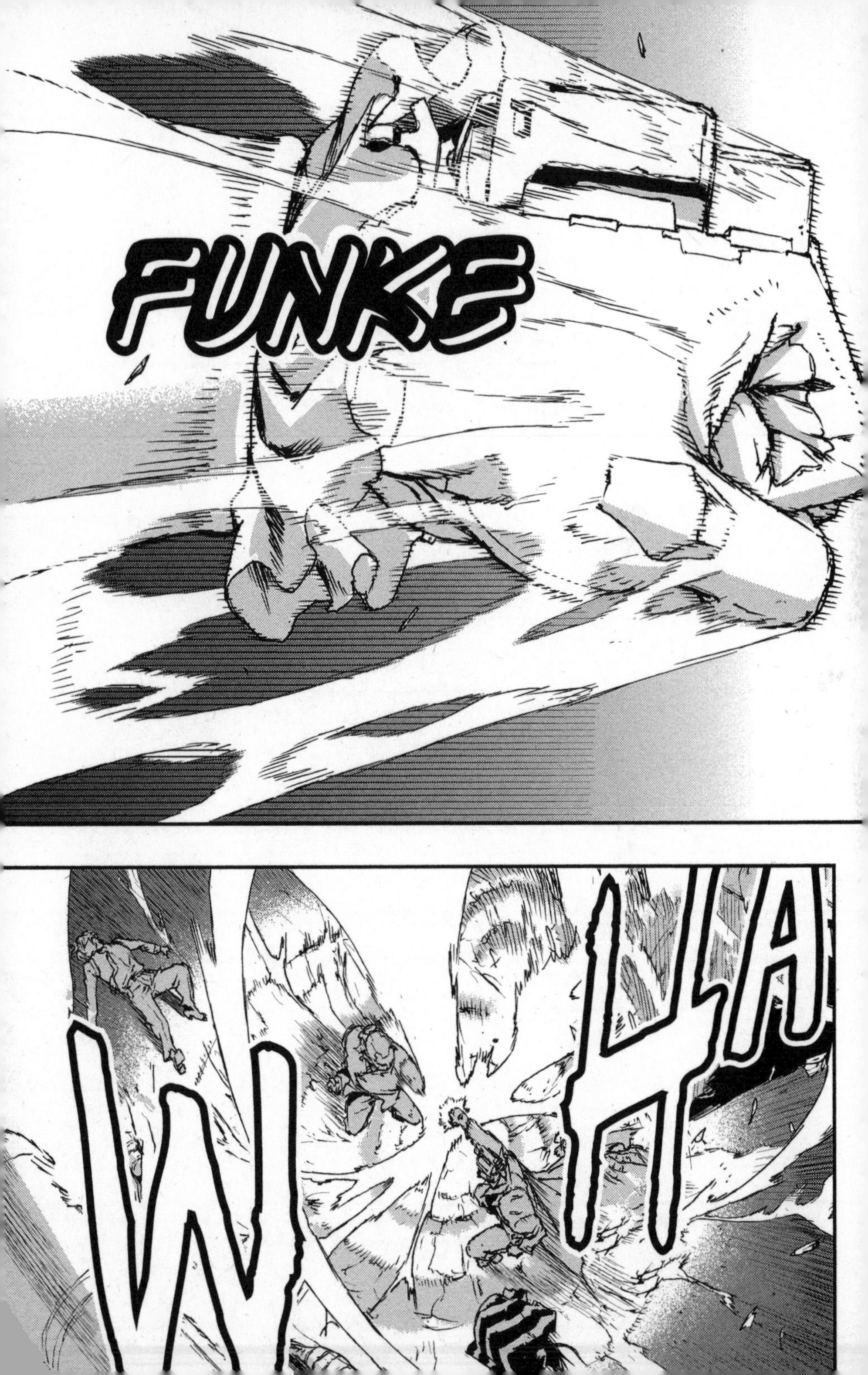
FUNKE
WHA

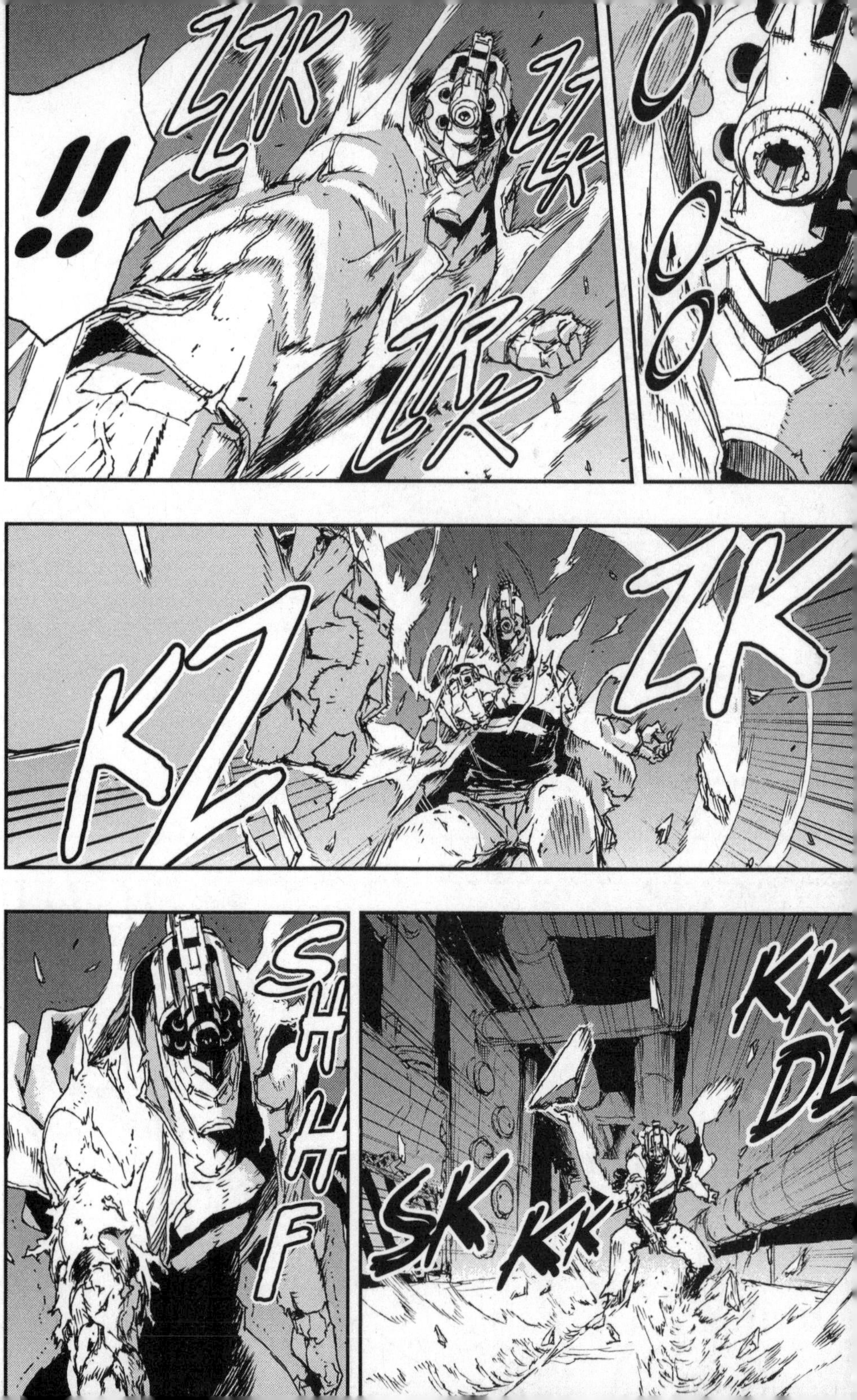
OOOO
ZZzk
ZZK
!!
ZZk
ZK
KZ
KK DL
SK KK
SHHHF

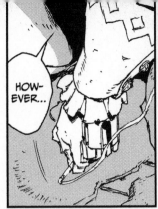

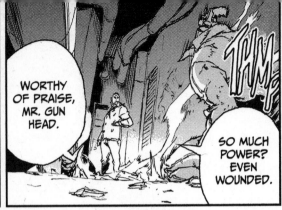

THMP
SO MUCH POWER? EVEN WOUNDED.
WORTHY OF PRAISE, MR. GUN HEAD.
HOW-EVER...
HOMEMADE, ISN'T IT? HOW UNUSUAL.
SIMILAR TO THAT CRUDE IMITATION TANEGASHIMA THAT THE KYUSEI FAMILY SELLS.
SNIFF
BUT THIS USES MUCH HIGHER QUALITY INGREDIENTS. HABITUAL USE OF SOMETHING THIS CONCENTRATED MUST MEAN YOUR NERVOUS SYSTEM IS IN BAD SHAPE.
KRUSH
ADD THE FATIGUE FROM THESE FIGHTS...
...AND I BET YOU CAN BARELY STAND.
...SLY OLD FOX.
YOU ARE ONE...

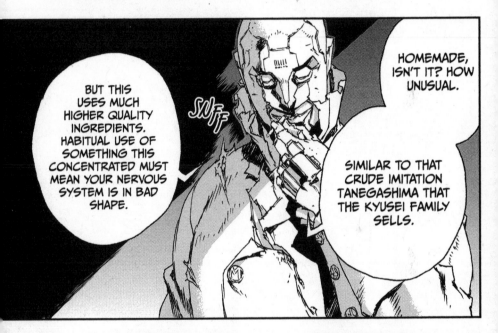

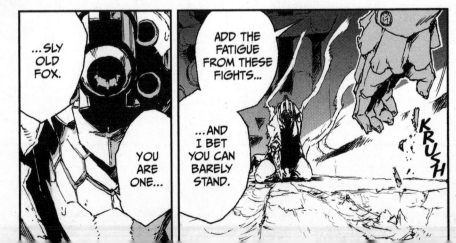

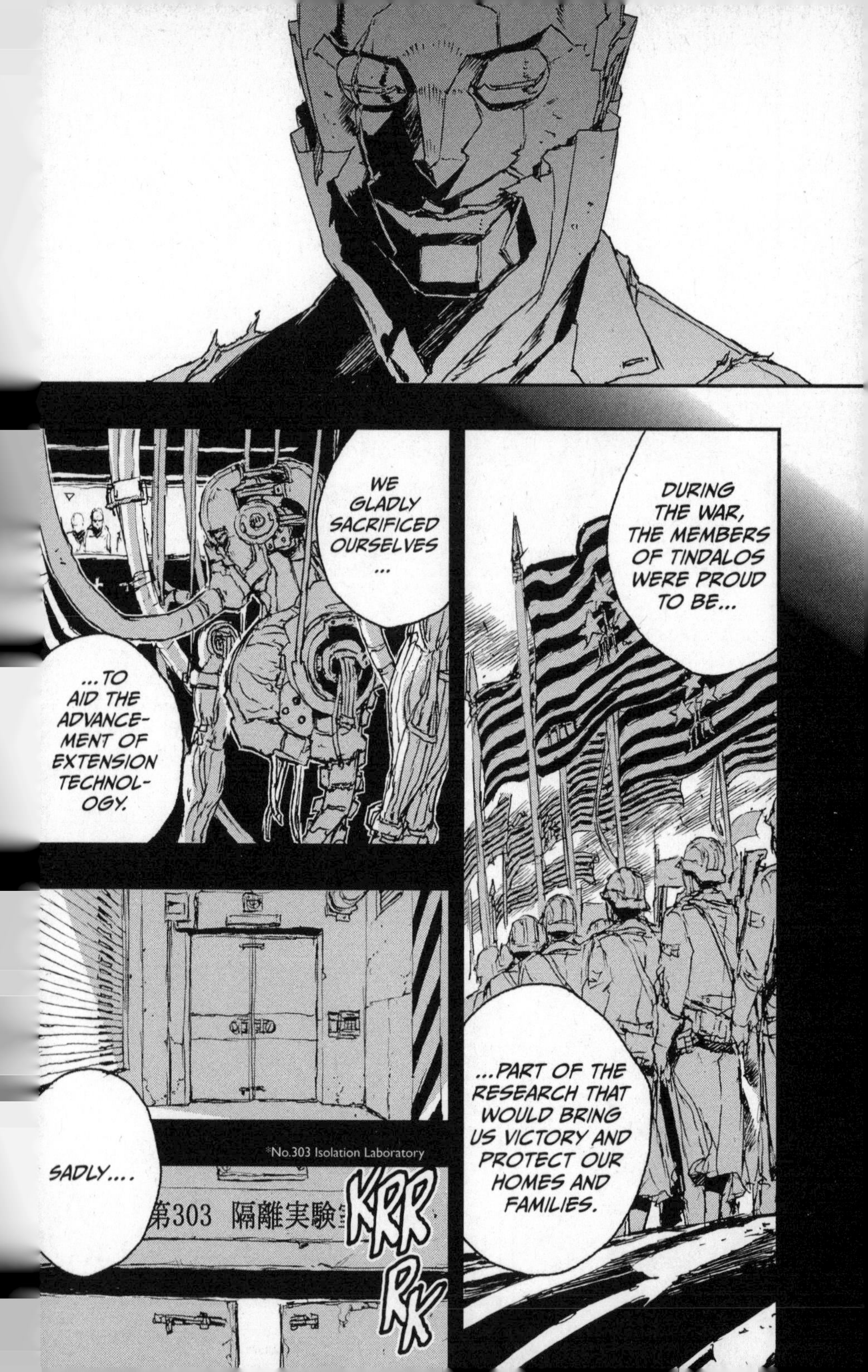
DURING THE WAR, THE MEMBERS OF TINDALOS WERE PROUD TO BE...
...PART OF THE RESEARCH THAT WOULD BRING US VICTORY AND PROTECT OUR HOMES AND FAMILIES.
WE GLADLY SACRIFICED OURSELVES ...
...TO AID THE ADVANCEMENT OF EXTENSION TECHNOLOGY.
SADLY....
第303 隔離実験
*No.303 Isolation Laboratory
KRRRK

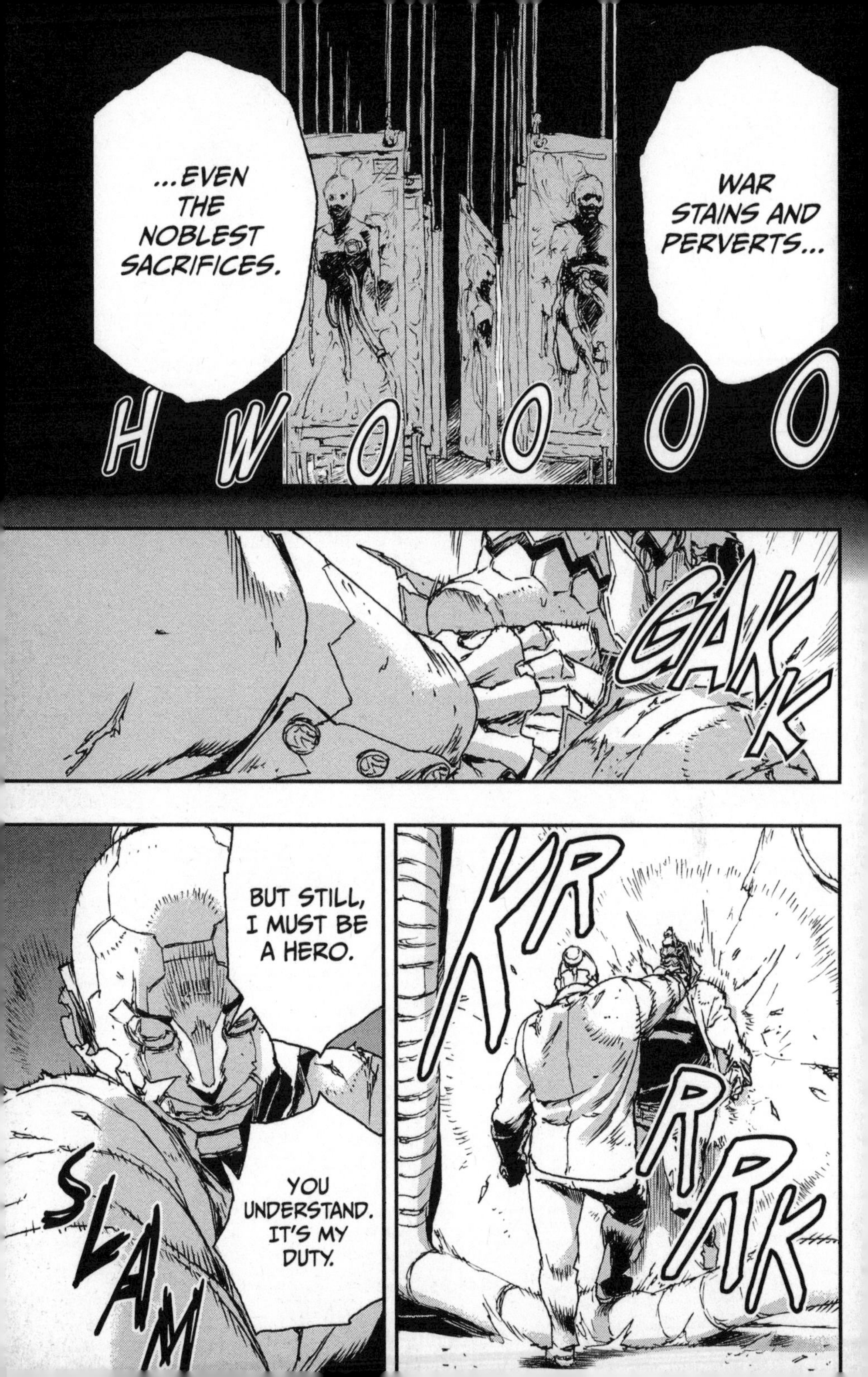
WAR STAINS AND PERVERTS...
...EVEN THE NOBLEST SACRIFICES.
HWOOOOO
GAKK
KRRRK
BUT STILL, I MUST BE A HERO.
YOU UNDERSTAND. IT'S MY DUTY.
SLAM

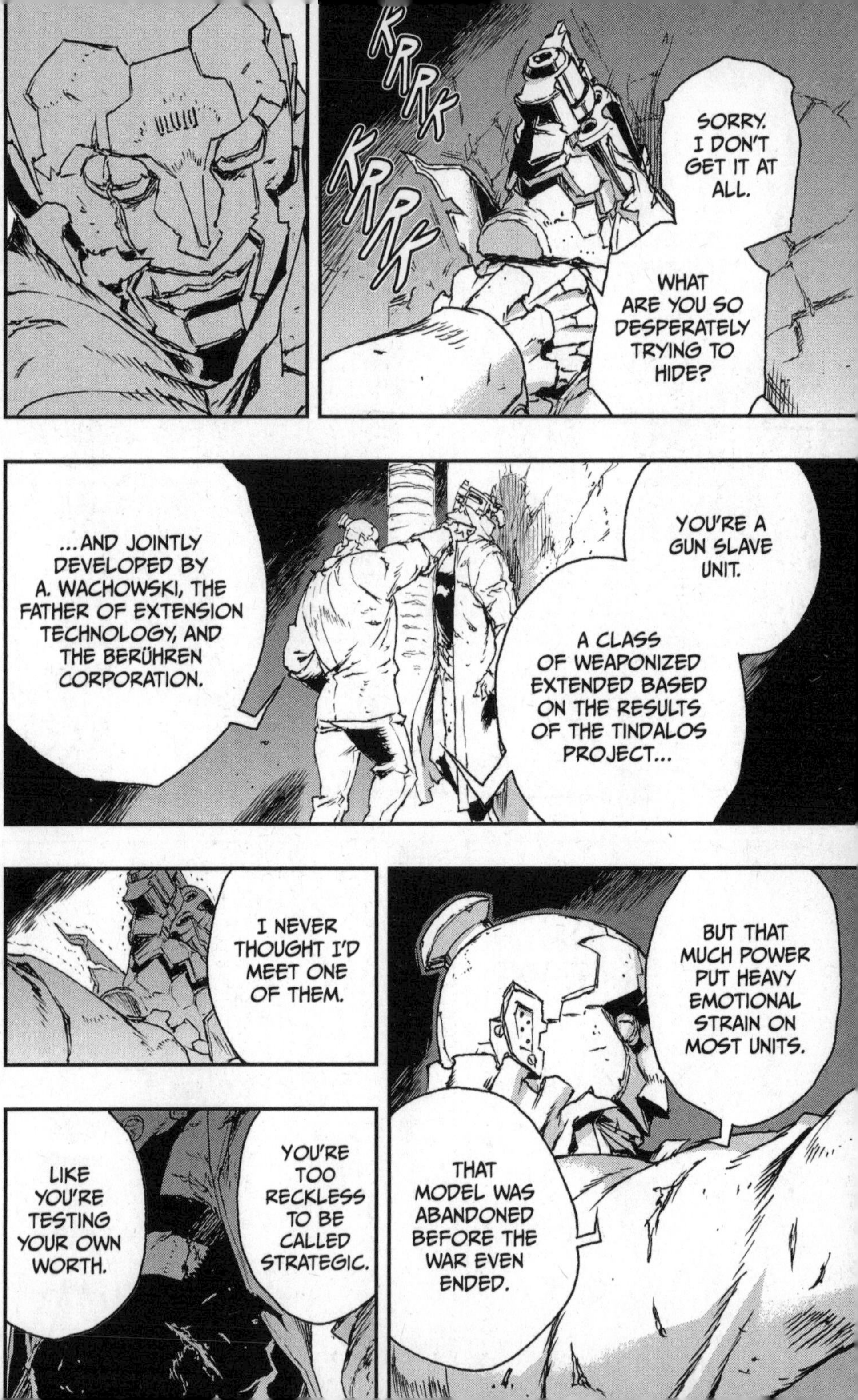
KRRK KRRK
SORRY. I DON'T GET IT AT ALL.
WHAT ARE YOU SO DESPERATELY TRYING TO HIDE?
YOU'RE A GUN SLAVE UNIT.
A CLASS OF WEAPONIZED EXTENDED BASED ON THE RESULTS OF THE TINDALOS PROJECT...
...AND JOINTLY DEVELOPED BY A. WACHOWSKI, THE FATHER OF EXTENSION TECHNOLOGY, AND THE BERÜHREN CORPORATION.
BUT THAT MUCH POWER PUT HEAVY EMOTIONAL STRAIN ON MOST UNITS.
THAT MODEL WAS ABANDONED BEFORE THE WAR EVEN ENDED.
I NEVER THOUGHT I'D MEET ONE OF THEM.
YOU'RE TOO RECKLESS TO BE CALLED STRATEGIC.
LIKE YOU'RE TESTING YOUR OWN WORTH.

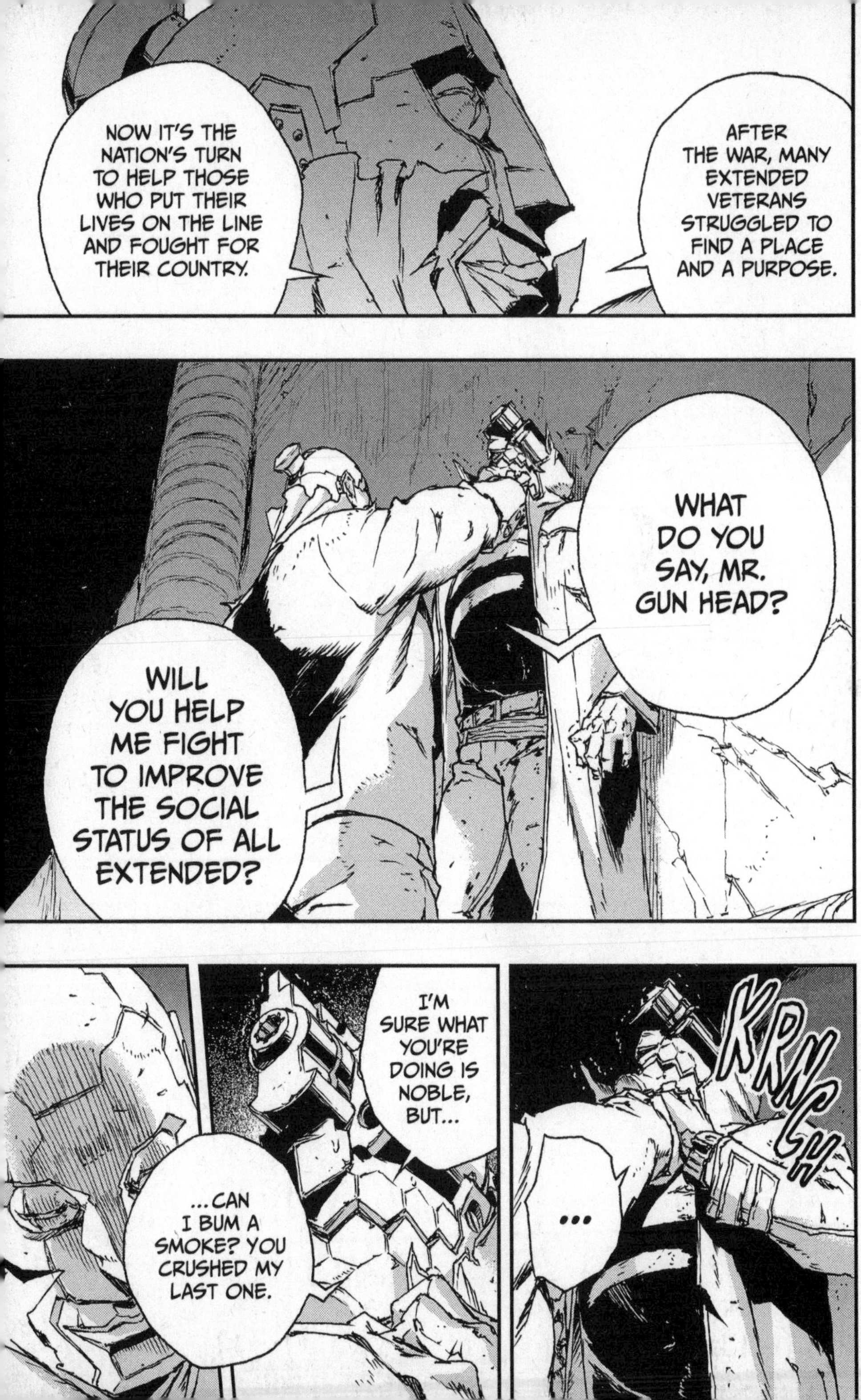
AFTER THE WAR, MANY EXTENDED VETERANS STRUGGLED TO FIND A PLACE AND A PURPOSE.
NOW IT'S THE NATION'S TURN TO HELP THOSE WHO PUT THEIR LIVES ON THE LINE AND FOUGHT FOR THEIR COUNTRY.
WHAT DO YOU SAY, MR. GUN HEAD?
WILL YOU HELP ME FIGHT TO IMPROVE THE SOCIAL STATUS OF ALL EXTENDED?
KRNCH
...
I'M SURE WHAT YOU'RE DOING IS NOBLE, BUT...
...CAN I BUM A SMOKE? YOU CRUSHED MY LAST ONE.

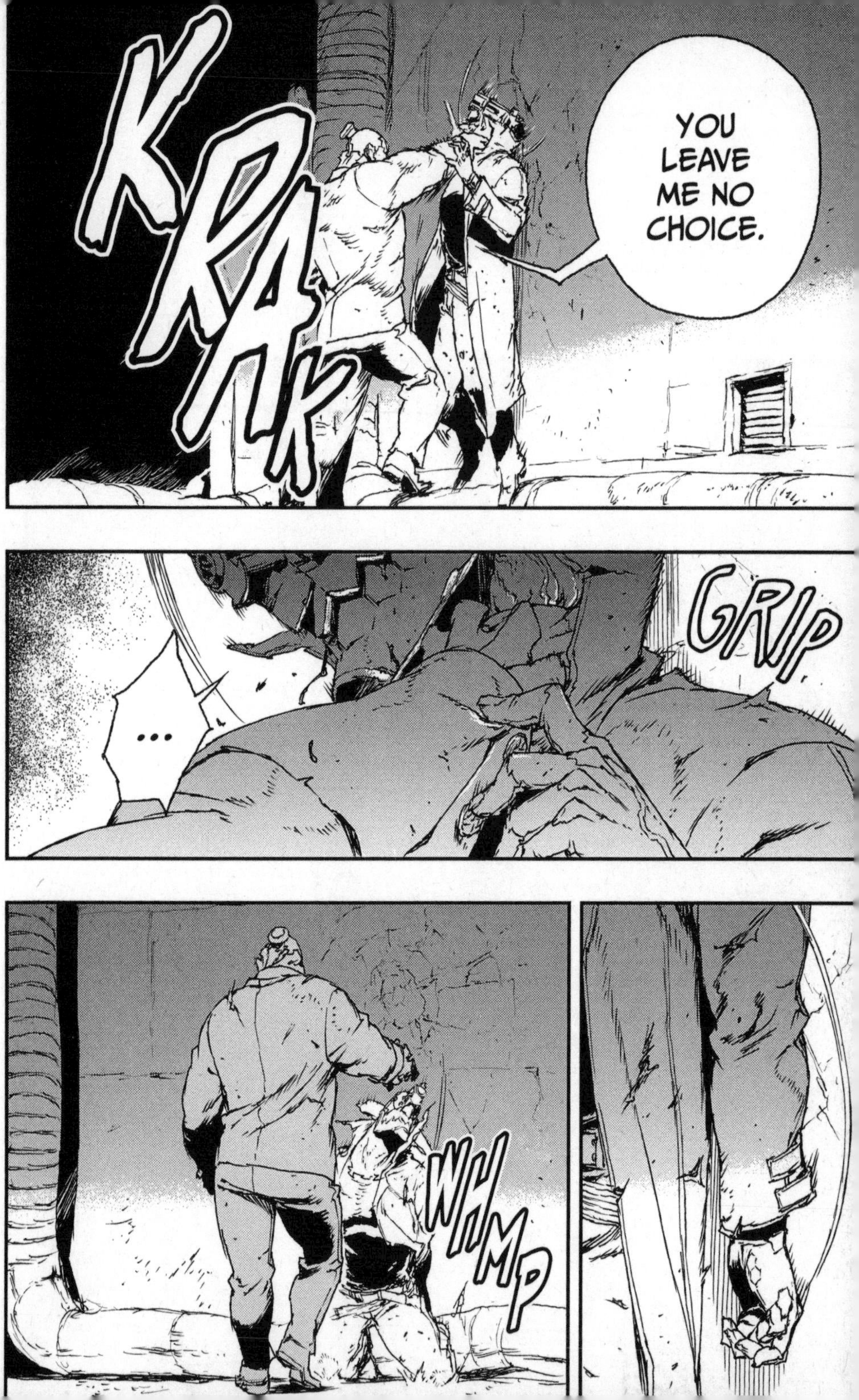
KRAK
YOU LEAVE ME NO CHOICE.
GRIP
...
WHUMP

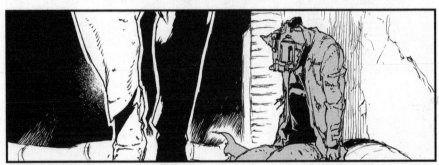

BUT
DO NOT
DESPAIR.

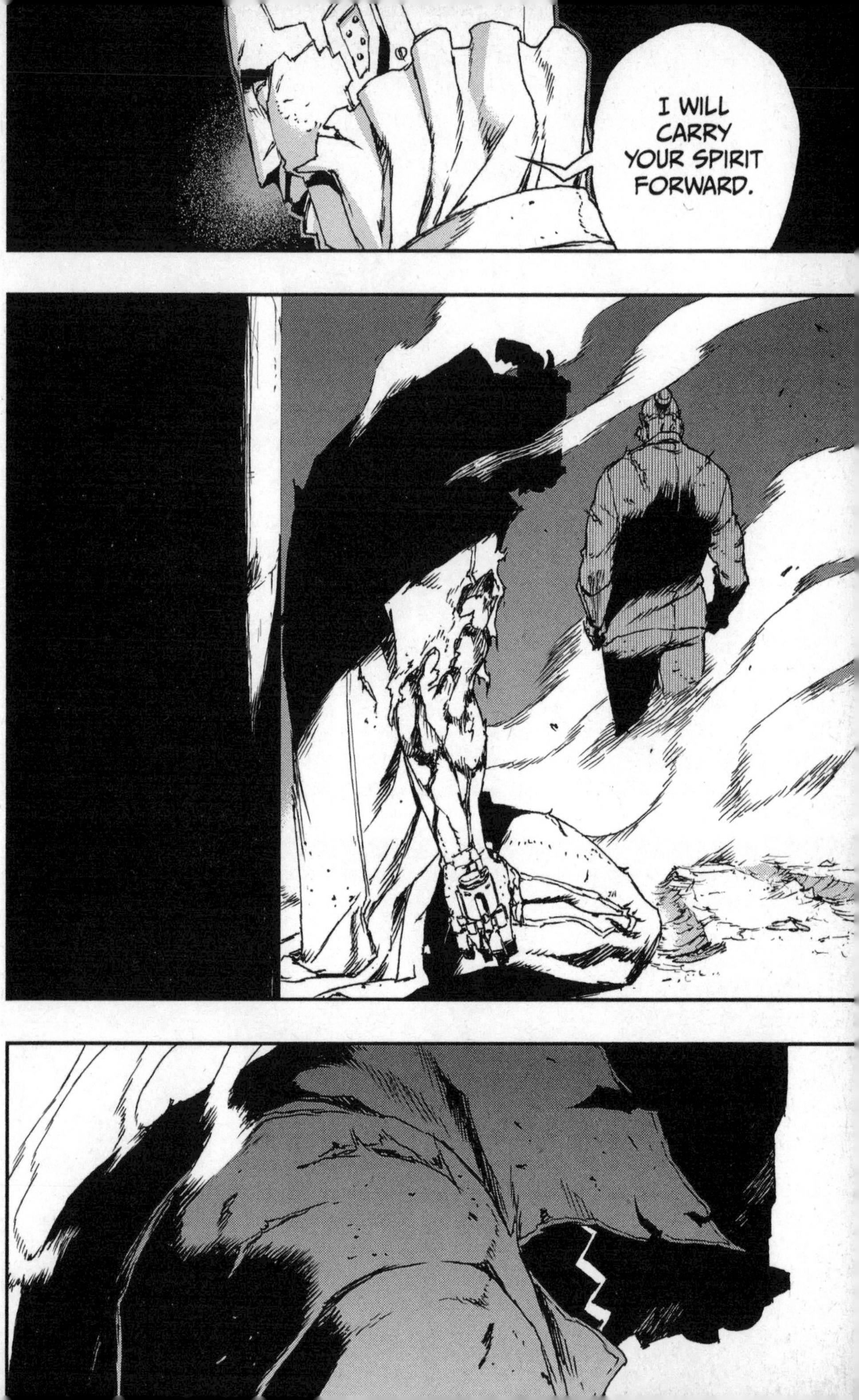
I WILL CARRY YOUR SPIRIT FORWARD.

Chapter 13
Madness

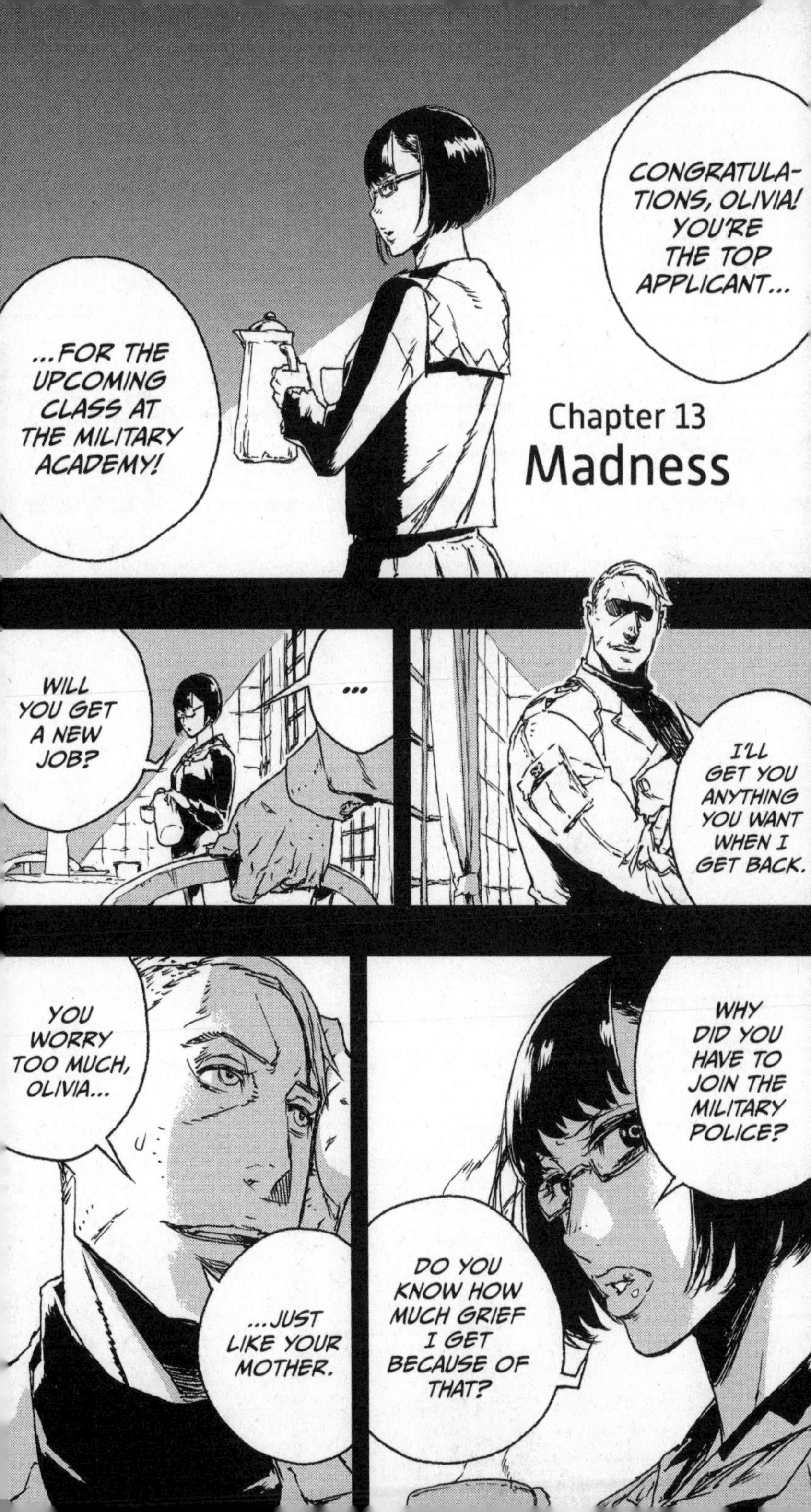

CONGRATULATIONS, OLIVIA! YOU'RE THE TOP APPLICANT...
...FOR THE UPCOMING CLASS AT THE MILITARY ACADEMY!
I'LL GET YOU ANYTHING YOU WANT WHEN I GET BACK.
...
WILL YOU GET A NEW JOB?
WHY DID YOU HAVE TO JOIN THE MILITARY POLICE?
DO YOU KNOW HOW MUCH GRIEF I GET BECAUSE OF THAT?
YOU WORRY TOO MUCH, OLIVIA...
...JUST LIKE YOUR MOTHER.

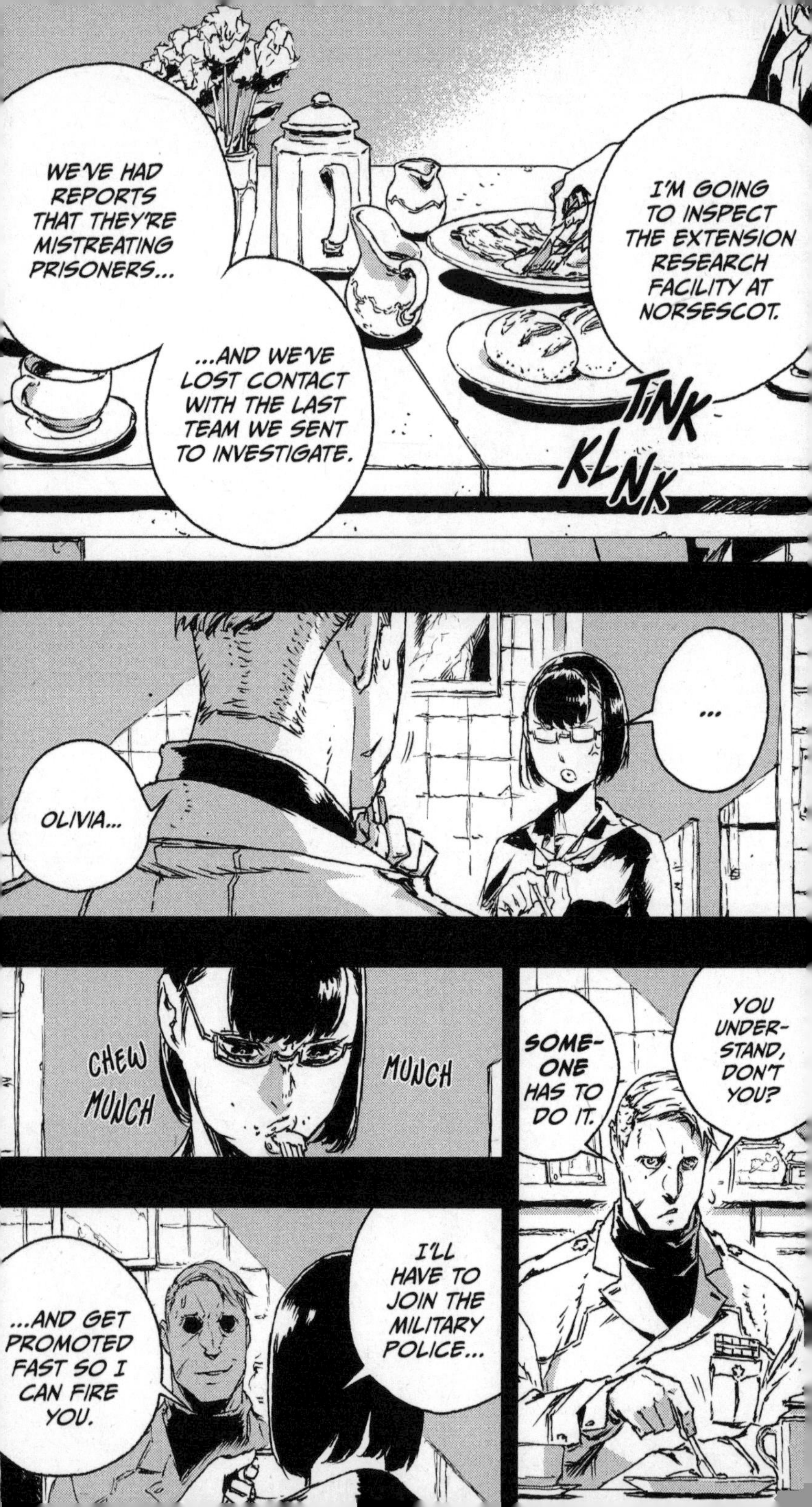
I'M GOING TO INSPECT THE EXTENSION RESEARCH FACILITY AT NORSESCOT.
TINK
KLNK
WE'VE HAD REPORTS THAT THEY'RE MISTREATING PRISONERS...
...AND WE'VE LOST CONTACT WITH THE LAST TEAM WE SENT TO INVESTIGATE.
...
OLIVIA...
YOU UNDERSTAND, DON'T YOU?
SOMEONE HAS TO DO IT.
MUNCH
CHEW
MUNCH
I'LL HAVE TO JOIN THE MILITARY POLICE...
...AND GET PROMOTED FAST SO I CAN FIRE YOU.

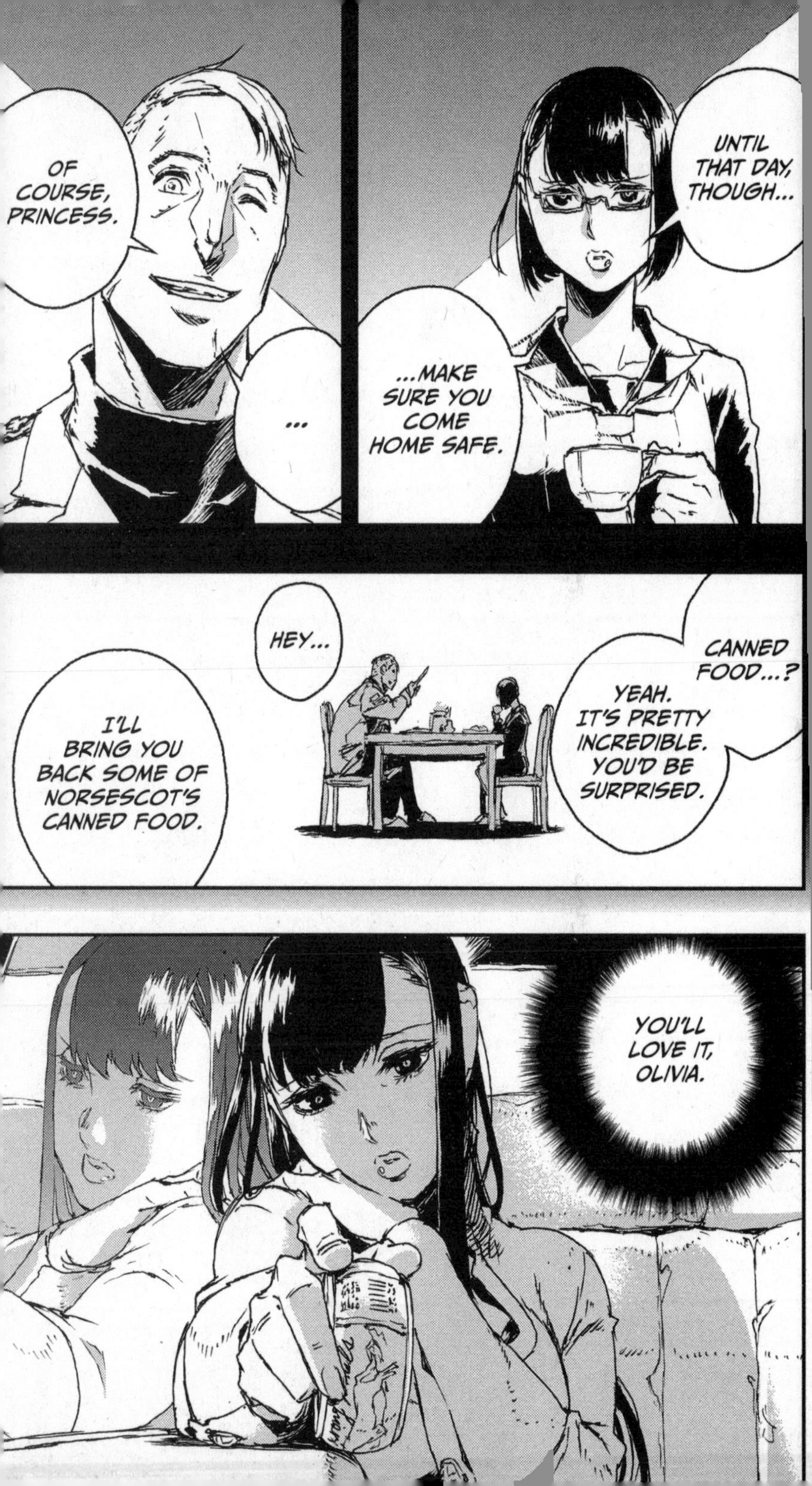
UNTIL THAT DAY, THOUGH...
...MAKE SURE YOU COME HOME SAFE.
OF COURSE, PRINCESS.
...
CANNED FOOD...?
YEAH. IT'S PRETTY INCREDIBLE. YOU'D BE SURPRISED.
HEY...
I'LL BRING YOU BACK SOME OF NORSESCOT'S CANNED FOOD.
YOU'LL LOVE IT, OLIVIA.

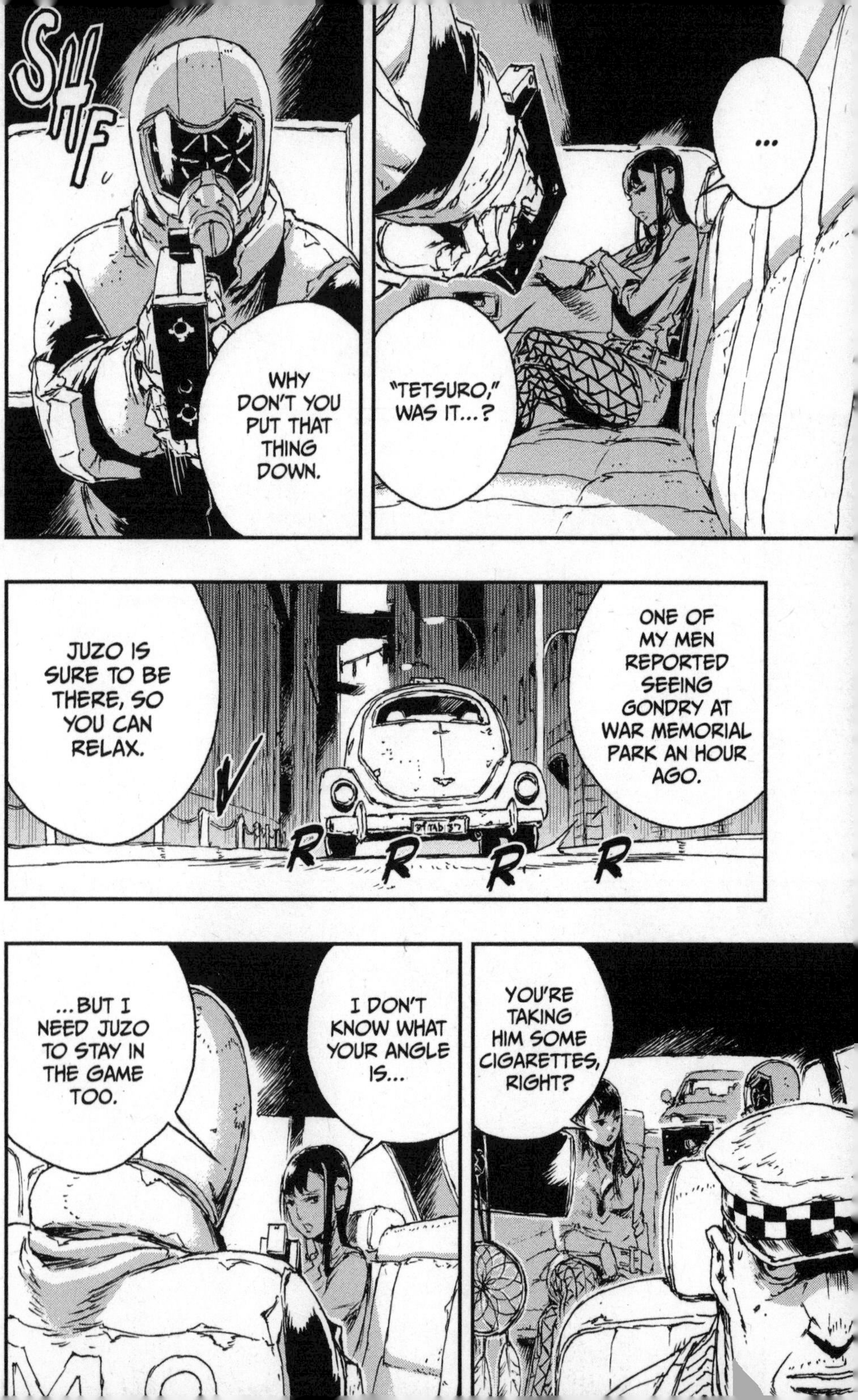
...
"TETSURO," WAS IT...?
SHF
WHY DON'T YOU PUT THAT THING DOWN.
ONE OF MY MEN REPORTED SEEING GONDRY AT WAR MEMORIAL PARK AN HOUR AGO.
JUZO IS SURE TO BE THERE, SO YOU CAN RELAX.
R R R R
YOU'RE TAKING HIM SOME CIGARETTES, RIGHT?
I DON'T KNOW WHAT YOUR ANGLE IS...
...BUT I NEED JUZO TO STAY IN THE GAME TOO.

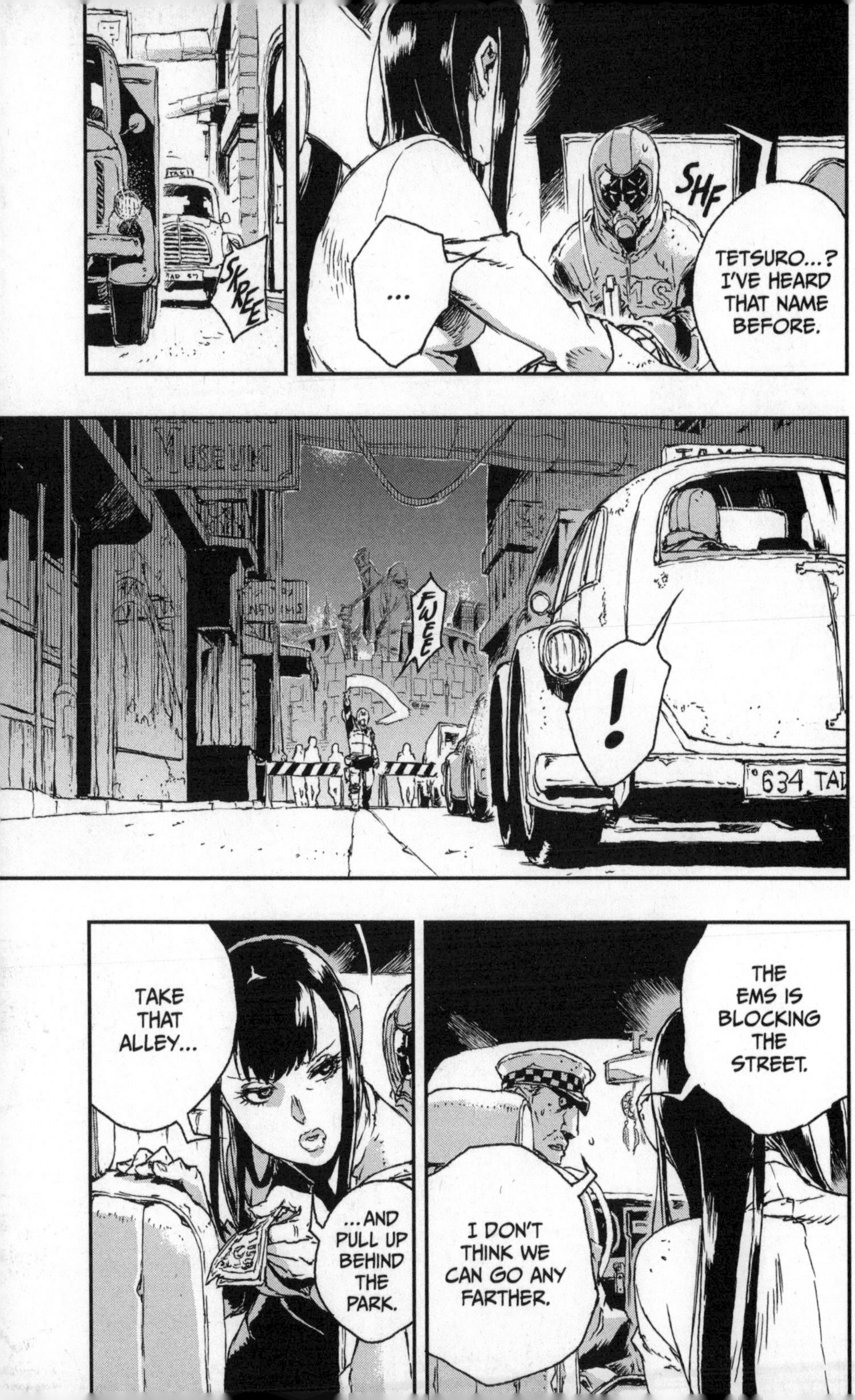
SHF
TETSURO...? I'VE HEARD THAT NAME BEFORE.
...
SKREE
!
FWEE
THE EMS IS BLOCKING THE STREET.
I DON'T THINK WE CAN GO ANY FARTHER.
TAKE THAT ALLEY...
...AND PULL UP BEHIND THE PARK.

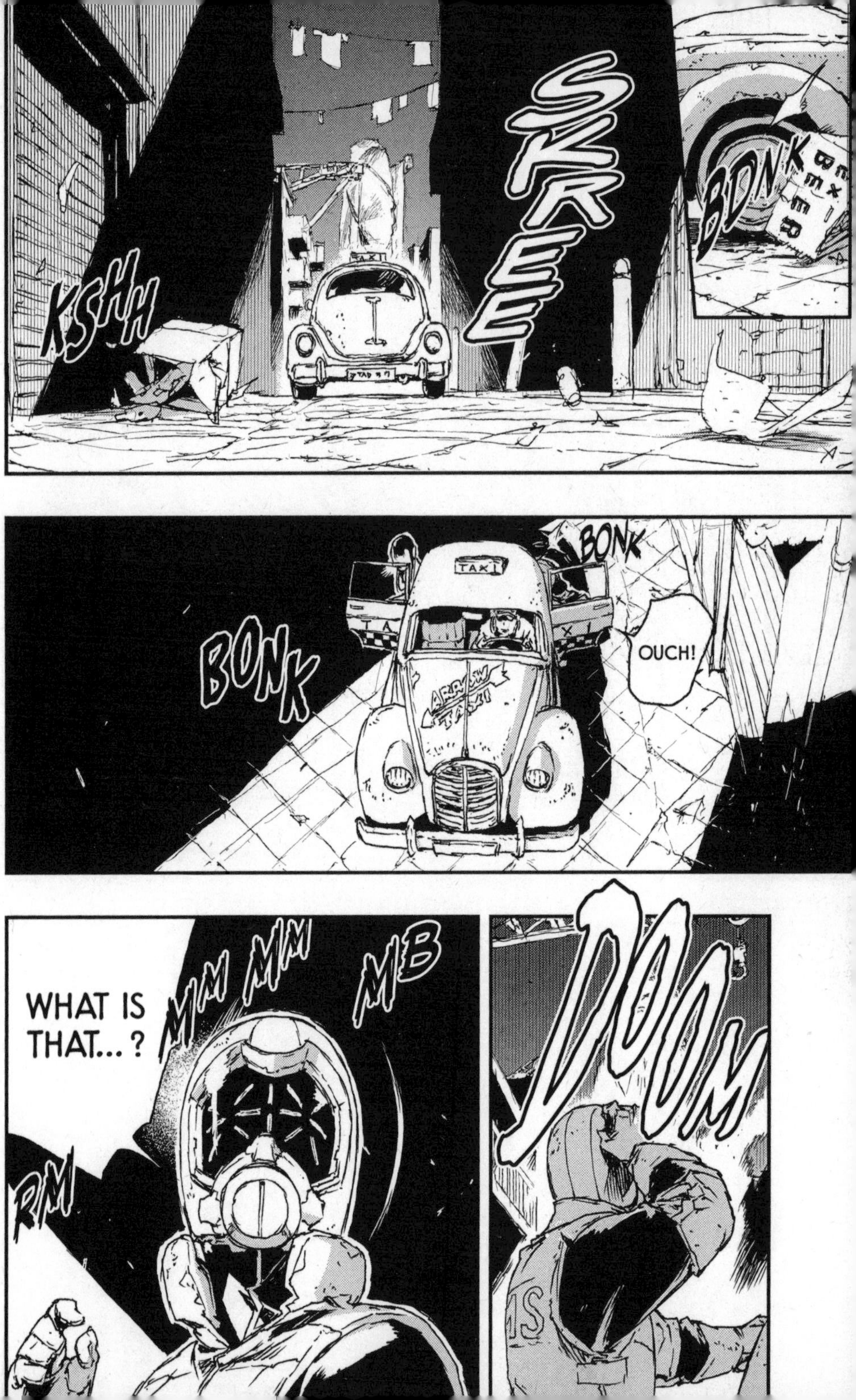
BONK
SKREE
KSHH
BONK
OUCH!
BONK
DOOM
MM MM MM
MB
WHAT IS THAT...?
RM

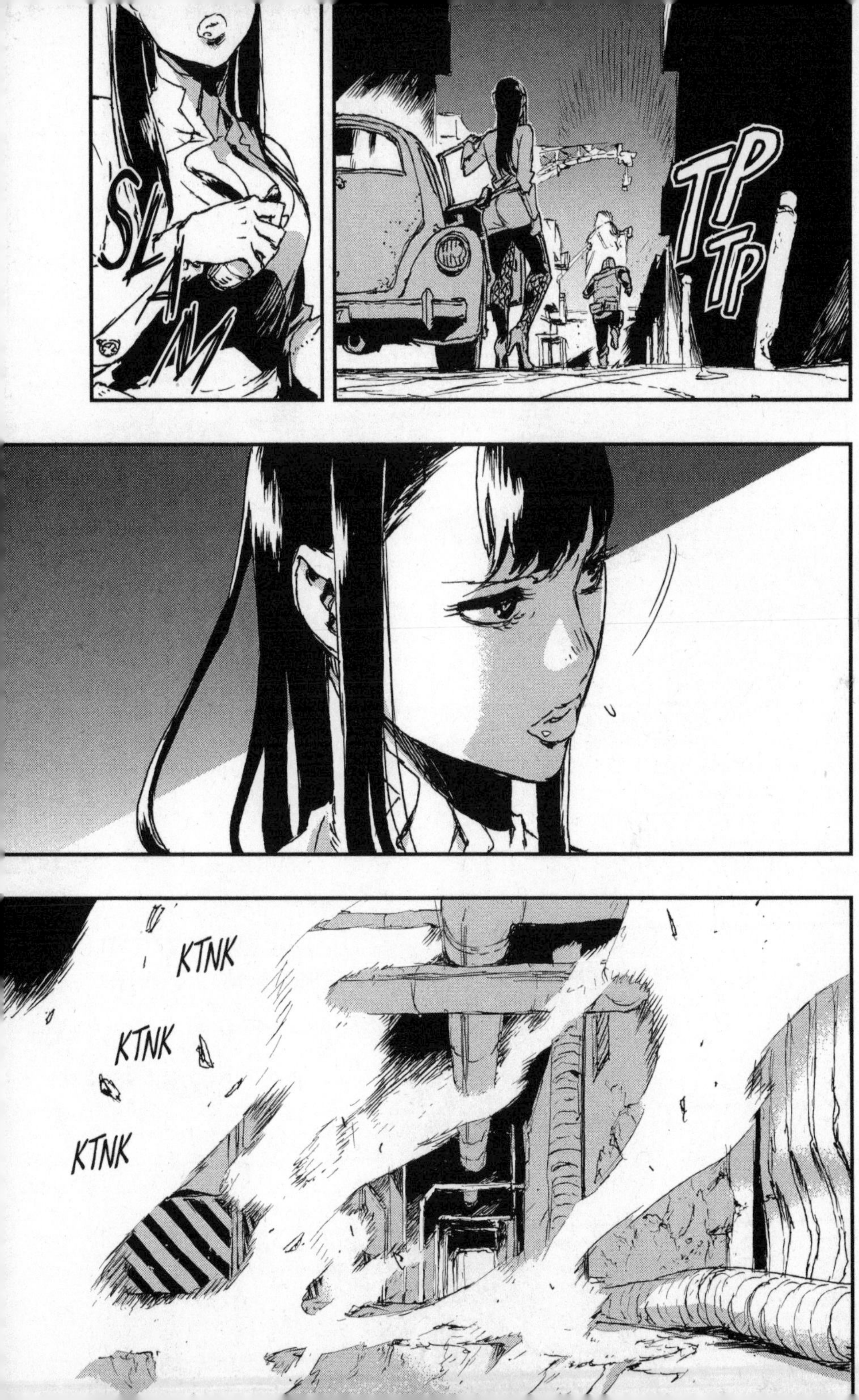
TP TP
SLAM
KTNK
KTNK
KTNK

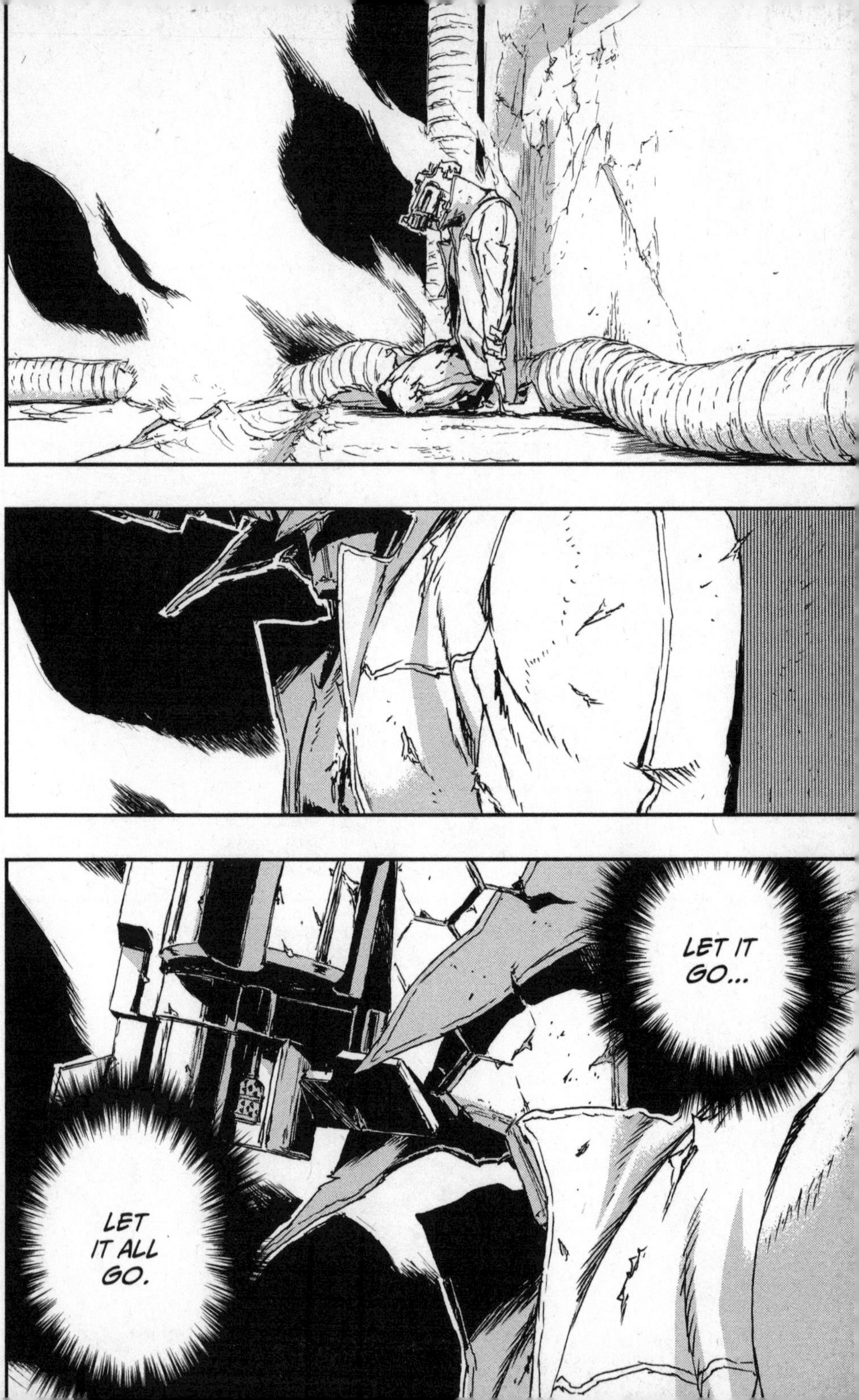
LET IT GO...
LET IT ALL GO.

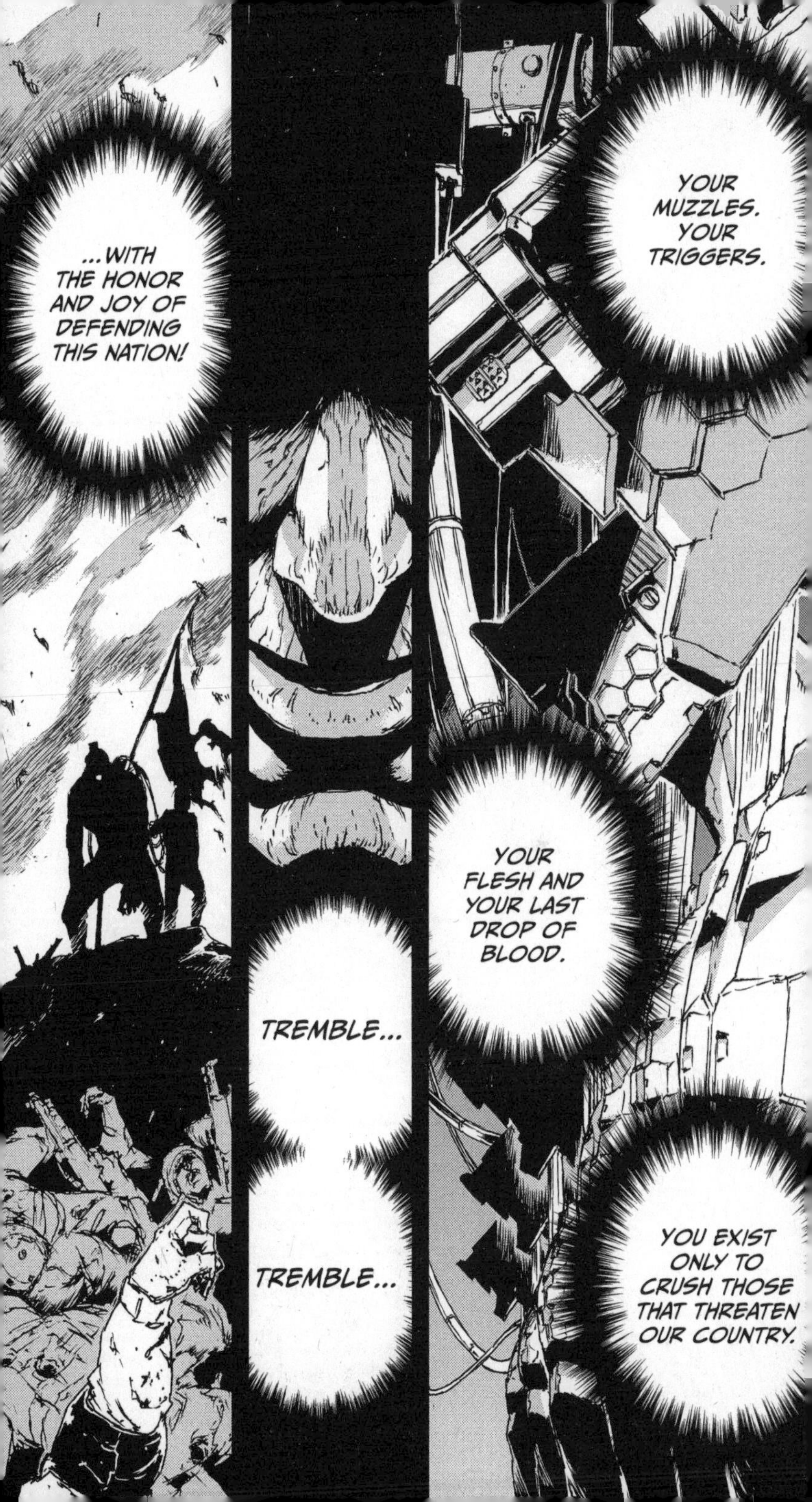
YOUR MUZZLES. YOUR TRIGGERS.
YOUR FLESH AND YOUR LAST DROP OF BLOOD.
YOU EXIST ONLY TO CRUSH THOSE THAT THREATEN OUR COUNTRY.
TREMBLE...
TREMBLE...
...WITH THE HONOR AND JOY OF DEFENDING THIS NATION!

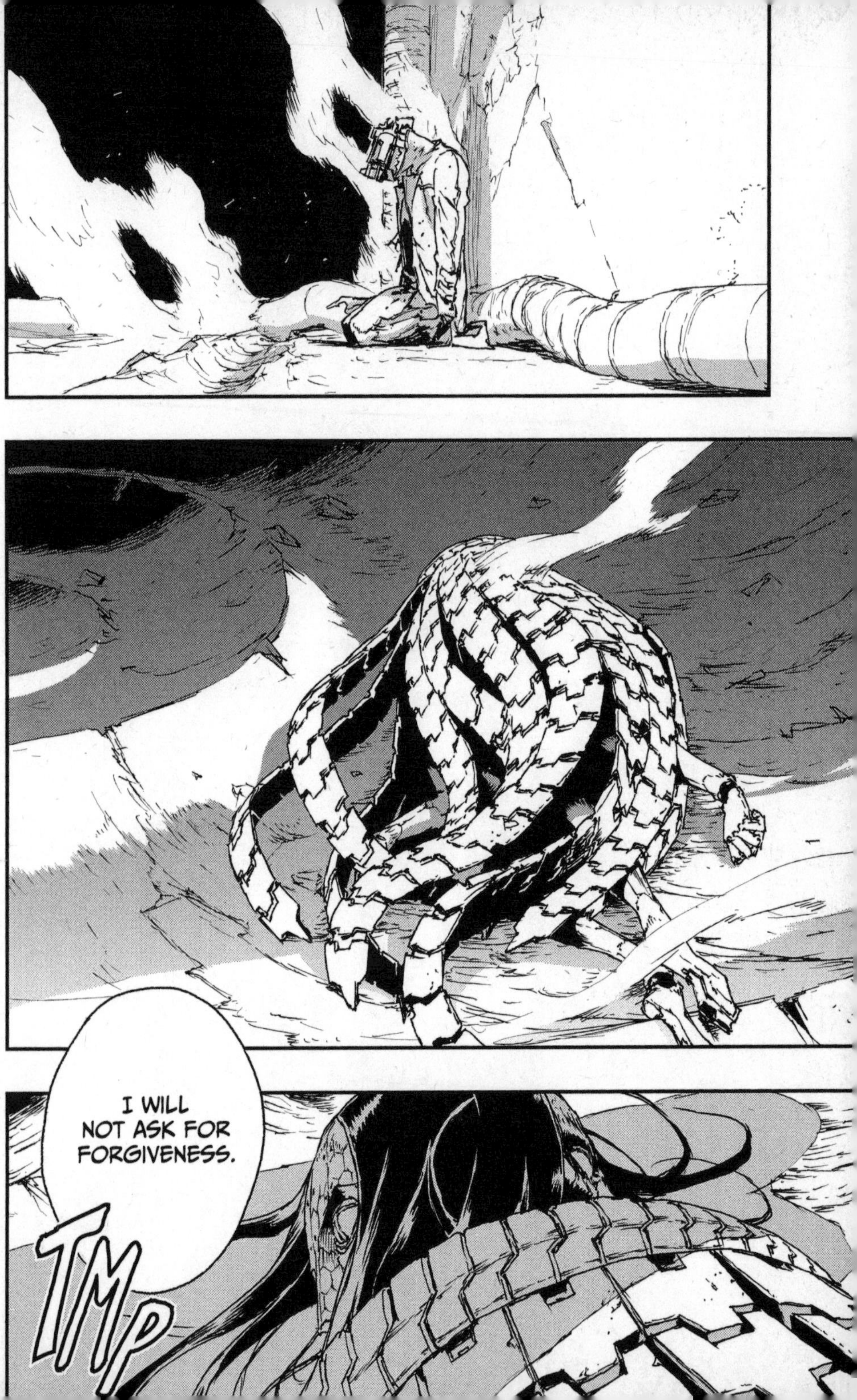
I WILL NOT ASK FOR FORGIVENESS.
TMP

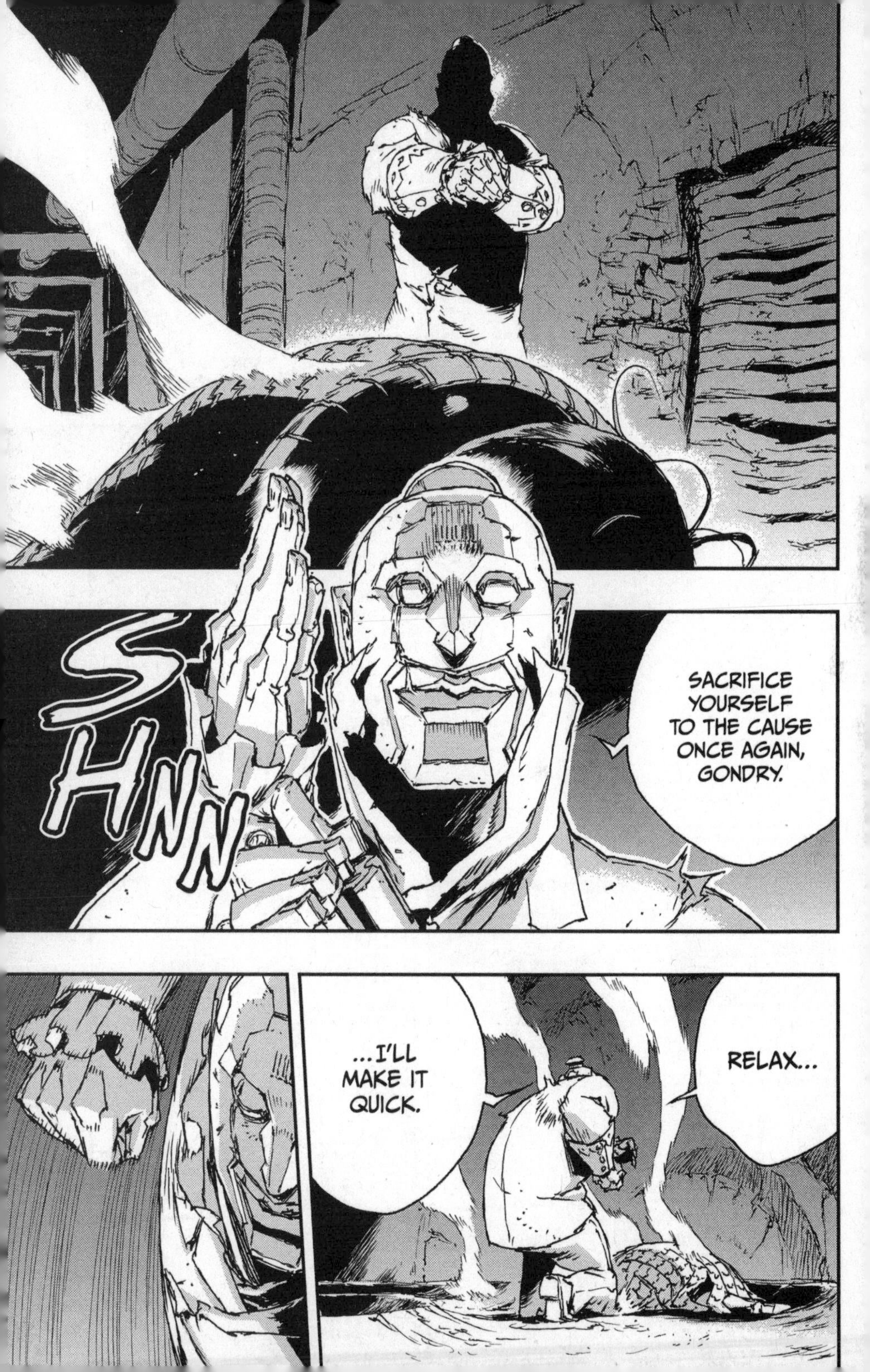
SACRIFICE YOURSELF TO THE CAUSE ONCE AGAIN, GONDRY.
SHNN
RELAX...
...I'LL MAKE IT QUICK.

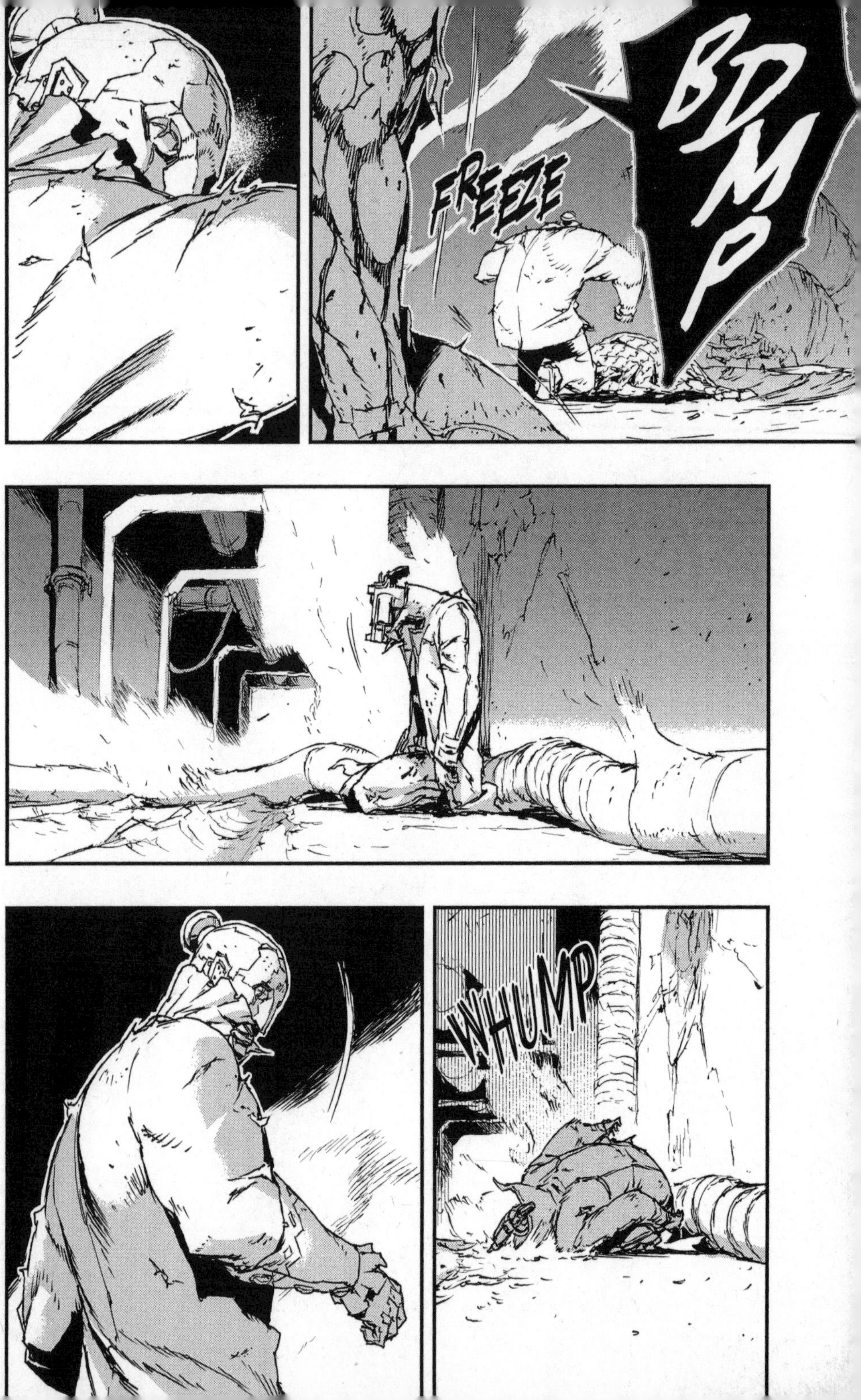
BDMP
FREEZE
WHUMP

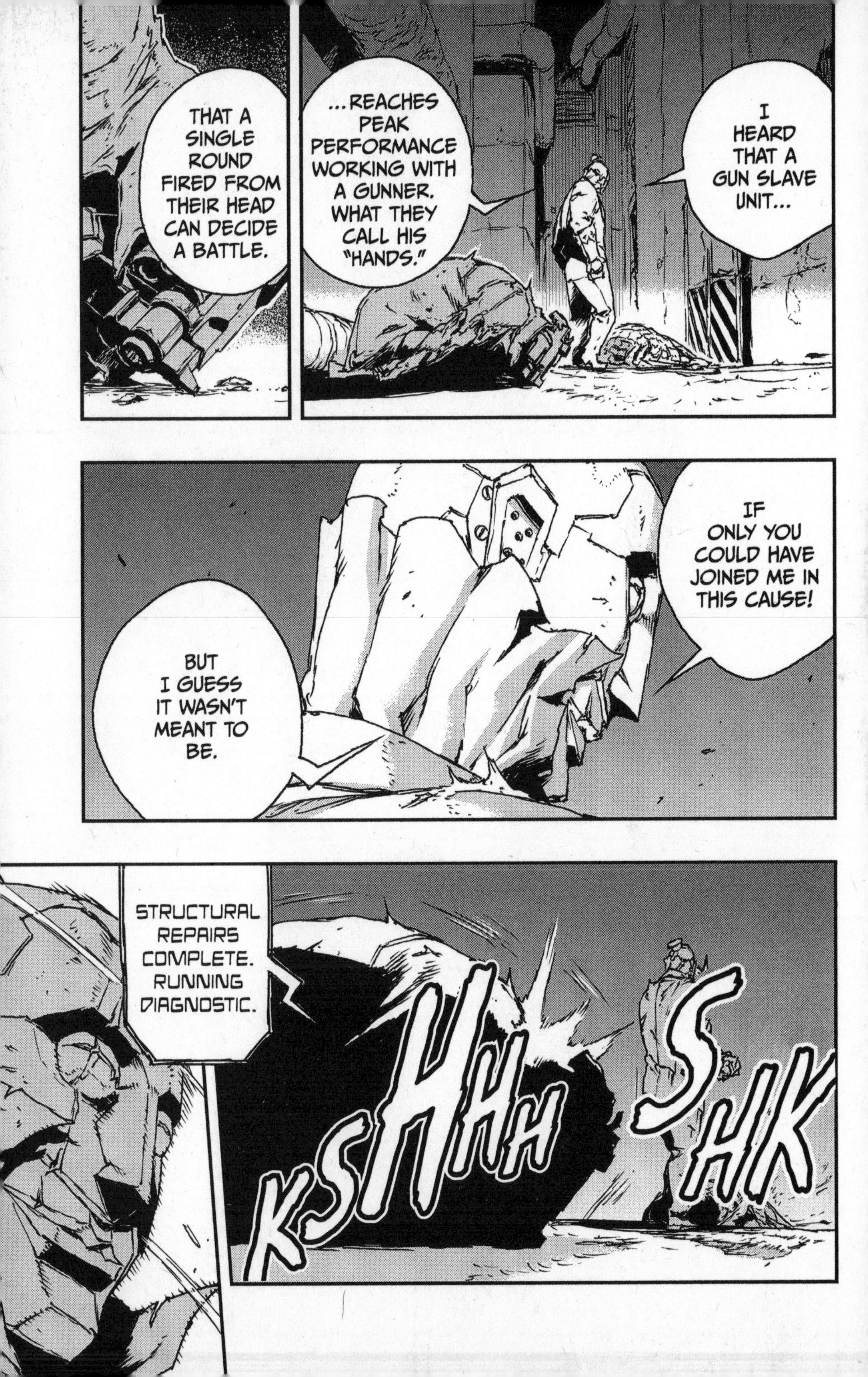
I HEARD THAT A GUN SLAVE UNIT...
...REACHES PEAK PERFORMANCE WORKING WITH A GUNNER. WHAT THEY CALL HIS "HANDS."
THAT A SINGLE ROUND FIRED FROM THEIR HEAD CAN DECIDE A BATTLE.
IF ONLY YOU COULD HAVE JOINED ME IN THIS CAUSE!
BUT I GUESS IT WASN'T MEANT TO BE.
STRUCTURAL REPAIRS COMPLETE. RUNNING DIAGNOSTIC.
SHK
KSHHH

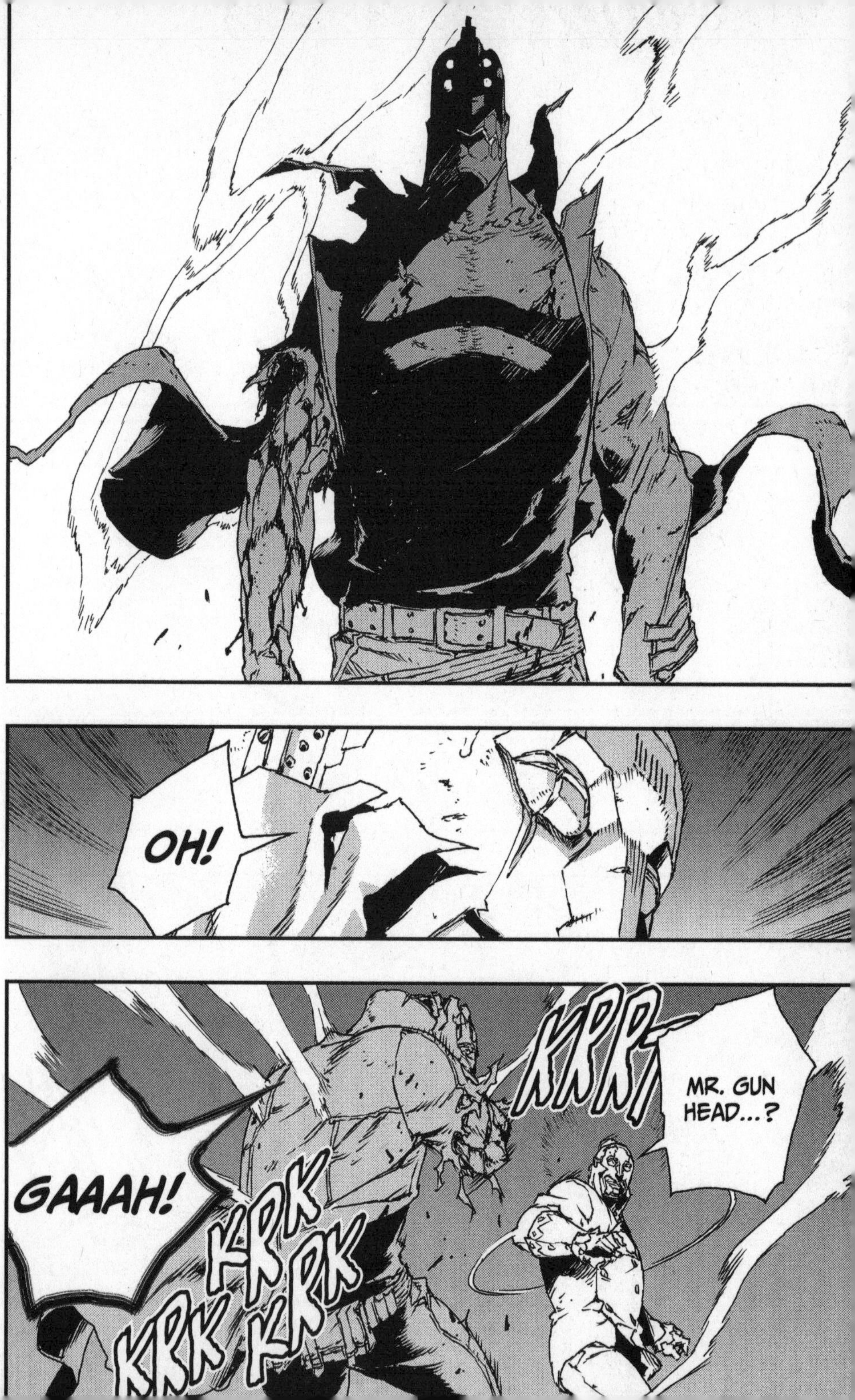
OH!
MR. GUN HEAD...?
KRRR
GAAAH!
KRK KRK KRK

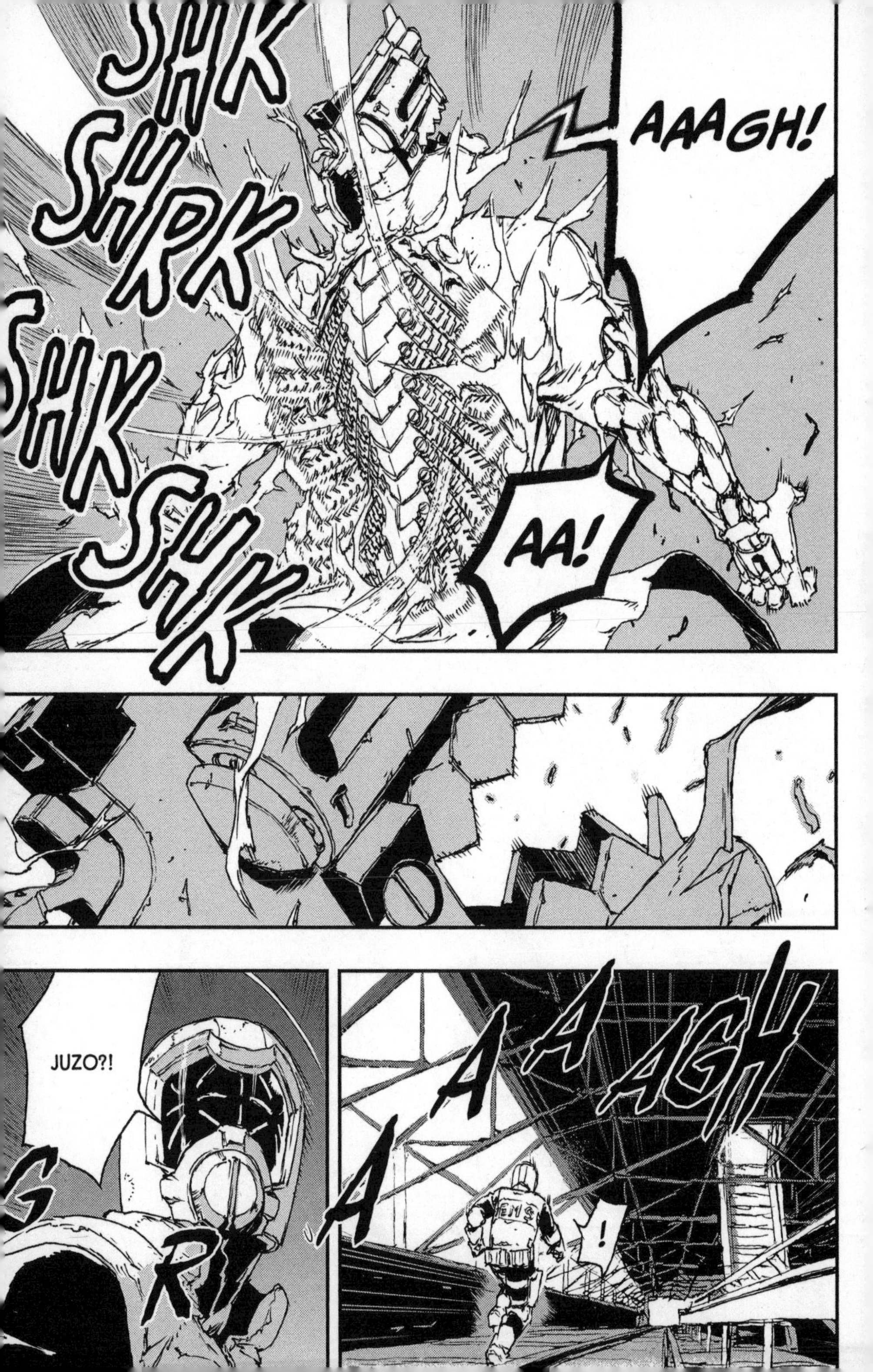
AAAGH!
AA!
SHK SHPK SHK SHK
A A A AGH
!
JUZO?!

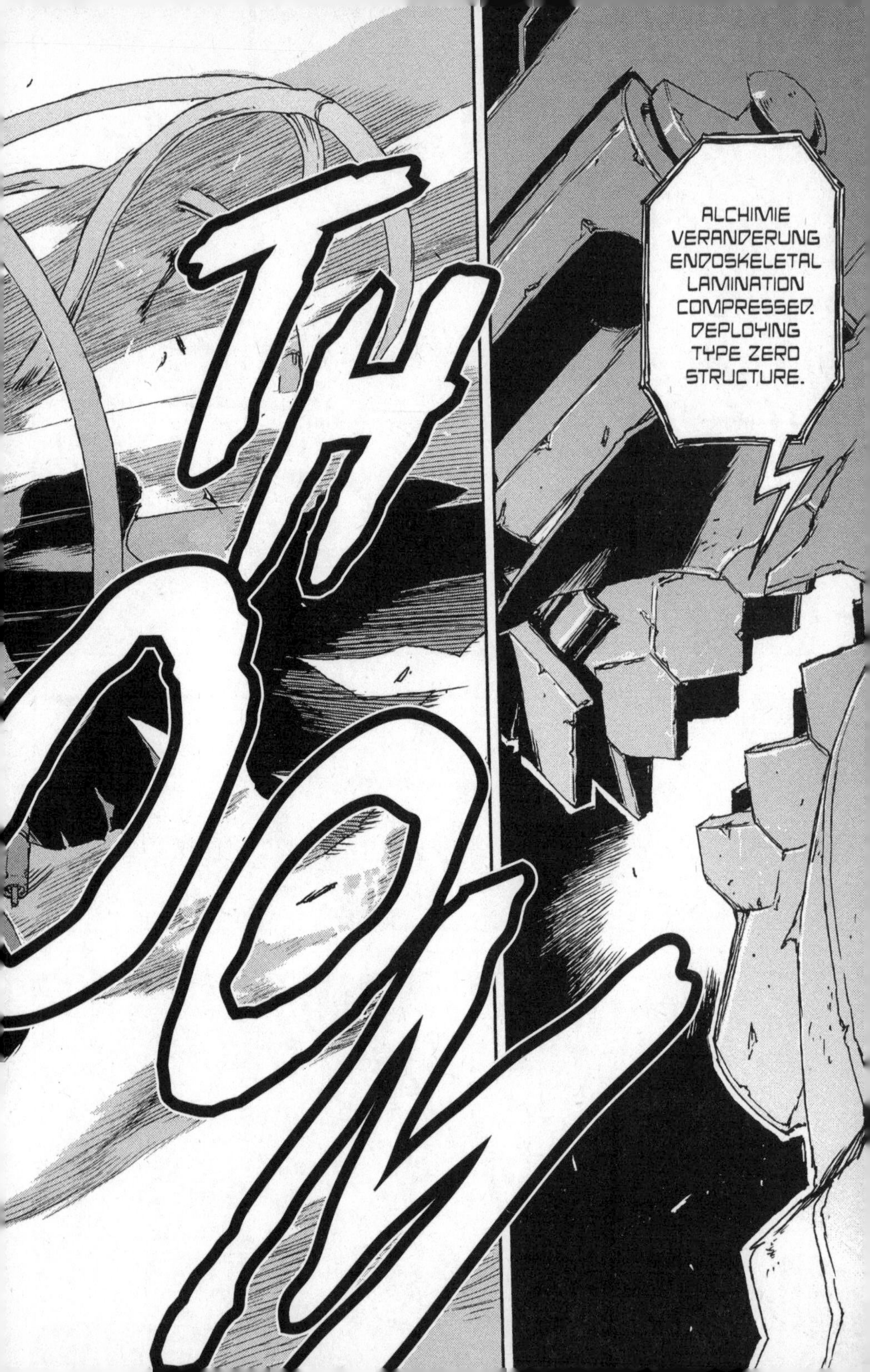
ALCHIMIE VERANDERUNG ENDOSKELETAL LAMINATION COMPRESSED. DEPLOYING TYPE ZERO STRUCTURE.
THOOM

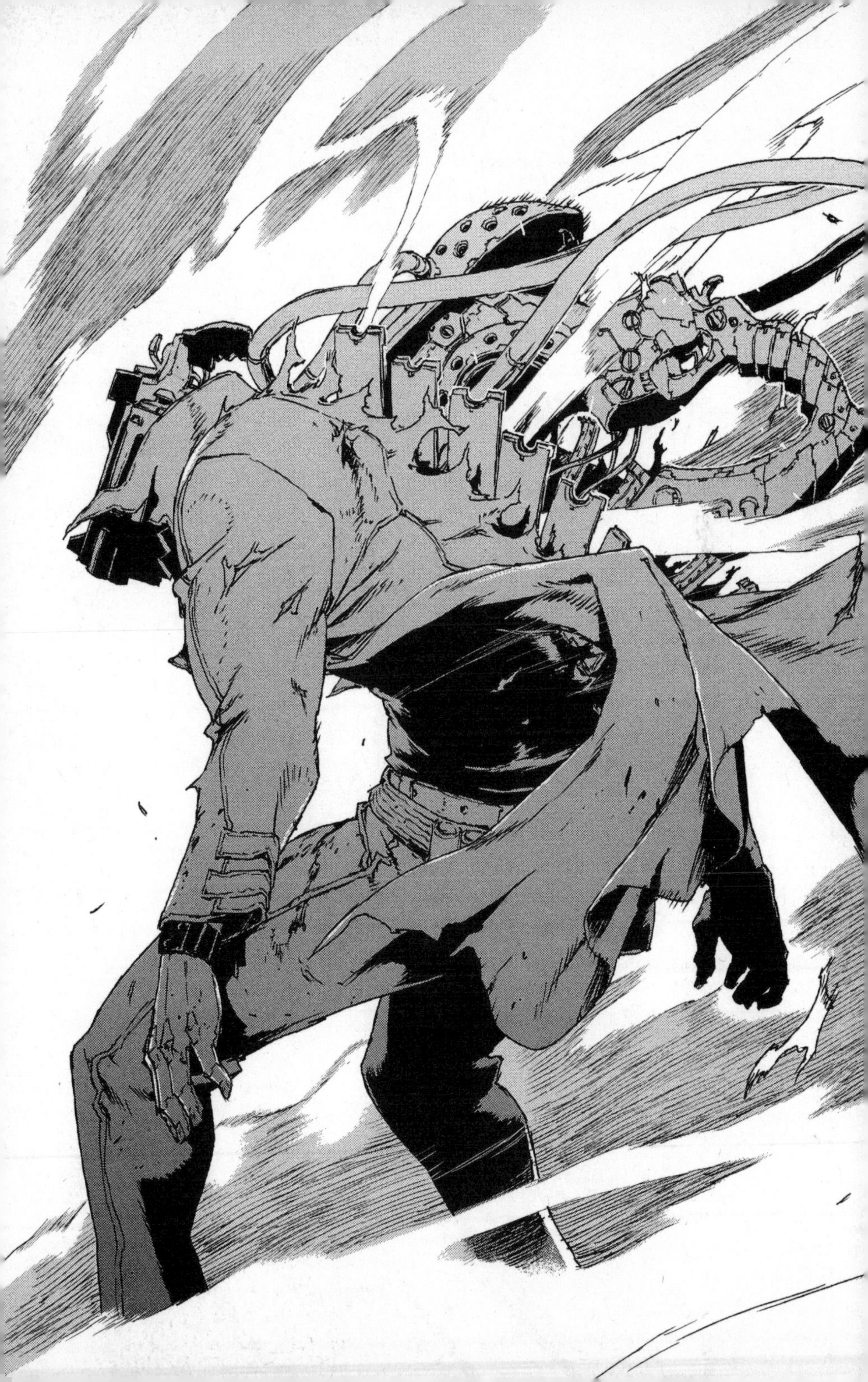

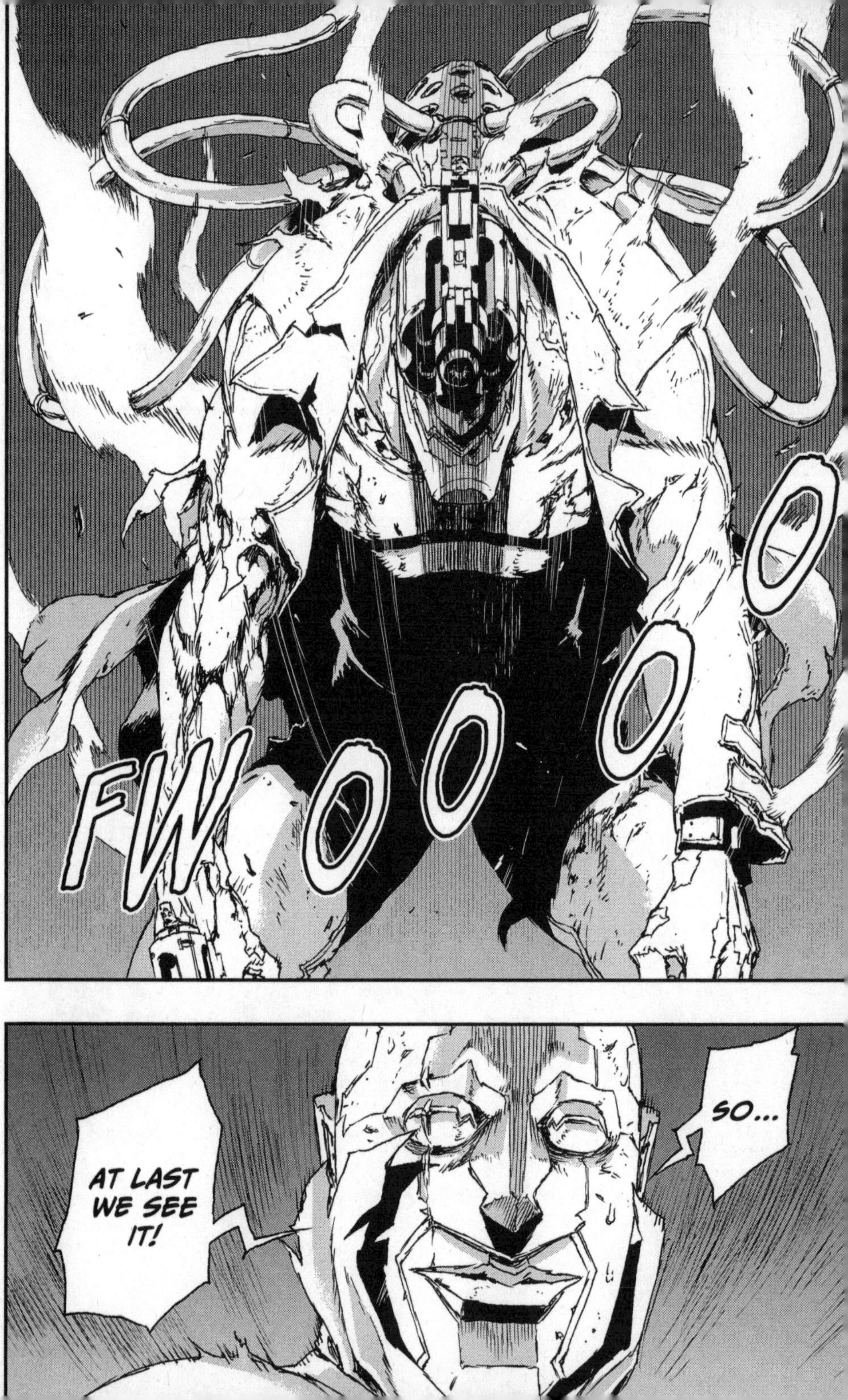
FWOOOOO
SO...
AT LAST WE SEE IT!

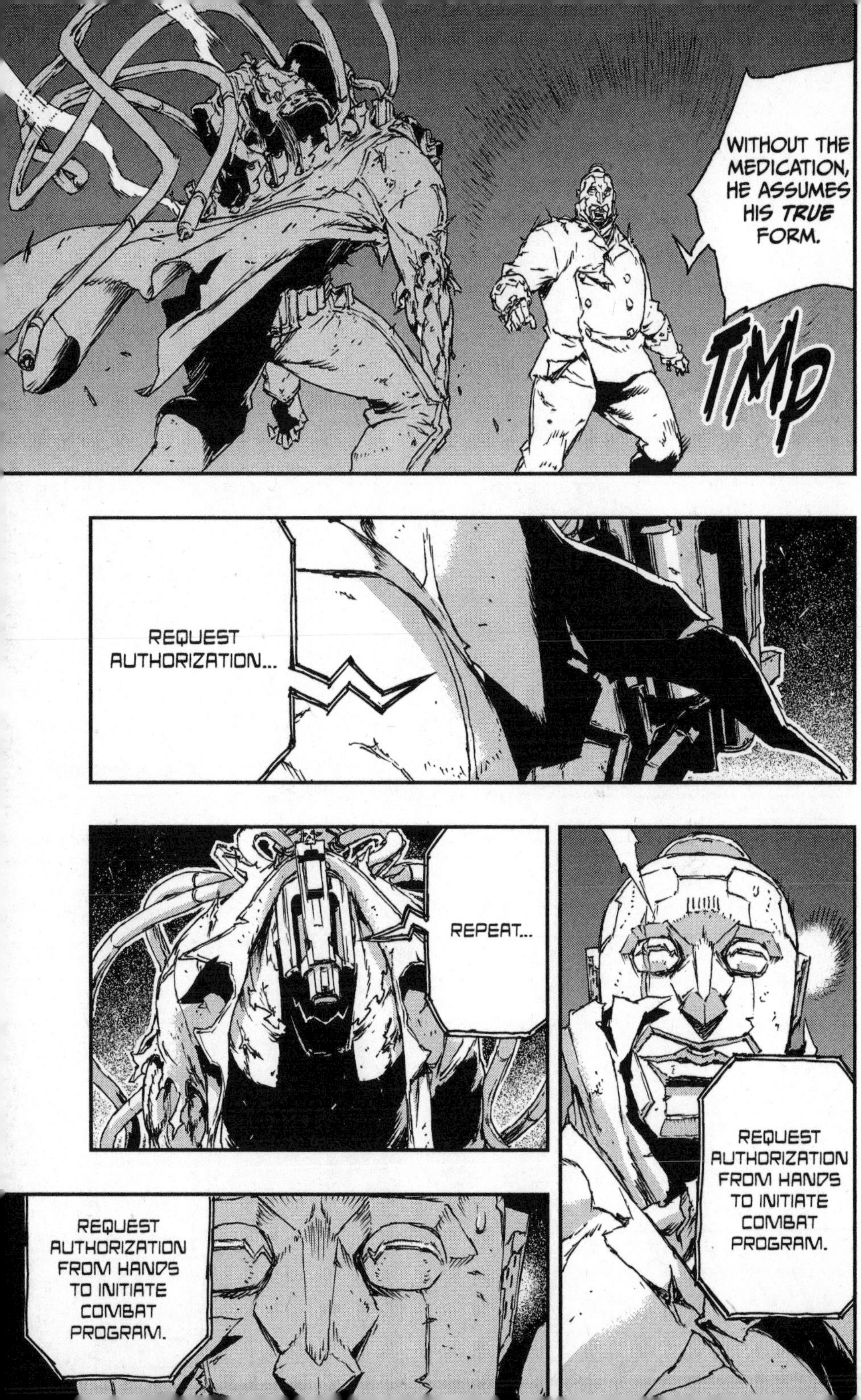
WITHOUT THE MEDICATION, HE ASSUMES HIS *TRUE* FORM.
TMP
REQUEST AUTHORIZATION...
REQUEST AUTHORIZATION FROM HANDS TO INITIATE COMBAT PROGRAM.
REPEAT...
REQUEST AUTHORIZATION FROM HANDS TO INITIATE COMBAT PROGRAM.

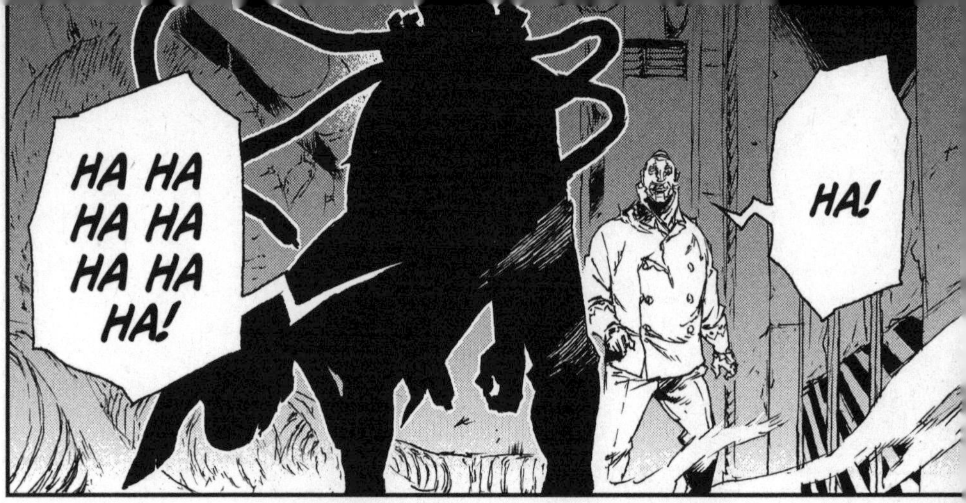
HA!
HA HA HA HA HA HA HA!

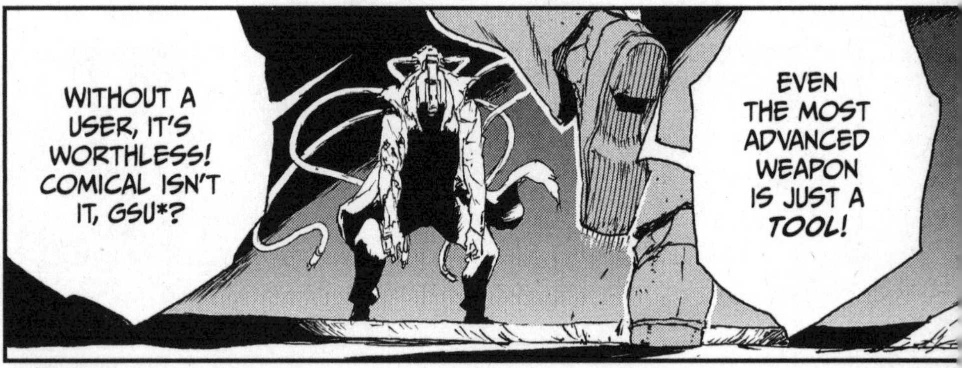
EVEN THE MOST ADVANCED WEAPON IS JUST A *TOOL*!
WITHOUT A USER, IT'S WORTHLESS! COMICAL ISN'T IT, GSU*?

*Gun Slave Unit

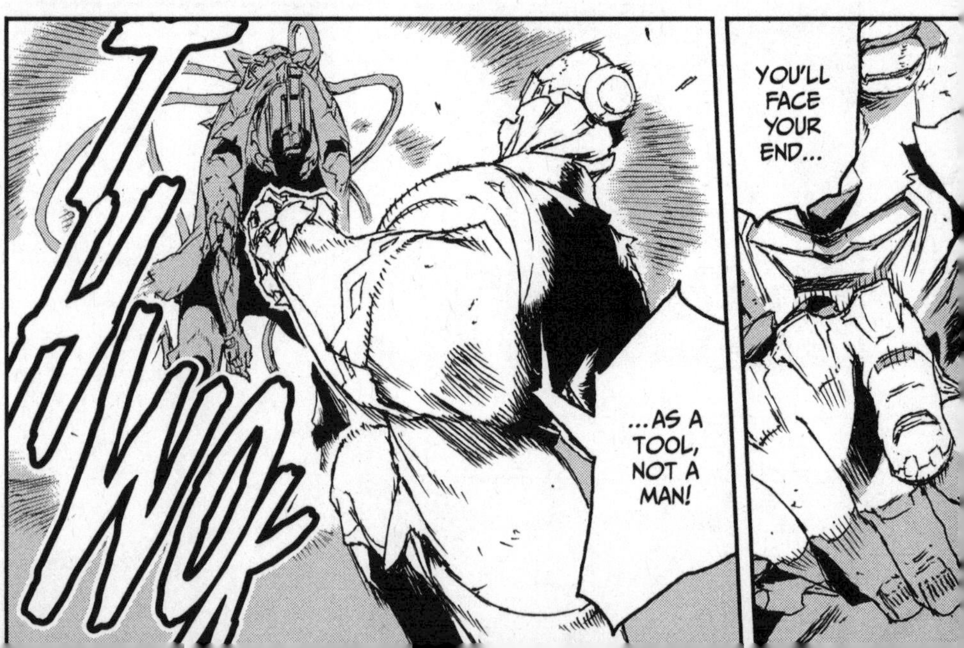
YOU'LL FACE YOUR END...
...AS A TOOL, NOT A MAN!

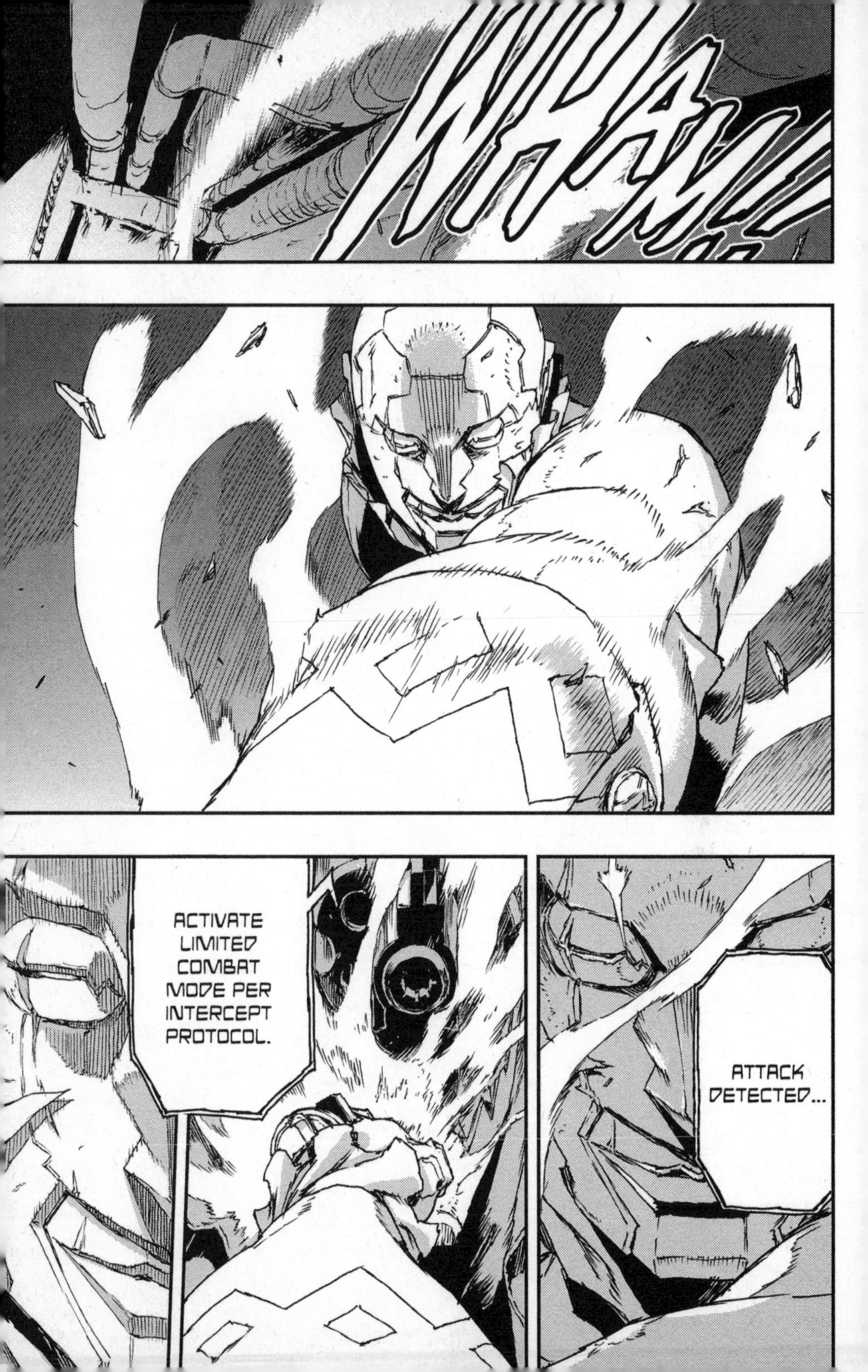
ATTACK DETECTED...
ACTIVATE LIMITED COMBAT MODE PER INTERCEPT PROTOCOL.

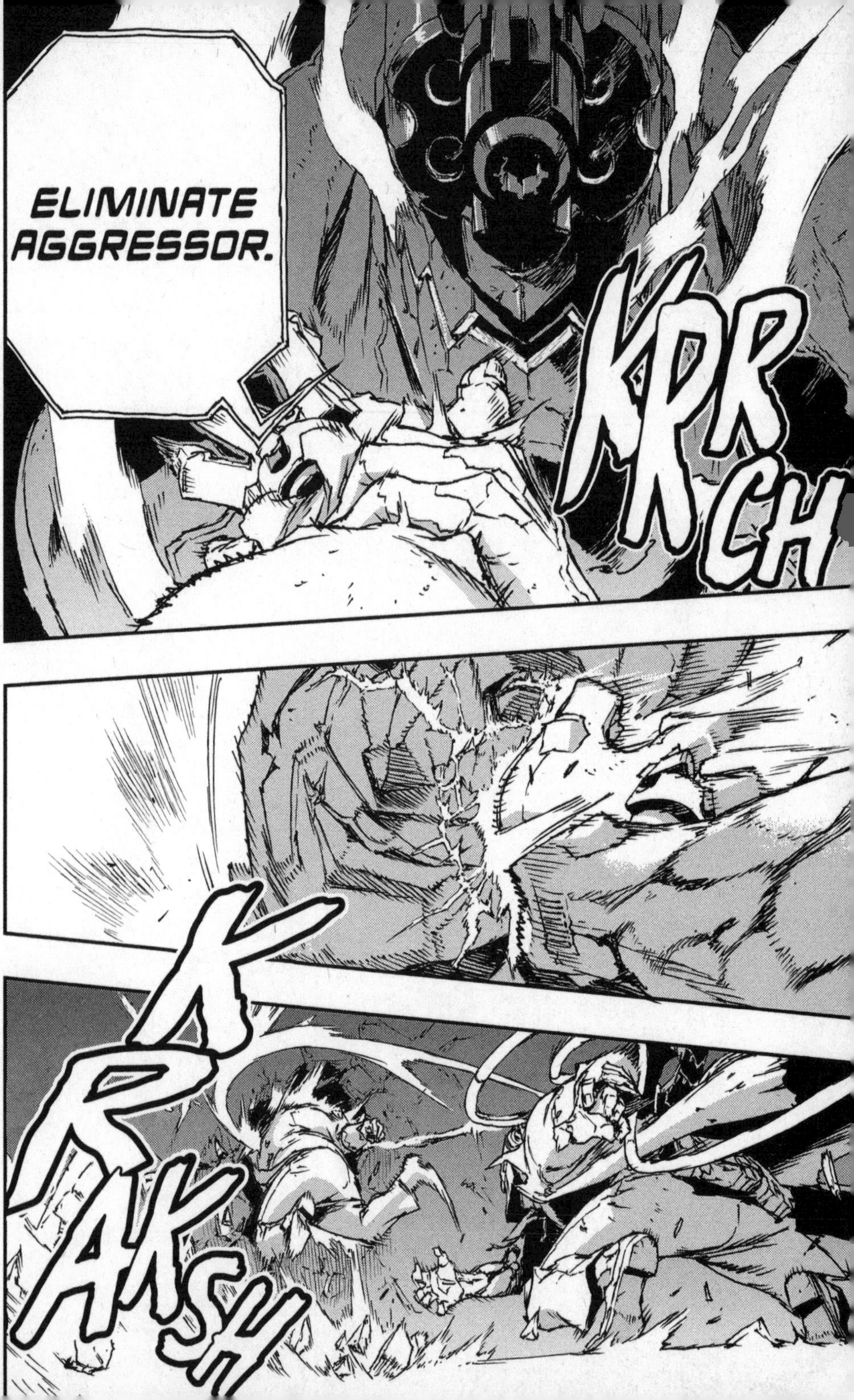ELIMINATE AGGRESSOR.
KRRCH
KRAKSH

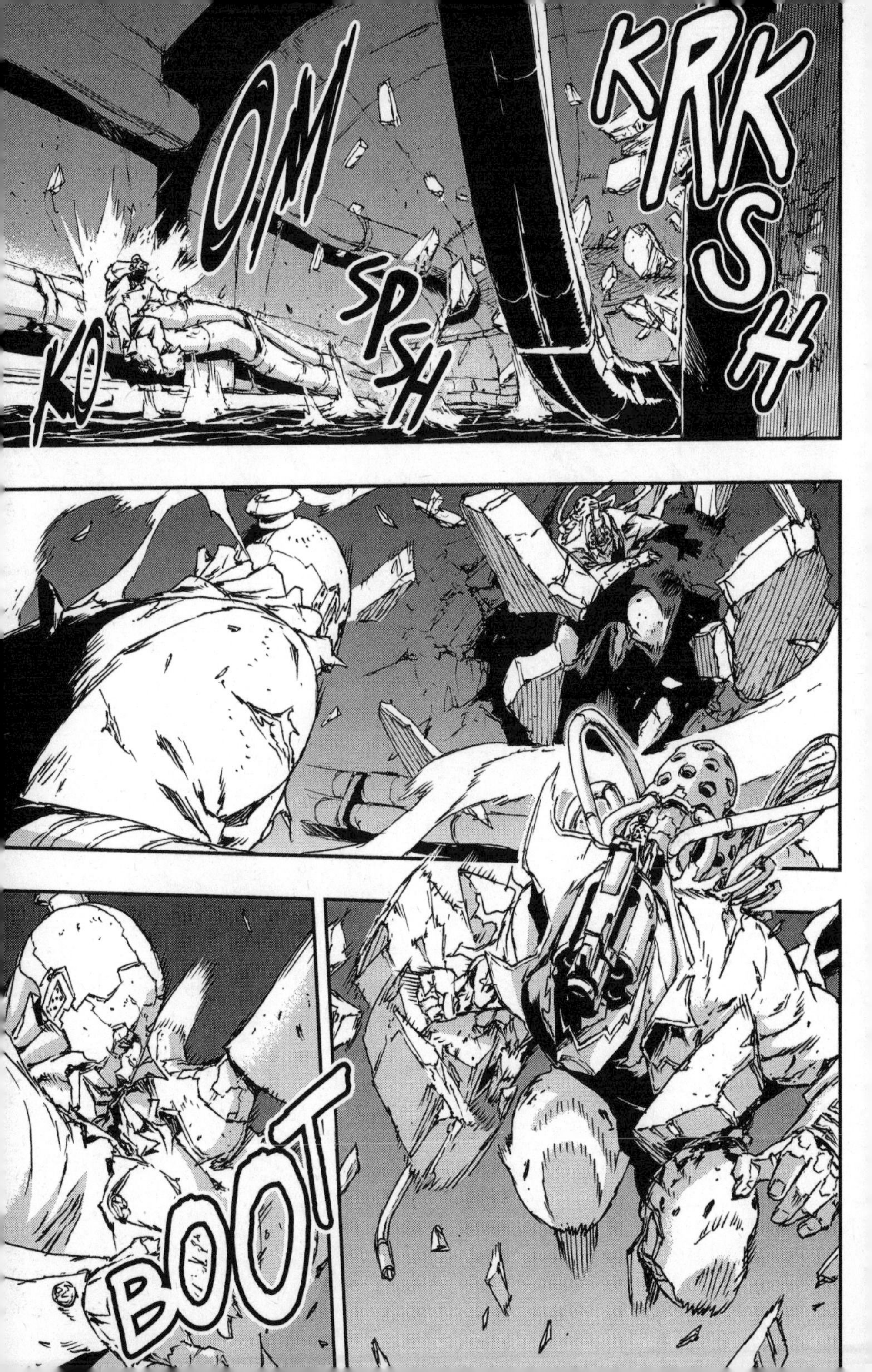
KRKSH
SPSH
KOOM
BOOT

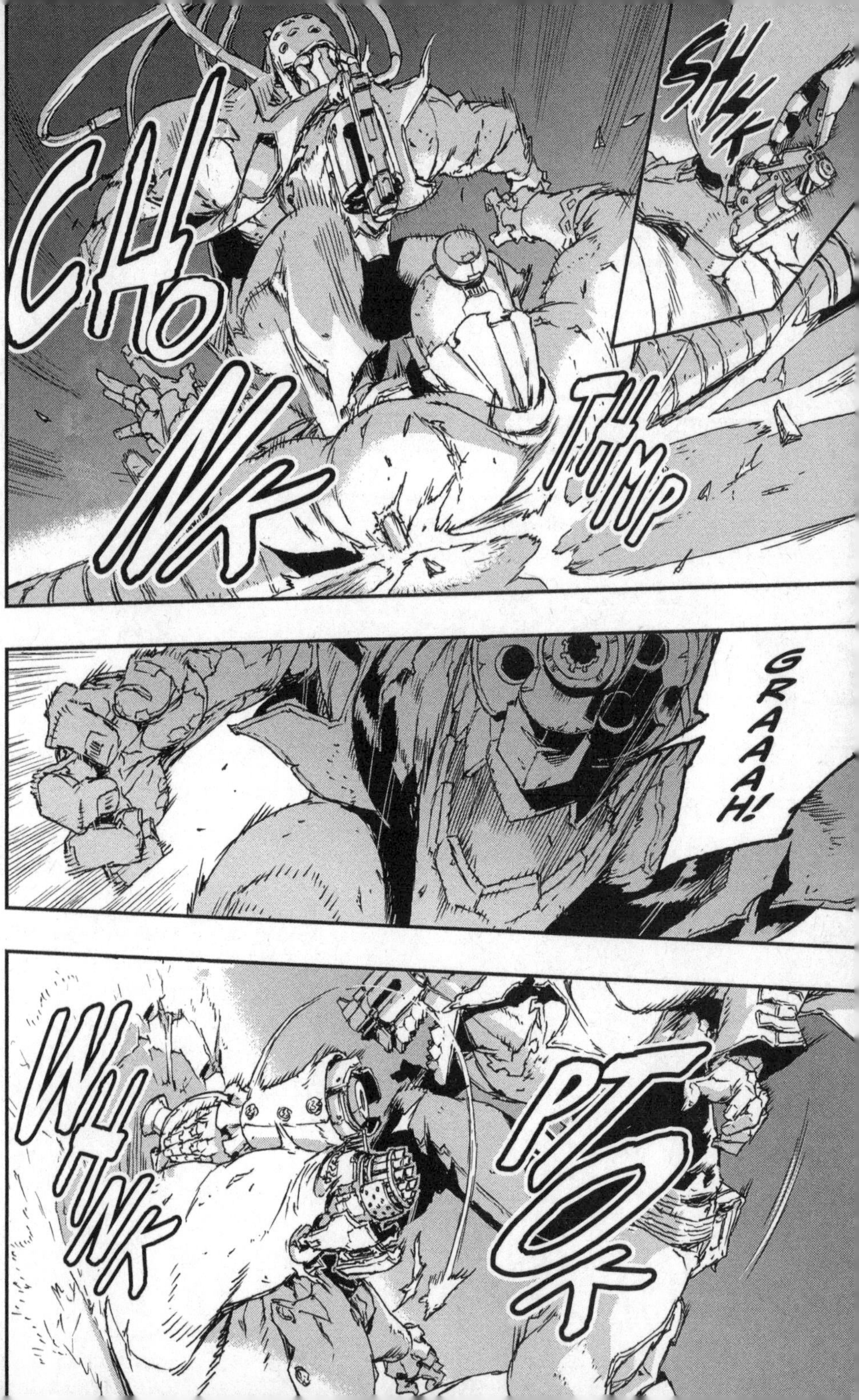
SHK
THMP
CHONK
GRAAAAH!
PTOK
WHUNK

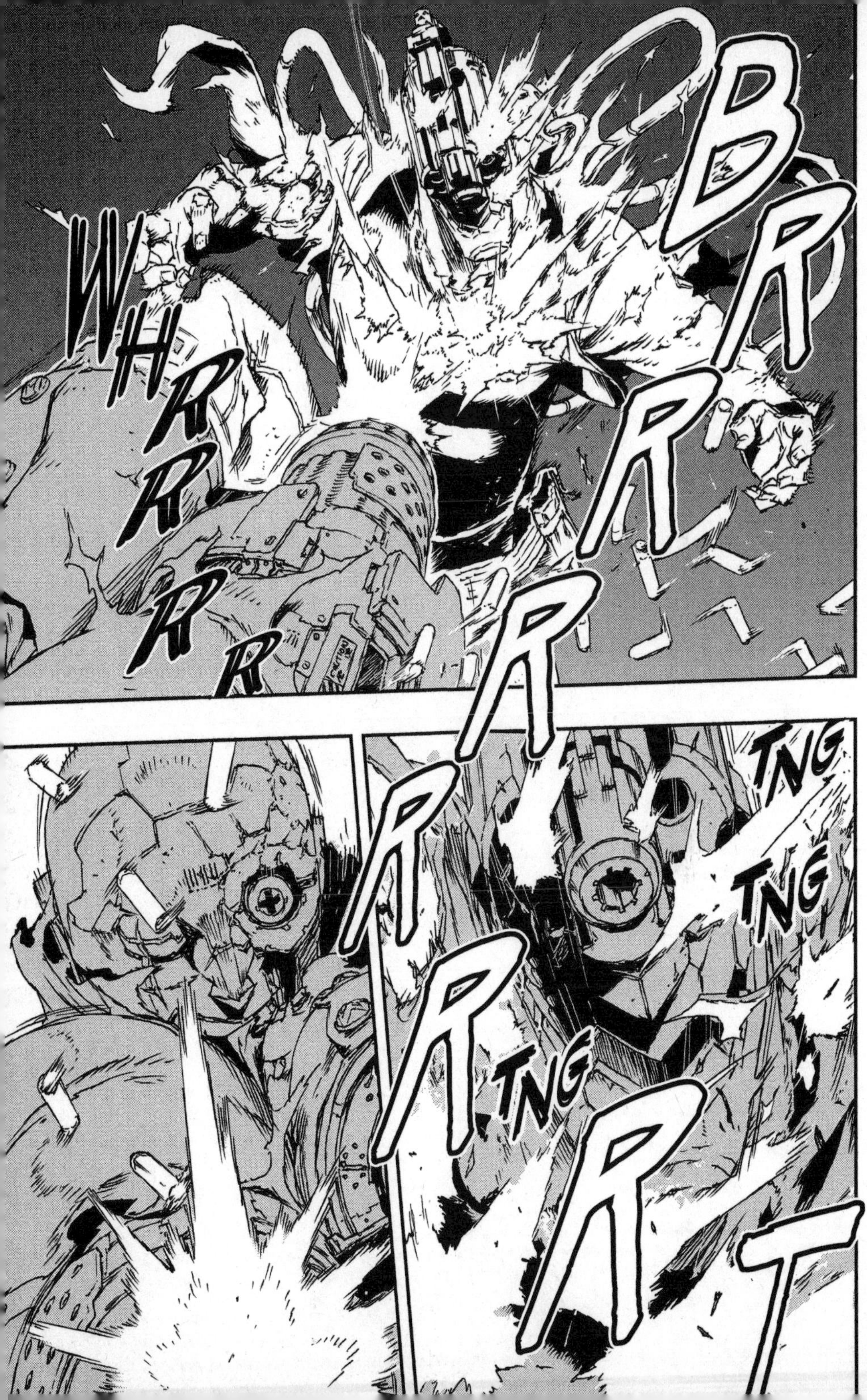
BRRRRRRT
WHRRRR
TNG
TNG
TNG

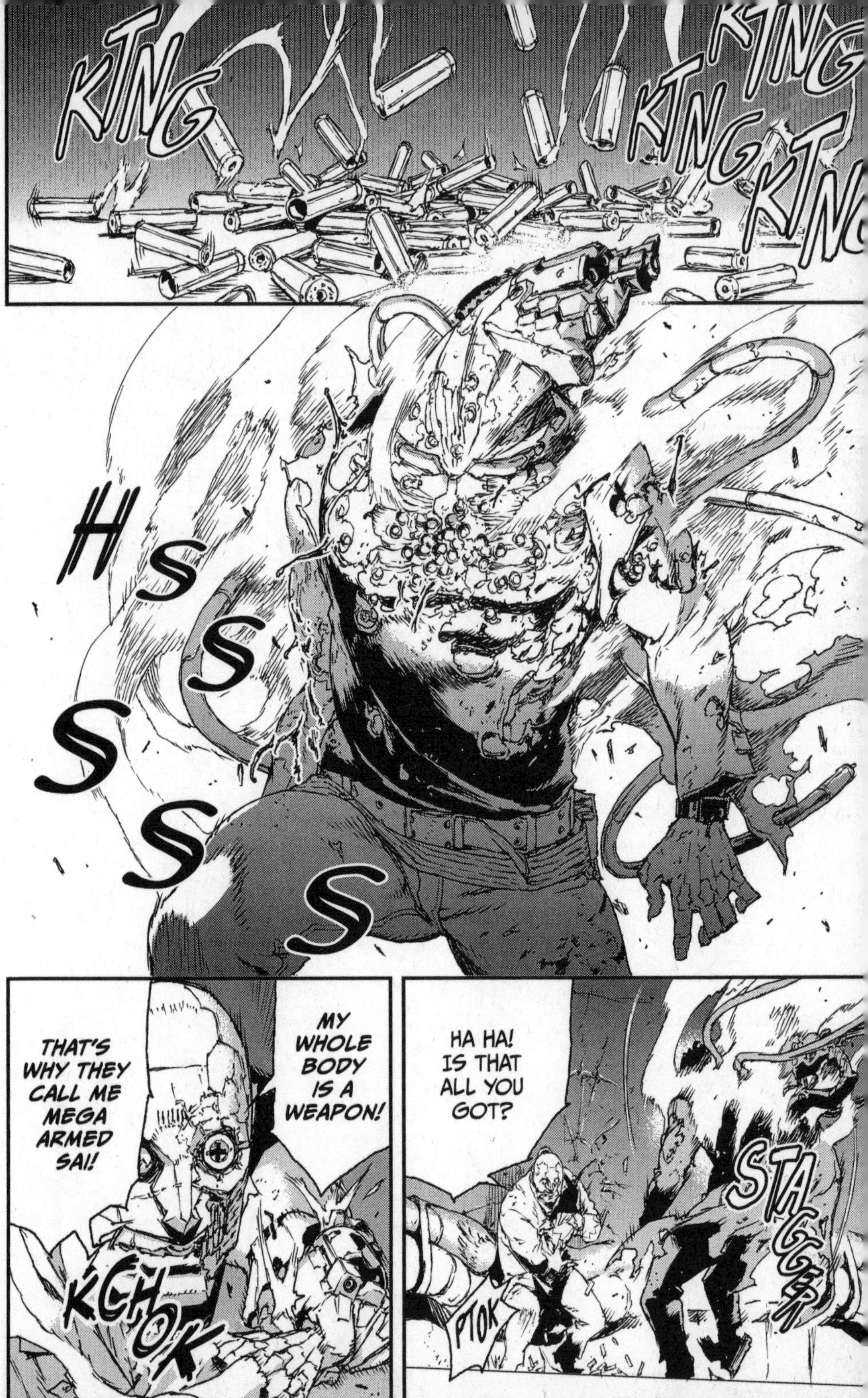
KING
KING
KING
KING
HSSSSS
HA HA! IS THAT ALL YOU GOT?
STAGGER
PTOK
MY WHOLE BODY IS A WEAPON!
THAT'S WHY THEY CALL ME MEGA ARMED SAI!
KCHOK

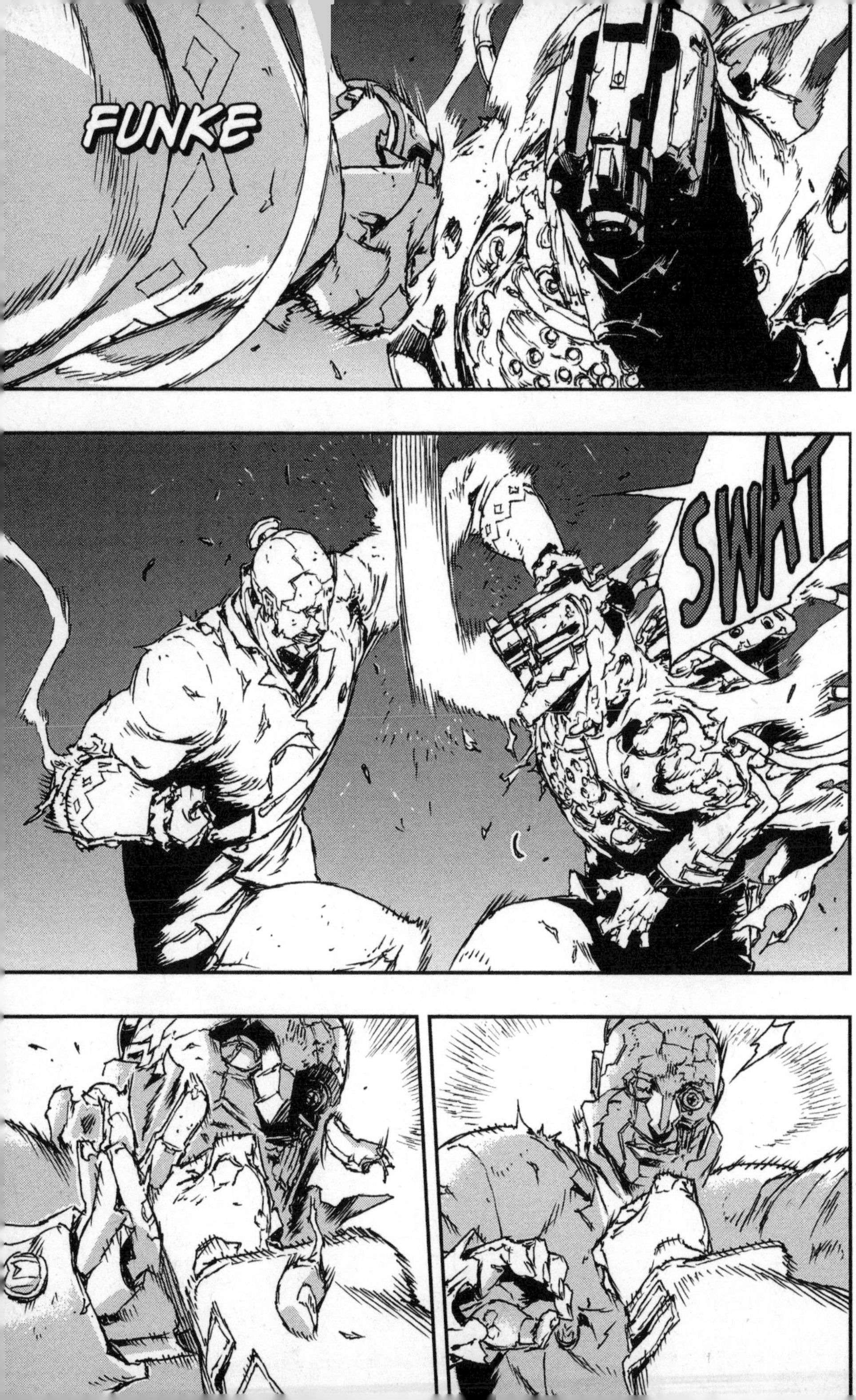
FUNKE
SWAT

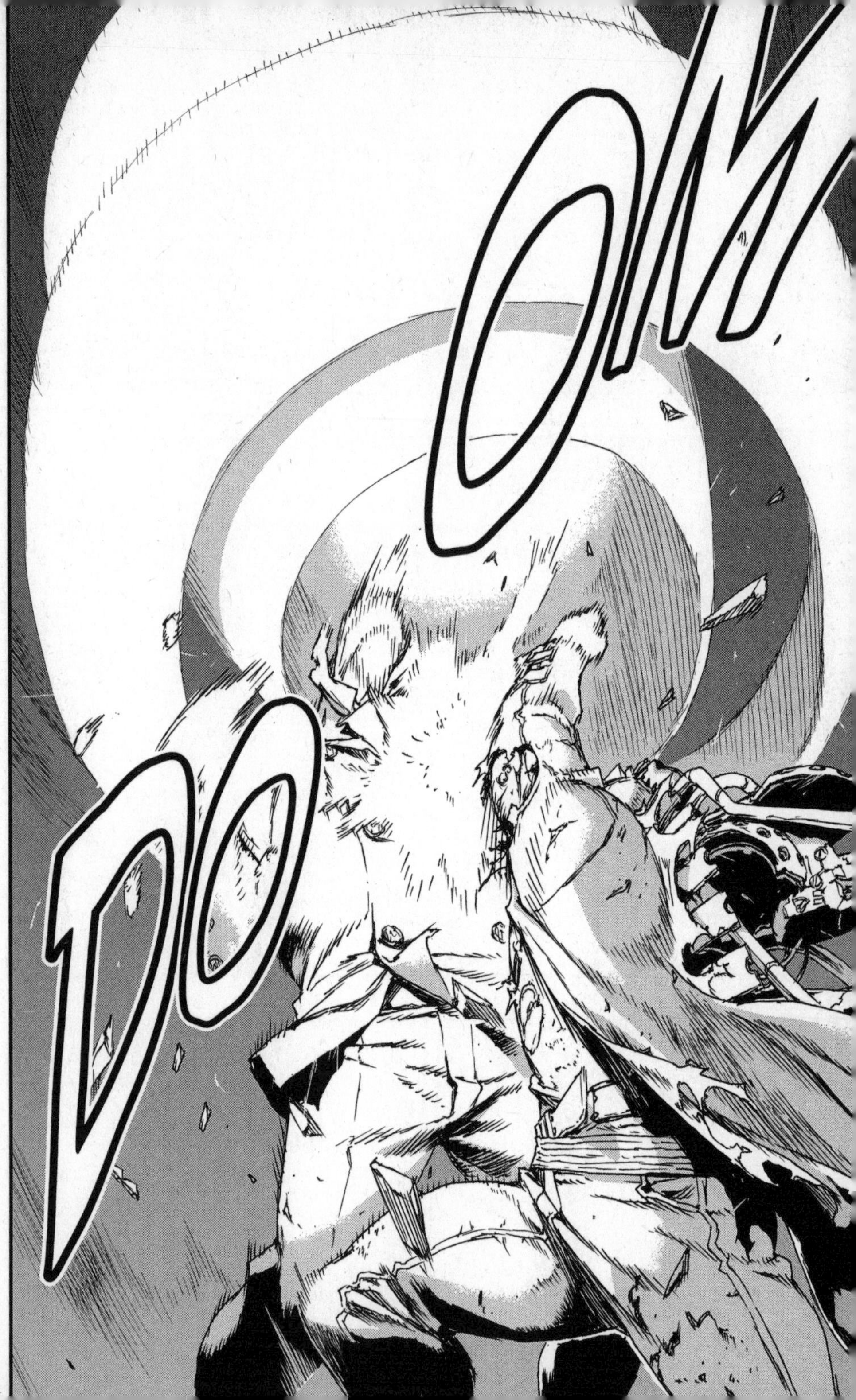
DOOM

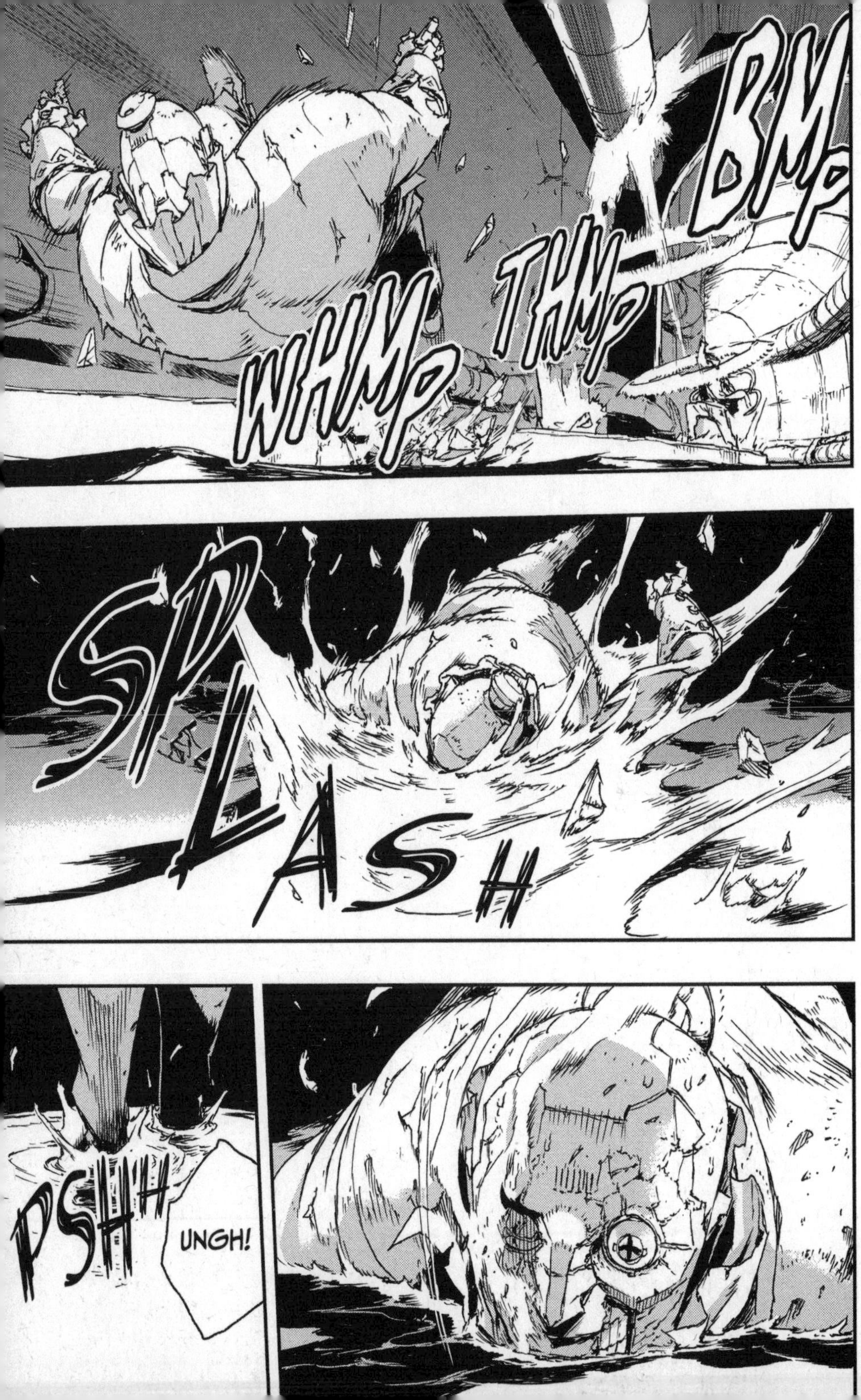
BMP
THMP
WHMP
SPLASH
UNGH!
PSHH

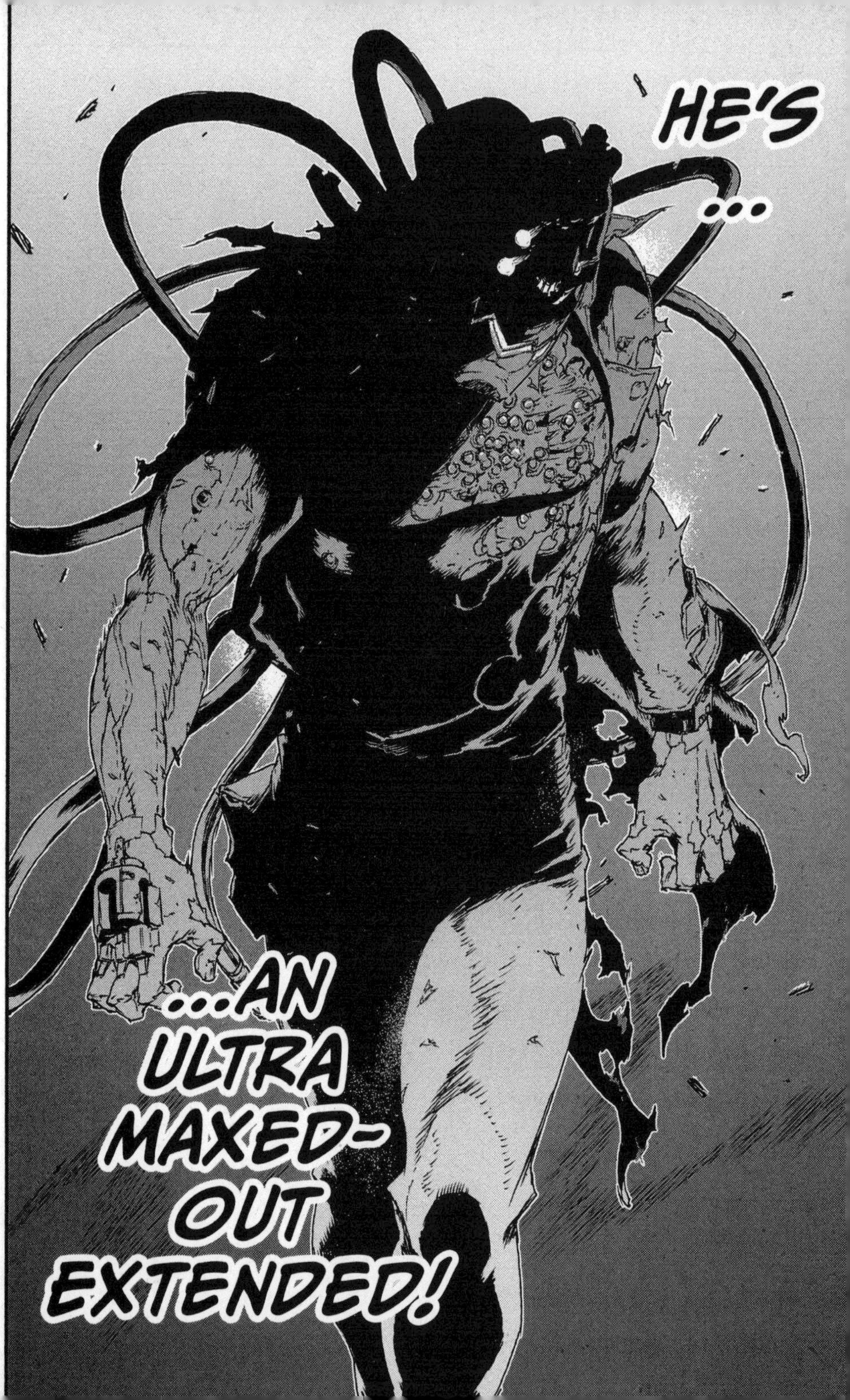
HE'S ...
...AN ULTRA MAXED-OUT EXTENDED!

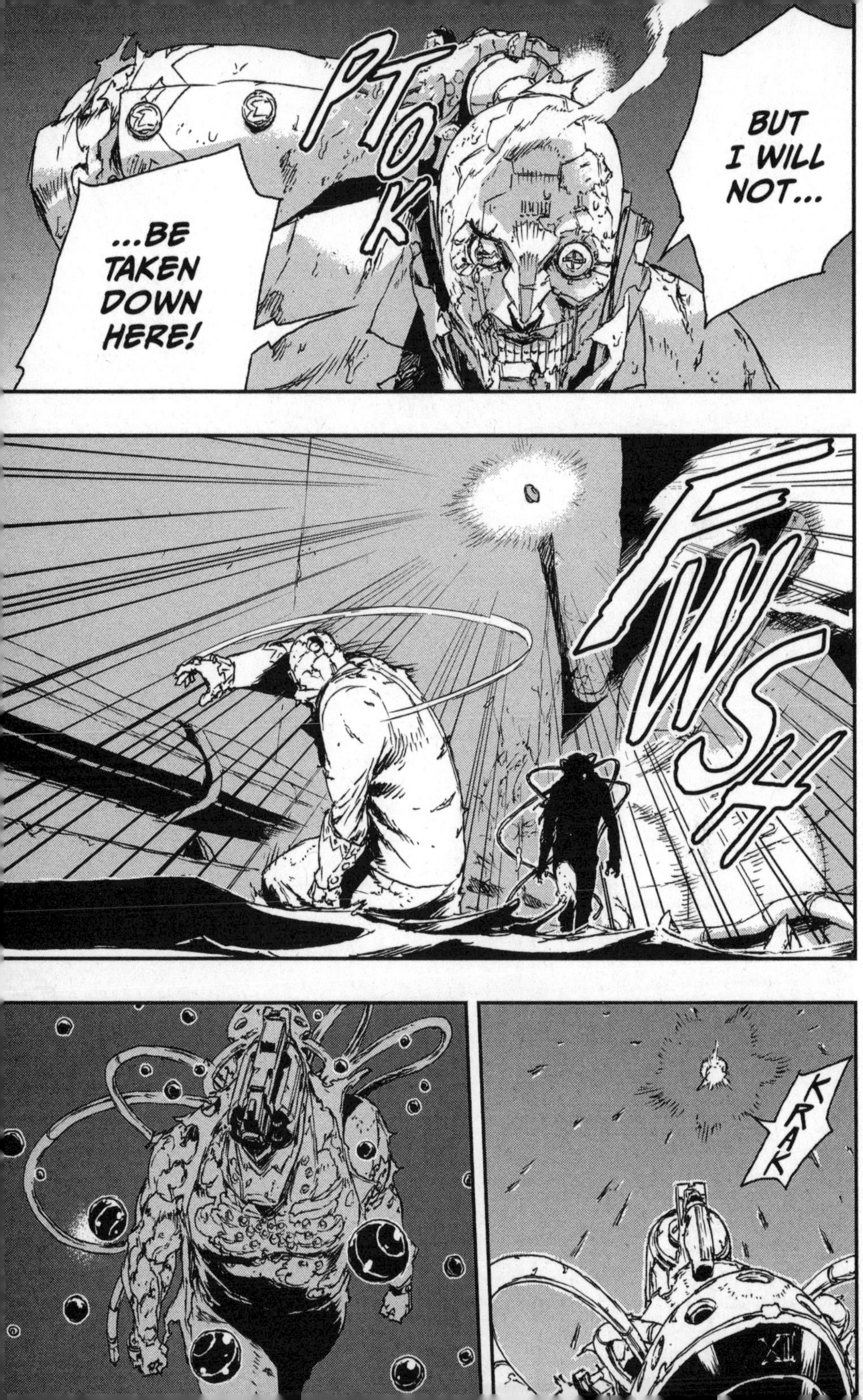
BUT I WILL NOT...
PTOK
...BE TAKEN DOWN HERE!
FWSH
KRAK

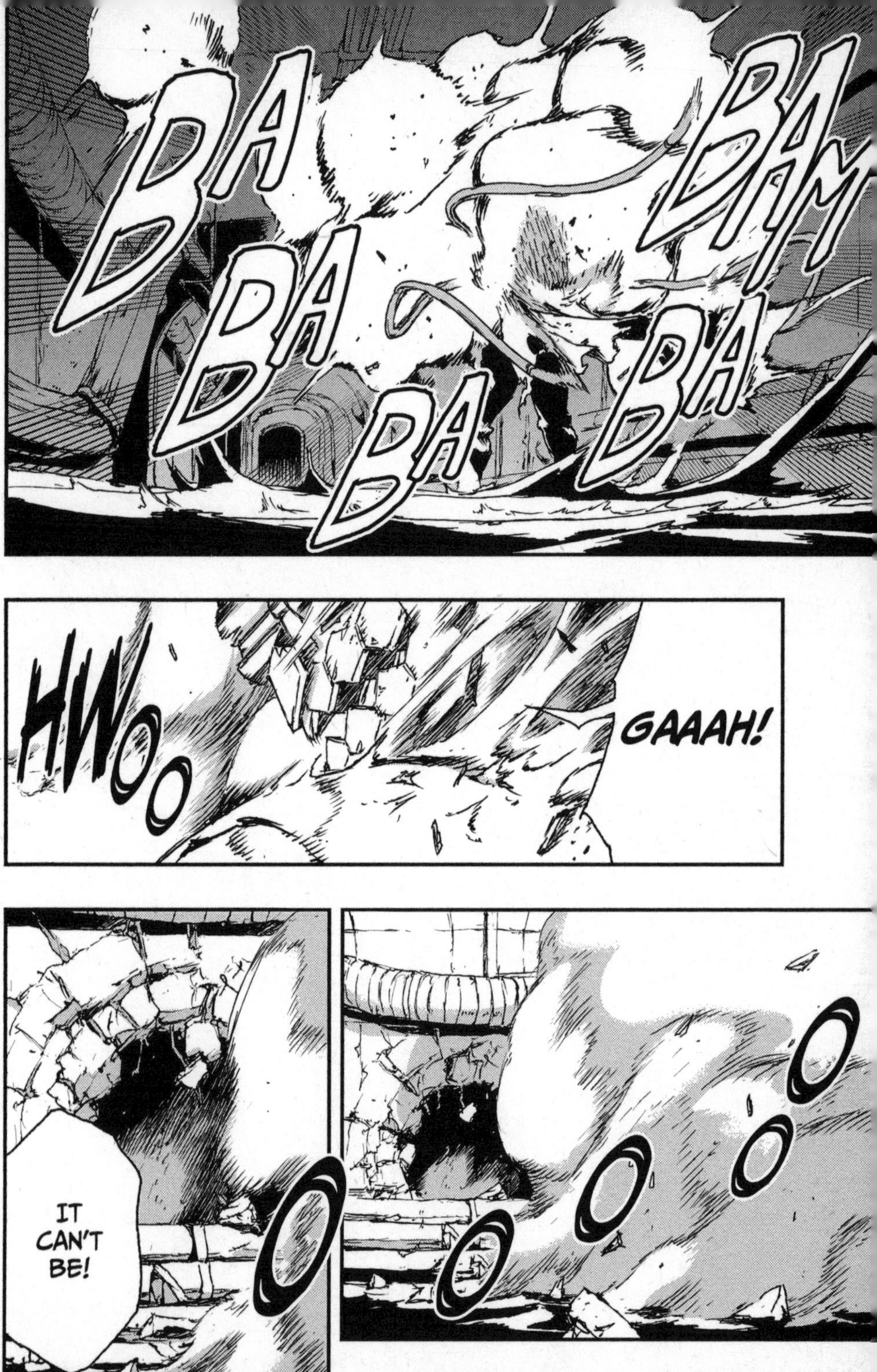
BA DA BA DA BA DA BA DAM
HWOO
GAAAH!
OOOO
IT CAN'T BE!

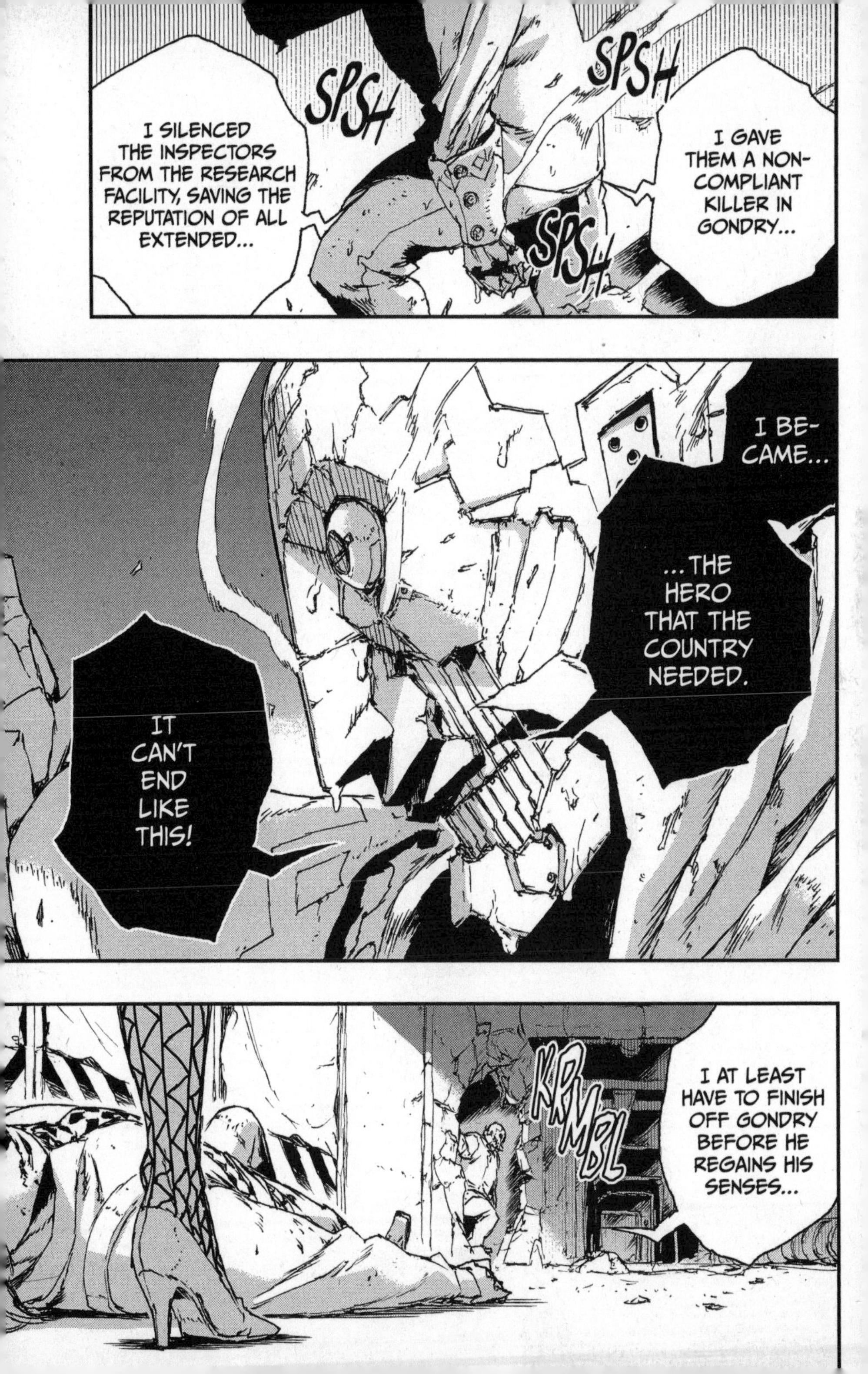
SPSH
I GAVE THEM A NON-COMPLIANT KILLER IN GONDRY...
SPSH
SPSH
I SILENCED THE INSPECTORS FROM THE RESEARCH FACILITY, SAVING THE REPUTATION OF ALL EXTENDED...
I BE-CAME...
...THE HERO THAT THE COUNTRY NEEDED.
IT CAN'T END LIKE THIS!
I AT LEAST HAVE TO FINISH OFF GONDRY BEFORE HE REGAINS HIS SENSES...
KRMBL

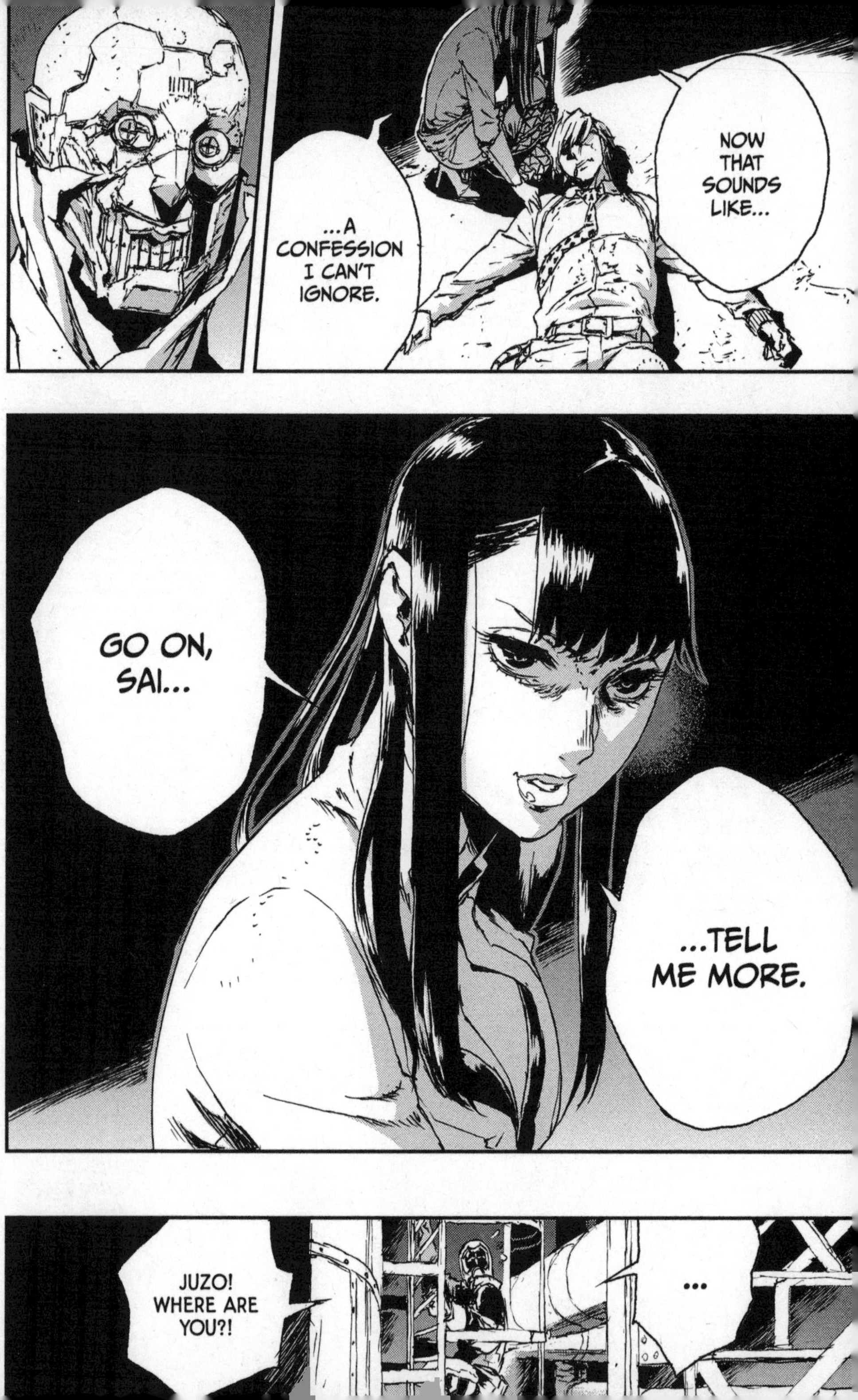
NOW THAT SOUNDS LIKE...
...A CONFESSION I CAN'T IGNORE.
GO ON, SAI...
...TELL ME MORE.
...
JUZO! WHERE ARE YOU?!

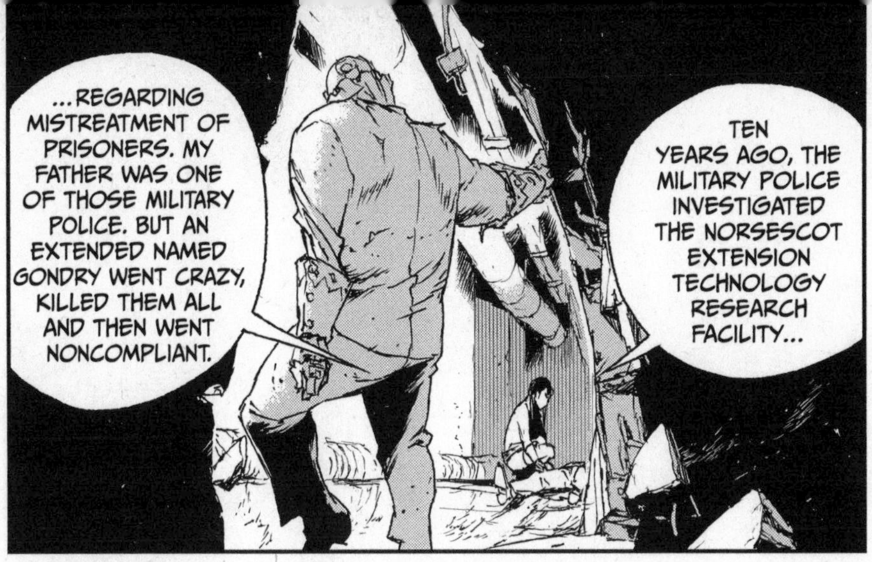
TEN YEARS AGO, THE MILITARY POLICE INVESTIGATED THE NORSESCOT EXTENSION TECHNOLOGY RESEARCH FACILITY...
...REGARDING MISTREATMENT OF PRISONERS. MY FATHER WAS ONE OF THOSE MILITARY POLICE. BUT AN EXTENDED NAMED GONDRY WENT CRAZY, KILLED THEM ALL AND THEN WENT NONCOMPLIANT.

Chapter 14
Will

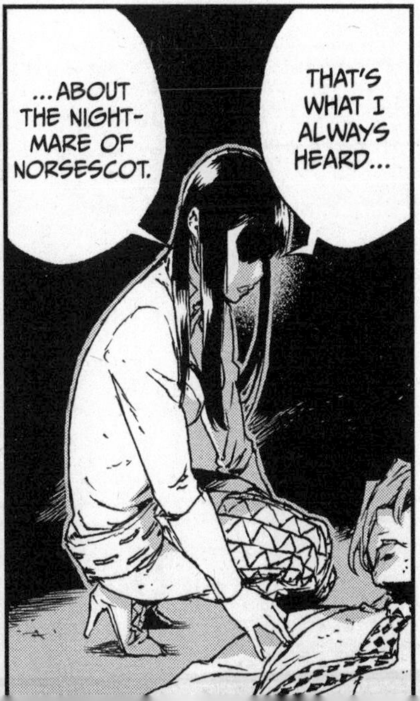
THAT'S WHAT I ALWAYS HEARD...
...ABOUT THE NIGHT-MARE OF NORSESCOT.

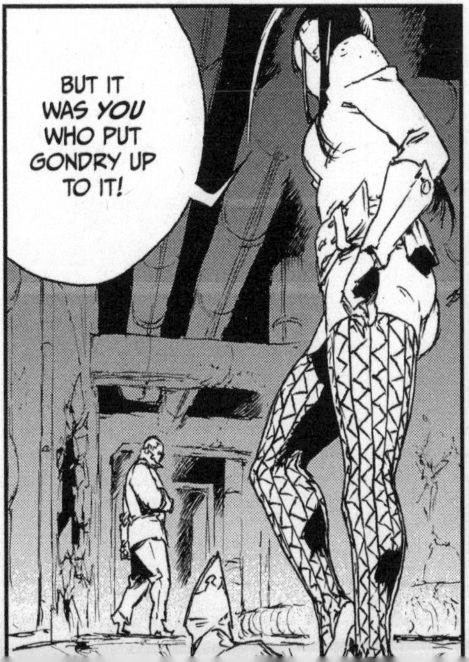
BUT IT WAS *YOU* WHO PUT GONDRY UP TO IT!

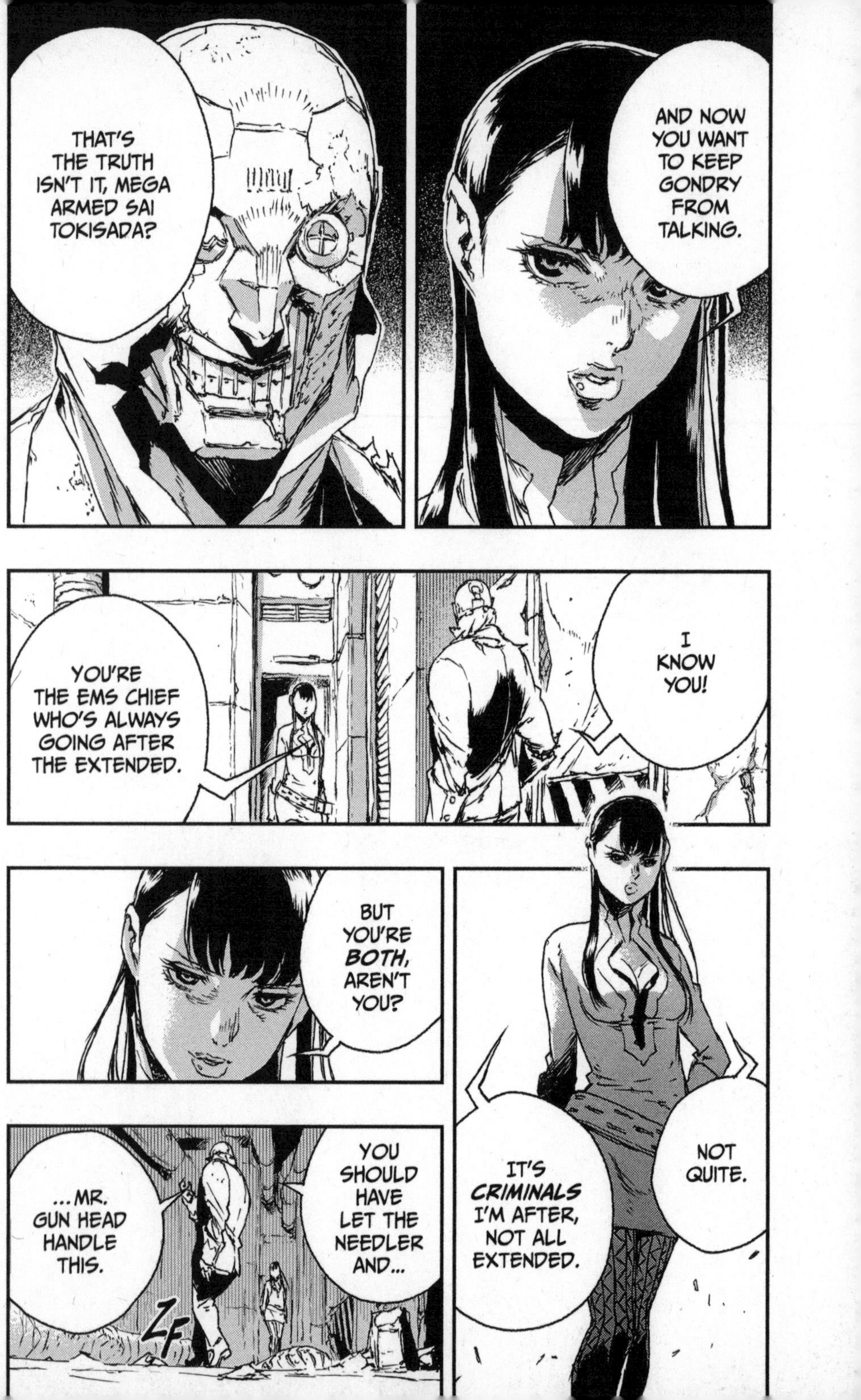
AND NOW YOU WANT TO KEEP GONDRY FROM TALKING.
THAT'S THE TRUTH ISN'T IT, MEGA ARMED SAI TOKISADA?
I KNOW YOU!
YOU'RE THE EMS CHIEF WHO'S ALWAYS GOING AFTER THE EXTENDED.
NOT QUITE.
IT'S *CRIMINALS* I'M AFTER, NOT ALL EXTENDED.
BUT YOU'RE *BOTH*, AREN'T YOU?
YOU SHOULD HAVE LET THE NEEDLER AND...
...MR. GUN HEAD HANDLE THIS.
ZF

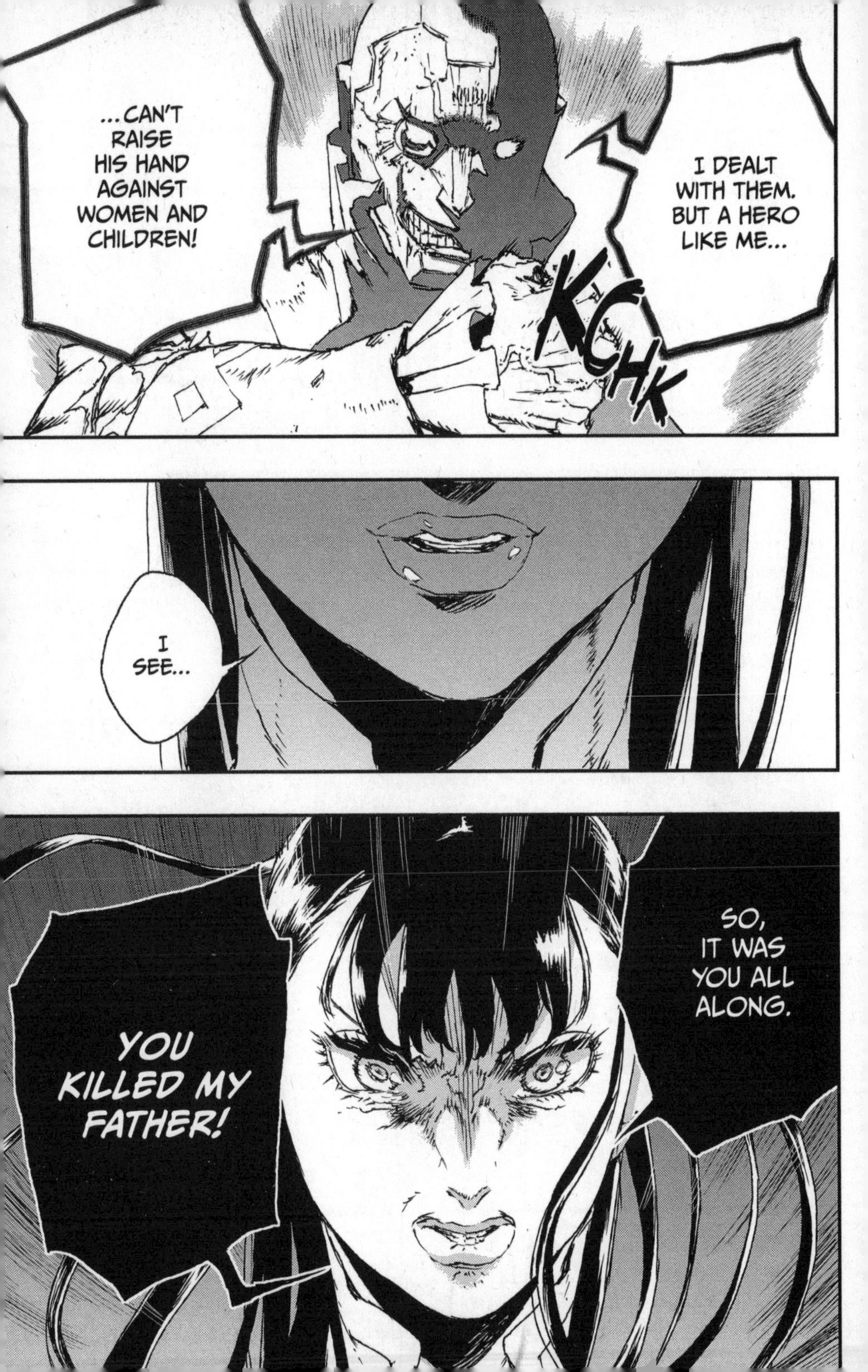
I DEALT WITH THEM. BUT A HERO LIKE ME...
...CAN'T RAISE HIS HAND AGAINST WOMEN AND CHILDREN!
KCHK
I SEE...
SO, IT WAS YOU ALL ALONG.
YOU KILLED MY FATHER!

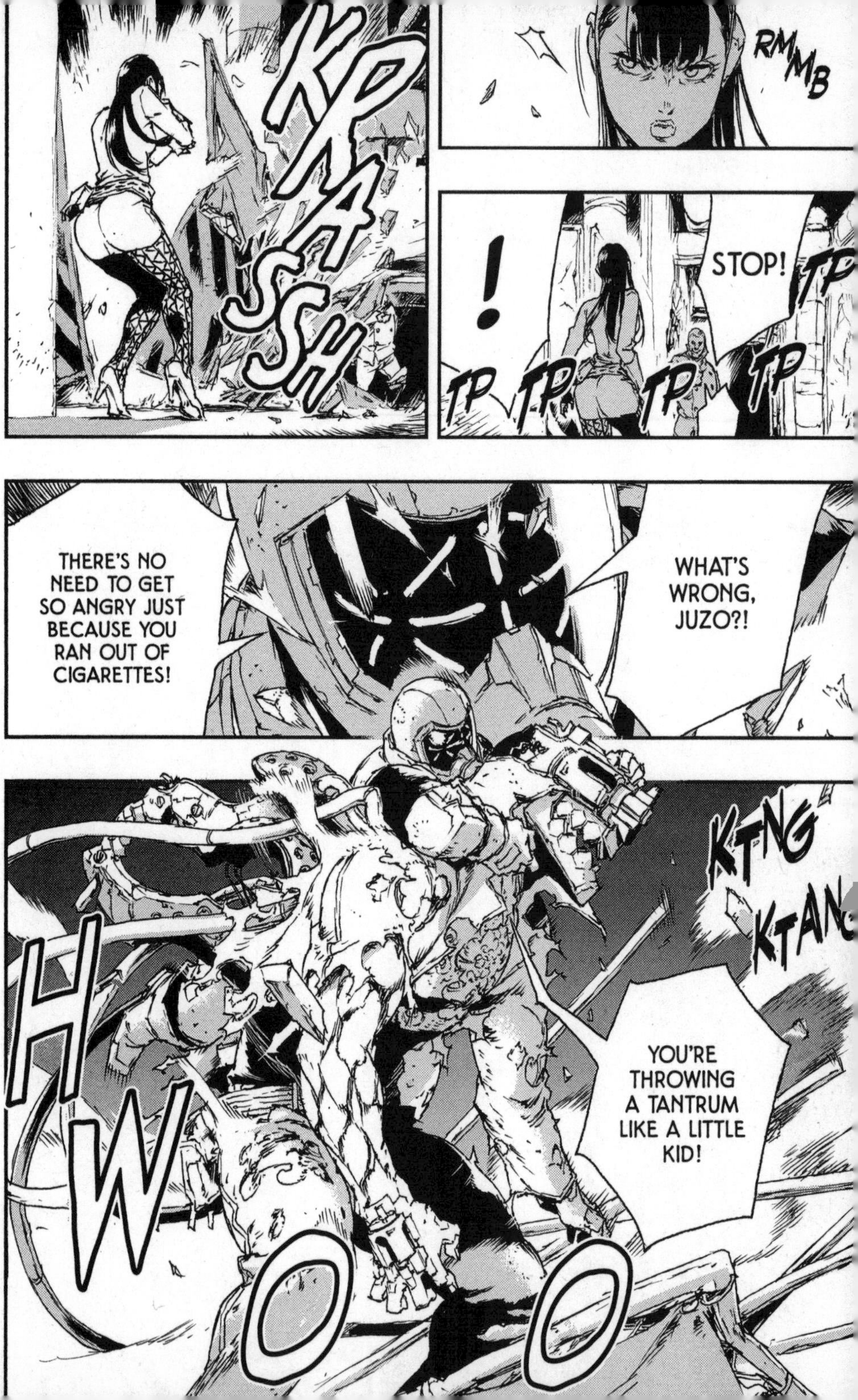
RMMB
!
STOP!
TP TP TP TP TP
KRASSH
WHAT'S WRONG, JUZO?!
THERE'S NO NEED TO GET SO ANGRY JUST BECAUSE YOU RAN OUT OF CIGARETTES!
KTNG
KTAN
YOU'RE THROWING A TANTRUM LIKE A LITTLE KID!
HWOO

HIS BODY ....

HIS MEDS WORE OFF! HE'S NON-COMPLIANT!

JUZO ?!

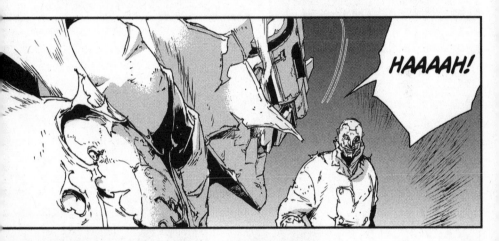

HAAAAH!

KTK

!!

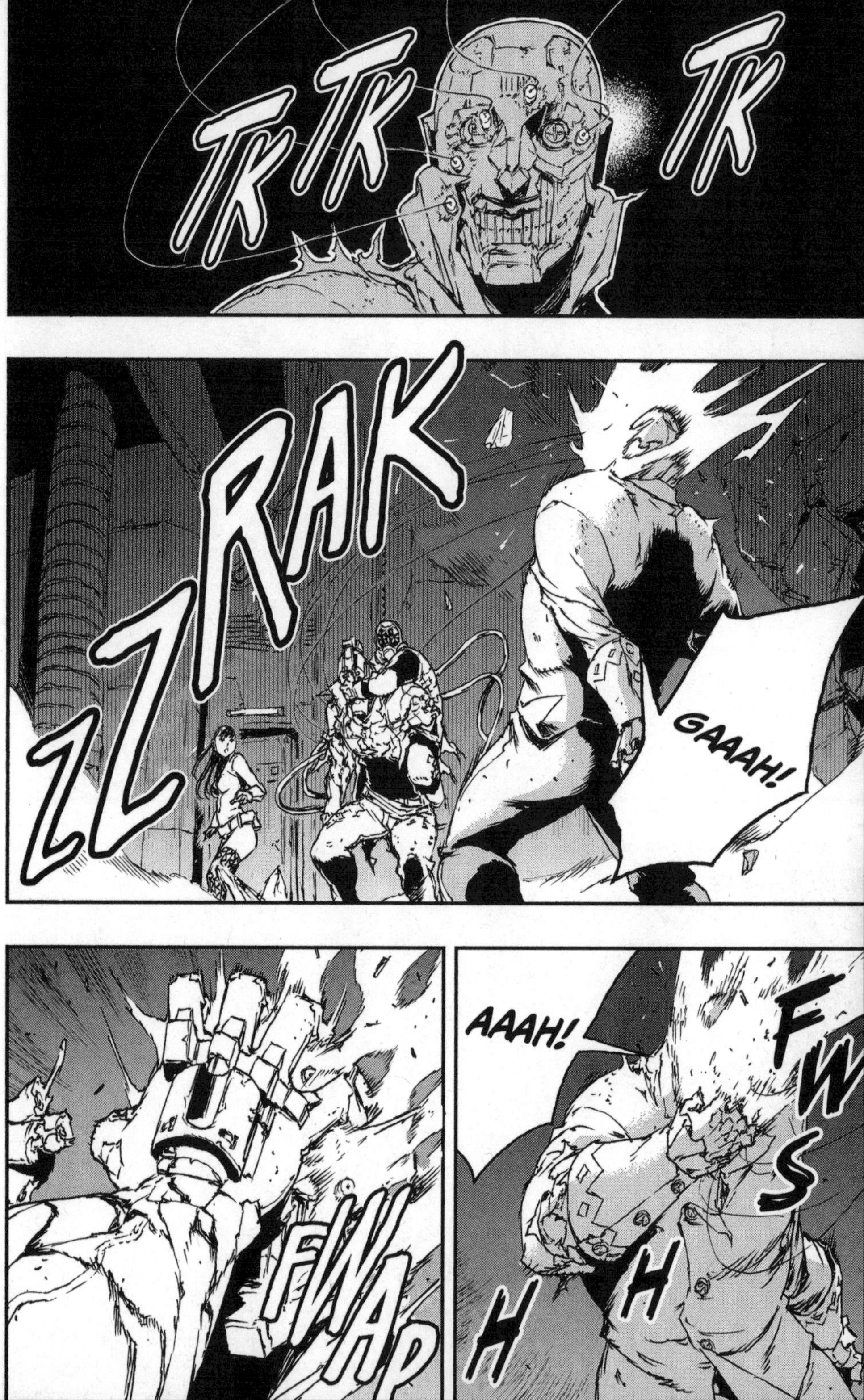
TKTK
TK
ZZRAK
GAAAH!
AAAH!
FWSHHH
FWAP

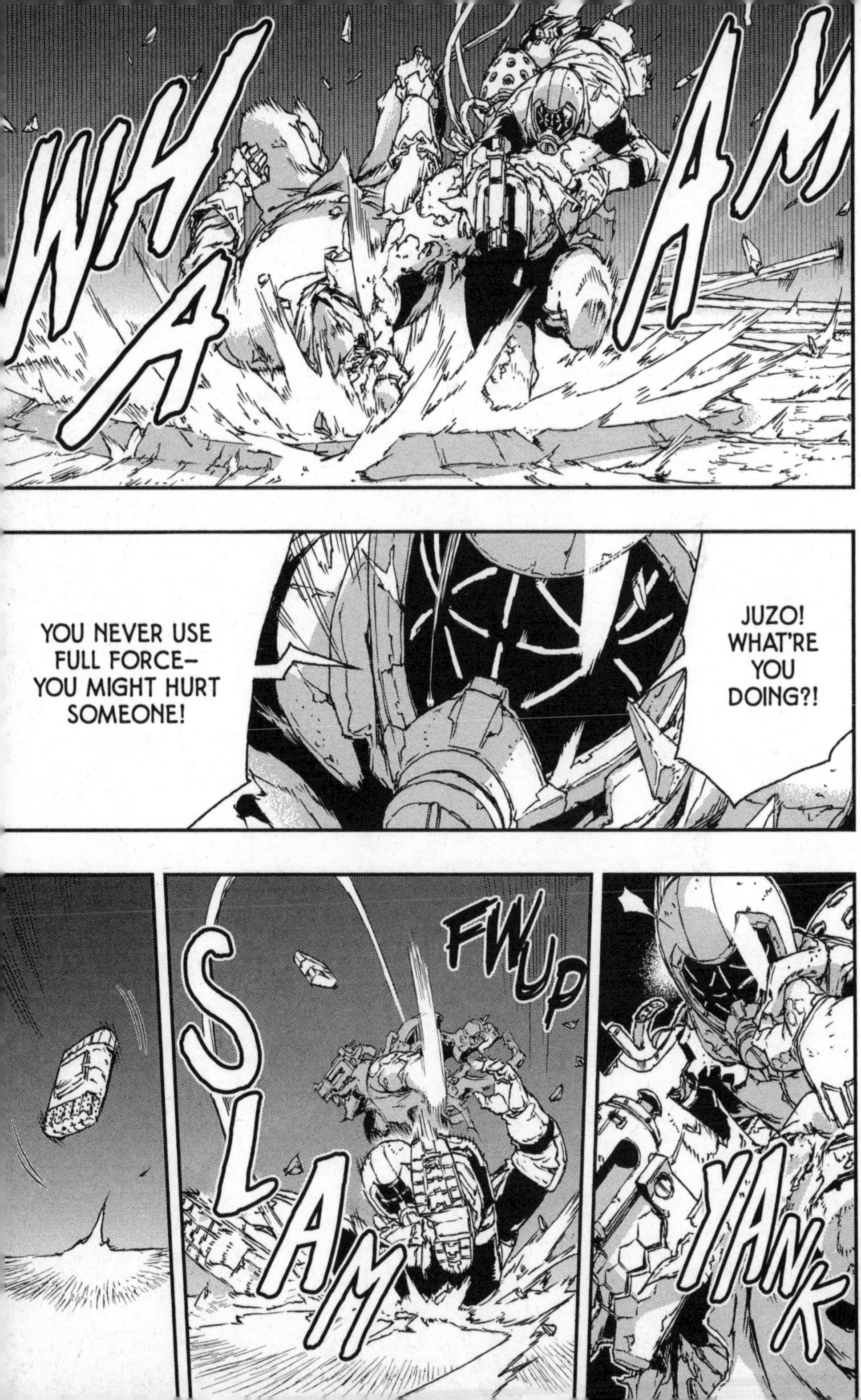
WHAAM
JUZO! WHAT'RE YOU DOING?!
YOU NEVER USE FULL FORCE— YOU MIGHT HURT SOMEONE!
YANK
FWUP
SLAM

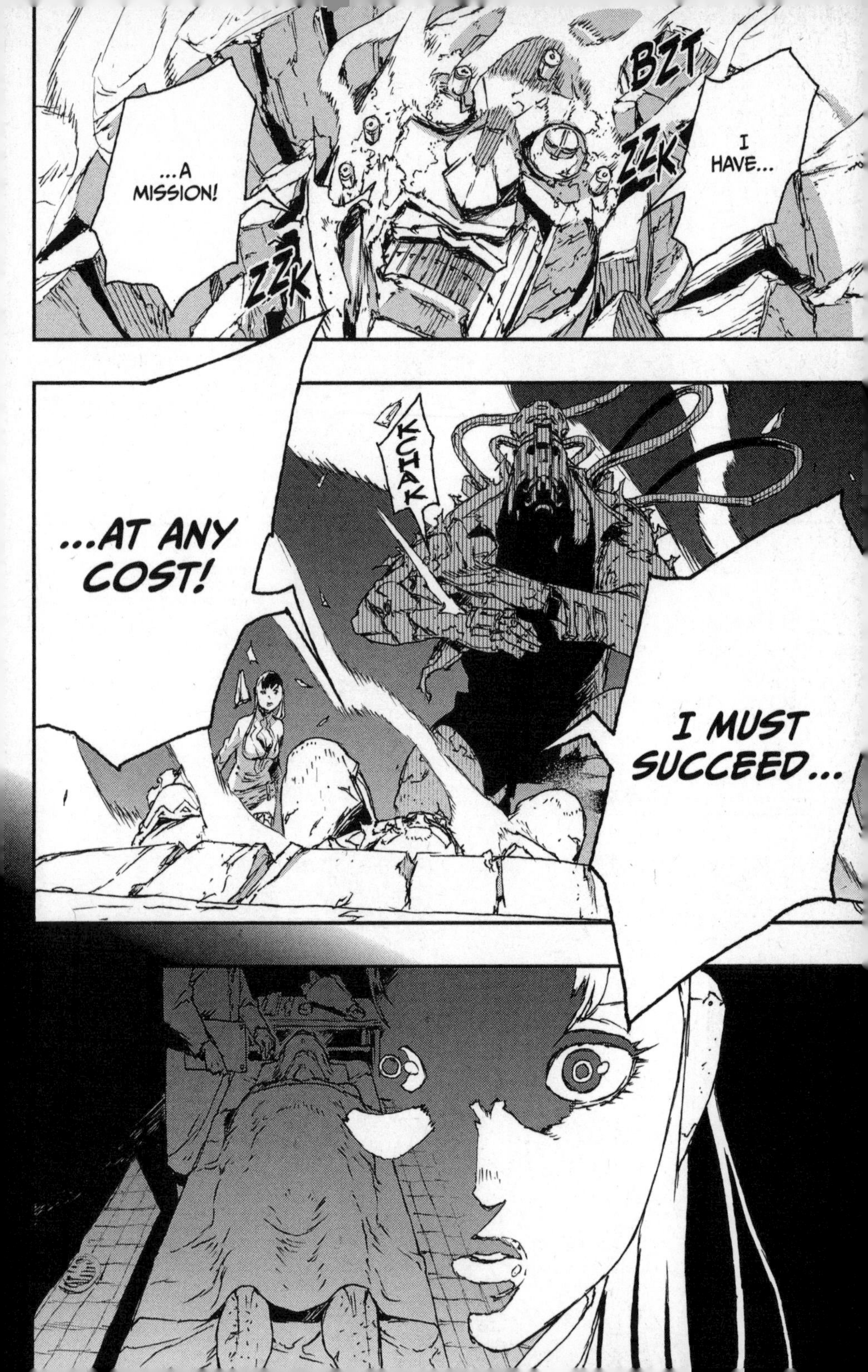
BZT
I HAVE...
ZZK
...A MISSION!
ZZK
KUCHAK
I MUST SUCCEED...
...AT ANY COST!

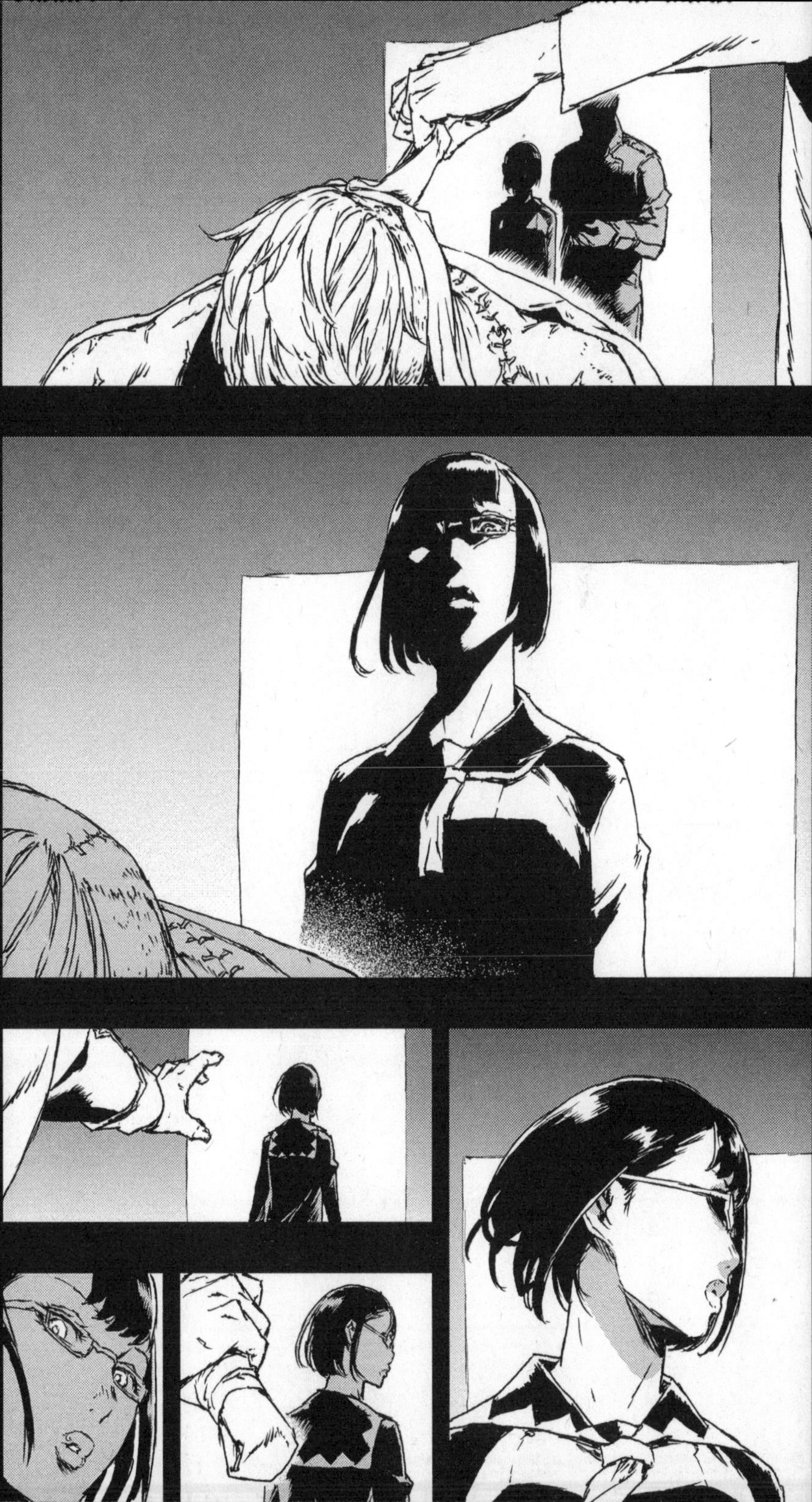

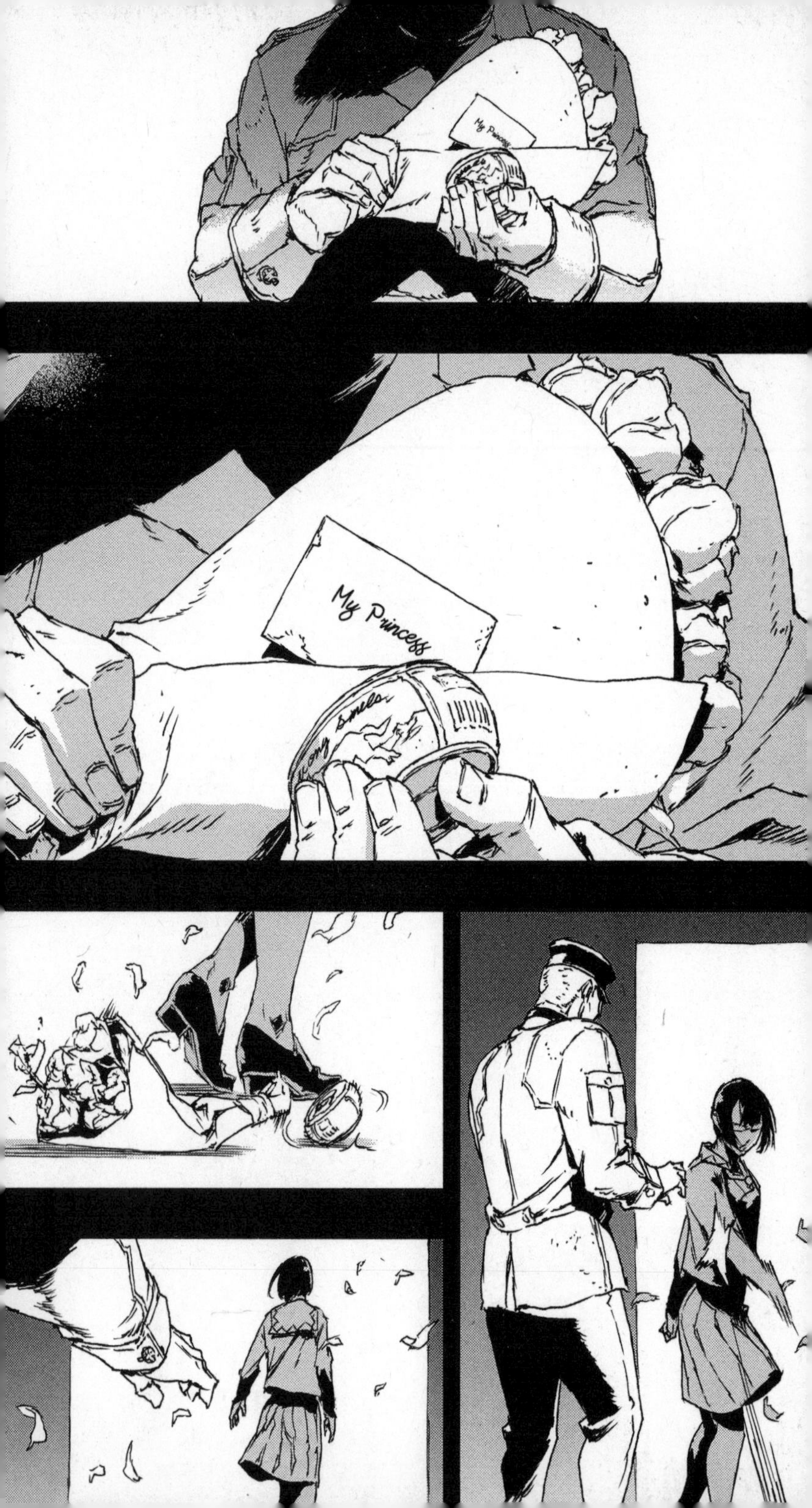
My Princess
My Princess

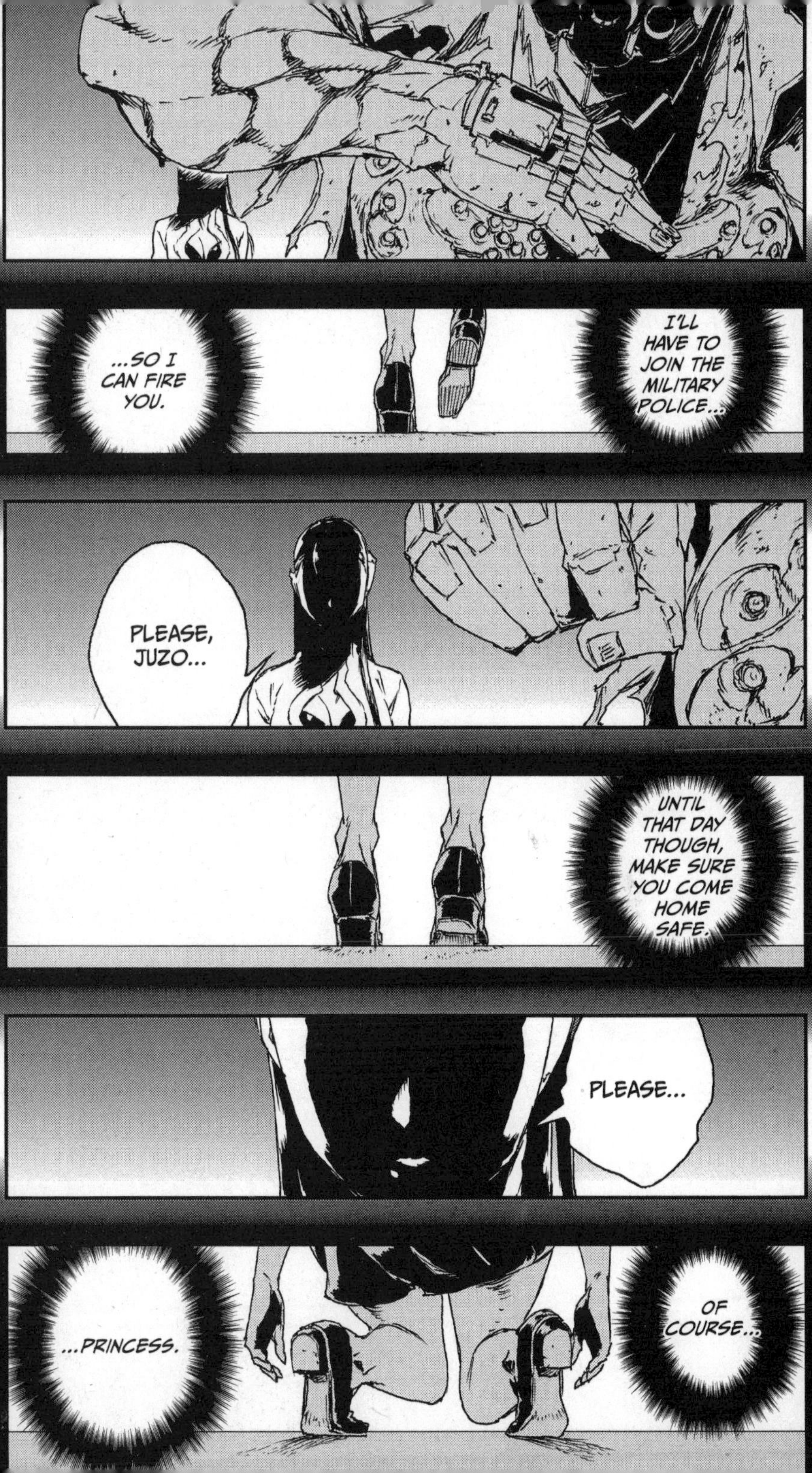
I'LL HAVE TO JOIN THE MILITARY POLICE...
...SO I CAN FIRE YOU.
PLEASE, JUZO...
UNTIL THAT DAY THOUGH, MAKE SURE YOU COME HOME SAFE.
PLEASE...
OF COURSE...
...PRINCESS.

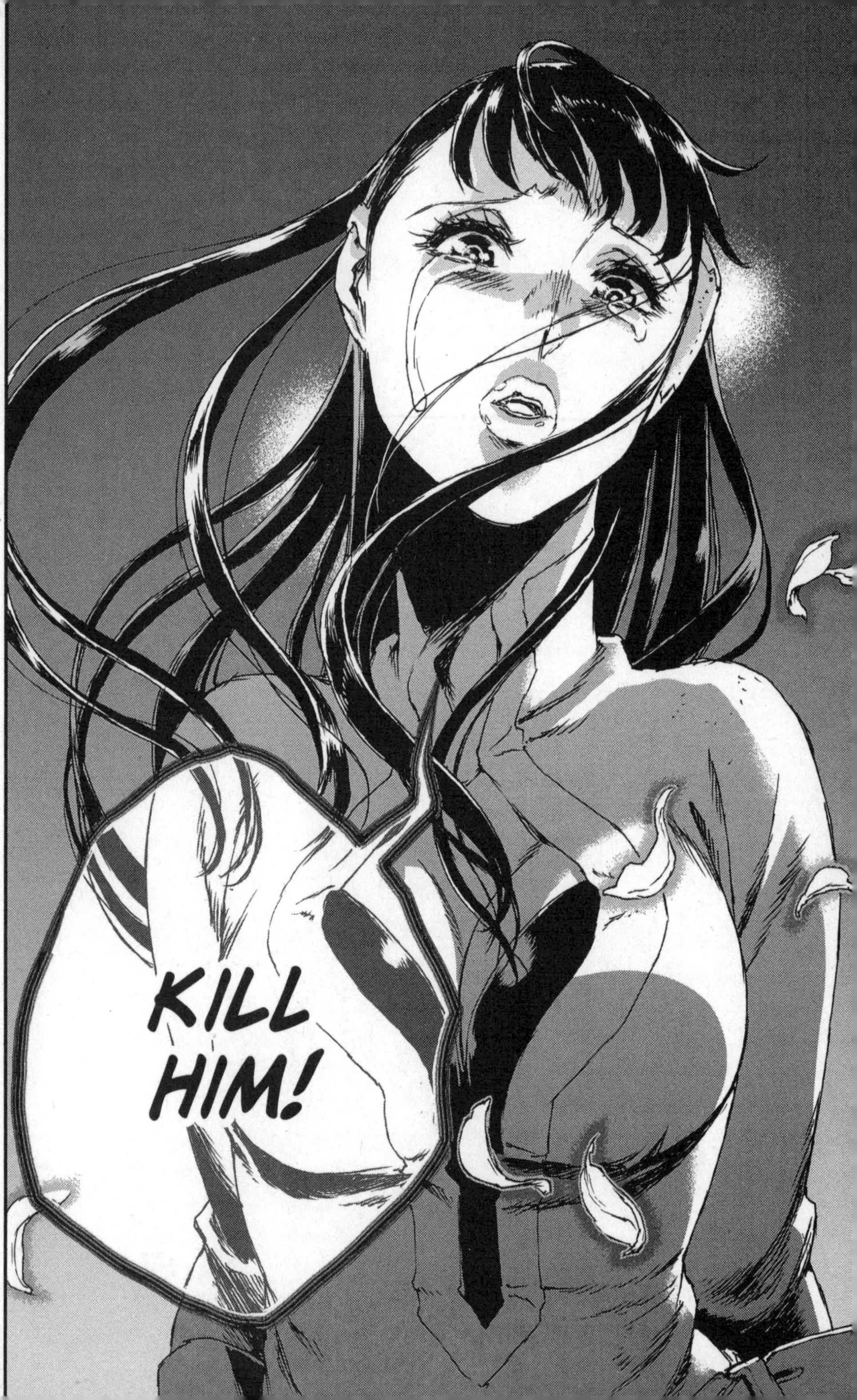
KILL HIM!

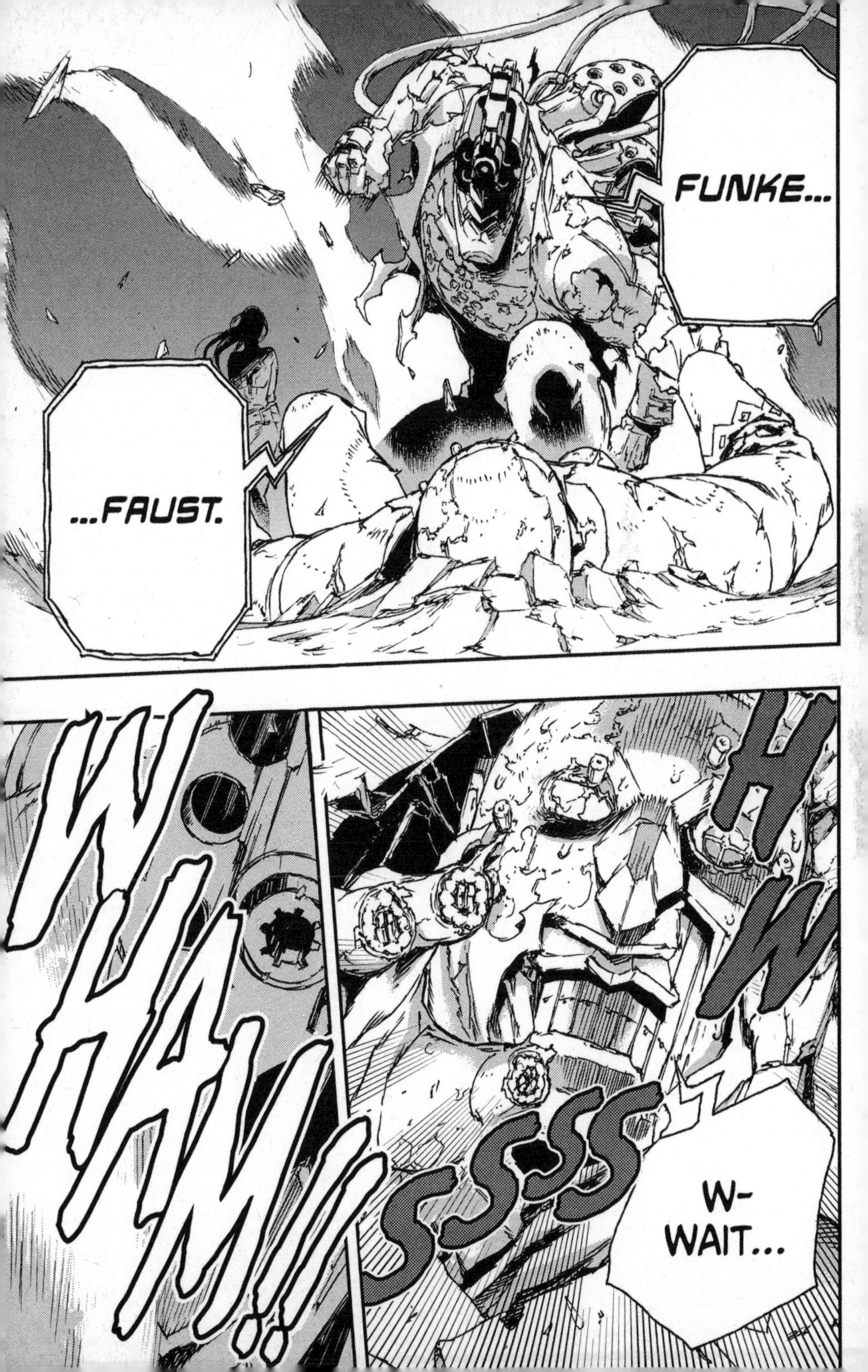
FUNKE...
...FAUST.
W-
WAIT...

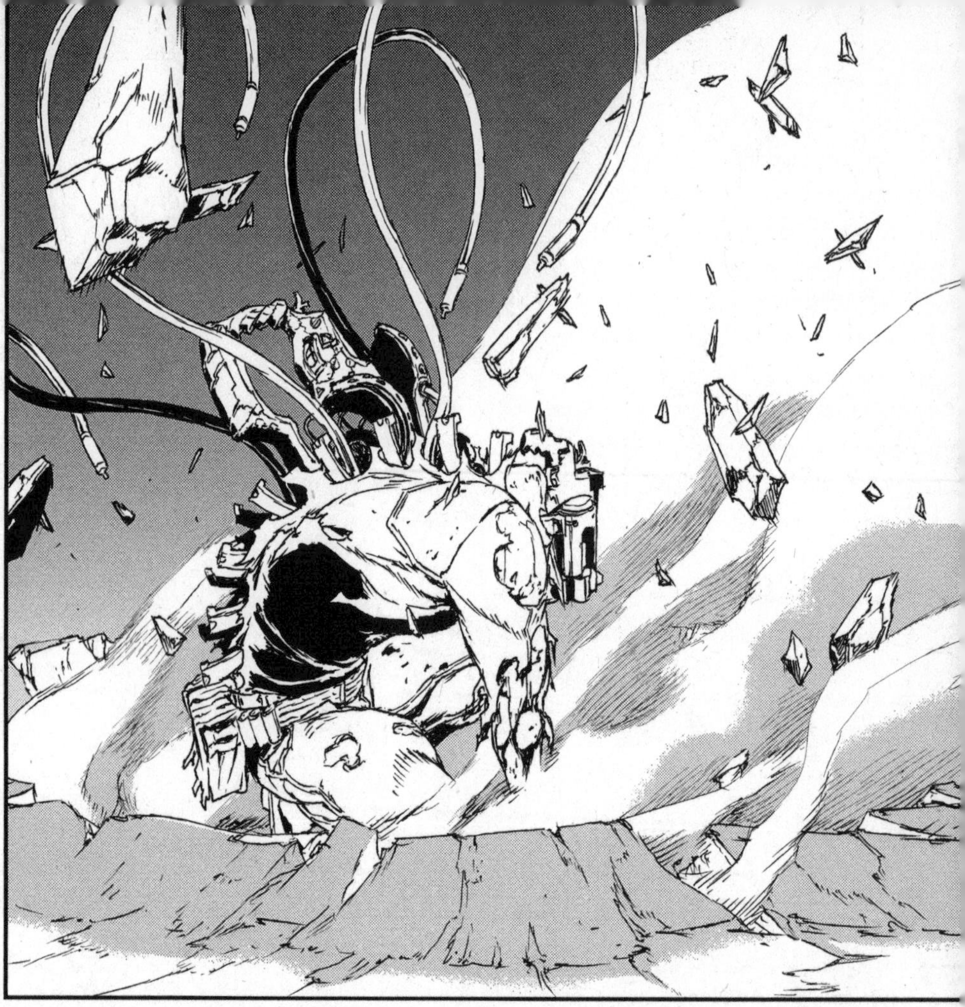

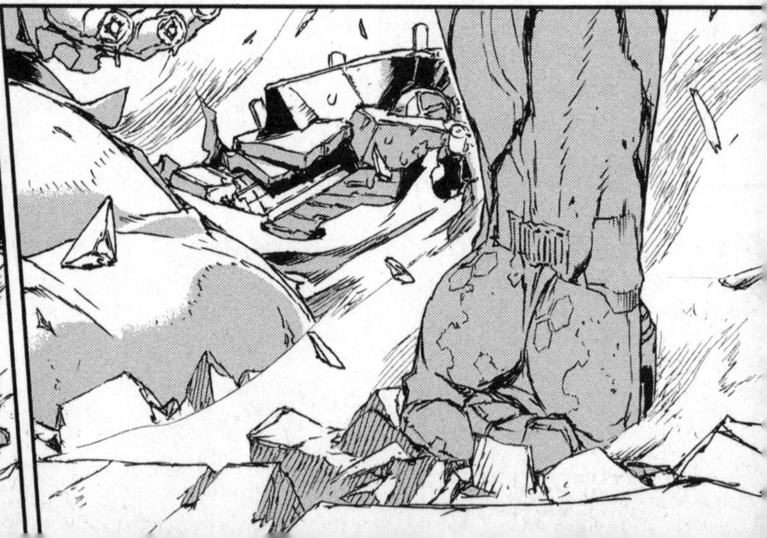

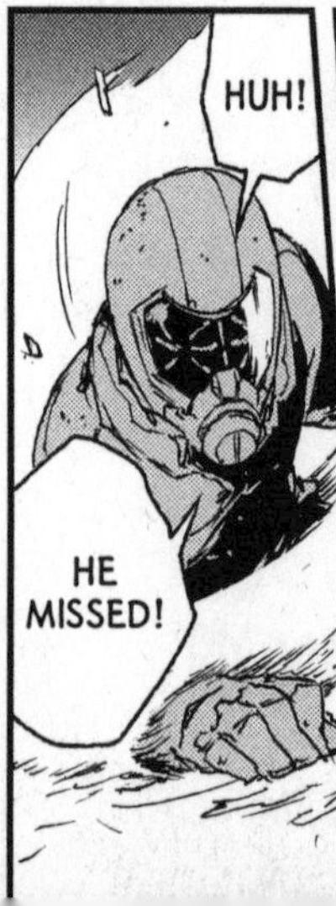
HUH!
HE MISSED!

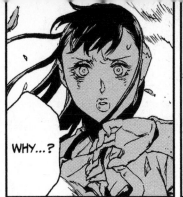

HWOOO
WHY...?
NOW WE'VE FINALLY GOT THE CHANCE...
...TO BRING GONDRY TO JUSTICE!
PLEASE, JUZO...
BRING HIM IN ALIVE!!

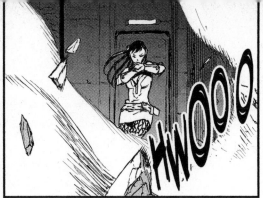

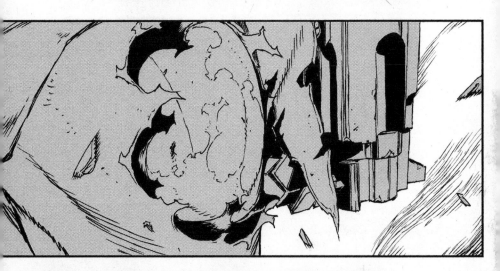

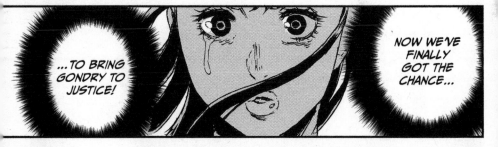

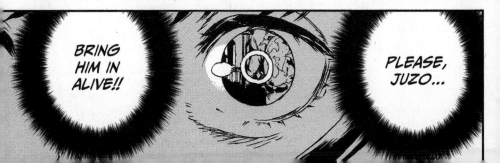

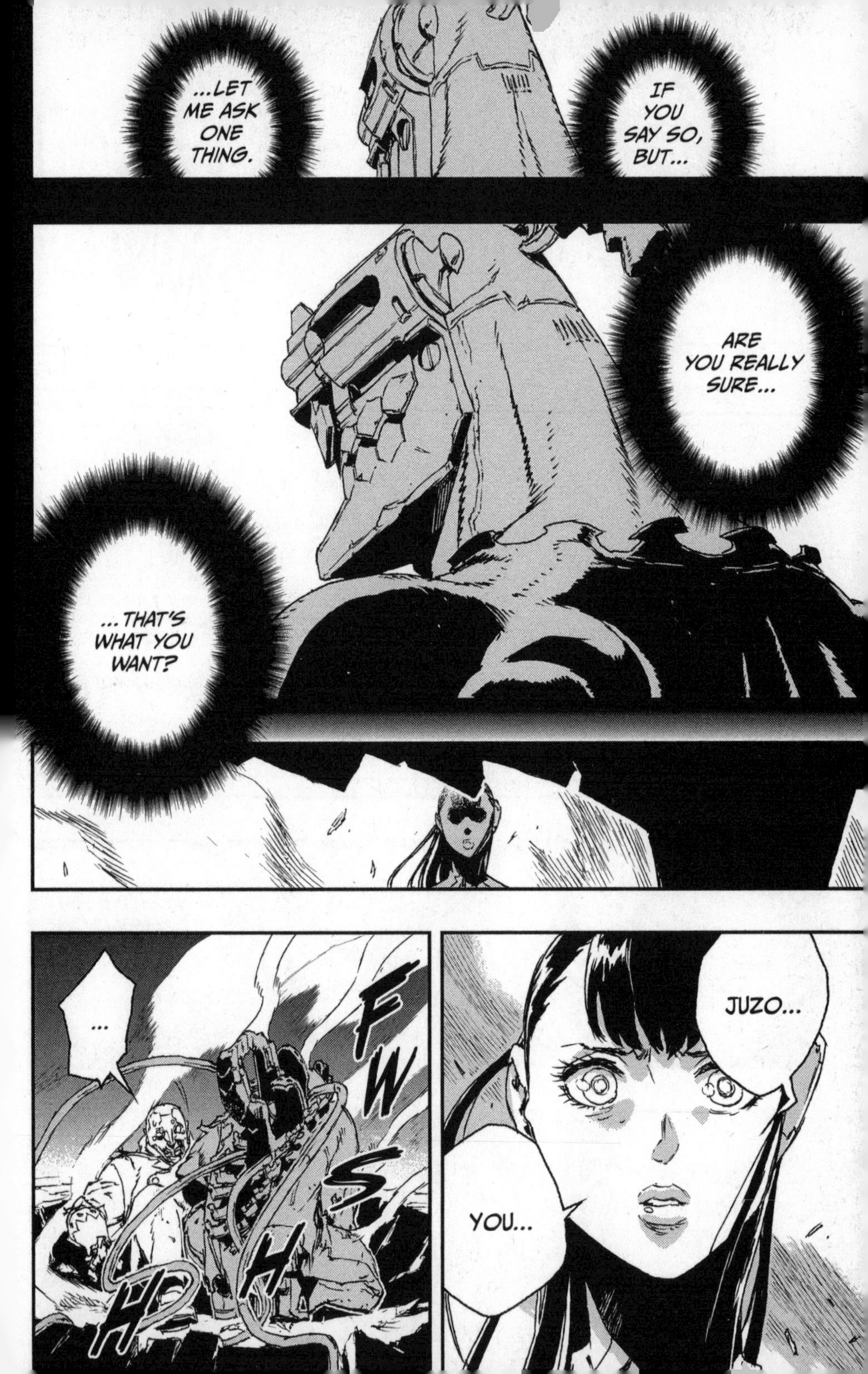
IF YOU SAY SO, BUT...
...LET ME ASK ONE THING.
ARE YOU REALLY SURE...
...THAT'S WHAT YOU WANT?
JUZO...
YOU...
...
FWSHH

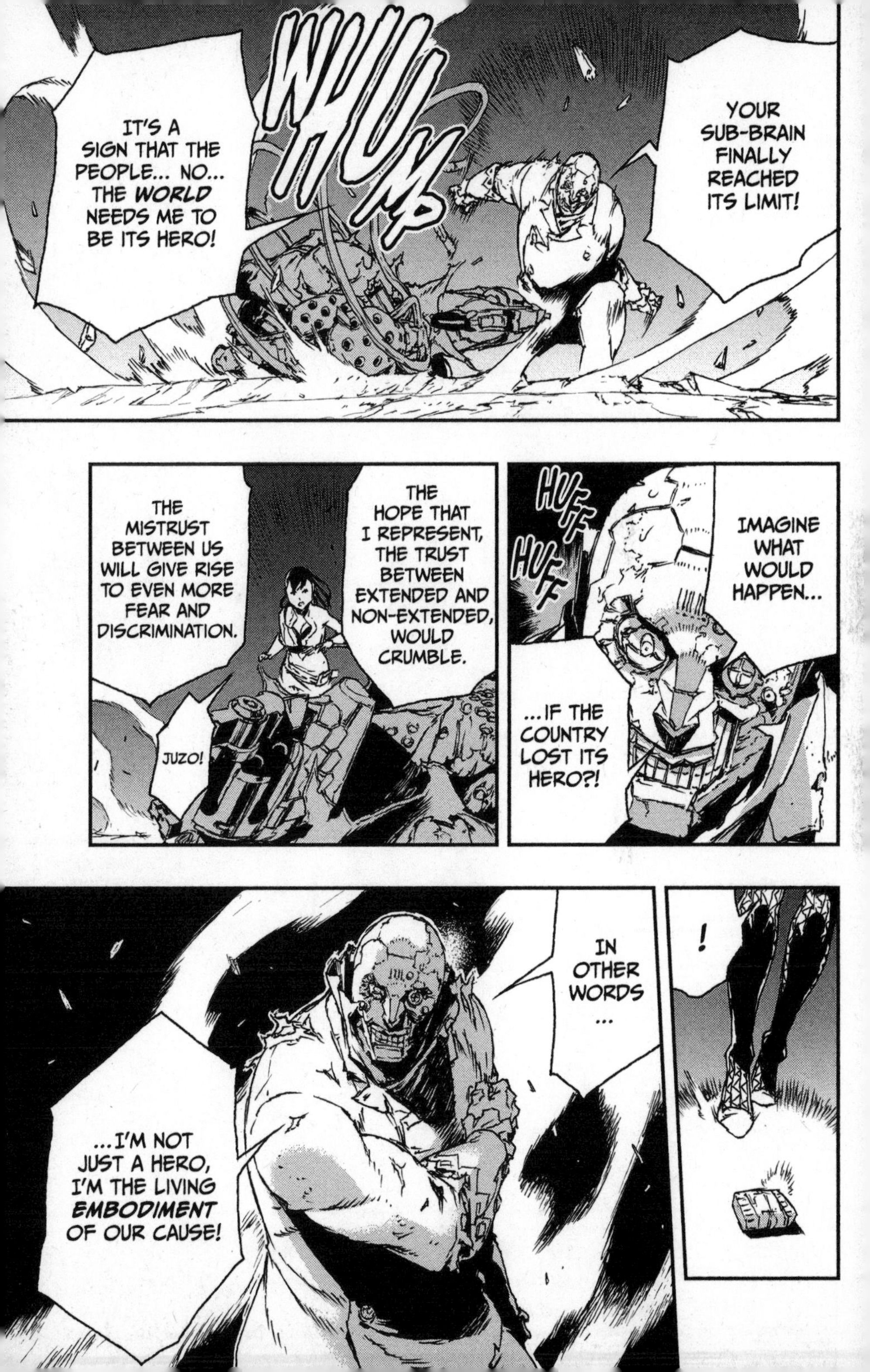
YOUR SUB-BRAIN FINALLY REACHED ITS LIMIT!
WHUMP
IT'S A SIGN THAT THE PEOPLE... NO... THE *WORLD* NEEDS ME TO BE ITS HERO!
IMAGINE WHAT WOULD HAPPEN...
HUFF HUFF
...IF THE COUNTRY LOST ITS HERO?!
THE HOPE THAT I REPRESENT, THE TRUST BETWEEN EXTENDED AND NON-EXTENDED, WOULD CRUMBLE.
THE MISTRUST BETWEEN US WILL GIVE RISE TO EVEN MORE FEAR AND DISCRIMINATION.
JUZO!
!
IN OTHER WORDS ...
...I'M NOT JUST A HERO, I'M THE LIVING *EMBODIMENT* OF OUR CAUSE!

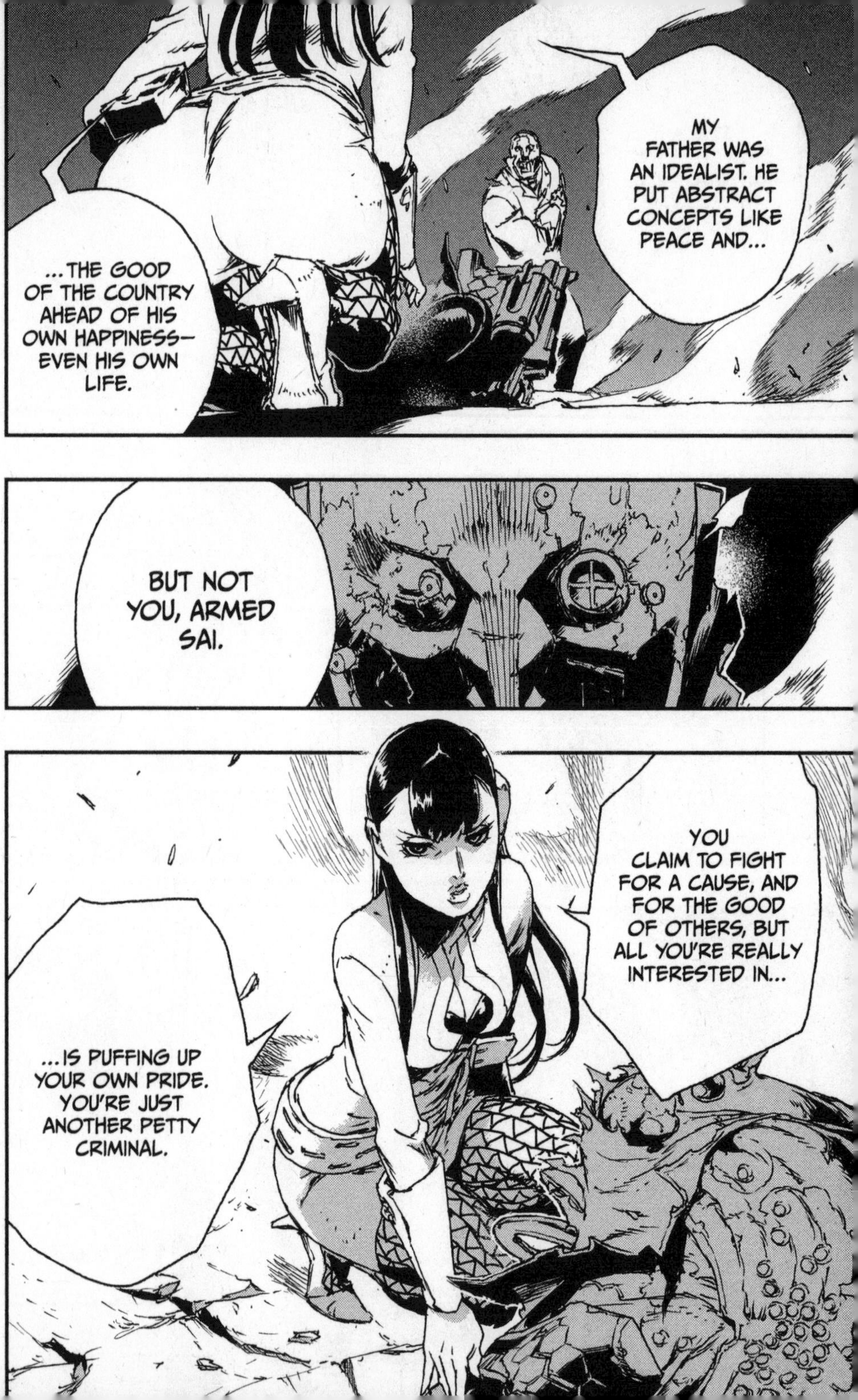
MY FATHER WAS AN IDEALIST. HE PUT ABSTRACT CONCEPTS LIKE PEACE AND...
...THE GOOD OF THE COUNTRY AHEAD OF HIS OWN HAPPINESS—EVEN HIS OWN LIFE.
BUT NOT YOU, ARMED SAI.
YOU CLAIM TO FIGHT FOR A CAUSE, AND FOR THE GOOD OF OTHERS, BUT ALL YOU'RE REALLY INTERESTED IN...
...IS PUFFING UP YOUR OWN PRIDE. YOU'RE JUST ANOTHER PETTY CRIMINAL.

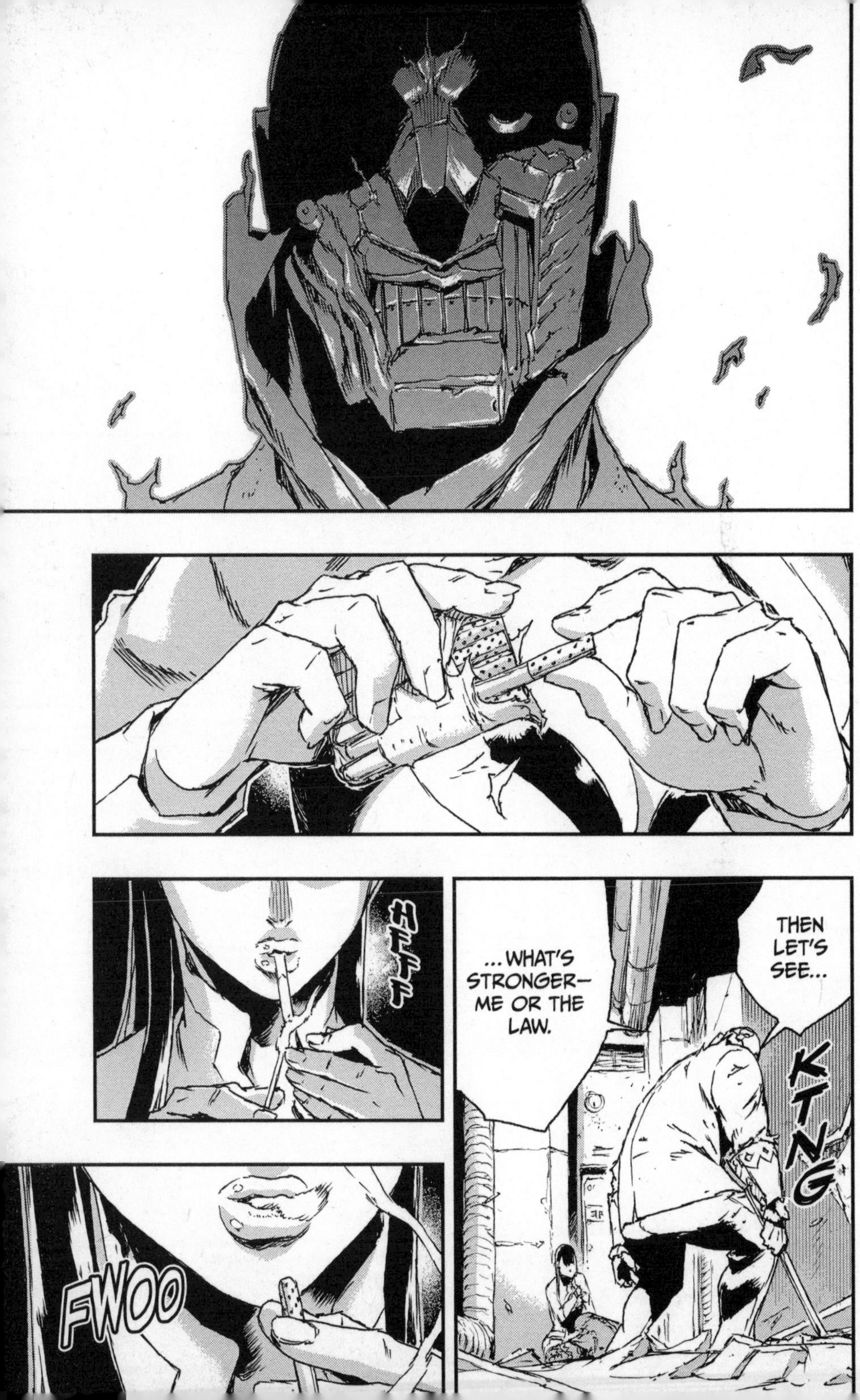
THEN LET'S SEE...
...WHAT'S STRONGER— ME OR THE LAW.
KTNG
HFFF
FWOO

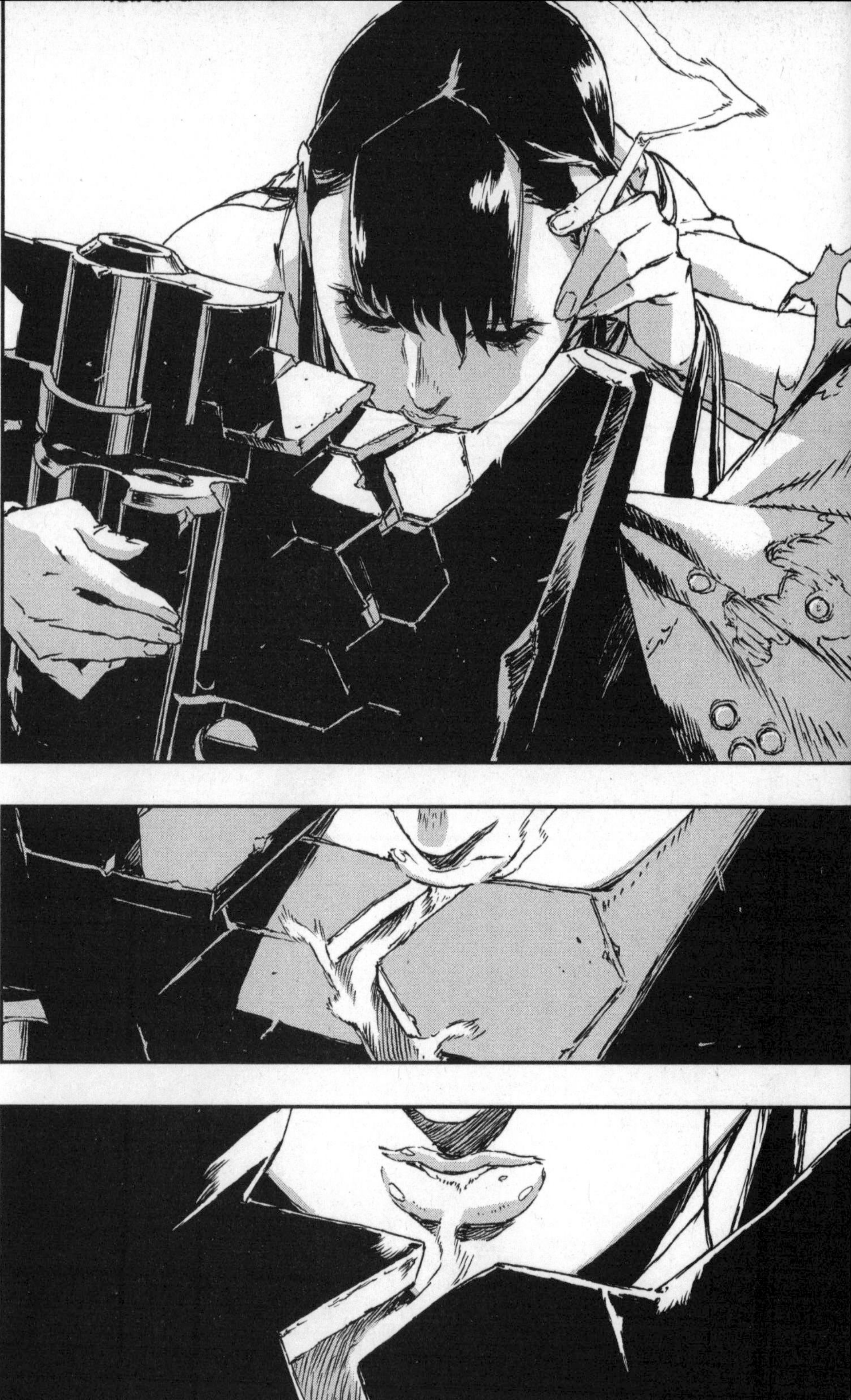

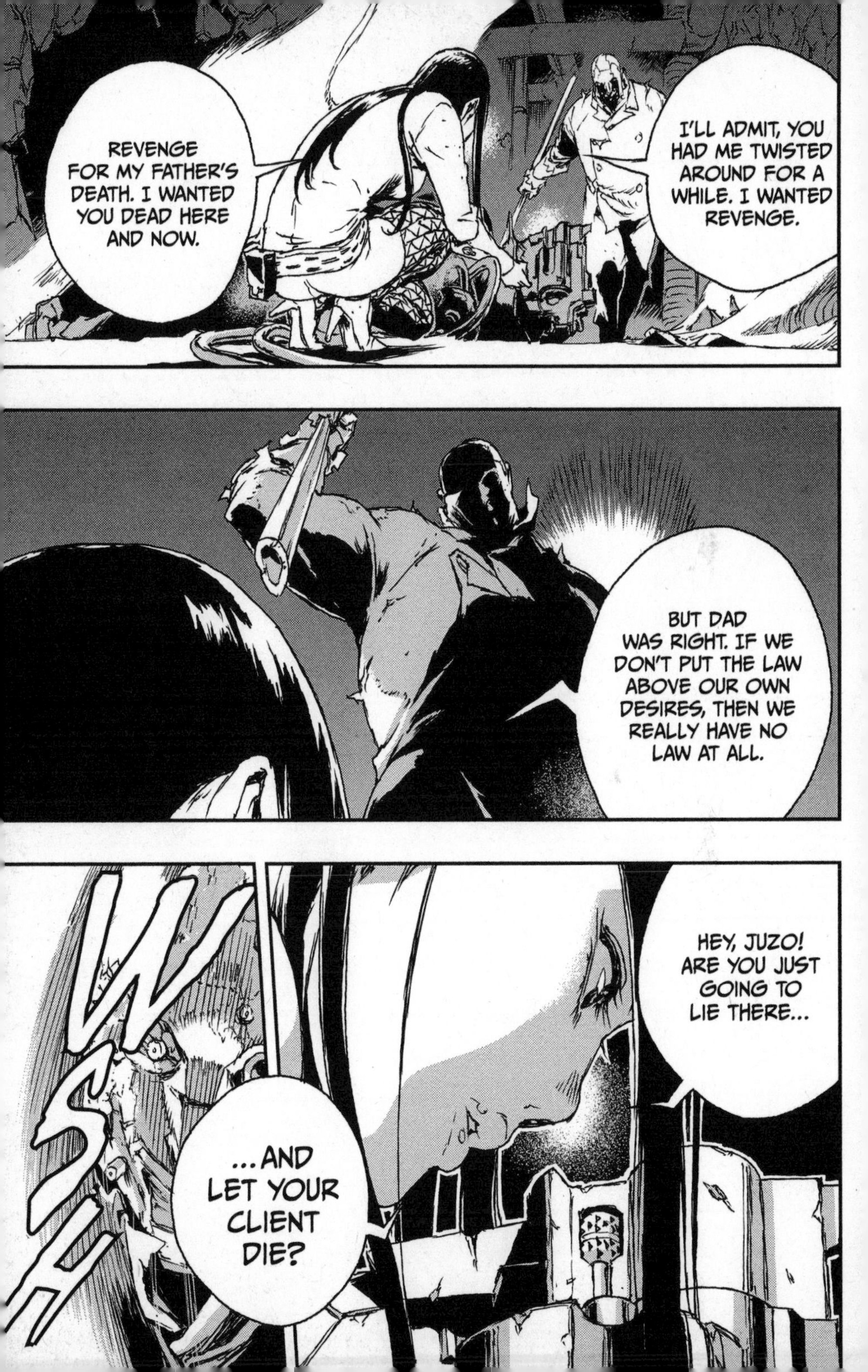
I'LL ADMIT, YOU HAD ME TWISTED AROUND FOR A WHILE. I WANTED REVENGE.
REVENGE FOR MY FATHER'S DEATH. I WANTED YOU DEAD HERE AND NOW.
BUT DAD WAS RIGHT. IF WE DON'T PUT THE LAW ABOVE OUR OWN DESIRES, THEN WE REALLY HAVE NO LAW AT ALL.
HEY, JUZO! ARE YOU JUST GOING TO LIE THERE...
...AND LET YOUR CLIENT DIE?
WSH

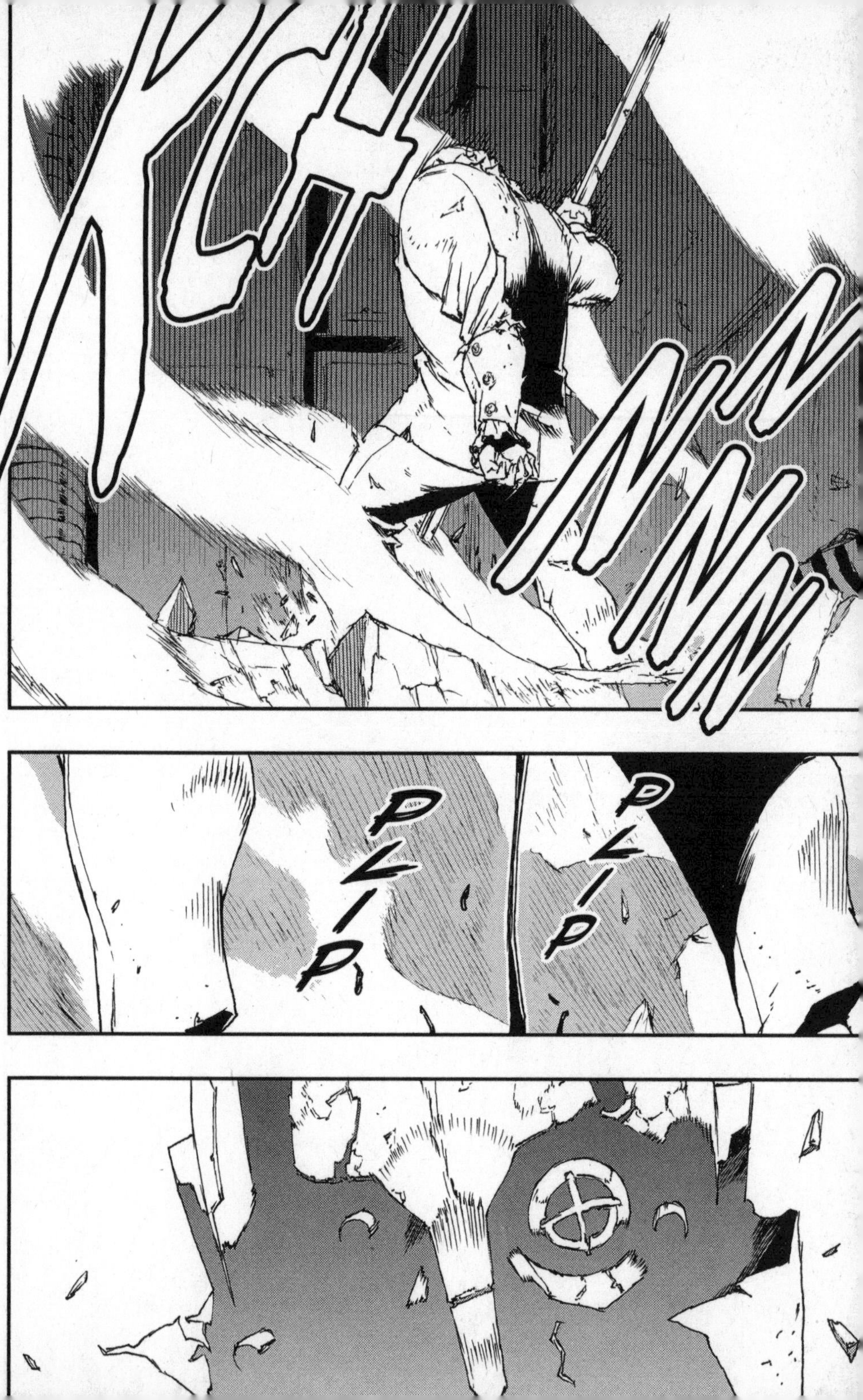
KCHNNNNN
PLIP
PLIP

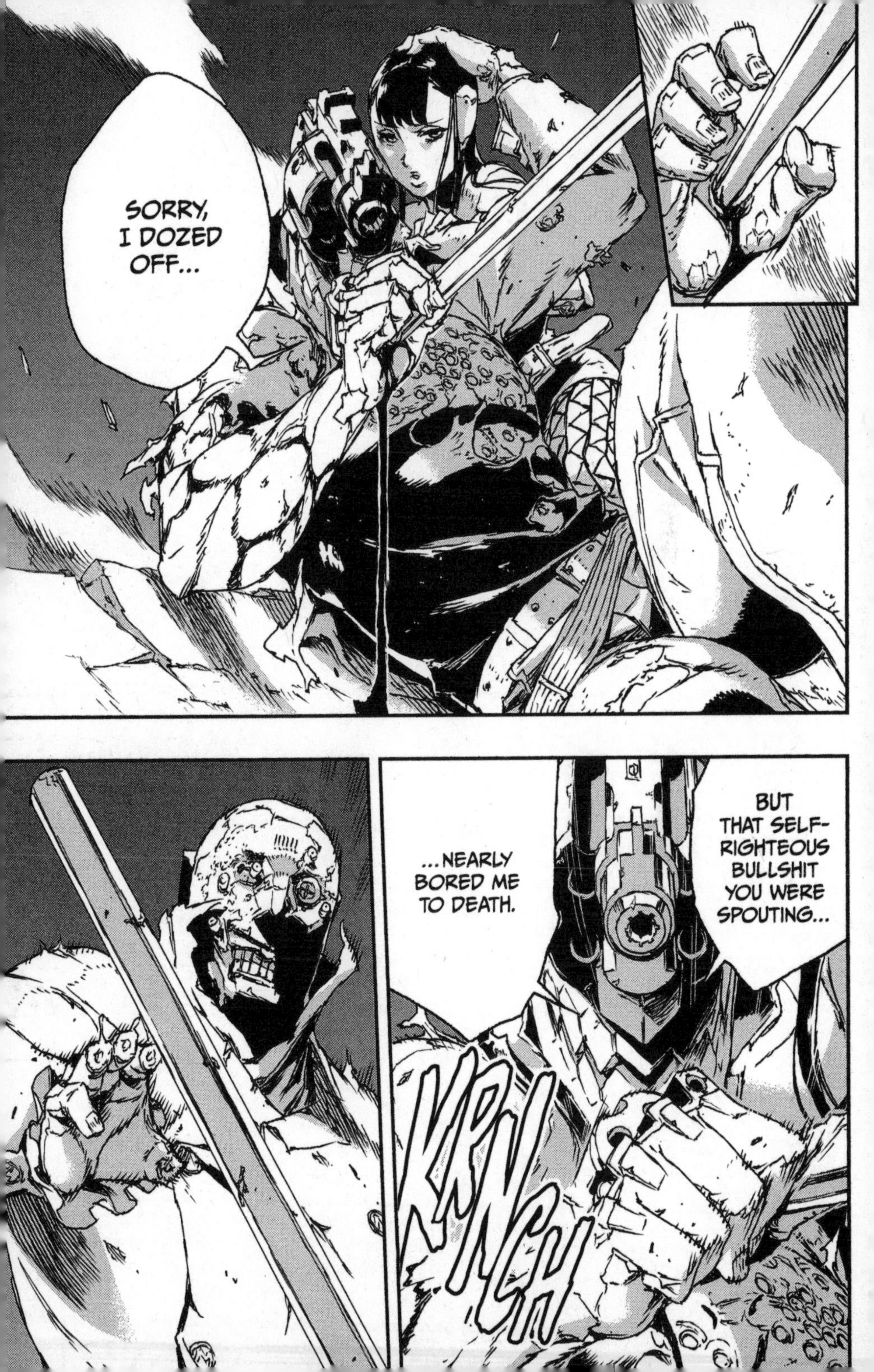
SORRY, I DOZED OFF...
BUT THAT SELF-RIGHTEOUS BULLSHIT YOU WERE SPOUTING...
...NEARLY BORED ME TO DEATH.
KRUNCH
!!!!!

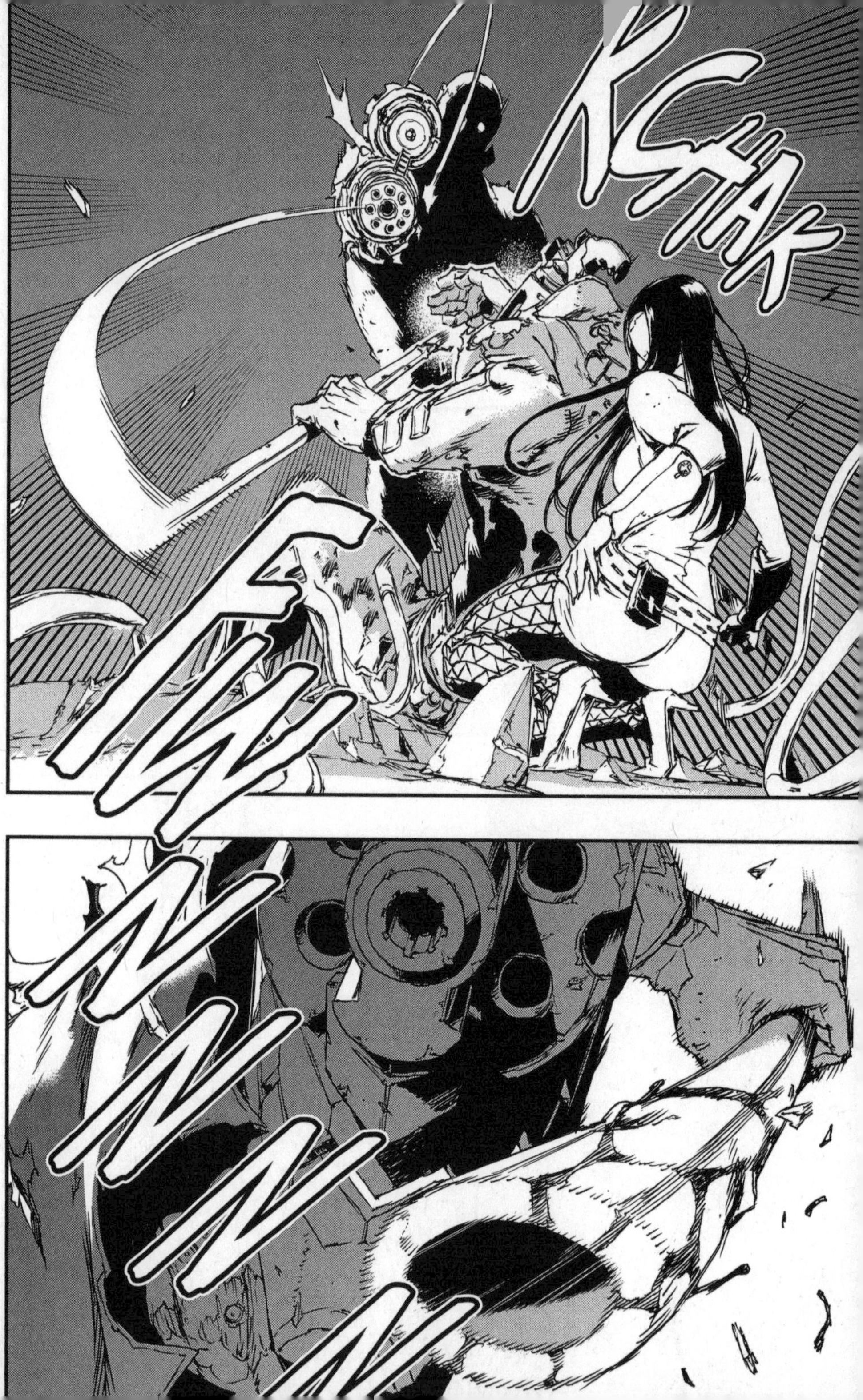
RSHAK
FWNNNNN

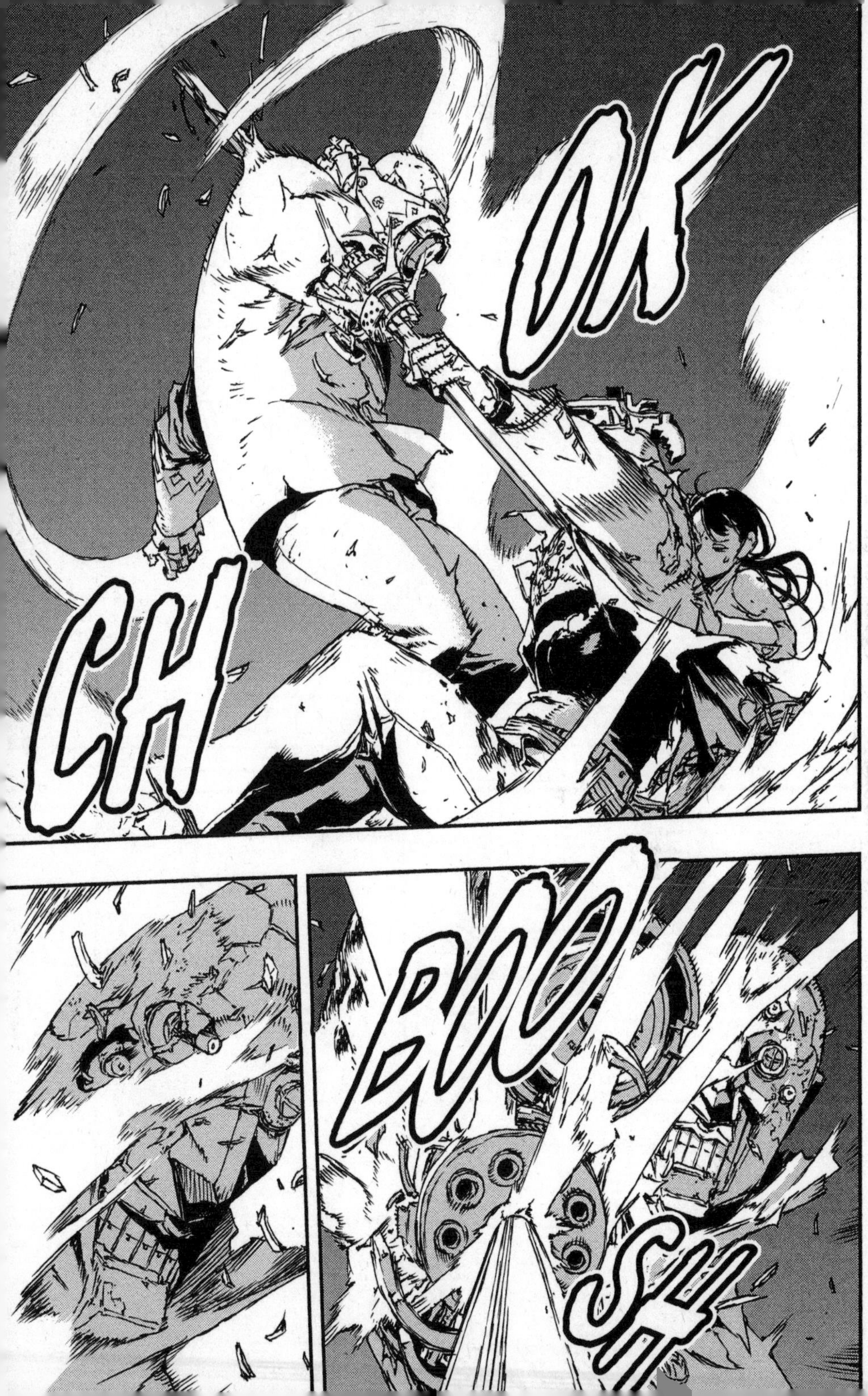
CHOK
BOOSH

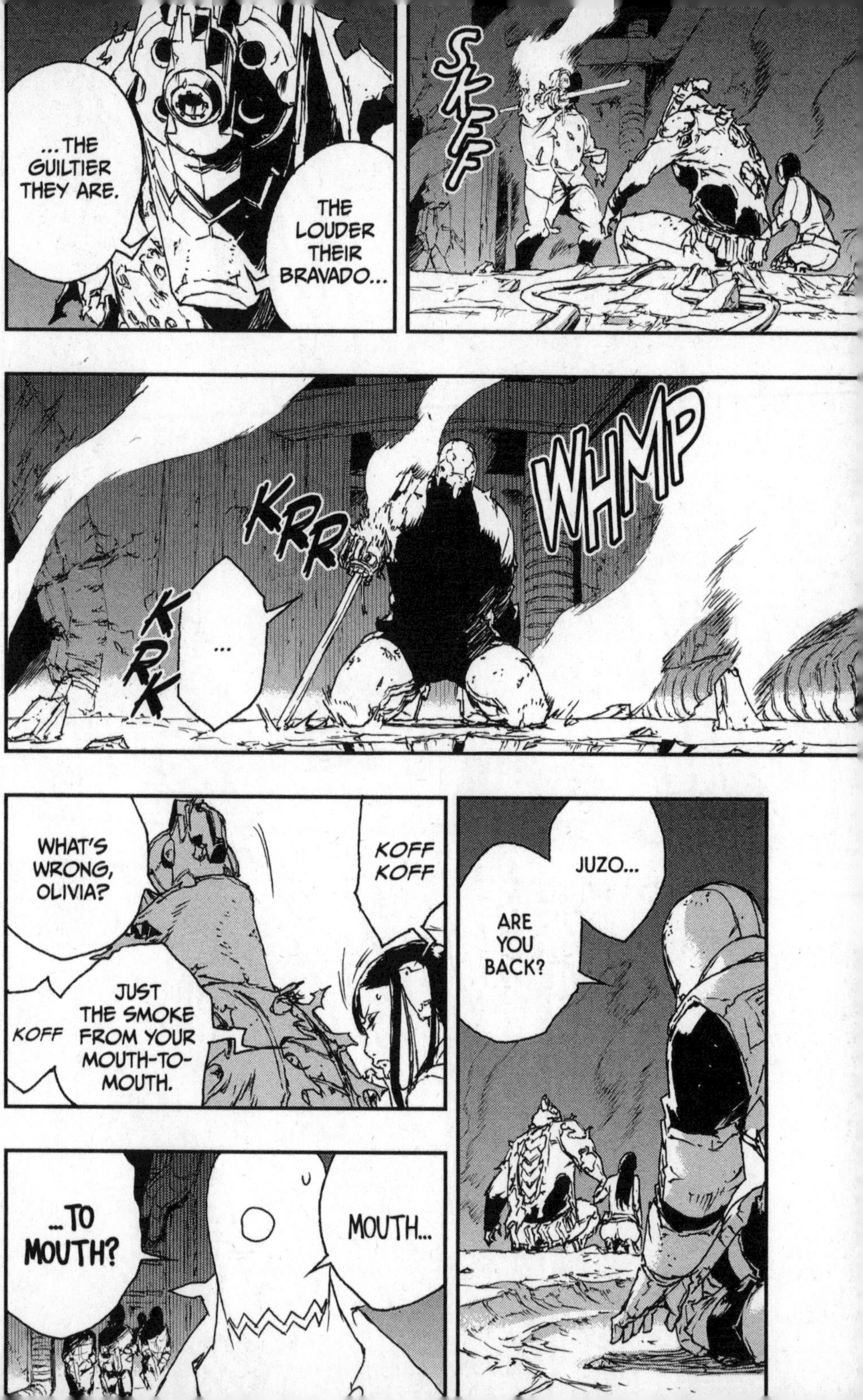
SKFF
THE LOUDER THEIR BRAVADO...
...THE GUILTIER THEY ARE.
WHMP
KRR
KRK
...
JUZO... ARE YOU BACK?
WHAT'S WRONG, OLIVIA?
KOFF KOFF
JUST THE SMOKE FROM YOUR MOUTH-TO-MOUTH.
KOFF
MOUTH...
...TO MOUTH?

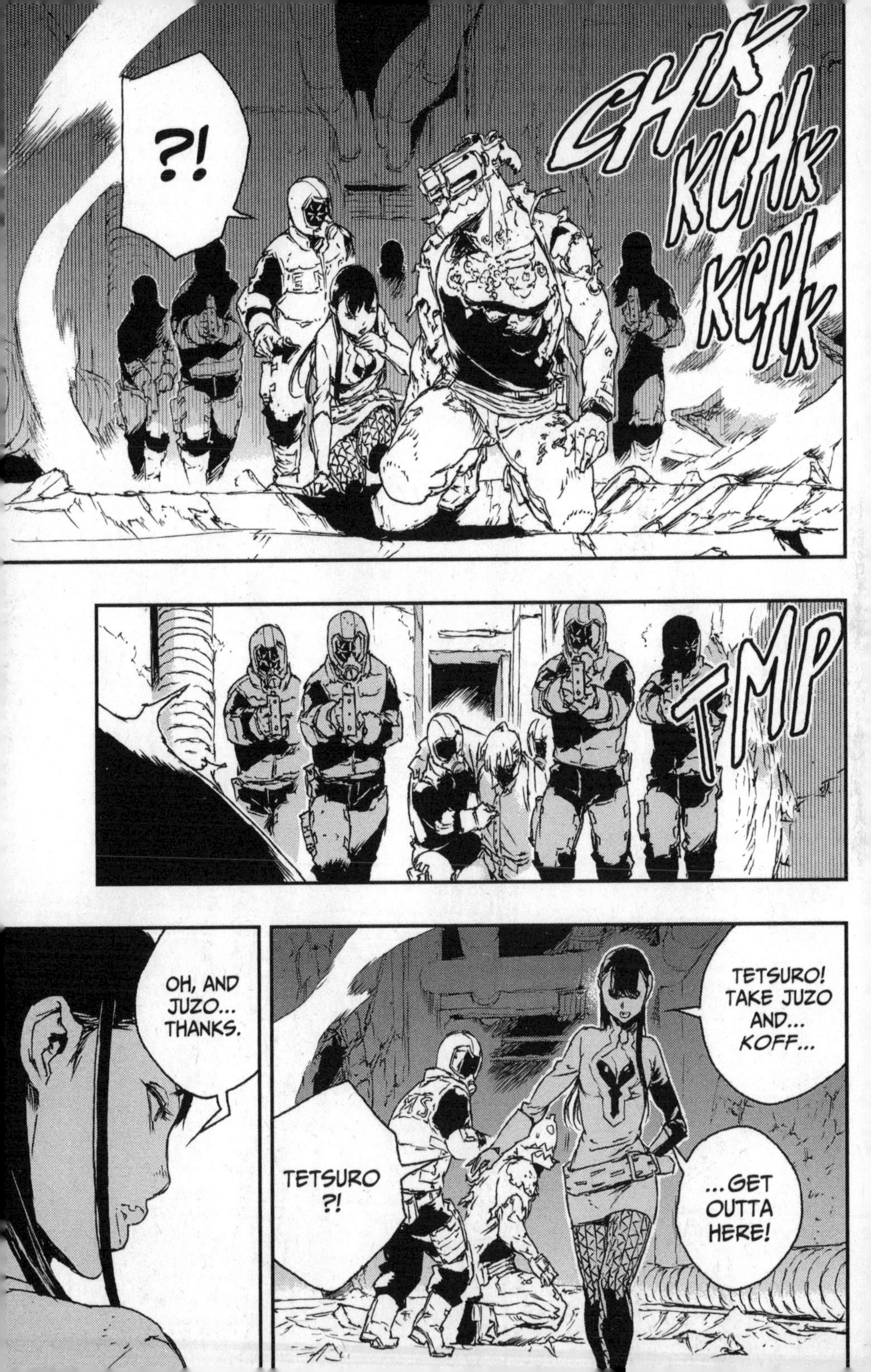
CHK KCHK KCHK
?!
TMP
TETSURO! TAKE JUZO AND... KOFF...
...GET OUTTA HERE!
TETSURO ?!
OH, AND JUZO... THANKS.

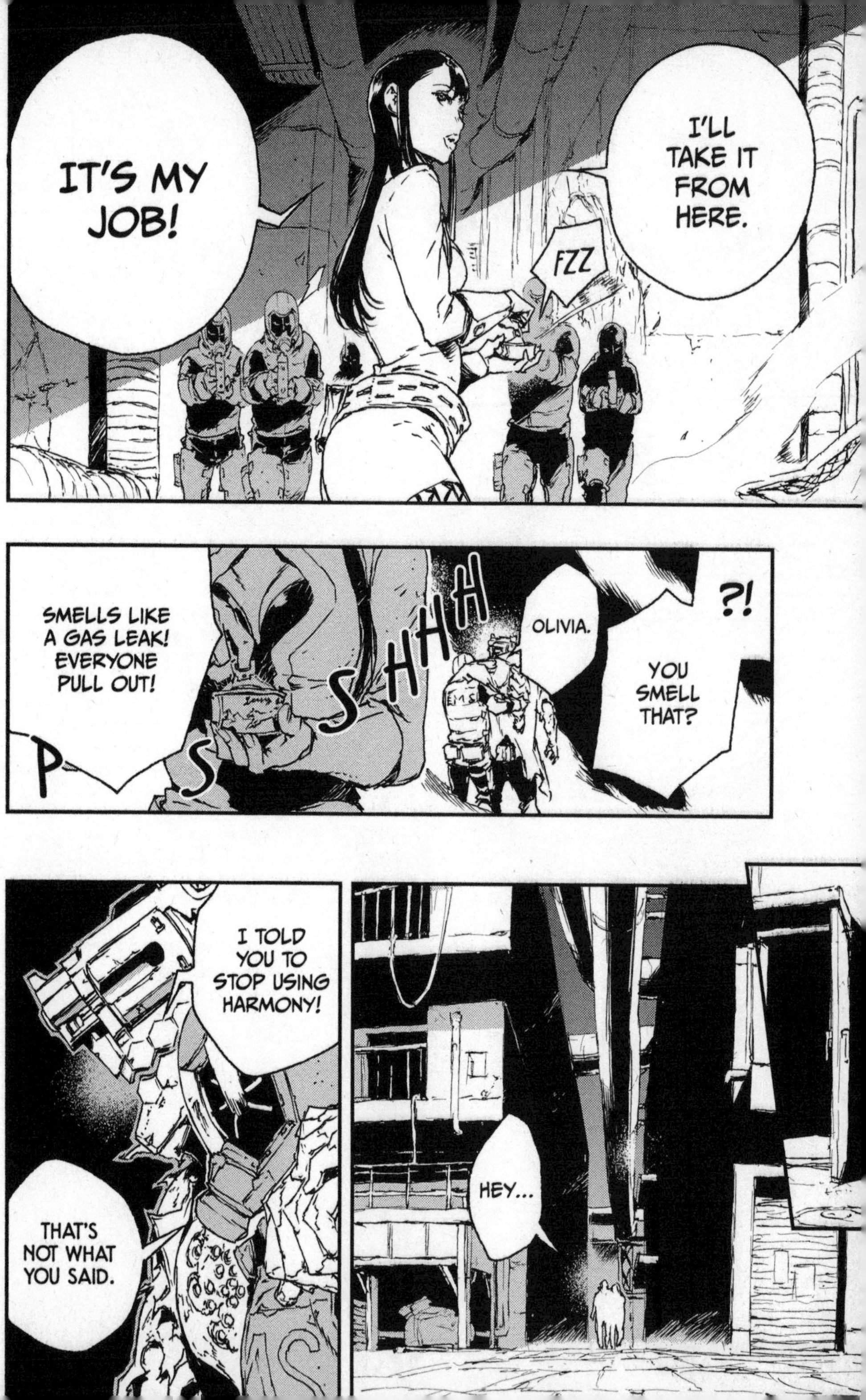
I'LL TAKE IT FROM HERE.
FZZ
IT'S MY JOB!
?!
OLIVIA.
YOU SMELL THAT?
SSHHH
SMELLS LIKE A GAS LEAK! EVERYONE PULL OUT!
P
HEY...
I TOLD YOU TO STOP USING HARMONY!
THAT'S NOT WHAT YOU SAID.

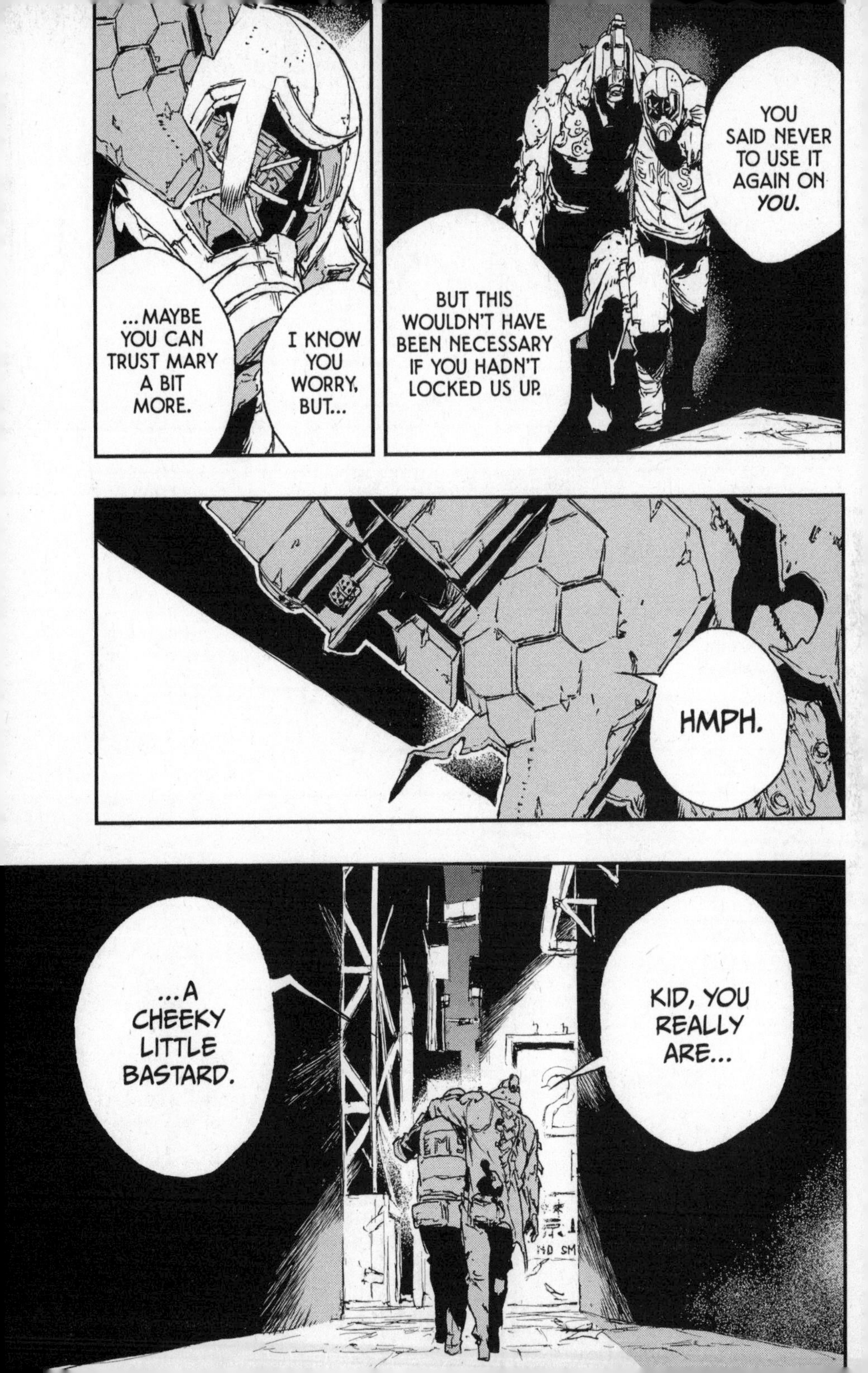
YOU SAID NEVER TO USE IT AGAIN ON *YOU.*
BUT THIS WOULDN'T HAVE BEEN NECESSARY IF YOU HADN'T LOCKED US UP.
I KNOW YOU WORRY, BUT...
...MAYBE YOU CAN TRUST MARY A BIT MORE.
HMPH.
KID, YOU REALLY ARE...
...A CHEEKY LITTLE BASTARD.

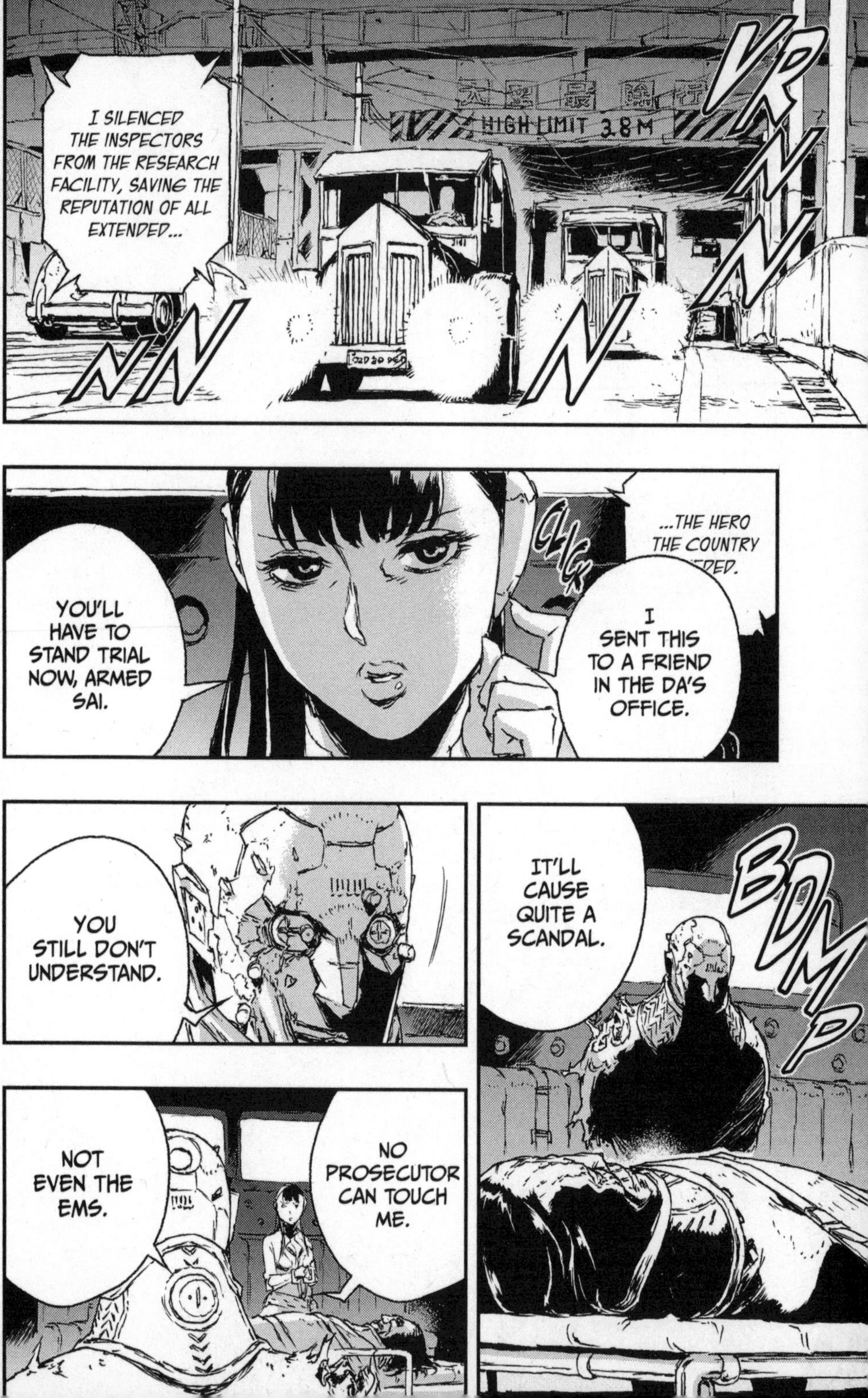
I SILENCED THE INSPECTORS FROM THE RESEARCH FACILITY, SAVING THE REPUTATION OF ALL EXTENDED...
HIGH LIMIT 3.8M
VRNNNN
N
NN
...THE HERO THE COUNTRY
EDED.
CLICK
I SENT THIS TO A FRIEND IN THE DA'S OFFICE.
YOU'LL HAVE TO STAND TRIAL NOW, ARMED SAI.
BDMP
IT'LL CAUSE QUITE A SCANDAL.
YOU STILL DON'T UNDERSTAND.
NO PROSECUTOR CAN TOUCH ME.
NOT EVEN THE EMS.

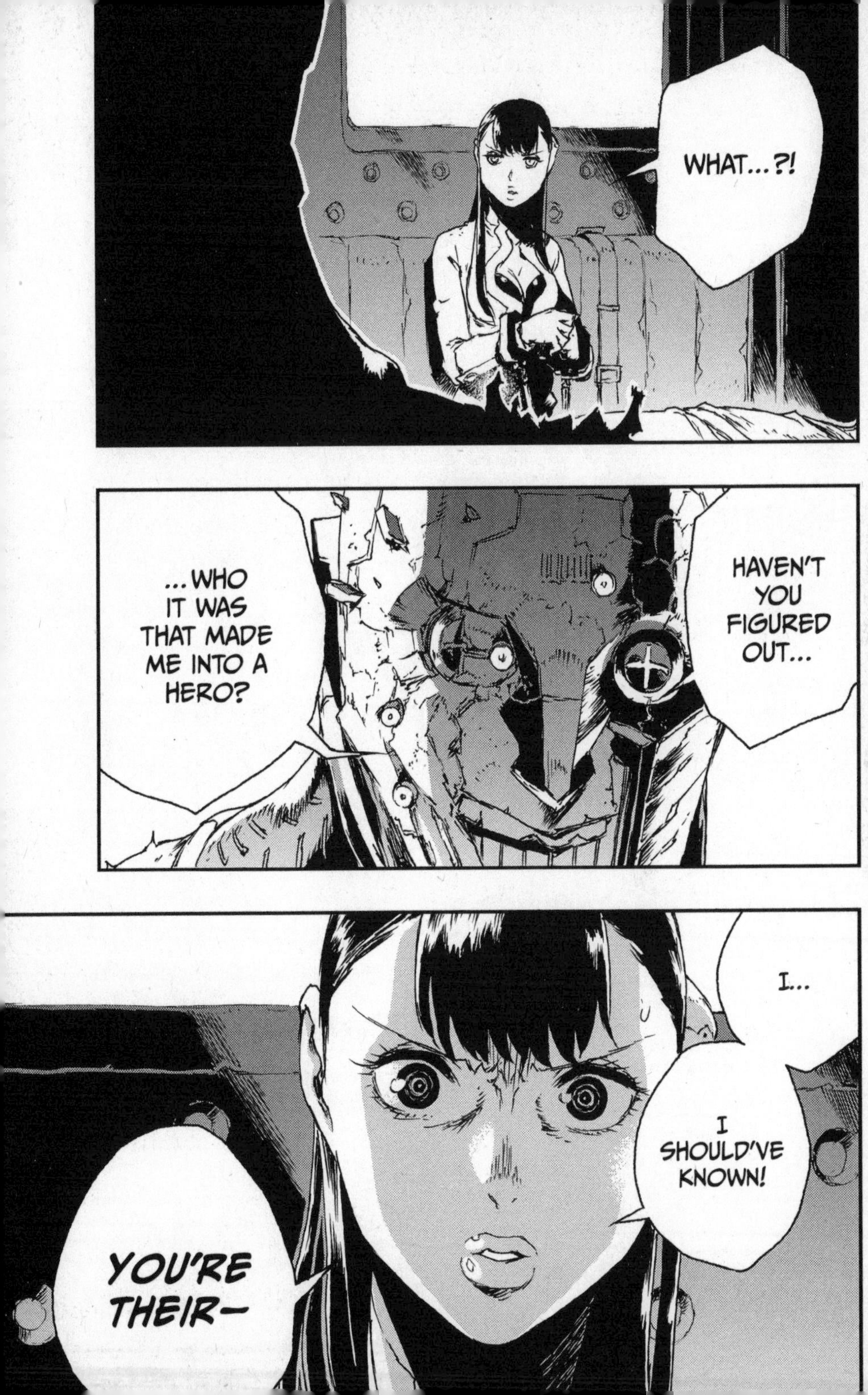
WHAT...?!
HAVEN'T YOU FIGURED OUT...
...WHO IT WAS THAT MADE ME INTO A HERO?
I...
I SHOULD'VE KNOWN!
YOU'RE THEIR—

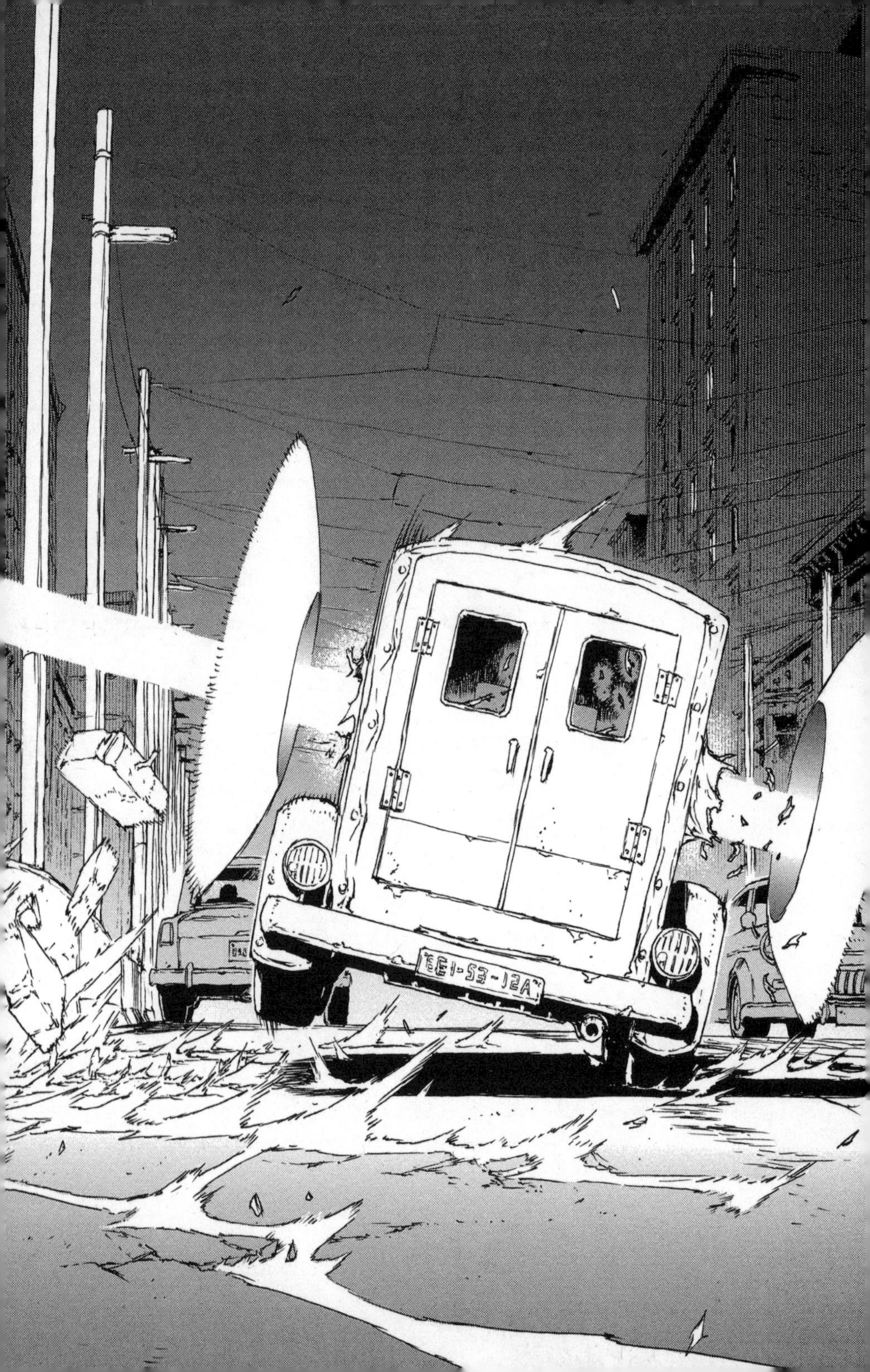

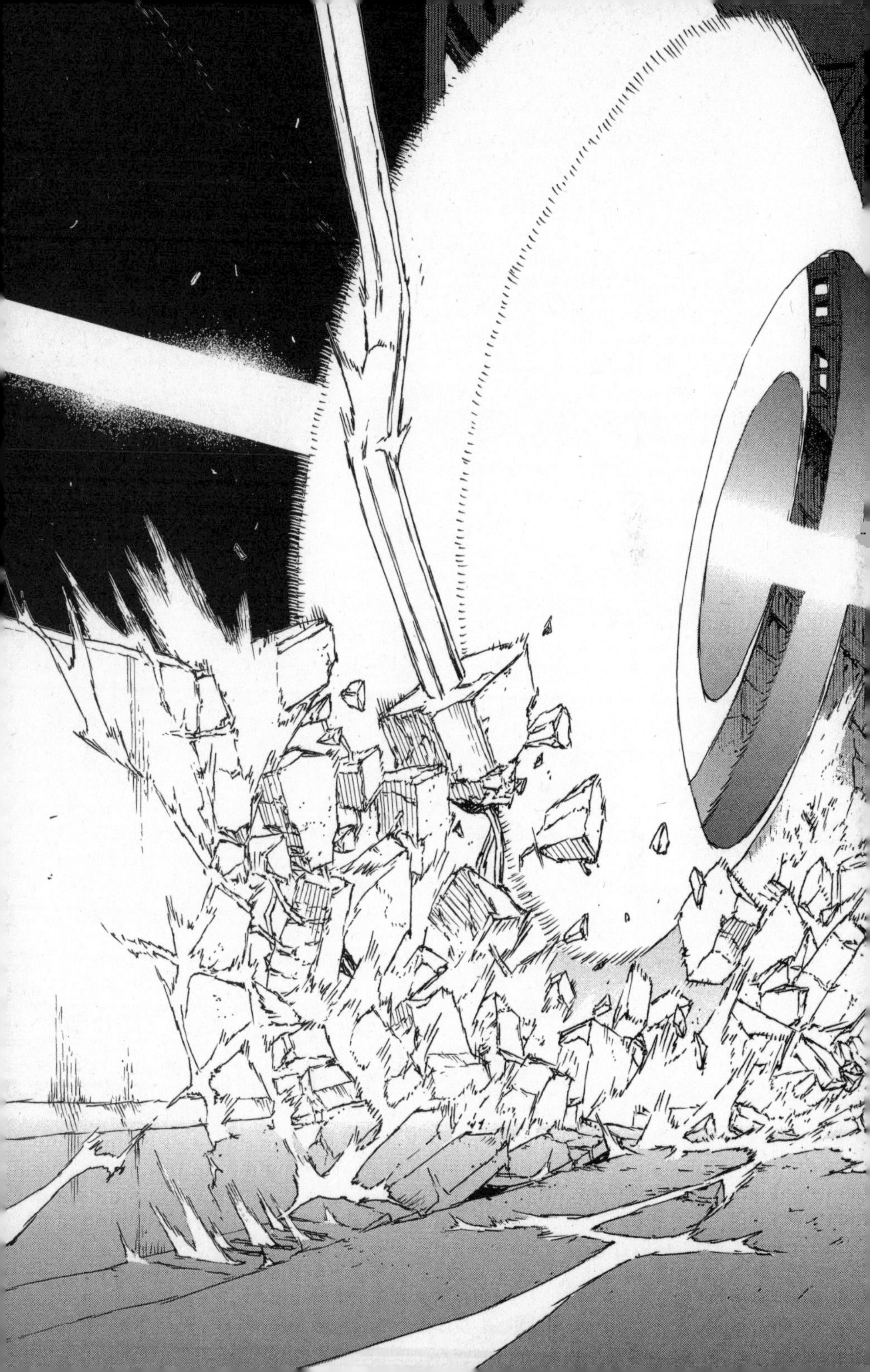

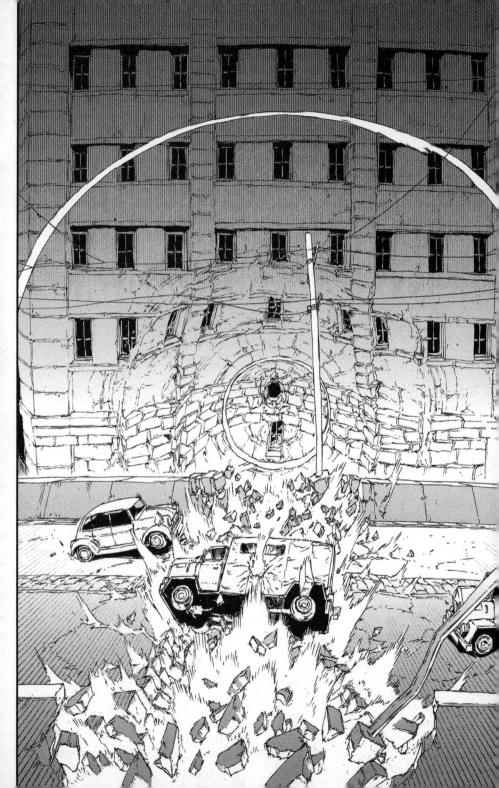

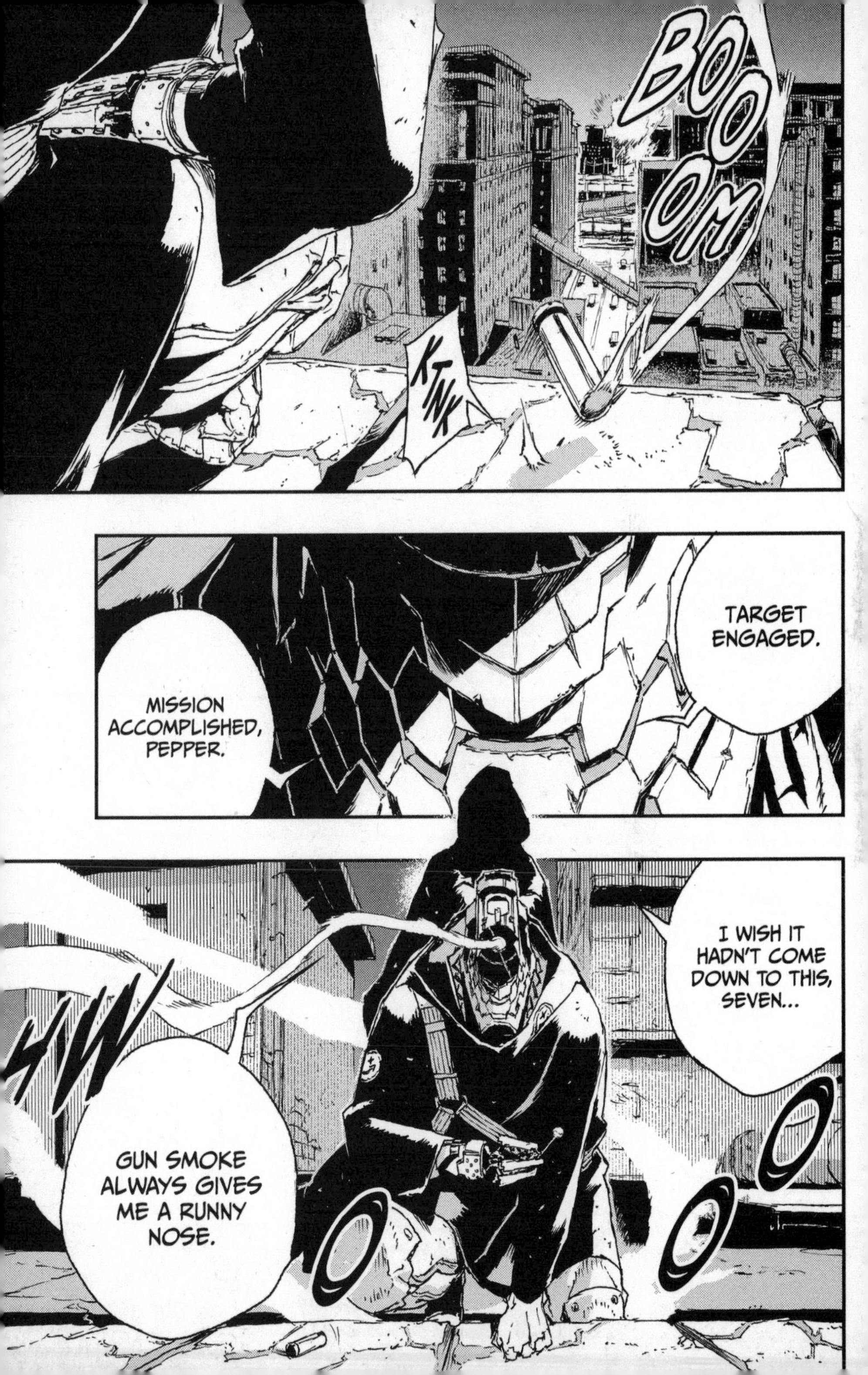
BOOOOM
KTINK
TARGET ENGAGED.
MISSION ACCOMPLISHED, PEPPER.
I WISH IT HADN'T COME DOWN TO THIS, SEVEN...
GUN SMOKE ALWAYS GIVES ME A RUNNY NOSE.

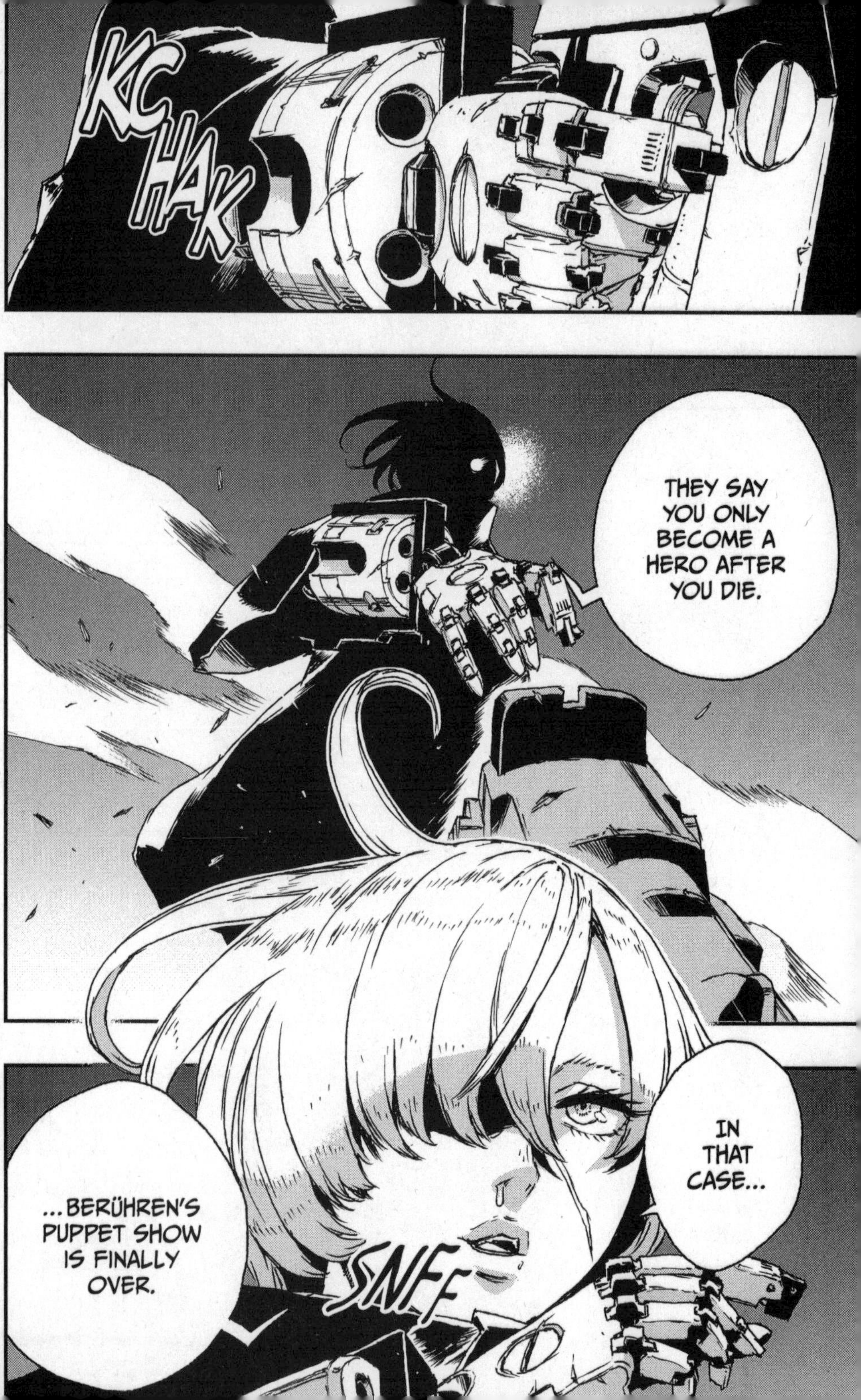
KCHAK
THEY SAY YOU ONLY BECOME A HERO AFTER YOU DIE.
IN THAT CASE...
...BERÜHREN'S PUPPET SHOW IS FINALLY OVER.
SNFF

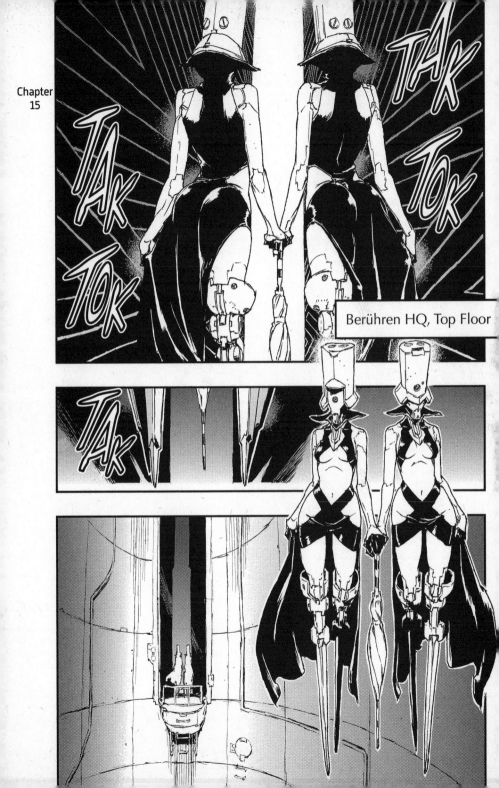

Chapter
15

Berühren HQ, Top Floor

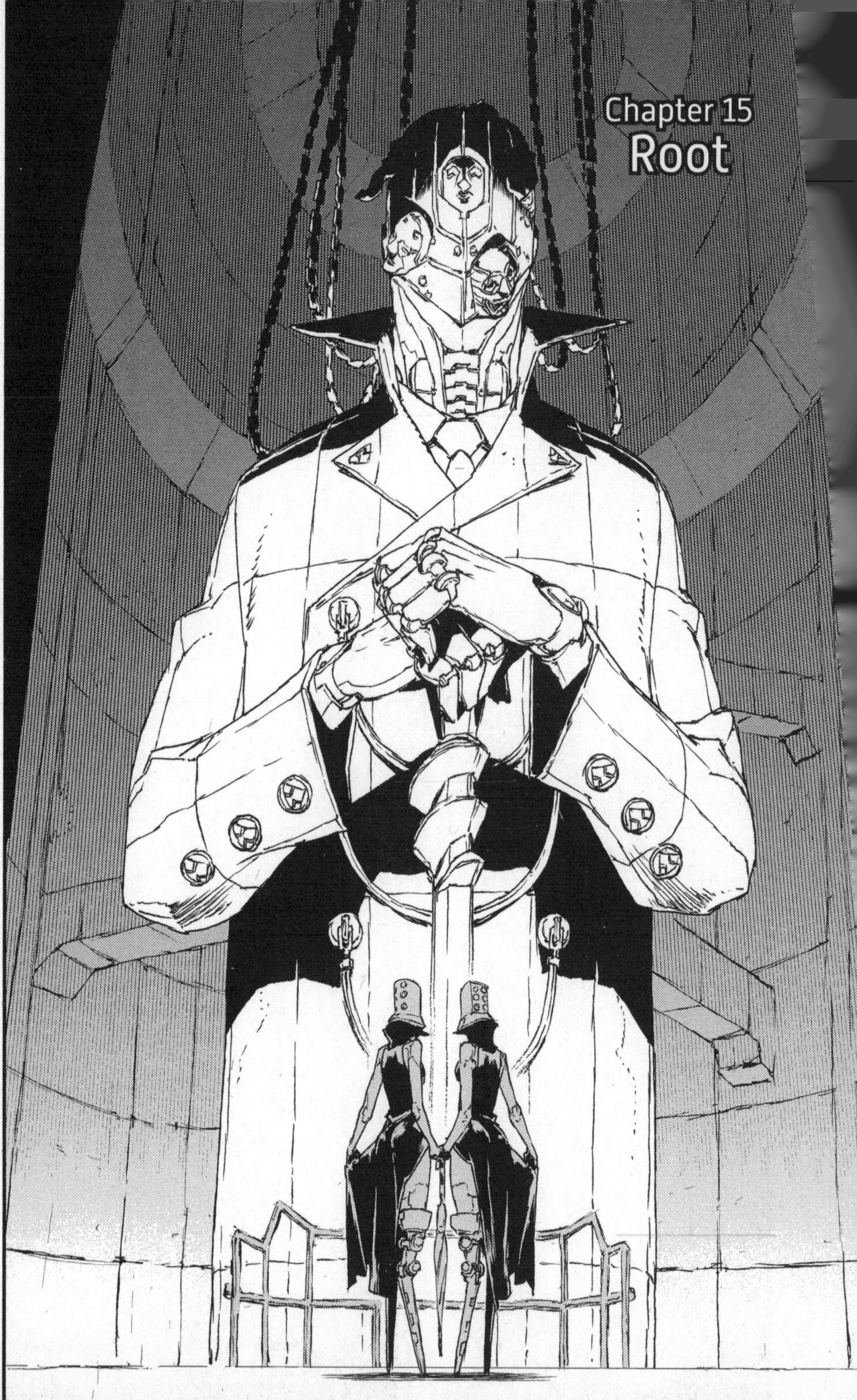
Chapter 15
Root

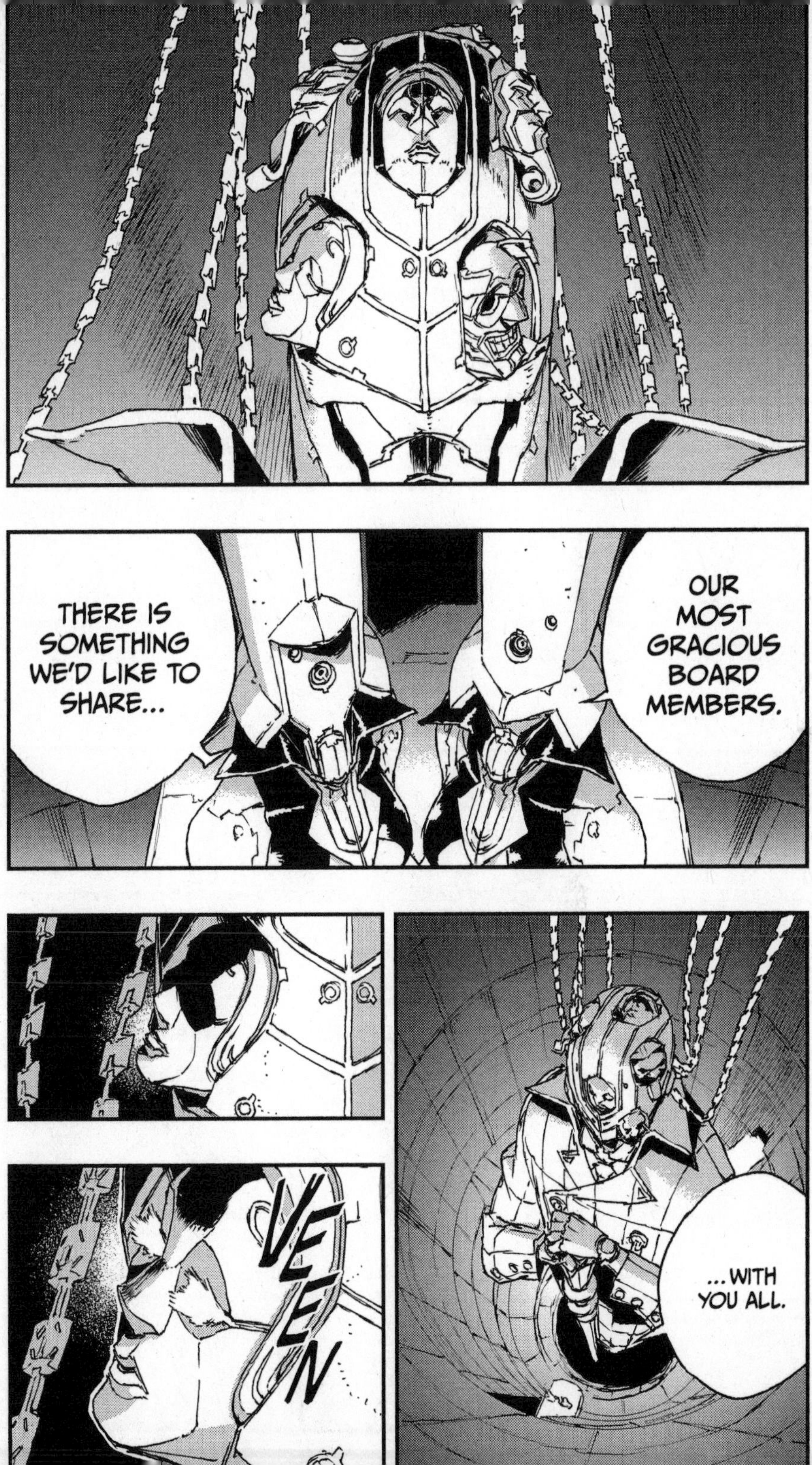
OUR MOST GRACIOUS BOARD MEMBERS.
THERE IS SOMETHING WE'D LIKE TO SHARE...
...WITH YOU ALL.
VEEEN

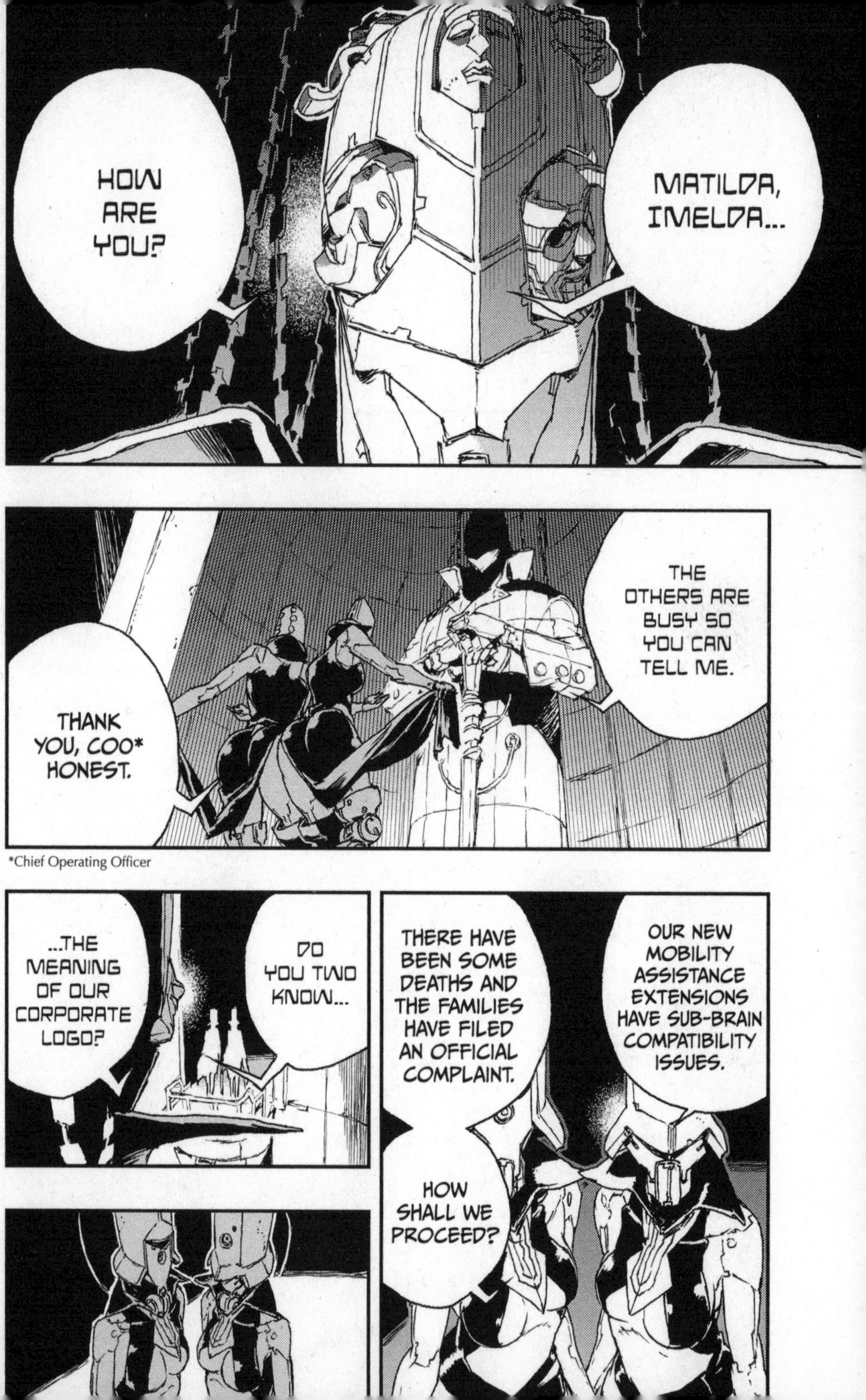
MATILDA, IMELDA...
HOW ARE YOU?
THE OTHERS ARE BUSY SO YOU CAN TELL ME.
THANK YOU, COO* HONEST.
OUR NEW MOBILITY ASSISTANCE EXTENSIONS HAVE SUB-BRAIN COMPATIBILITY ISSUES.
THERE HAVE BEEN SOME DEATHS AND THE FAMILIES HAVE FILED AN OFFICIAL COMPLAINT.
HOW SHALL WE PROCEED?
DO YOU TWO KNOW...
...THE MEANING OF OUR CORPORATE LOGO?
*Chief Operating Officer

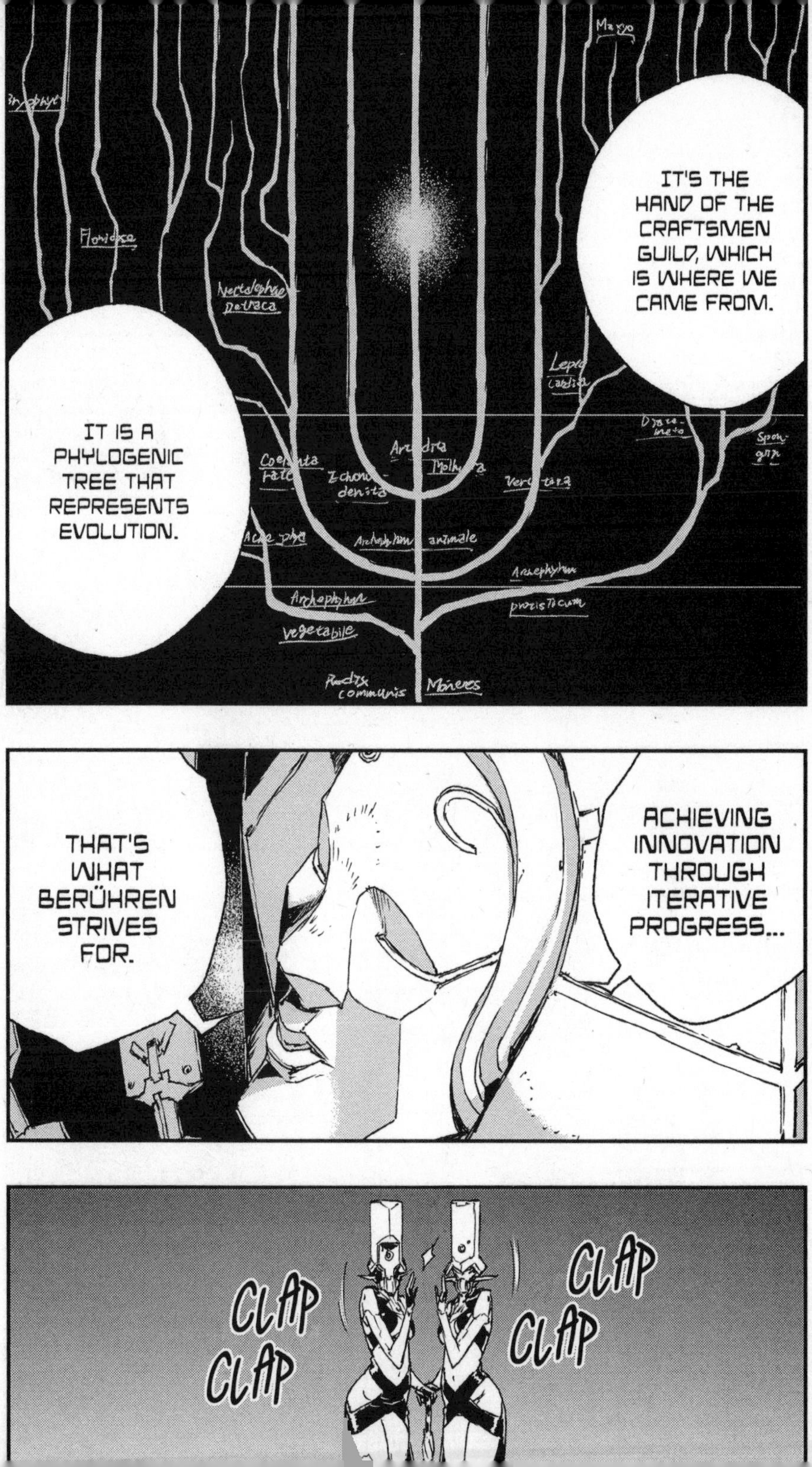
IT'S THE HAND OF THE CRAFTSMEN GUILD, WHICH IS WHERE WE CAME FROM.
IT IS A PHYLOGENIC TREE THAT REPRESENTS EVOLUTION.
ACHIEVING INNOVATION THROUGH ITERATIVE PROGRESS...
THAT'S WHAT BERÜHREN STRIVES FOR.
CLAP
CLAP
CLAP
CLAP

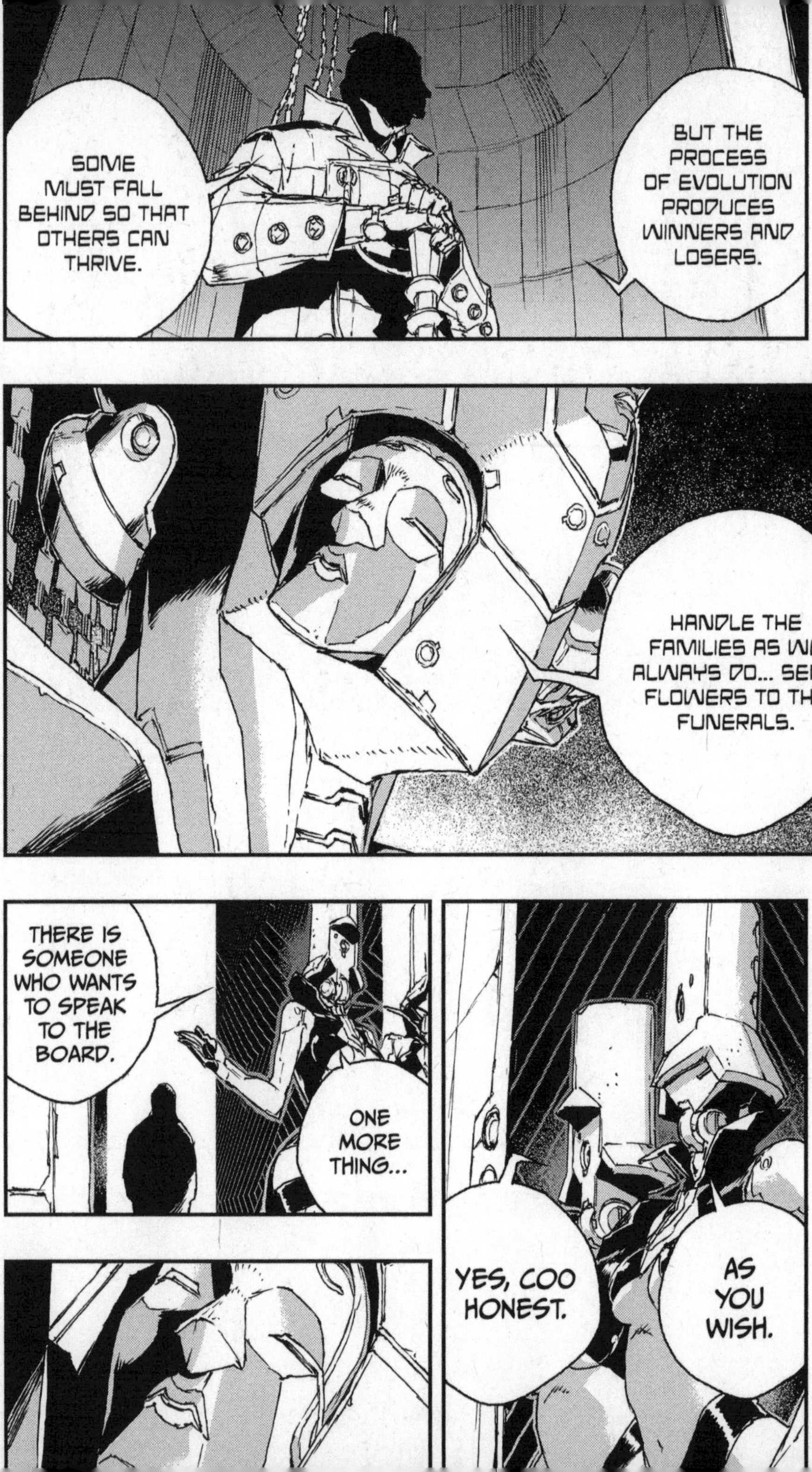
BUT THE PROCESS OF EVOLUTION PRODUCES WINNERS AND LOSERS.
SOME MUST FALL BEHIND SO THAT OTHERS CAN THRIVE.
HANDLE THE FAMILIES AS WE ALWAYS DO... SEND FLOWERS TO THE FUNERALS.
AS YOU WISH.
YES, COO HONEST.
ONE MORE THING...
THERE IS SOMEONE WHO WANTS TO SPEAK TO THE BOARD.

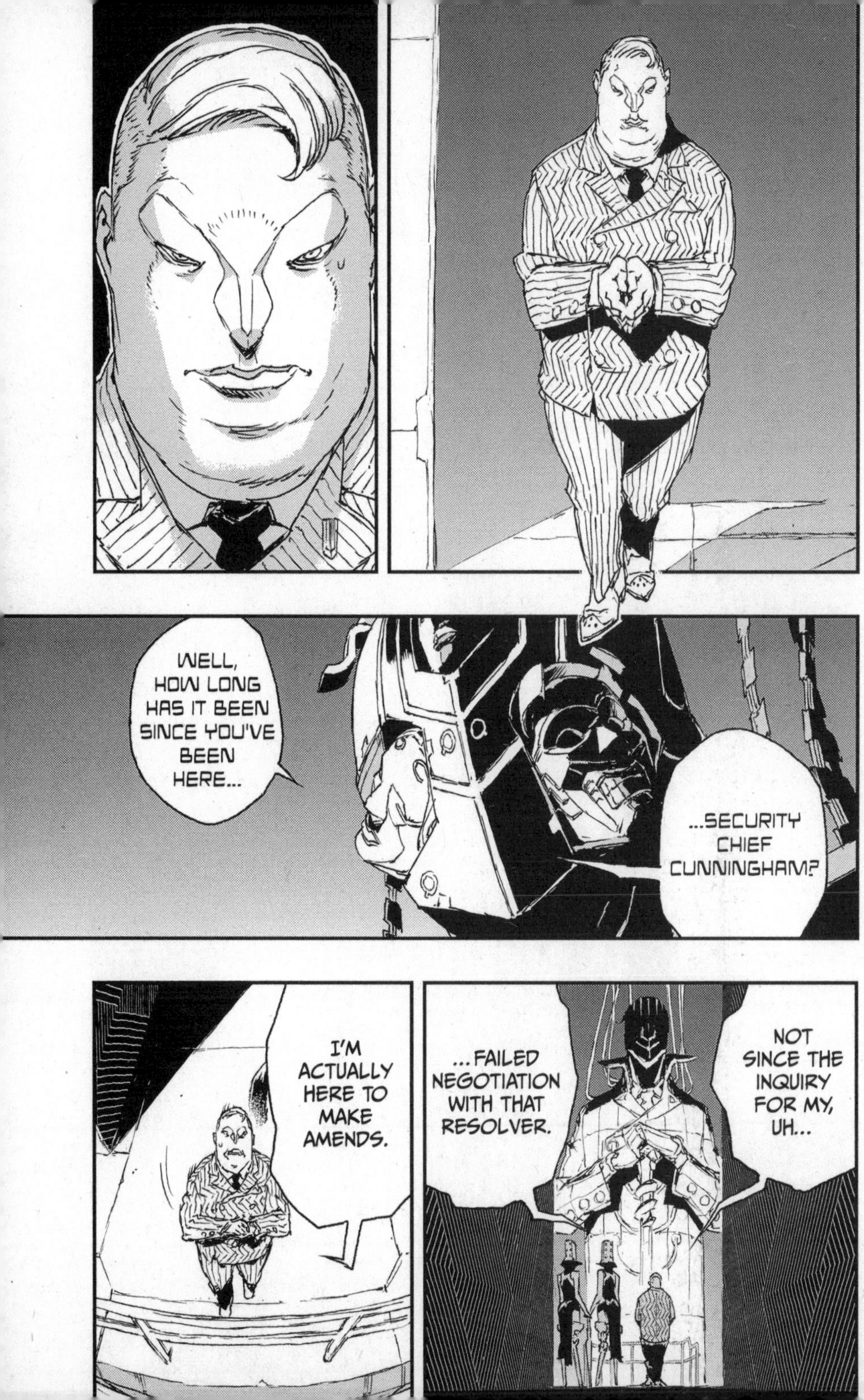

WELL, HOW LONG HAS IT BEEN SINCE YOU'VE BEEN HERE...
...SECURITY CHIEF CUNNINGHAM?
NOT SINCE THE INQUIRY FOR MY, UH...
...FAILED NEGOTIATION WITH THAT RESOLVER.
I'M ACTUALLY HERE TO MAKE AMENDS.

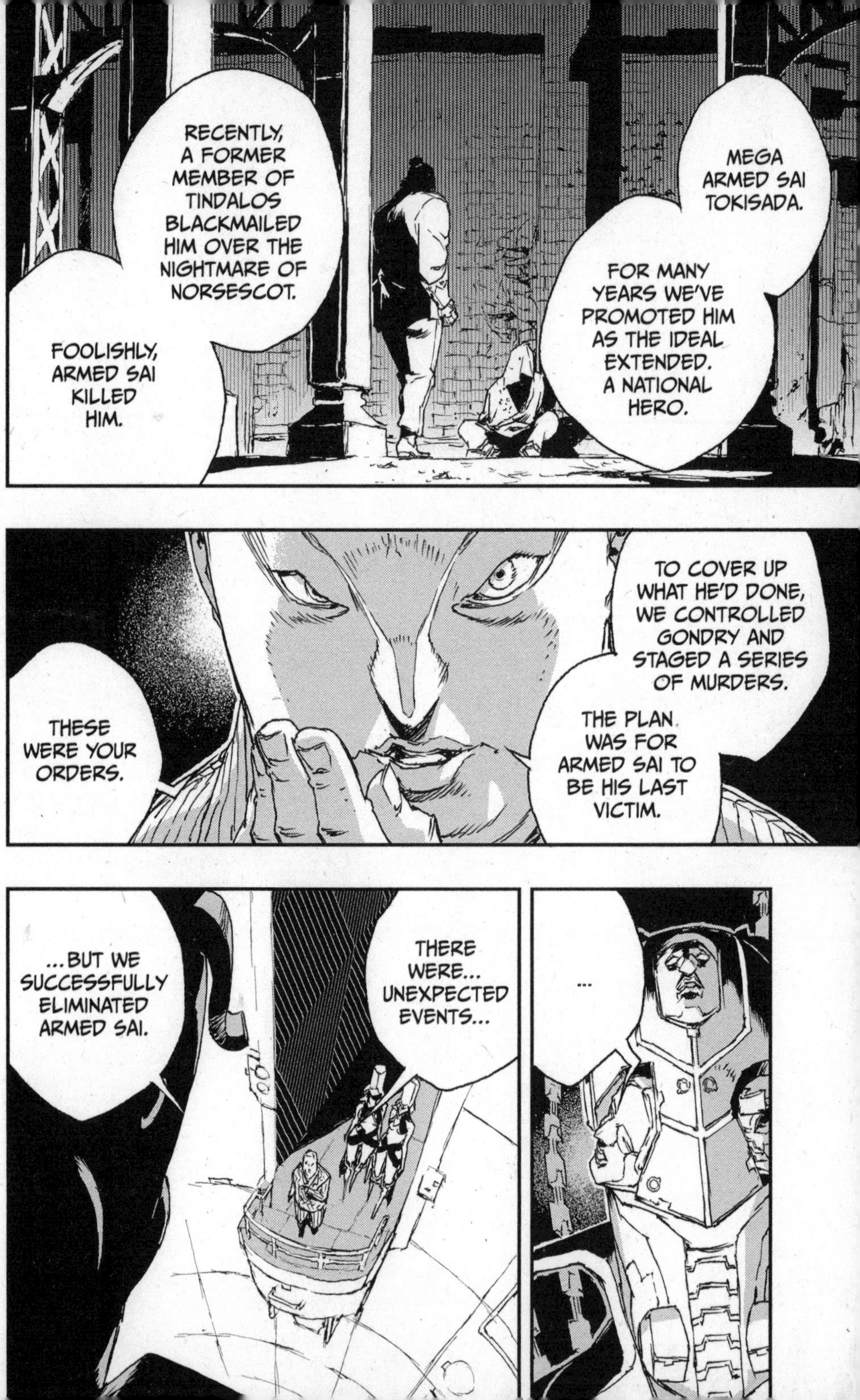
MEGA ARMED SAI TOKISADA.
FOR MANY YEARS WE'VE PROMOTED HIM AS THE IDEAL EXTENDED. A NATIONAL HERO.
RECENTLY, A FORMER MEMBER OF TINDALOS BLACKMAILED HIM OVER THE NIGHTMARE OF NORSESCOT.
FOOLISHLY, ARMED SAI KILLED HIM.
TO COVER UP WHAT HE'D DONE, WE CONTROLLED GONDRY AND STAGED A SERIES OF MURDERS.
THE PLAN WAS FOR ARMED SAI TO BE HIS LAST VICTIM.
THESE WERE YOUR ORDERS.
...
THERE WERE... UNEXPECTED EVENTS...
...BUT WE SUCCESSFULLY ELIMINATED ARMED SAI.

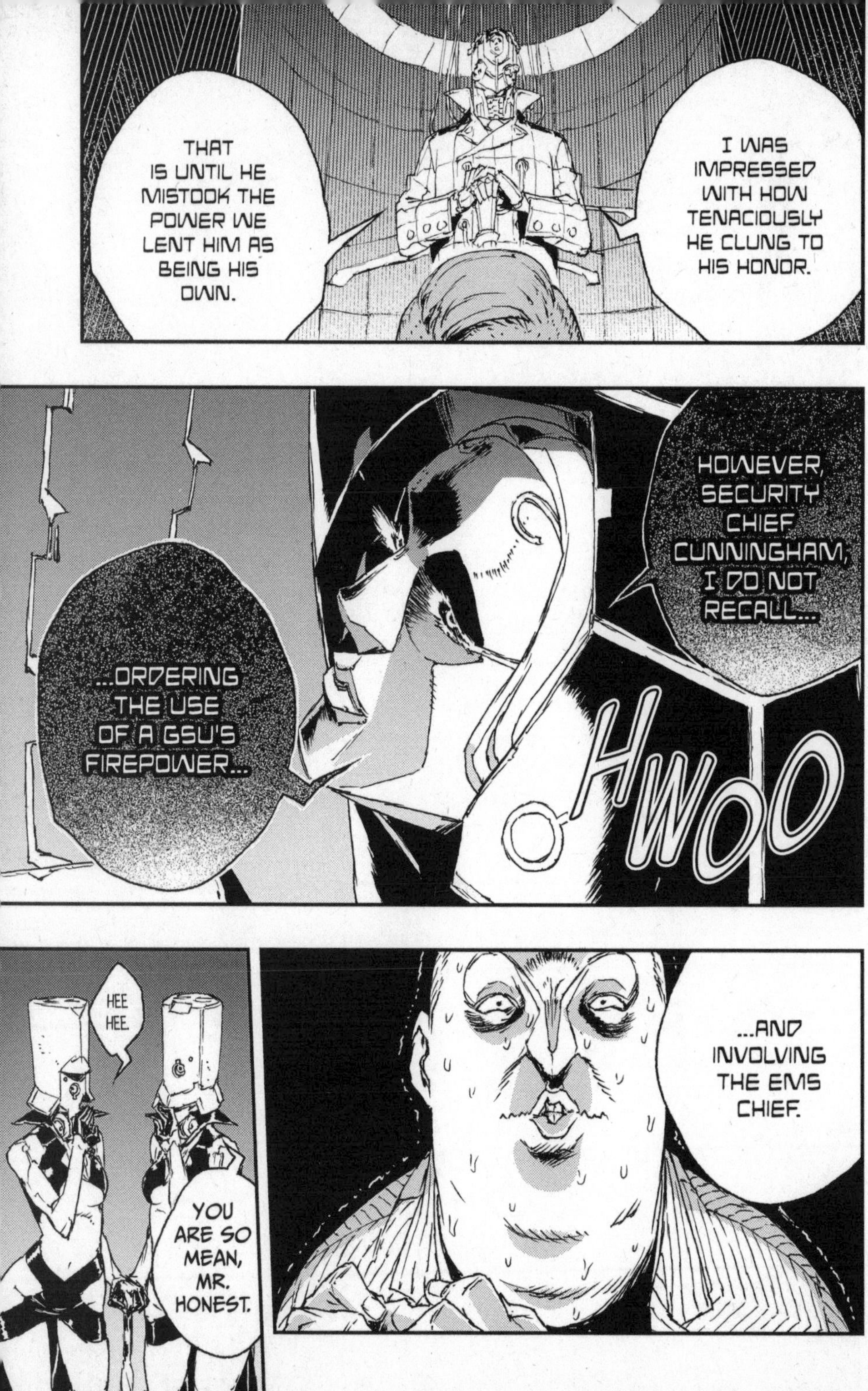
I WAS IMPRESSED WITH HOW TENACIOUSLY HE CLUNG TO HIS HONOR.
THAT IS UNTIL HE MISTOOK THE POWER WE LENT HIM AS BEING HIS OWN.
HOWEVER, SECURITY CHIEF CUNNINGHAM, I DO NOT RECALL...
HWOO
...ORDERING THE USE OF A GSU'S FIREPOWER...
...AND INVOLVING THE EMS CHIEF.
HEE HEE.
YOU ARE SO MEAN, MR. HONEST.

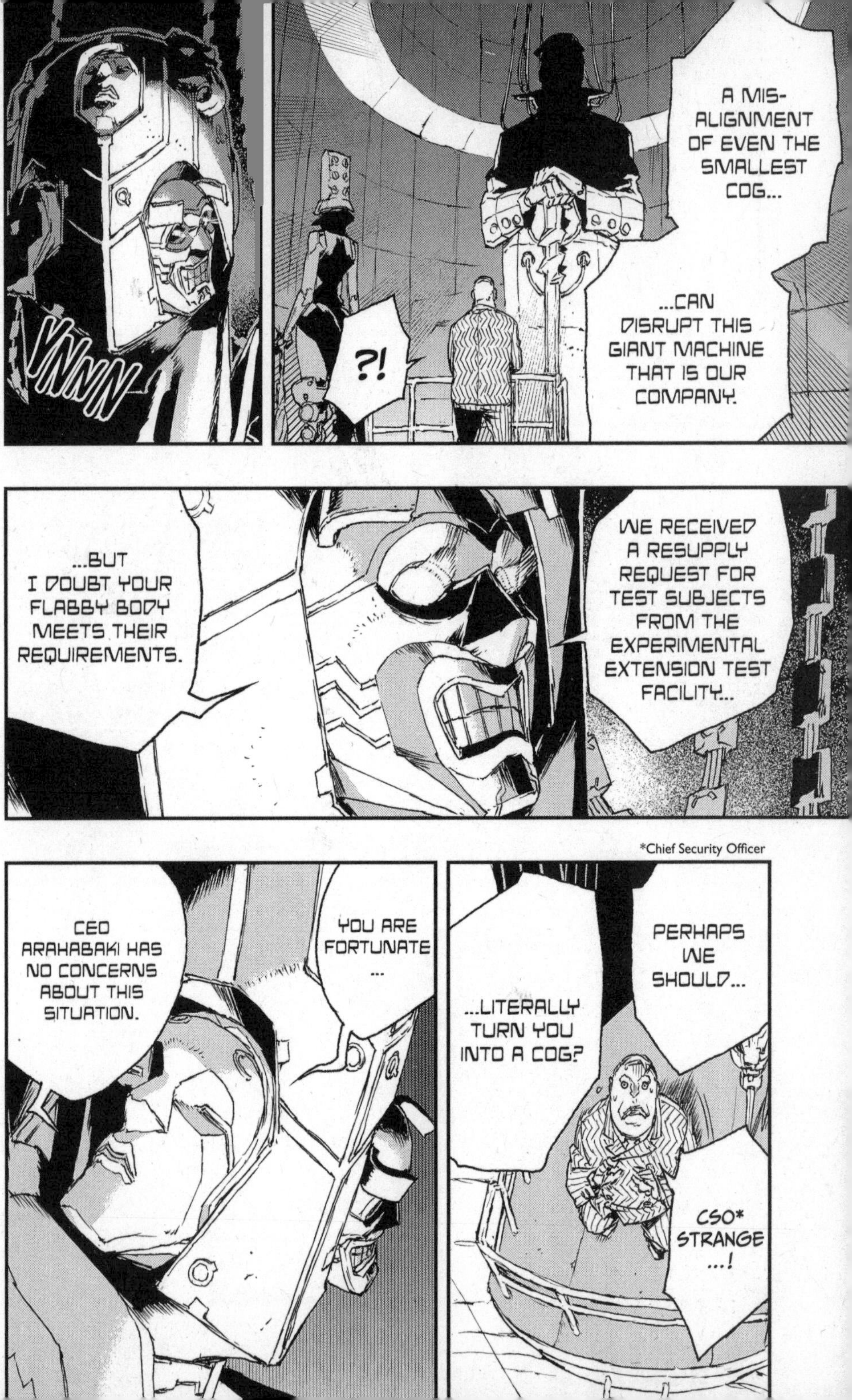
A MIS-ALIGNMENT OF EVEN THE SMALLEST COG...
...CAN DISRUPT THIS GIANT MACHINE THAT IS OUR COMPANY.
?!
VNNN
WE RECEIVED A RESUPPLY REQUEST FOR TEST SUBJECTS FROM THE EXPERIMENTAL EXTENSION TEST FACILITY...
...BUT I DOUBT YOUR FLABBY BODY MEETS THEIR REQUIREMENTS.
*Chief Security Officer
PERHAPS WE SHOULD...
...LITERALLY TURN YOU INTO A COG?
CSO* STRANGE ...!
YOU ARE FORTUNATE ...
CEO ARAHABAKI HAS NO CONCERNS ABOUT THIS SITUATION.

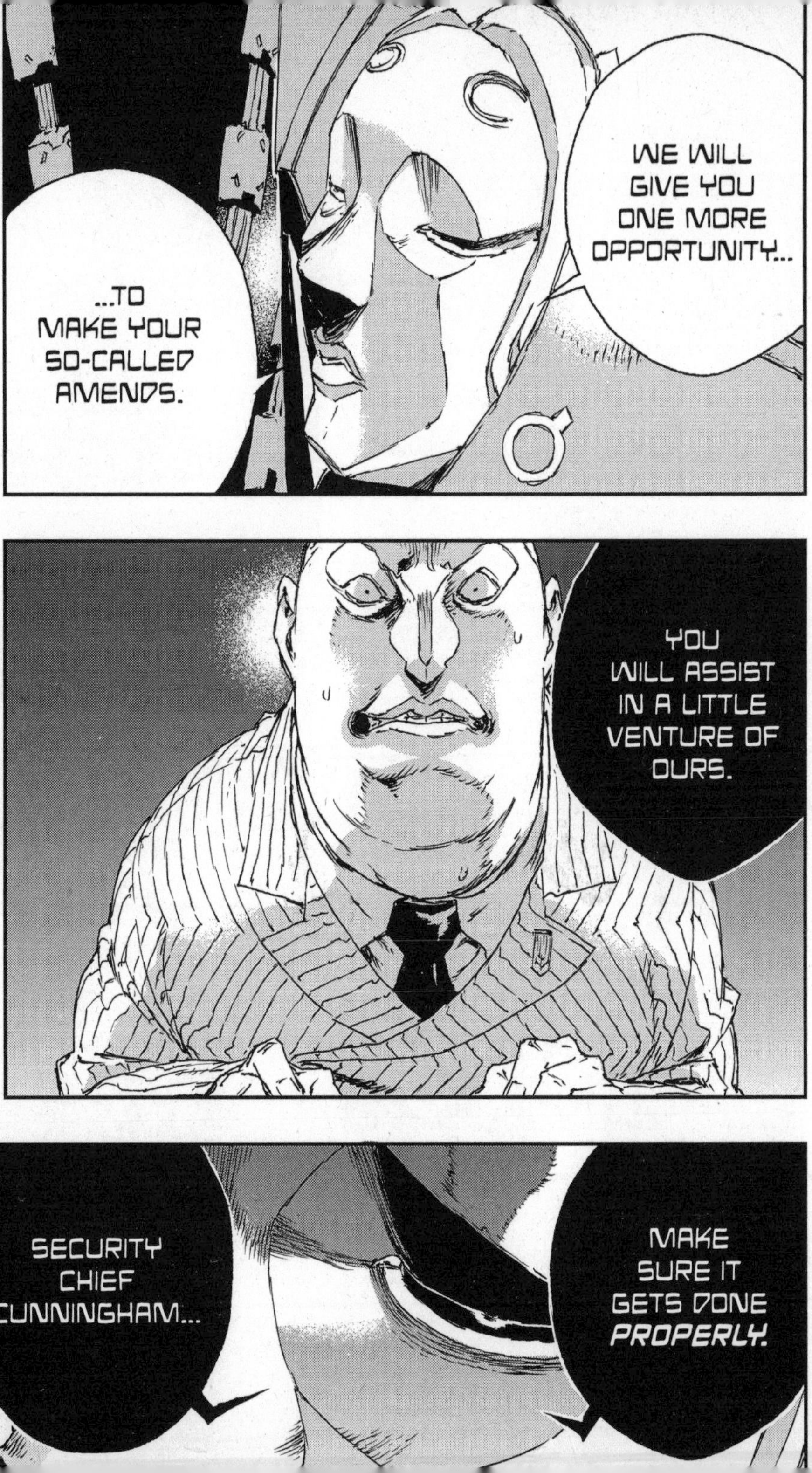
WE WILL GIVE YOU ONE MORE OPPORTUNITY...
...TO MAKE YOUR SO-CALLED AMENDS.
YOU WILL ASSIST IN A LITTLE VENTURE OF OURS.
MAKE SURE IT GETS DONE *PROPERLY*.
SECURITY CHIEF CUNNINGHAM...

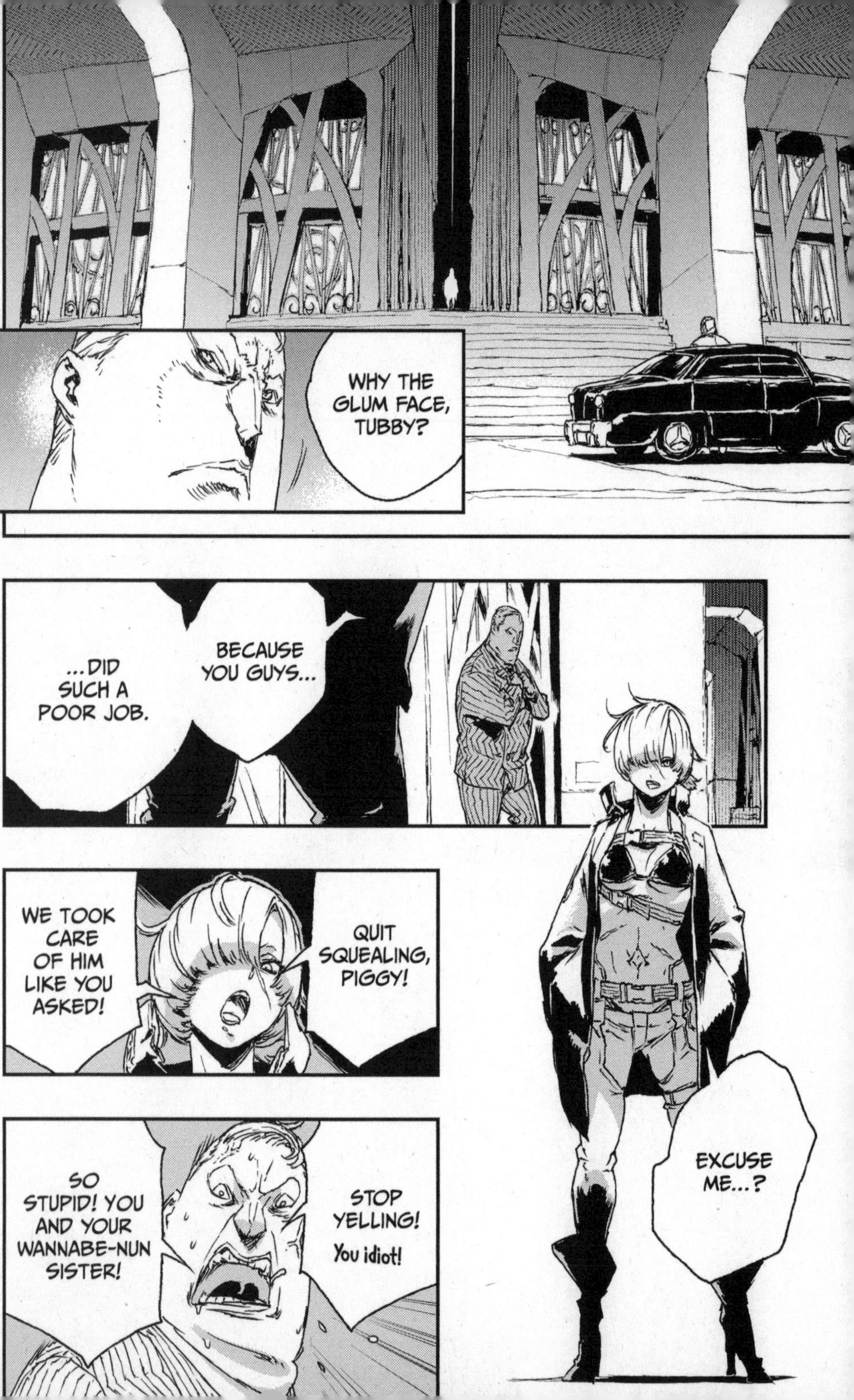
WHY THE GLUM FACE, TUBBY?
BECAUSE YOU GUYS...
...DID SUCH A POOR JOB.
QUIT SQUEALING, PIGGY!
WE TOOK CARE OF HIM LIKE YOU ASKED!
STOP YELLING!
You idiot!
SO STUPID! YOU AND YOUR WANNABE-NUN SISTER!
EXCUSE ME...?

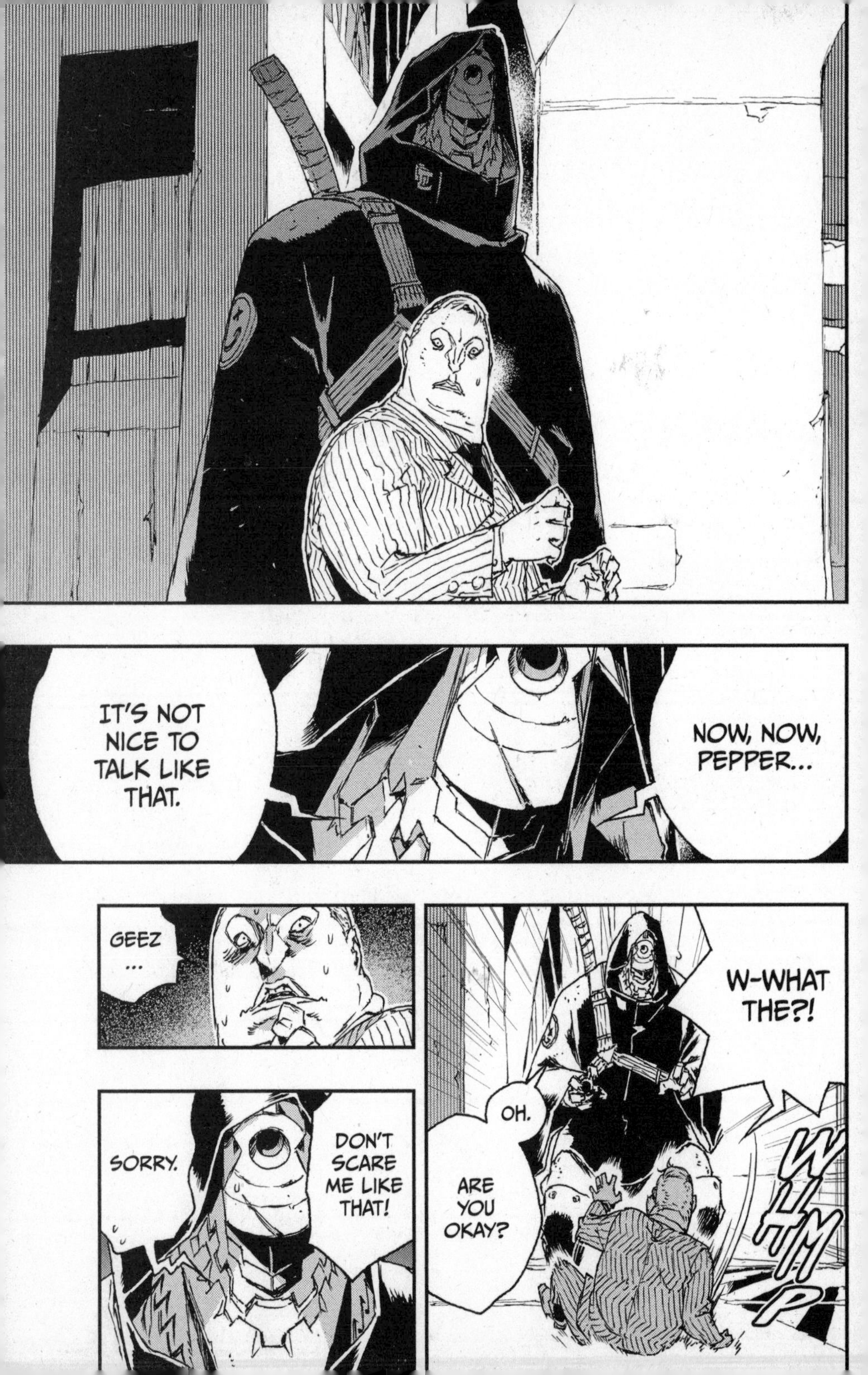
NOW, NOW, PEPPER...
IT'S NOT NICE TO TALK LIKE THAT.
W-WHAT THE?!
WHMP
OH.
ARE YOU OKAY?
GEEZ ...
DON'T SCARE ME LIKE THAT!
SORRY.

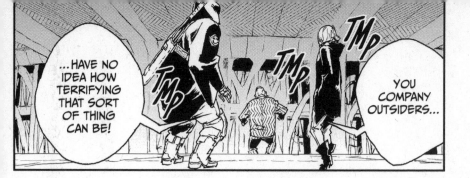

TMP
TMP
TMP
YOU COMPANY OUTSIDERS...
...HAVE NO IDEA HOW TERRIFYING THAT SORT OF THING CAN BE!
A HALF-CENTURY-LONG WAR WAS BROUGHT TO AN END...
...BY THE WURZEL—THE MYSTERIOUS FOUNDERS OF BERÜHREN.
THEY WERE AT WORK BEHIND-THE-SCENES BEFORE THE WAR, AND SOME SAY THEY WERE EVEN THE ONES WHO ACTUALLY STARTED IT.
I MUST DO SOME-THING...
...OR ELSE I'M—

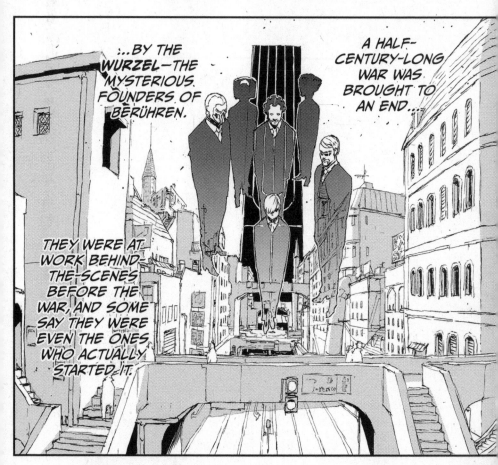

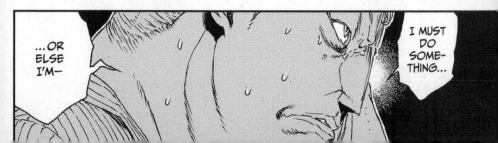

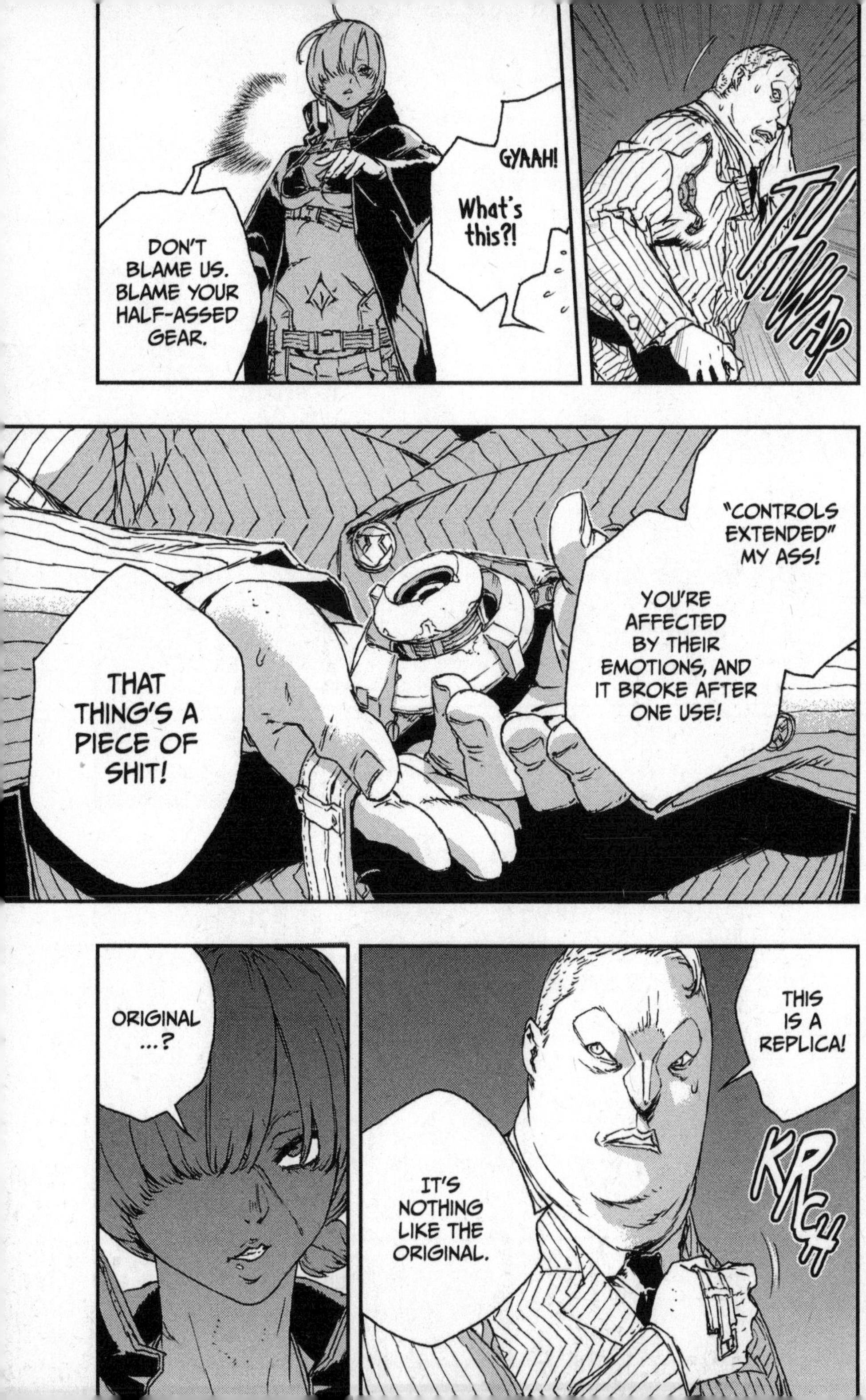
THWAP
GYAAH!
What's this?!
DON'T BLAME US. BLAME YOUR HALF-ASSED GEAR.
"CONTROLS EXTENDED" MY ASS!
YOU'RE AFFECTED BY THEIR EMOTIONS, AND IT BROKE AFTER ONE USE!
THAT THING'S A PIECE OF SHIT!
THIS IS A REPLICA!
KRCH
IT'S NOTHING LIKE THE ORIGINAL.
ORIGINAL ...?

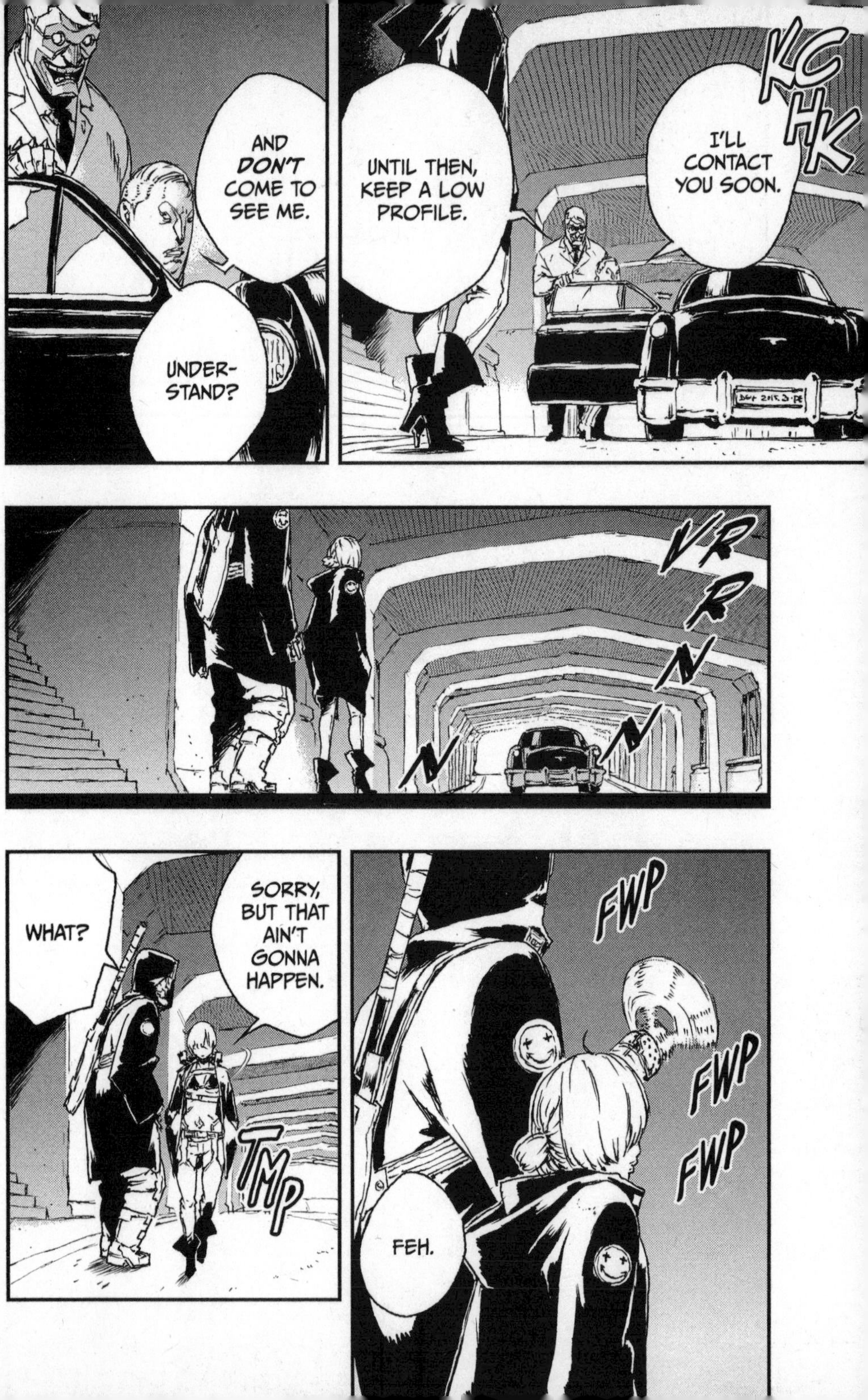
KCHK
I'LL CONTACT YOU SOON.
UNTIL THEN, KEEP A LOW PROFILE.
AND DON'T COME TO SEE ME.
UNDER-STAND?
VRRNNN
FWP
FWP
FWP
FEH.
SORRY, BUT THAT AIN'T GONNA HAPPEN.
WHAT?
TMP

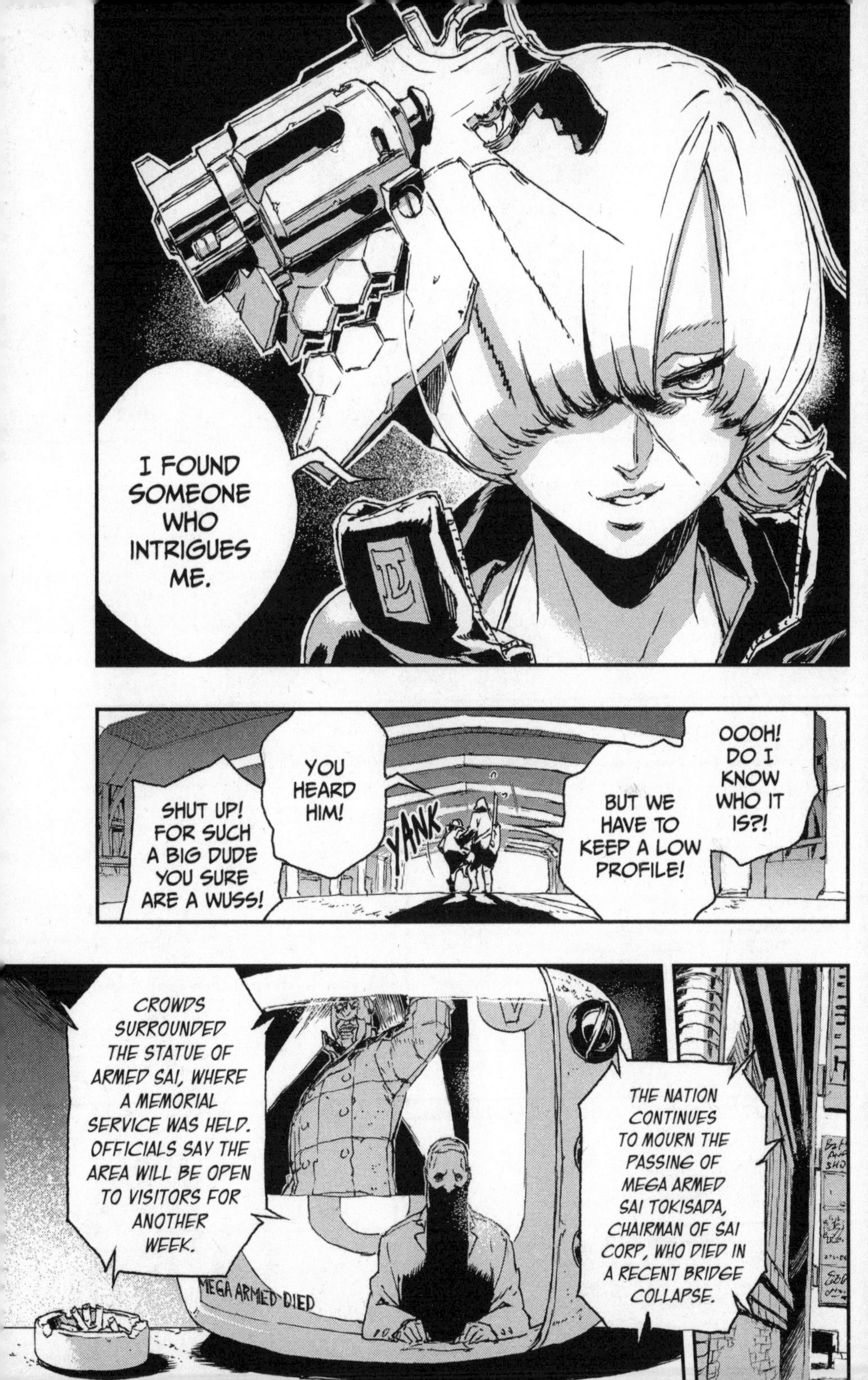
I FOUND SOMEONE WHO INTRIGUES ME.
OOOH! DO I KNOW WHO IT IS?!
BUT WE HAVE TO KEEP A LOW PROFILE!
YOU HEARD HIM!
YANK
SHUT UP! FOR SUCH A BIG DUDE YOU SURE ARE A WUSS!
THE NATION CONTINUES TO MOURN THE PASSING OF MEGA ARMED SAI TOKISADA, CHAIRMAN OF SAI CORP, WHO DIED IN A RECENT BRIDGE COLLAPSE.
CROWDS SURROUNDED THE STATUE OF ARMED SAI, WHERE A MEMORIAL SERVICE WAS HELD. OFFICIALS SAY THE AREA WILL BE OPEN TO VISITORS FOR ANOTHER WEEK.
MEGA ARMED DIED

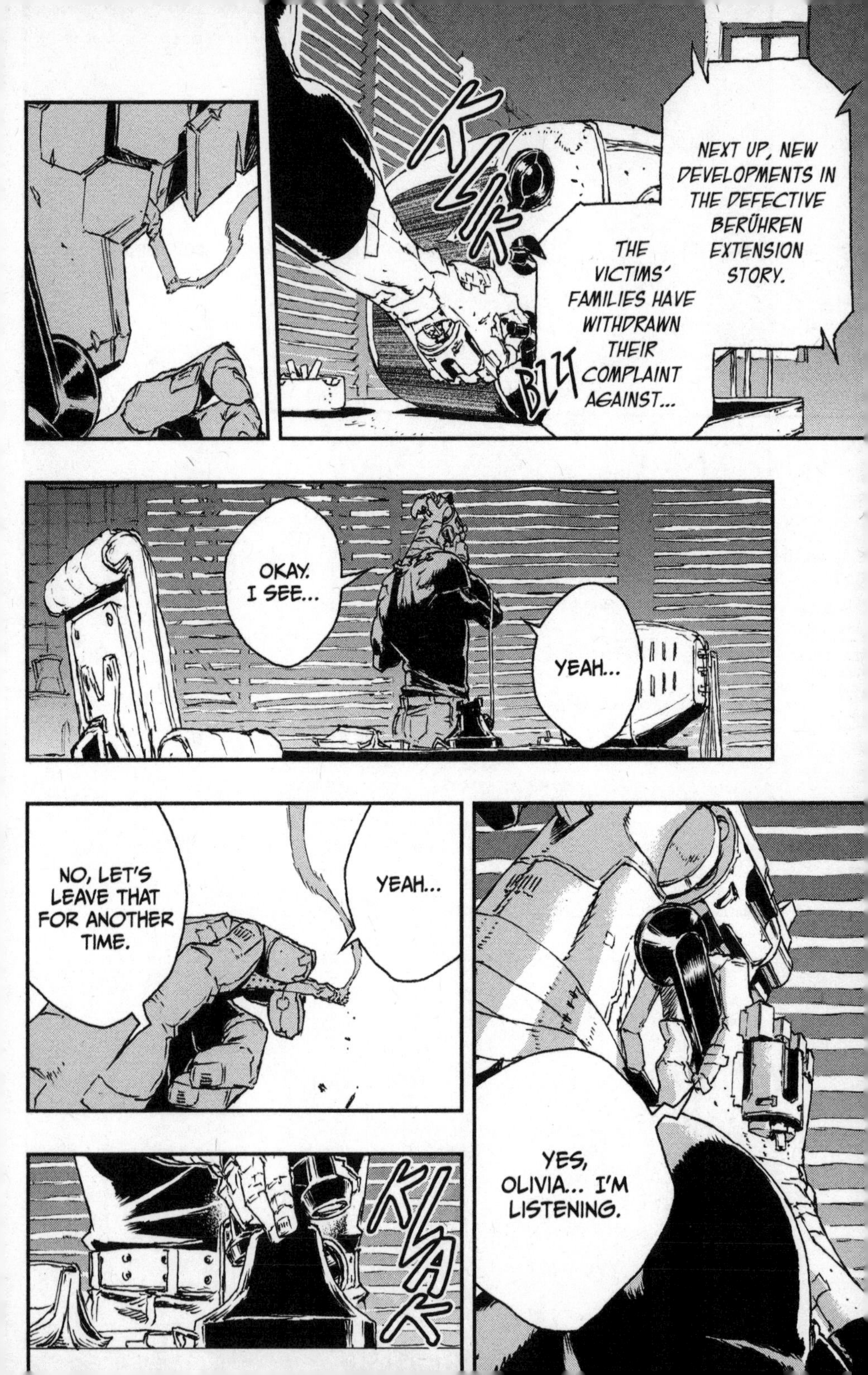
NEXT UP, NEW DEVELOPMENTS IN THE DEFECTIVE BERÜHREN EXTENSION STORY.
THE VICTIMS' FAMILIES HAVE WITHDRAWN THEIR COMPLAINT AGAINST...
KLIK
BZZT
YEAH...
OKAY. I SEE...
YES, OLIVIA... I'M LISTENING.
YEAH...
NO, LET'S LEAVE THAT FOR ANOTHER TIME.
KLAK

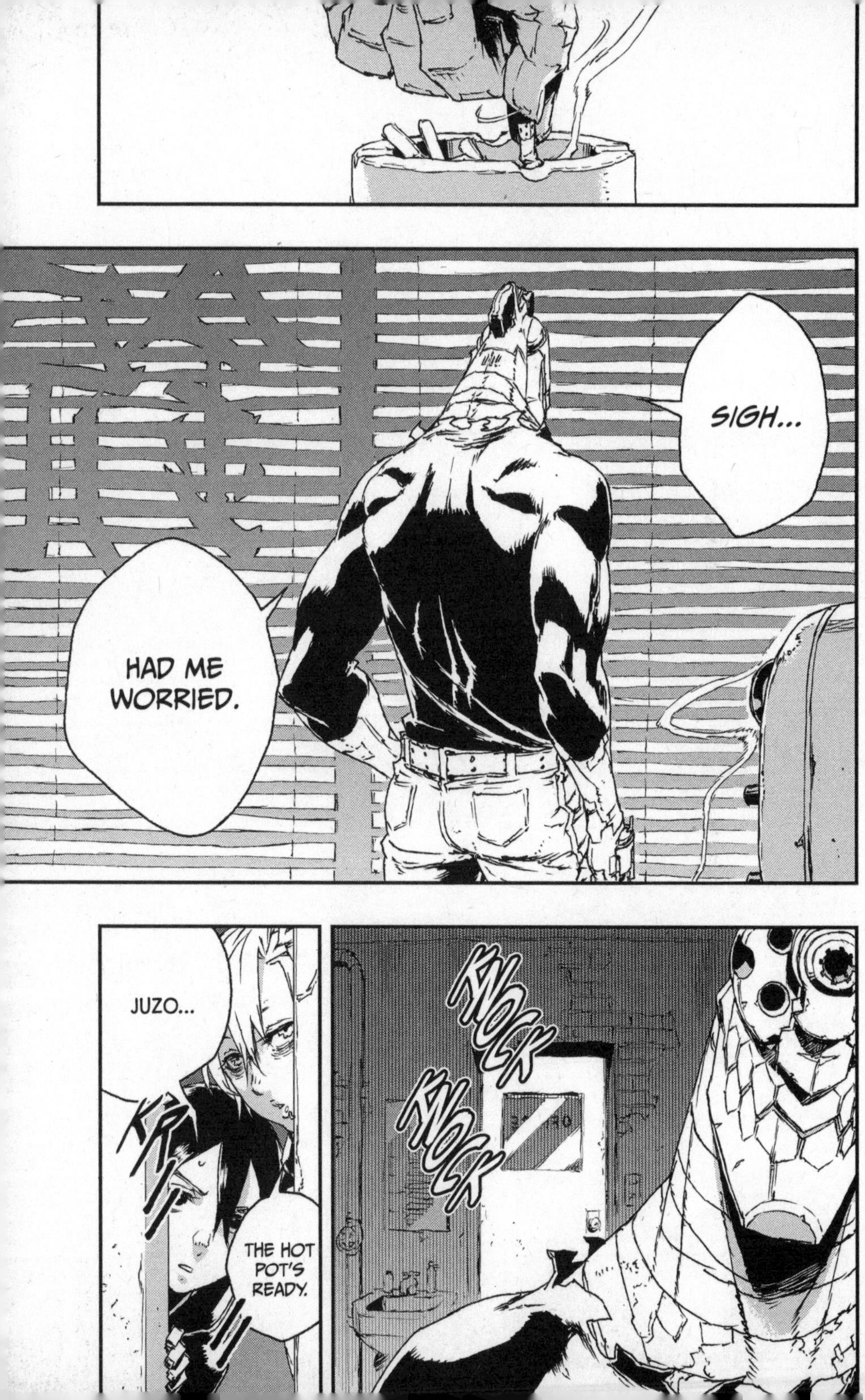
SIGH...
HAD ME WORRIED.
KNOCK KNOCK
JUZO...
THE HOT POT'S READY.

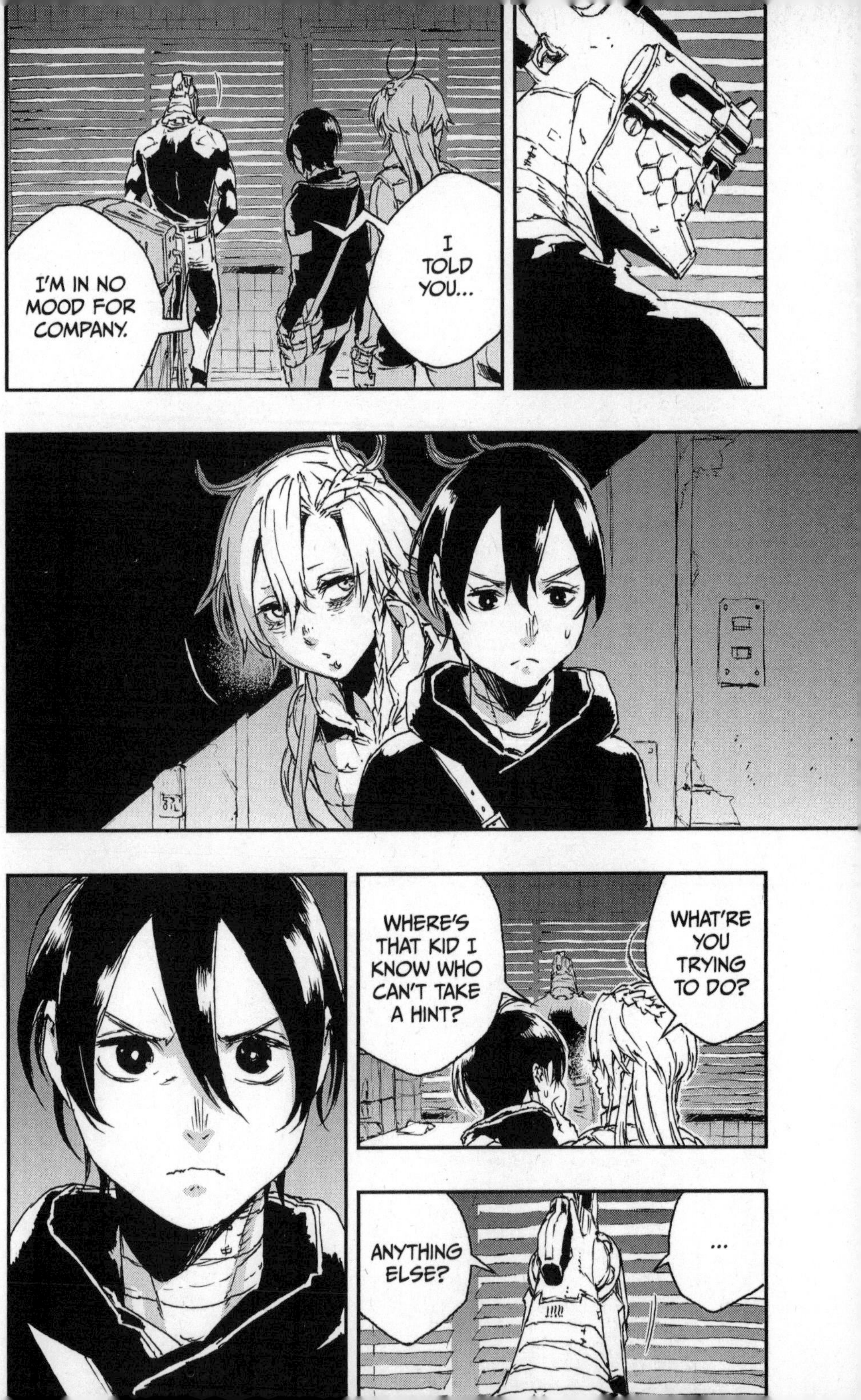
I TOLD YOU...
I'M IN NO MOOD FOR COMPANY.
WHAT'RE YOU TRYING TO DO?
WHERE'S THAT KID I KNOW WHO CAN'T TAKE A HINT?
...
ANYTHING ELSE?

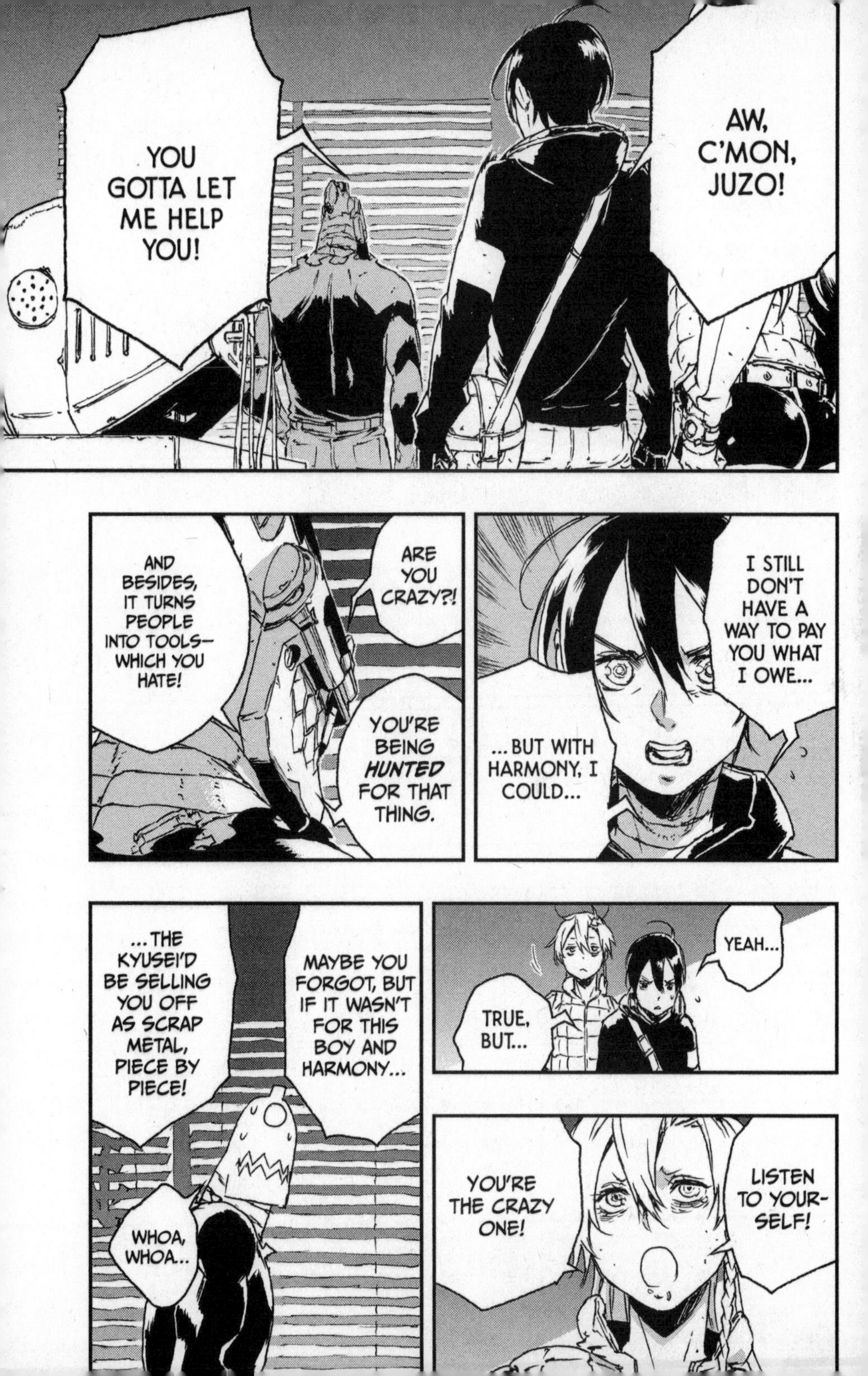
AW, C'MON, JUZO!
YOU GOTTA LET ME HELP YOU!
I STILL DON'T HAVE A WAY TO PAY YOU WHAT I OWE...
...BUT WITH HARMONY, I COULD...
ARE YOU CRAZY?!
YOU'RE BEING *HUNTED* FOR THAT THING.
AND BESIDES, IT TURNS PEOPLE INTO TOOLS—WHICH YOU HATE!
YEAH...
TRUE, BUT...
LISTEN TO YOUR-SELF!
YOU'RE THE CRAZY ONE!
MAYBE YOU FORGOT, BUT IF IT WASN'T FOR THIS BOY AND HARMONY...
...THE KYUSEI'D BE SELLING YOU OFF AS SCRAP METAL, PIECE BY PIECE!
WHOA, WHOA...

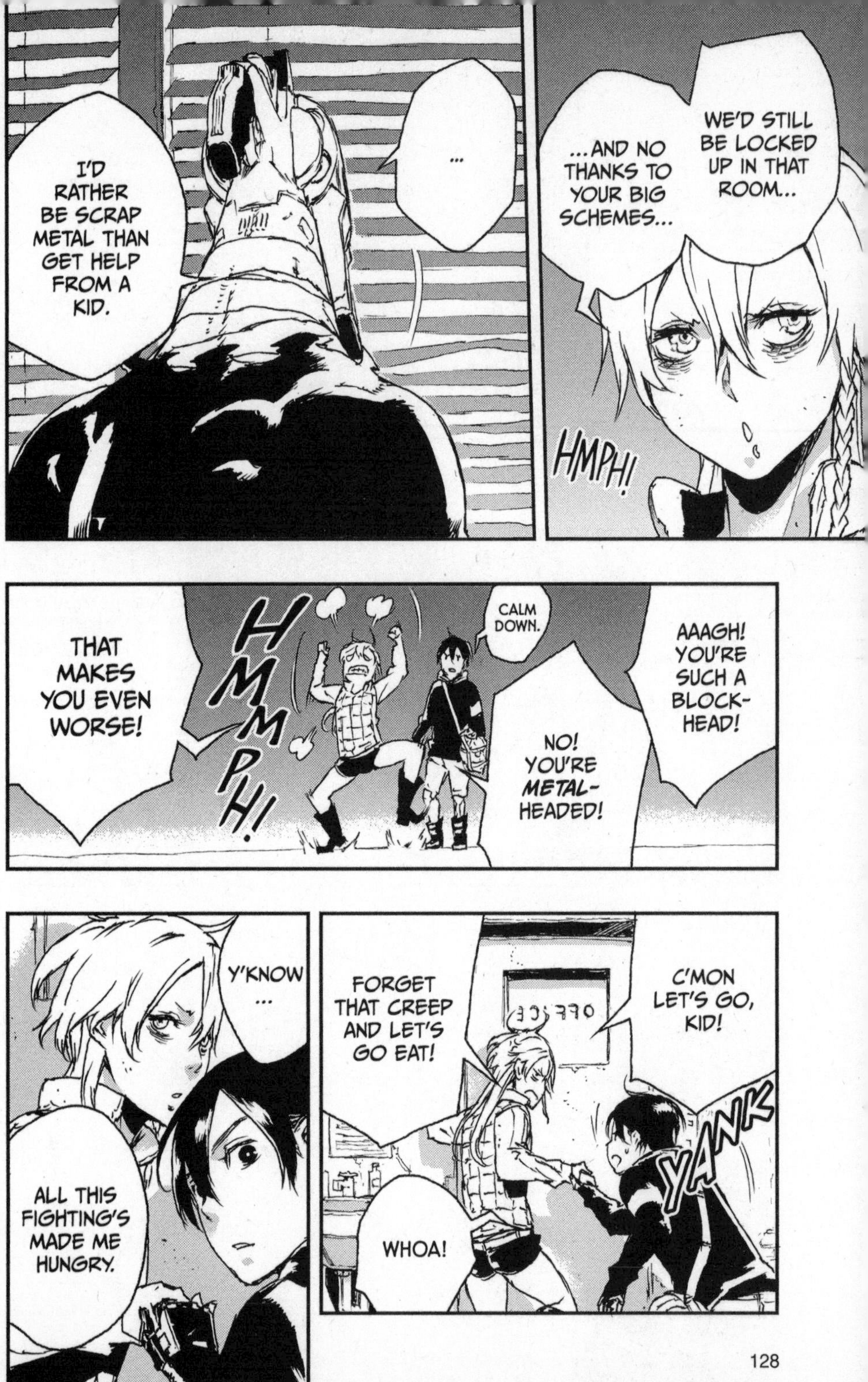
WE'D STILL BE LOCKED UP IN THAT ROOM...
...AND NO THANKS TO YOUR BIG SCHEMES...
HMPH!
...
I'D RATHER BE SCRAP METAL THAN GET HELP FROM A KID.
AAAGH! YOU'RE SUCH A BLOCK-HEAD!
CALM DOWN.
NO! YOU'RE *METAL*-HEADED!
HMMPH!
THAT MAKES YOU EVEN WORSE!
C'MON LET'S GO, KID!
YANK
FORGET THAT CREEP AND LET'S GO EAT!
WHOA!
Y'KNOW ...
ALL THIS FIGHTING'S MADE ME HUNGRY.

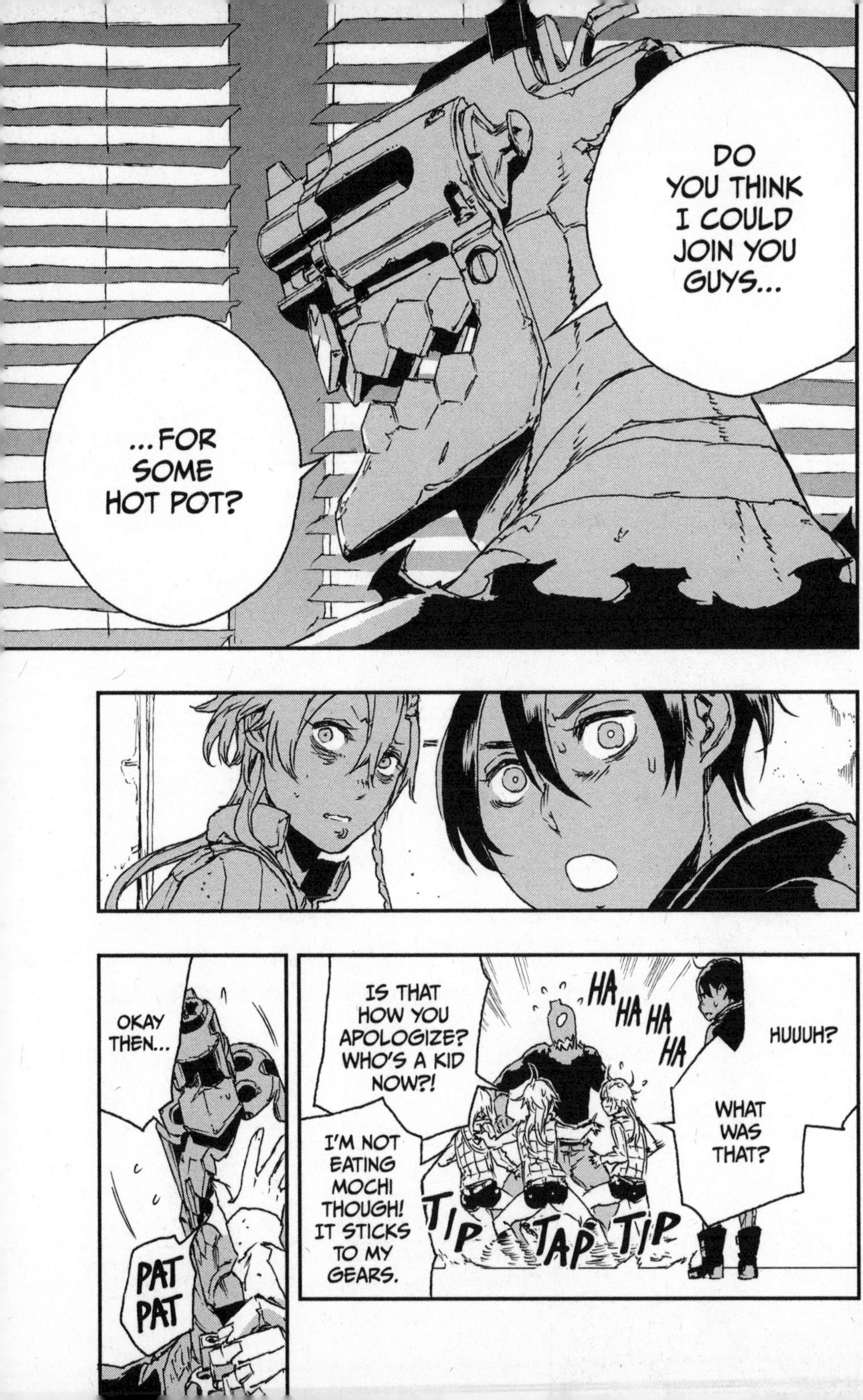
DO YOU THINK I COULD JOIN YOU GUYS...
...FOR SOME HOT POT?
HUUUH?
WHAT WAS THAT?
HA HA HA HA
IS THAT HOW YOU APOLOGIZE? WHO'S A KID NOW?!
I'M NOT EATING MOCHI THOUGH! IT STICKS TO MY GEARS.
TIP TAP TIP
OKAY THEN...
PAT PAT

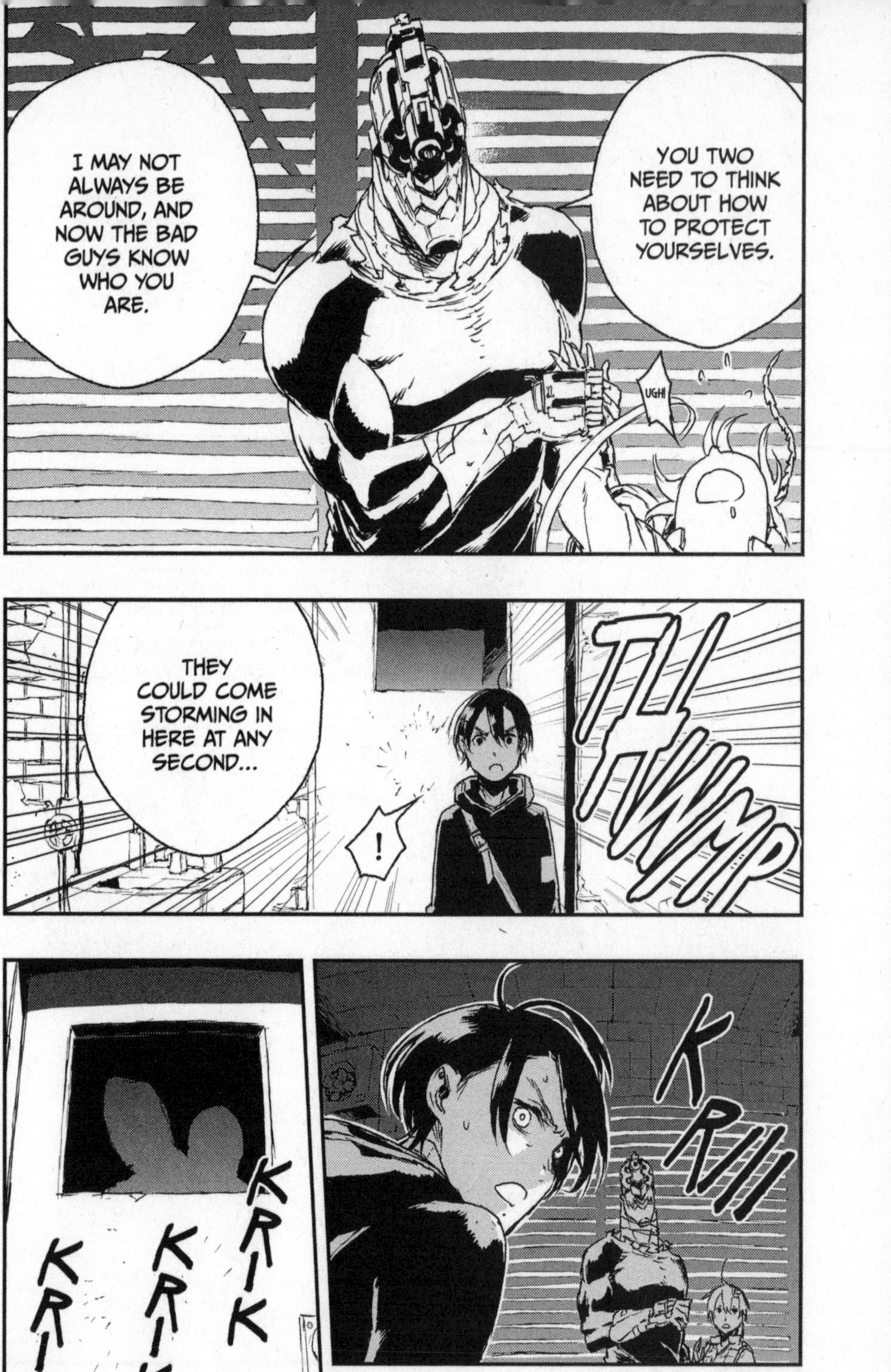
YOU TWO NEED TO THINK ABOUT HOW TO PROTECT YOURSELVES.
I MAY NOT ALWAYS BE AROUND, AND NOW THE BAD GUYS KNOW WHO YOU ARE.
UGH!
THWUMP
THEY COULD COME STORMING IN HERE AT ANY SECOND...
!
KRIII
KRIK
KRIK
KRIK

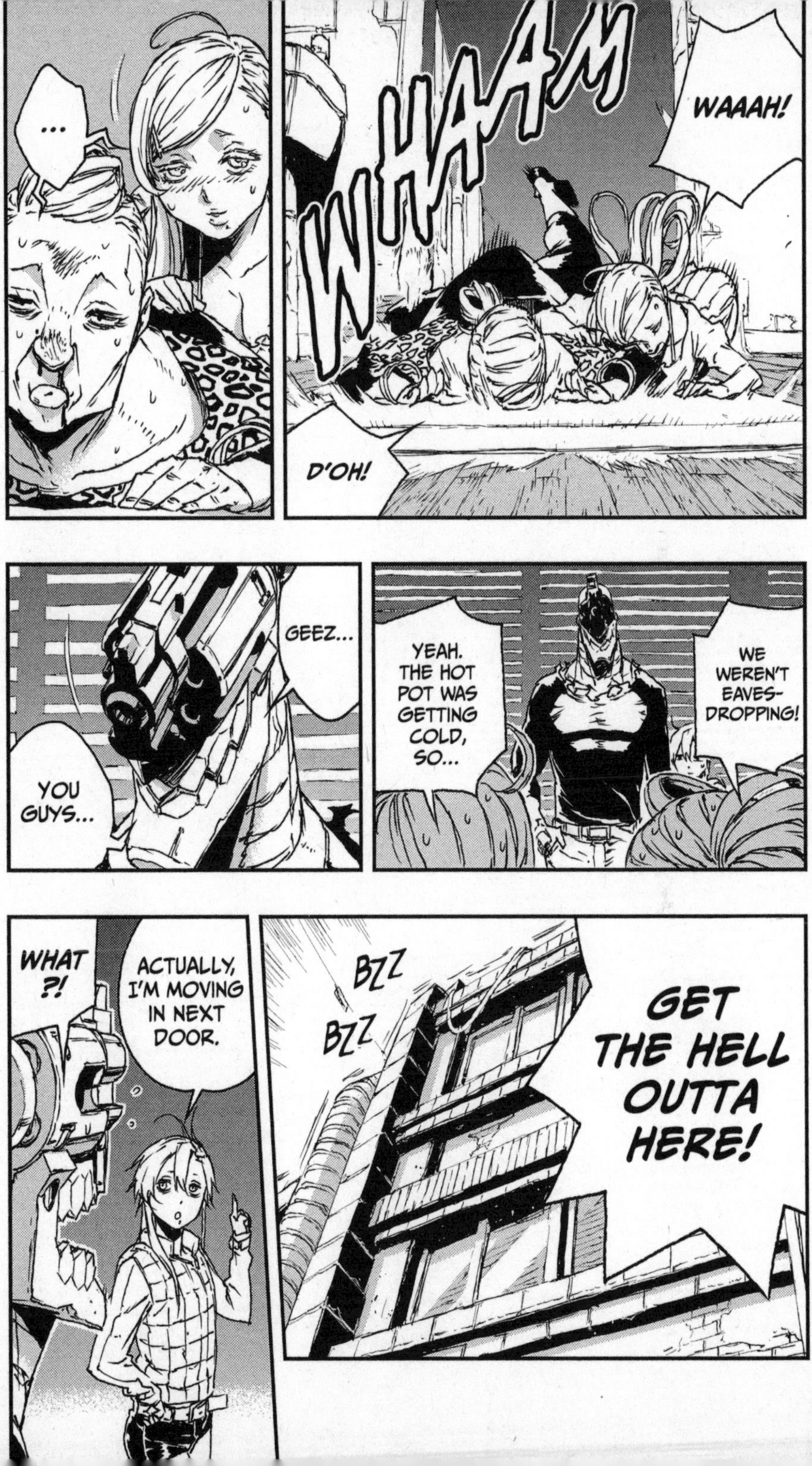
WAAAH!
WHAAM
D'OH!
...
WE WEREN'T EAVES-DROPPING!
YEAH. THE HOT POT WAS GETTING COLD, SO...
GEEZ...
YOU GUYS...
BZZ
BZZ
GET THE HELL OUTTA HERE!
ACTUALLY, I'M MOVING IN NEXT DOOR.
WHAT?!

NO GUNS LIFE

The gunsmoke drifts, the muzzle talks

Chapter 16

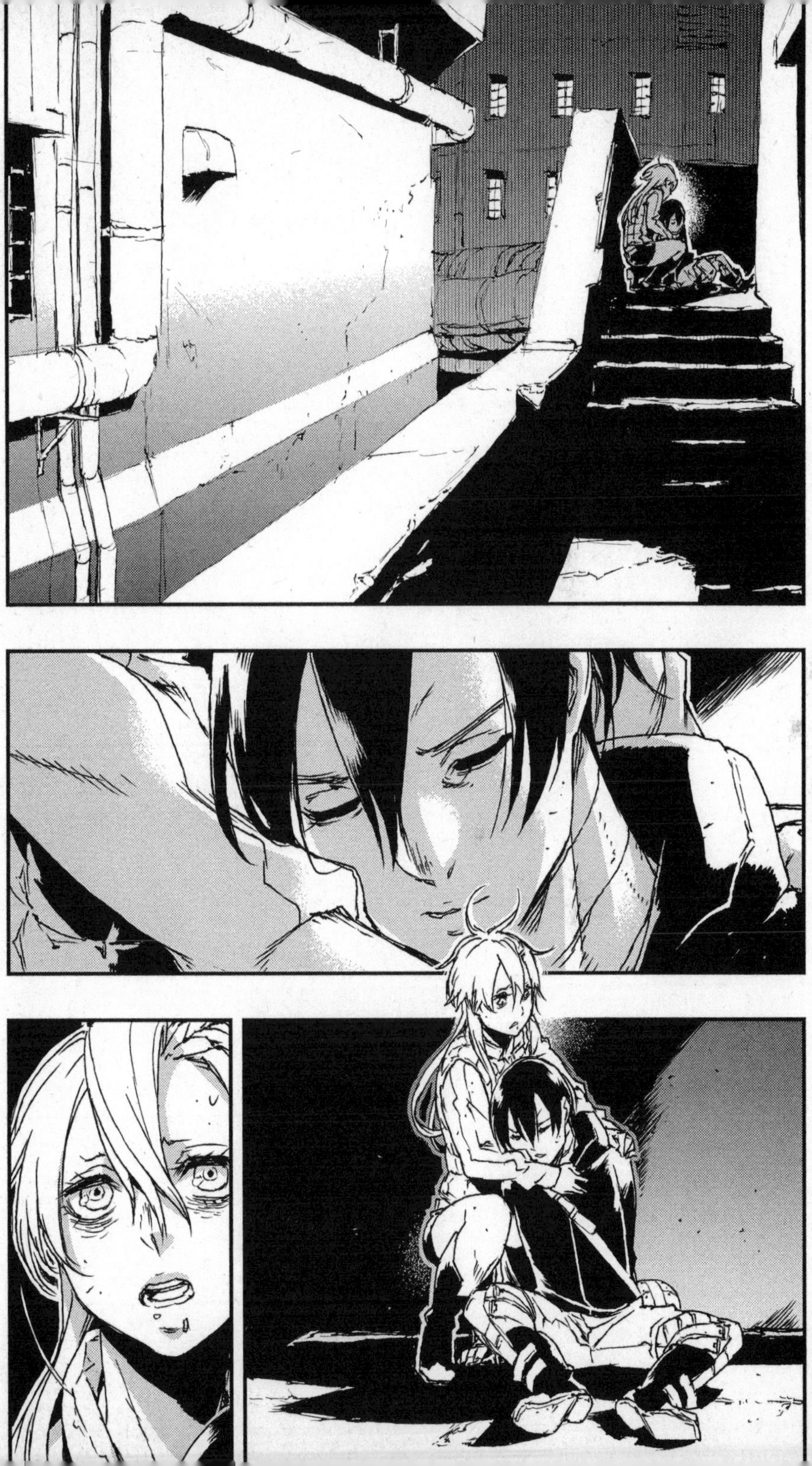

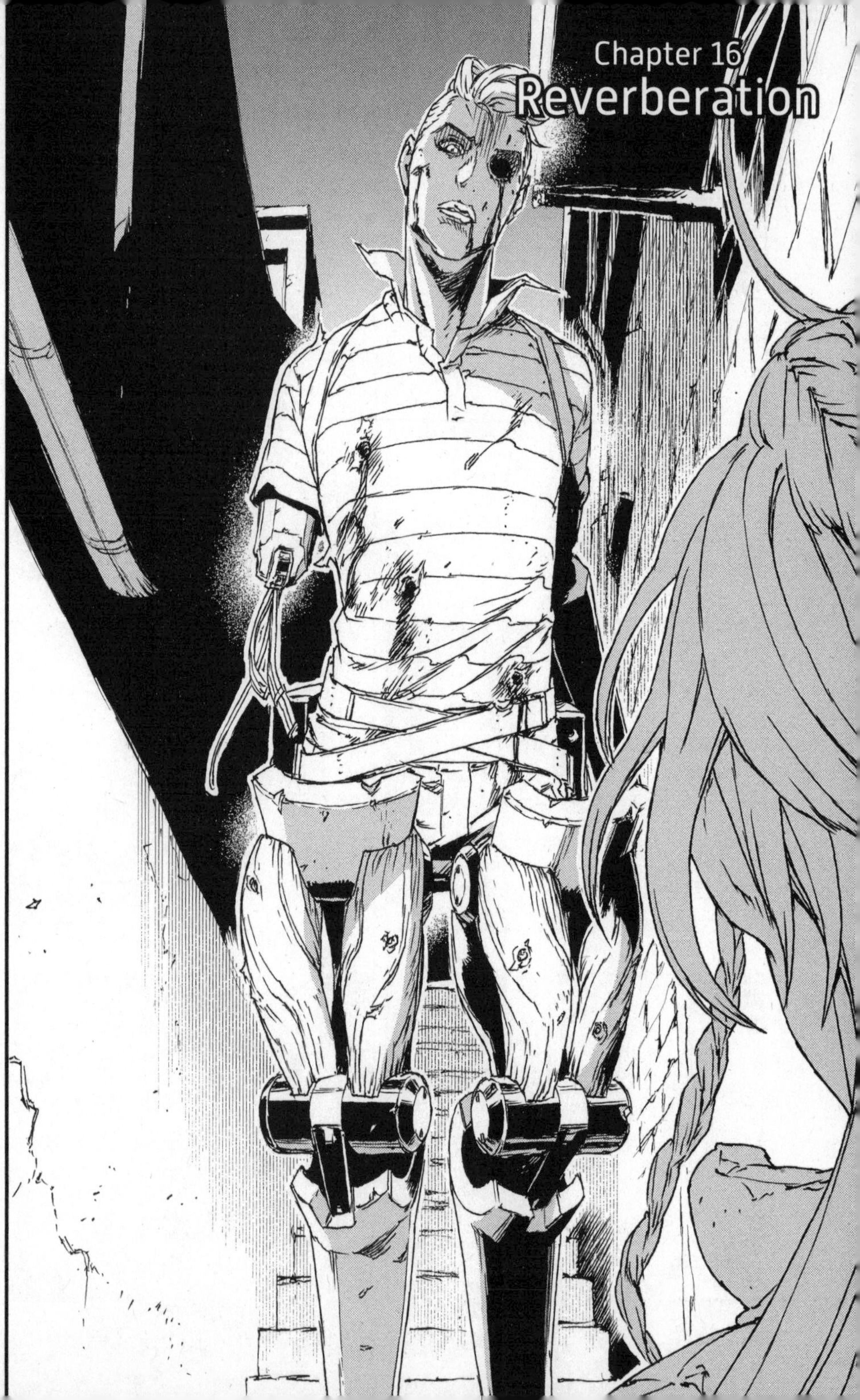
Chapter 16
Reverberation

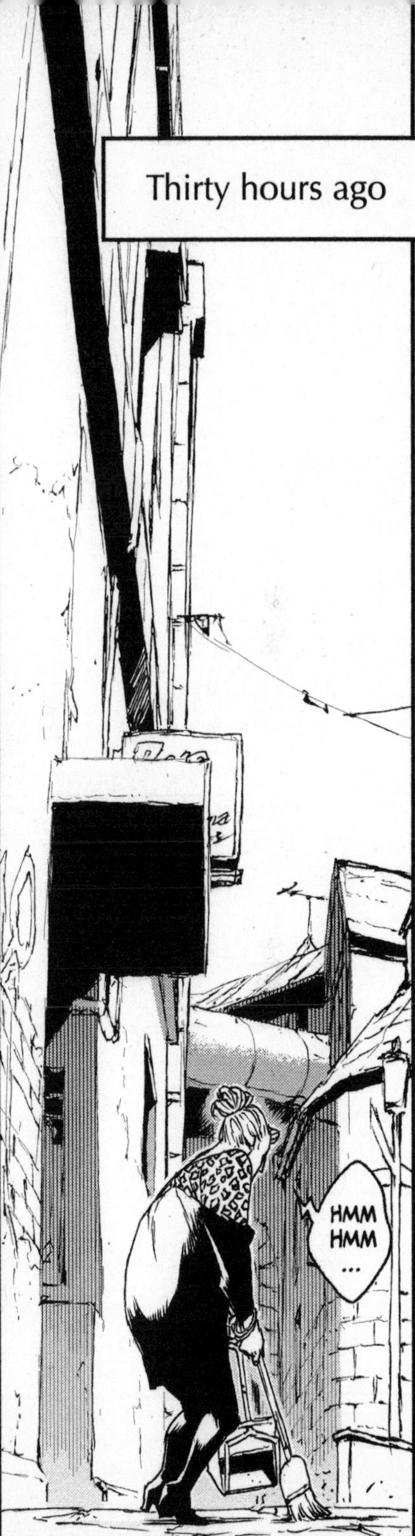
Thirty hours ago
HMM HMM ...

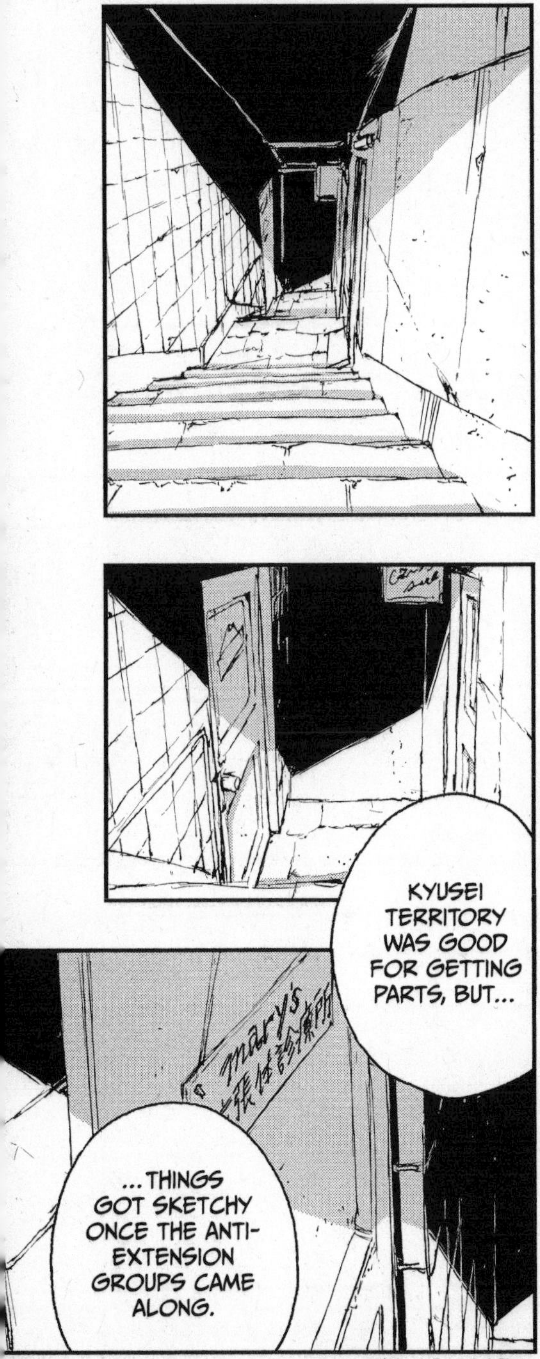
KYUSEI TERRITORY WAS GOOD FOR GETTING PARTS, BUT...
mary's
...THINGS GOT SKETCHY ONCE THE ANTI-EXTENSION GROUPS CAME ALONG.

*Mary's Extended Clinic

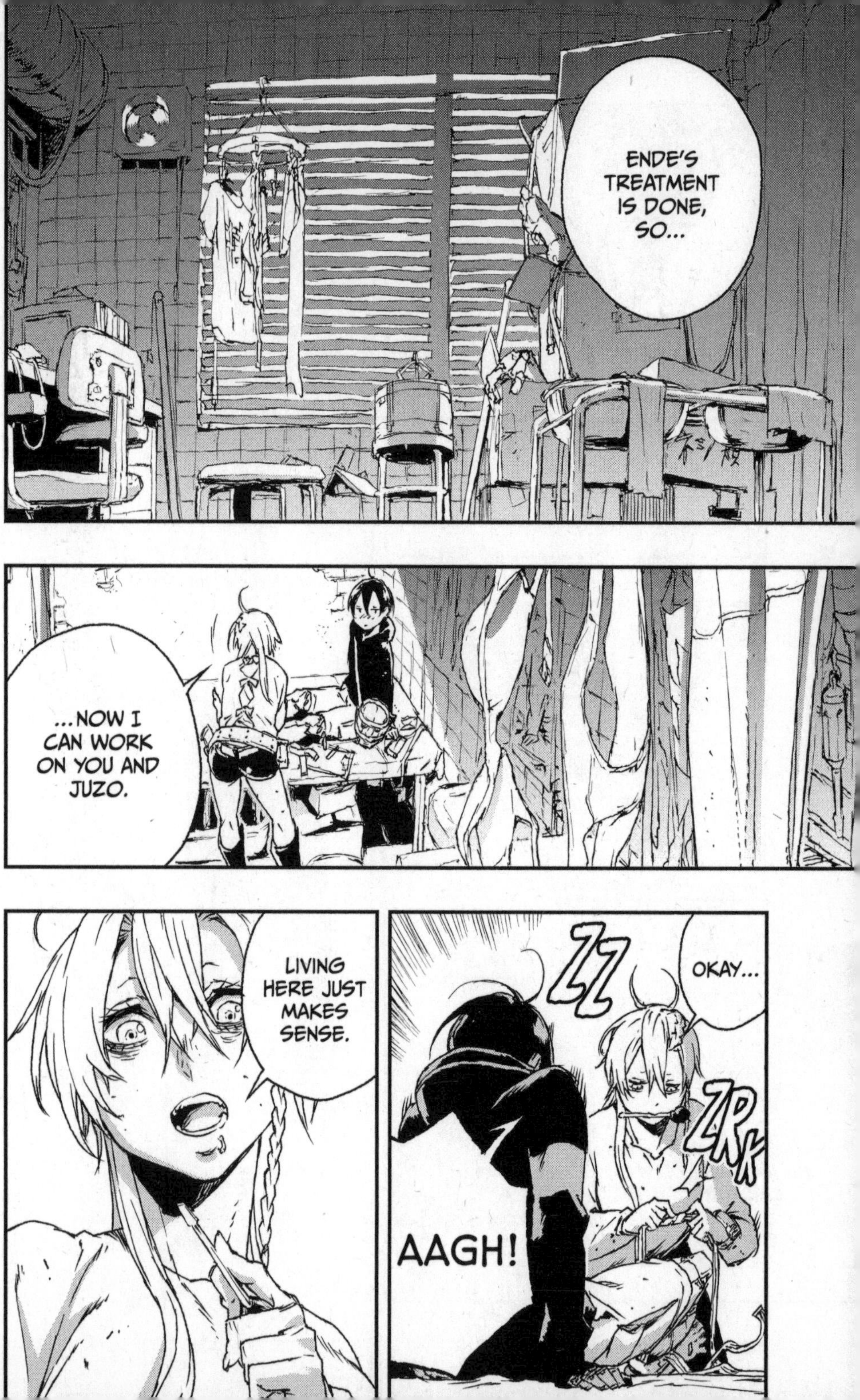
ENDE'S TREATMENT IS DONE, SO...
...NOW I CAN WORK ON YOU AND JUZO.
OKAY...
ZZ
ZRK
AAGH!
LIVING HERE JUST MAKES SENSE.

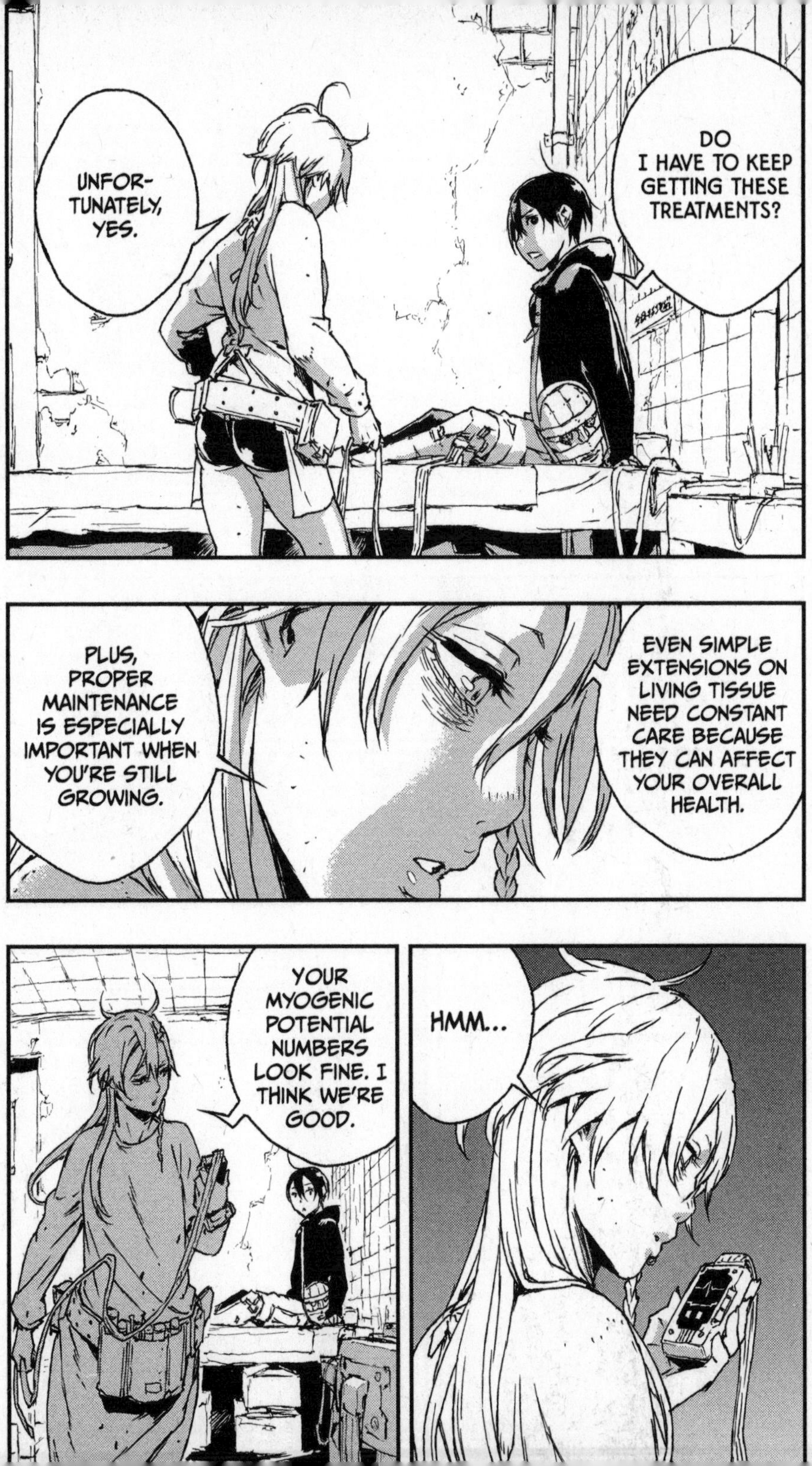
DO I HAVE TO KEEP GETTING THESE TREATMENTS?
UNFOR-TUNATELY, YES.
EVEN SIMPLE EXTENSIONS ON LIVING TISSUE NEED CONSTANT CARE BECAUSE THEY CAN AFFECT YOUR OVERALL HEALTH.
PLUS, PROPER MAINTENANCE IS ESPECIALLY IMPORTANT WHEN YOU'RE STILL GROWING.
HMM...
YOUR MYOGENIC POTENTIAL NUMBERS LOOK FINE. I THINK WE'RE GOOD.

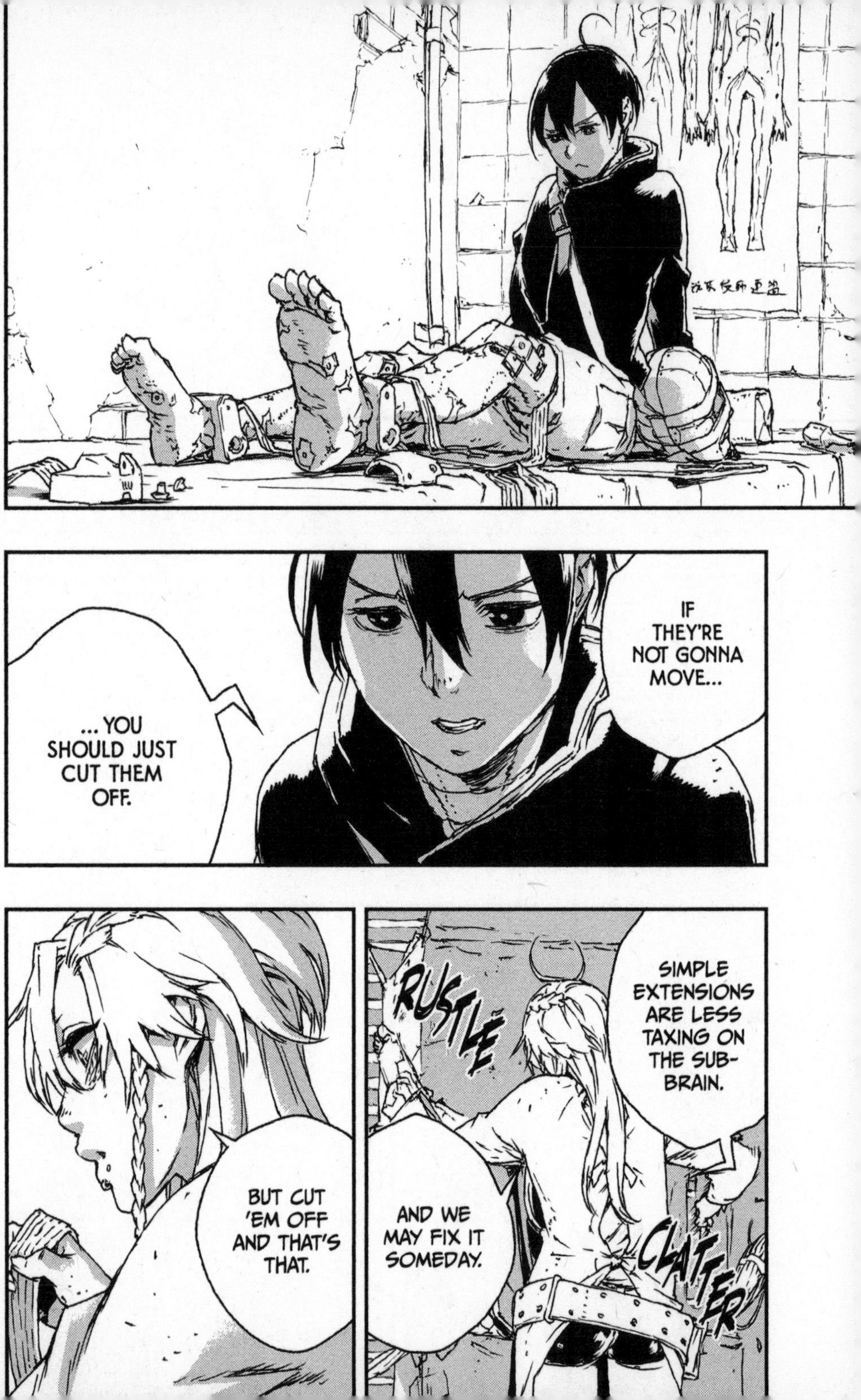
IF THEY'RE NOT GONNA MOVE...
...YOU SHOULD JUST CUT THEM OFF.
SIMPLE EXTENSIONS ARE LESS TAXING ON THE SUB-BRAIN.
RUSTLE
CLATTER
AND WE MAY FIX IT SOMEDAY.
BUT CUT 'EM OFF AND THAT'S THAT.

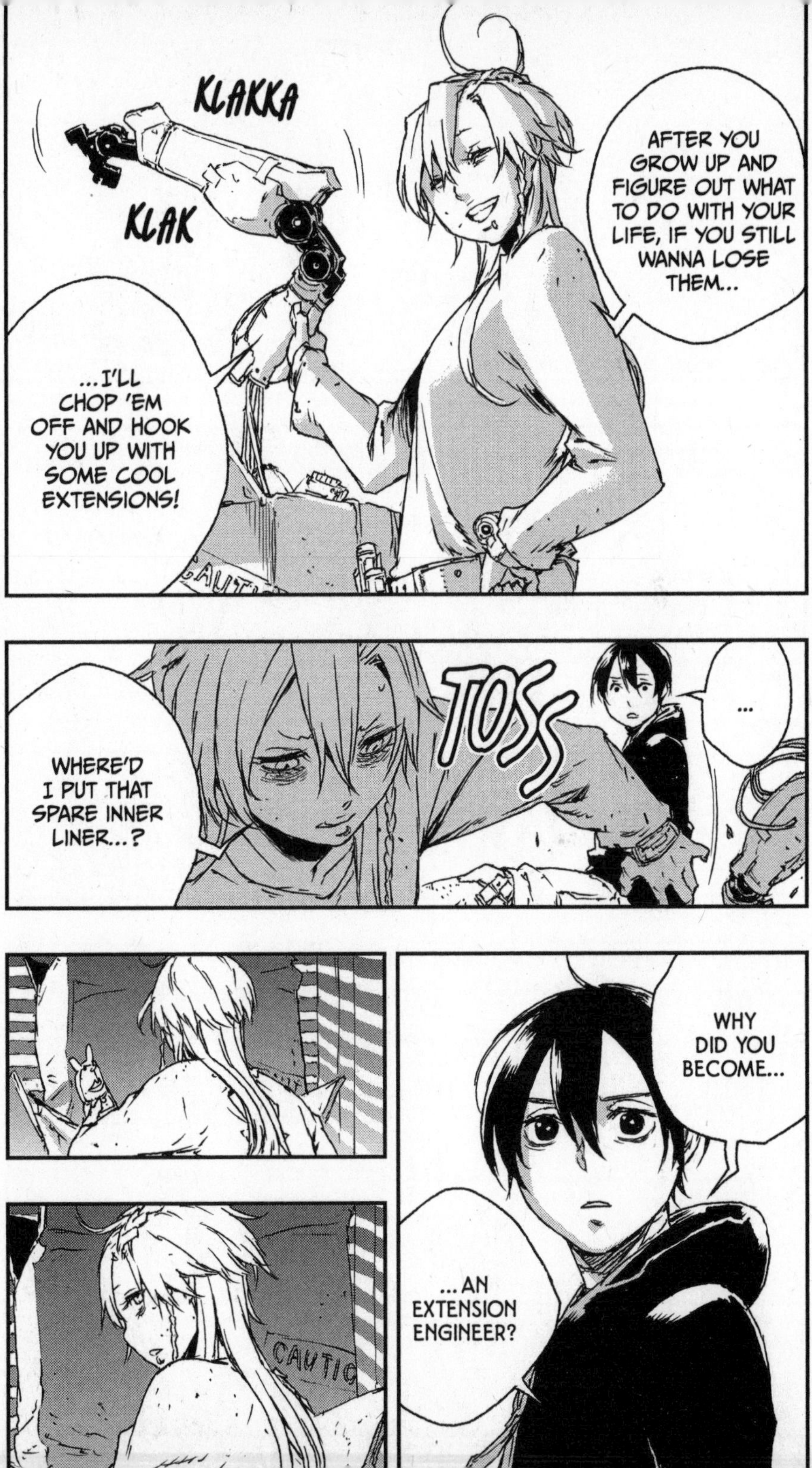
AFTER YOU GROW UP AND FIGURE OUT WHAT TO DO WITH YOUR LIFE, IF YOU STILL WANNA LOSE THEM...
KLAKKA
KLAK
...I'LL CHOP 'EM OFF AND HOOK YOU UP WITH SOME COOL EXTENSIONS!
...
TOSS
WHERE'D I PUT THAT SPARE INNER LINER...?
WHY DID YOU BECOME...
...AN EXTENSION ENGINEER?

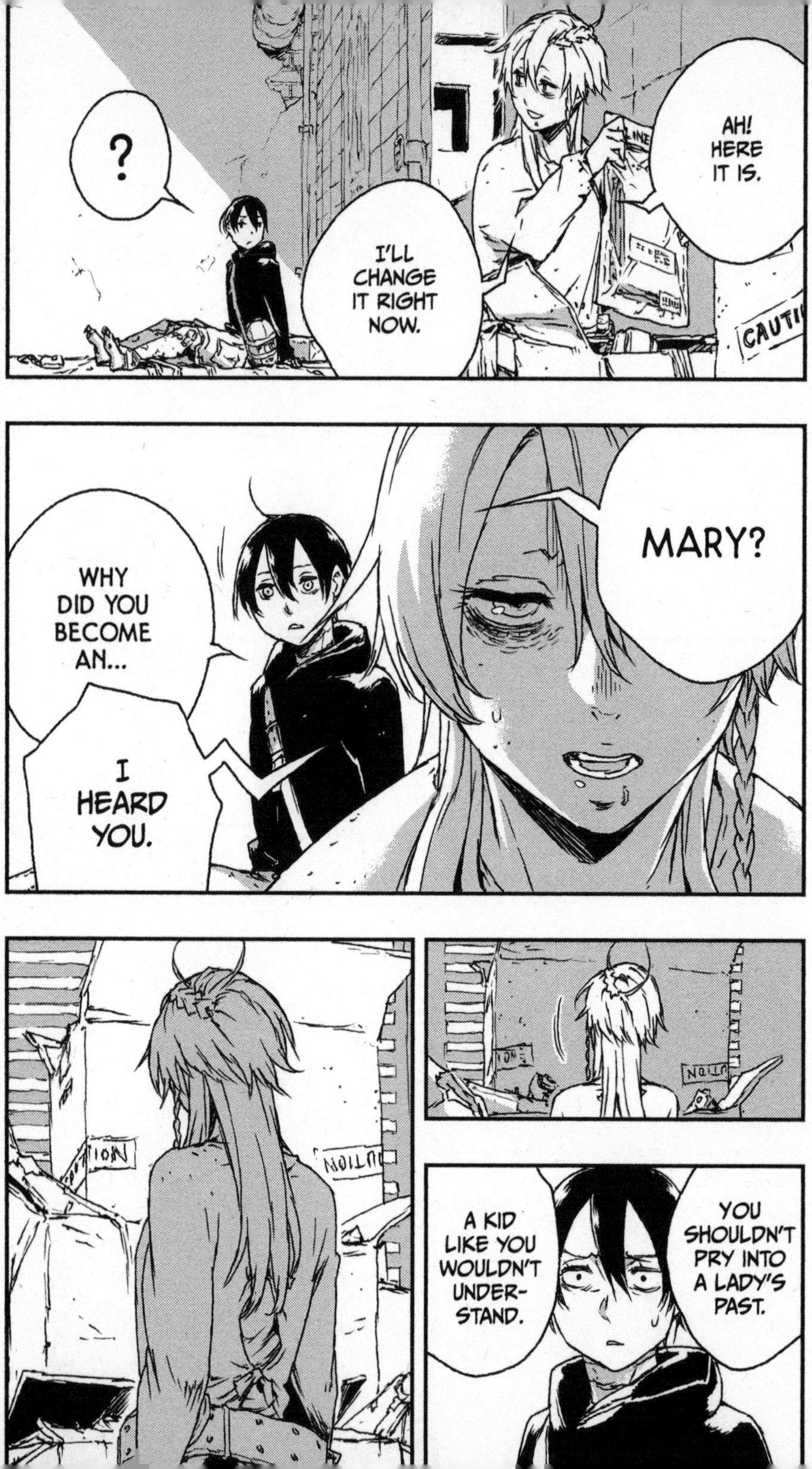
AH! HERE IT IS.
I'LL CHANGE IT RIGHT NOW.
?
MARY?
WHY DID YOU BECOME AN...
I HEARD YOU.
YOU SHOULDN'T PRY INTO A LADY'S PAST.
A KID LIKE YOU WOULDN'T UNDER-STAND.

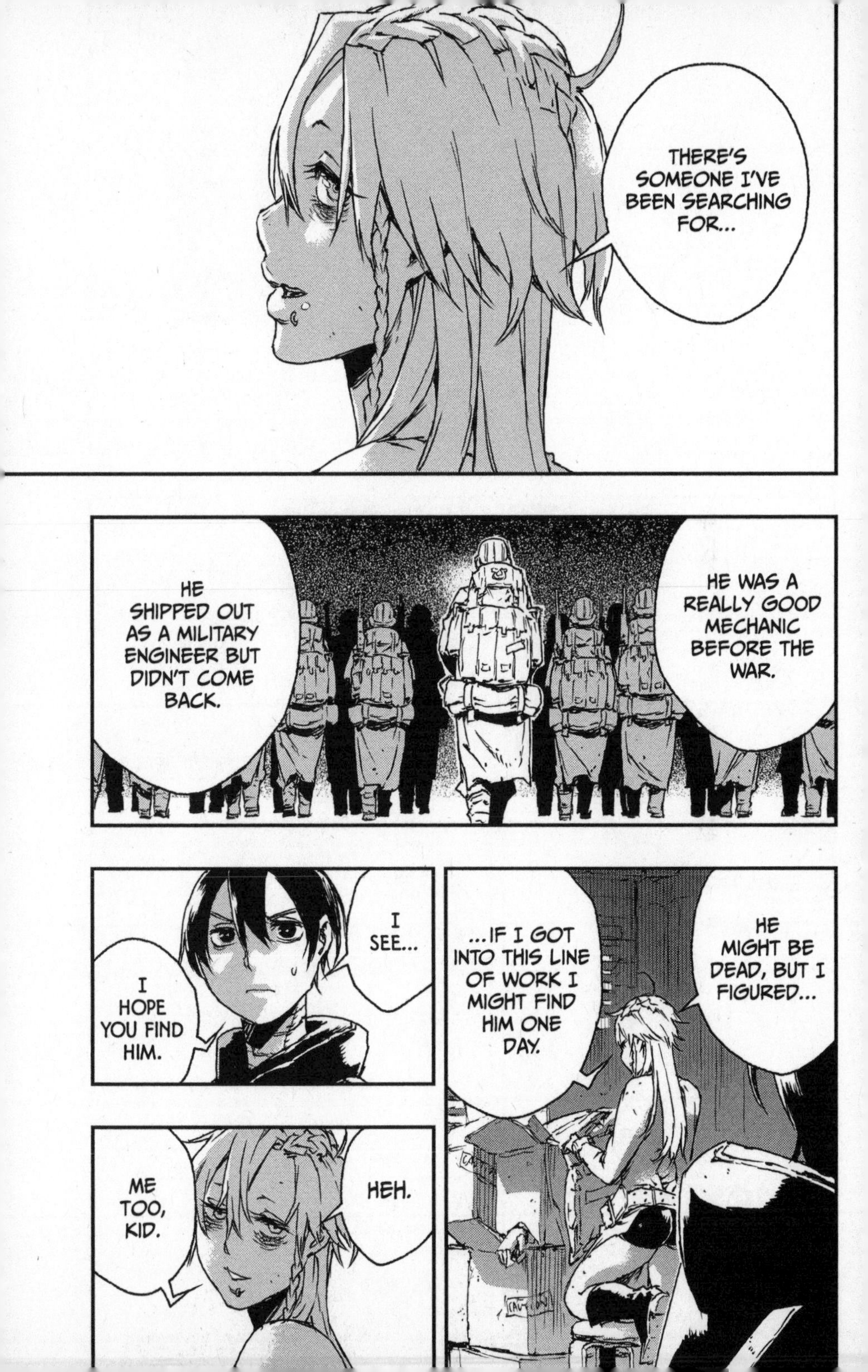
THERE'S SOMEONE I'VE BEEN SEARCHING FOR...
HE WAS A REALLY GOOD MECHANIC BEFORE THE WAR.
HE SHIPPED OUT AS A MILITARY ENGINEER BUT DIDN'T COME BACK.
HE MIGHT BE DEAD, BUT I FIGURED...
...IF I GOT INTO THIS LINE OF WORK I MIGHT FIND HIM ONE DAY.
I SEE...
I HOPE YOU FIND HIM.
HEH.
ME TOO, KID.

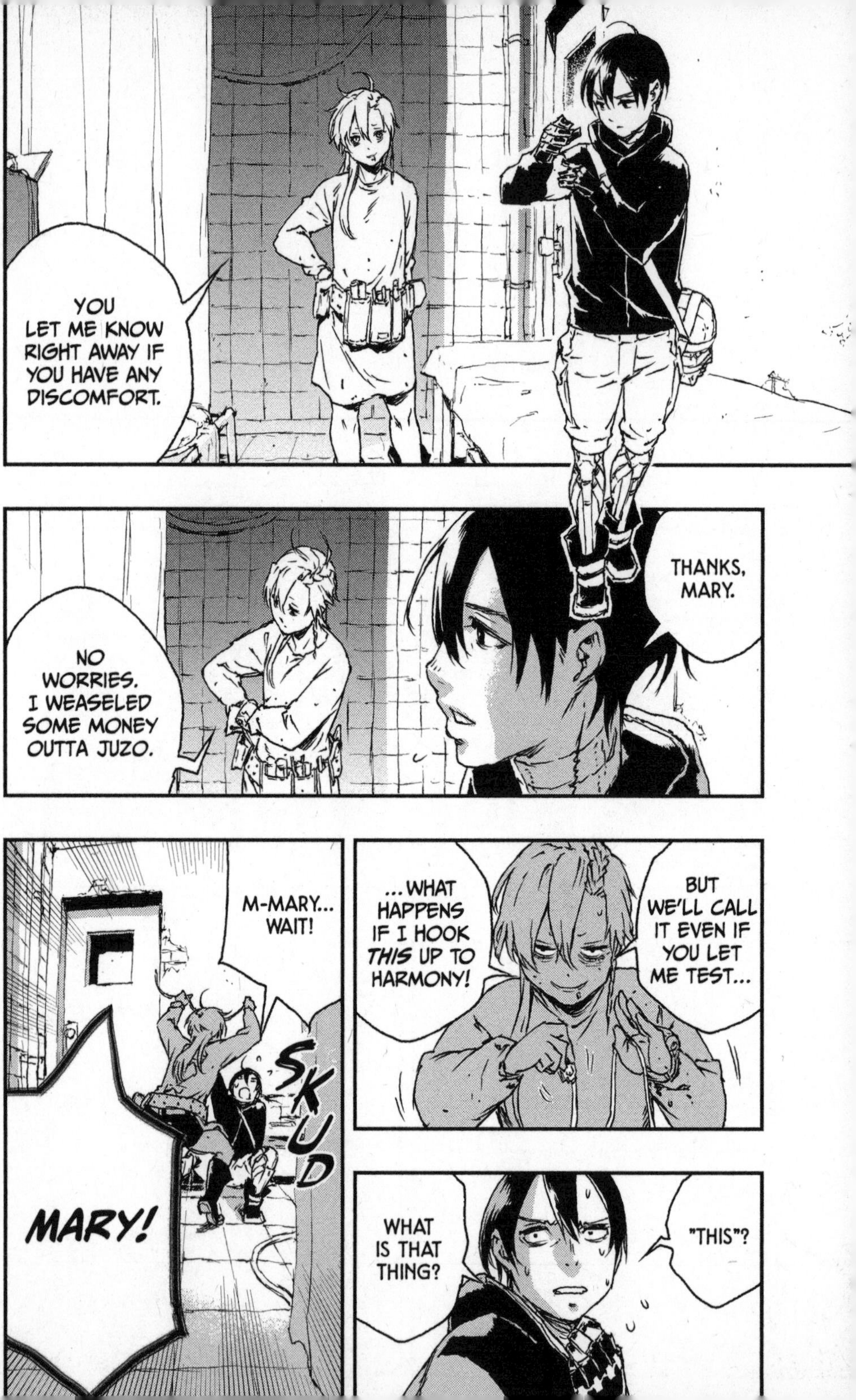
YOU LET ME KNOW RIGHT AWAY IF YOU HAVE ANY DISCOMFORT.
THANKS, MARY.
NO WORRIES. I WEASELED SOME MONEY OUTTA JUZO.
BUT WE'LL CALL IT EVEN IF YOU LET ME TEST...
...WHAT HAPPENS IF I HOOK *THIS* UP TO HARMONY!
"THIS"?
WHAT IS THAT THING?
M-MARY... WAIT!
SKUD
MARY!

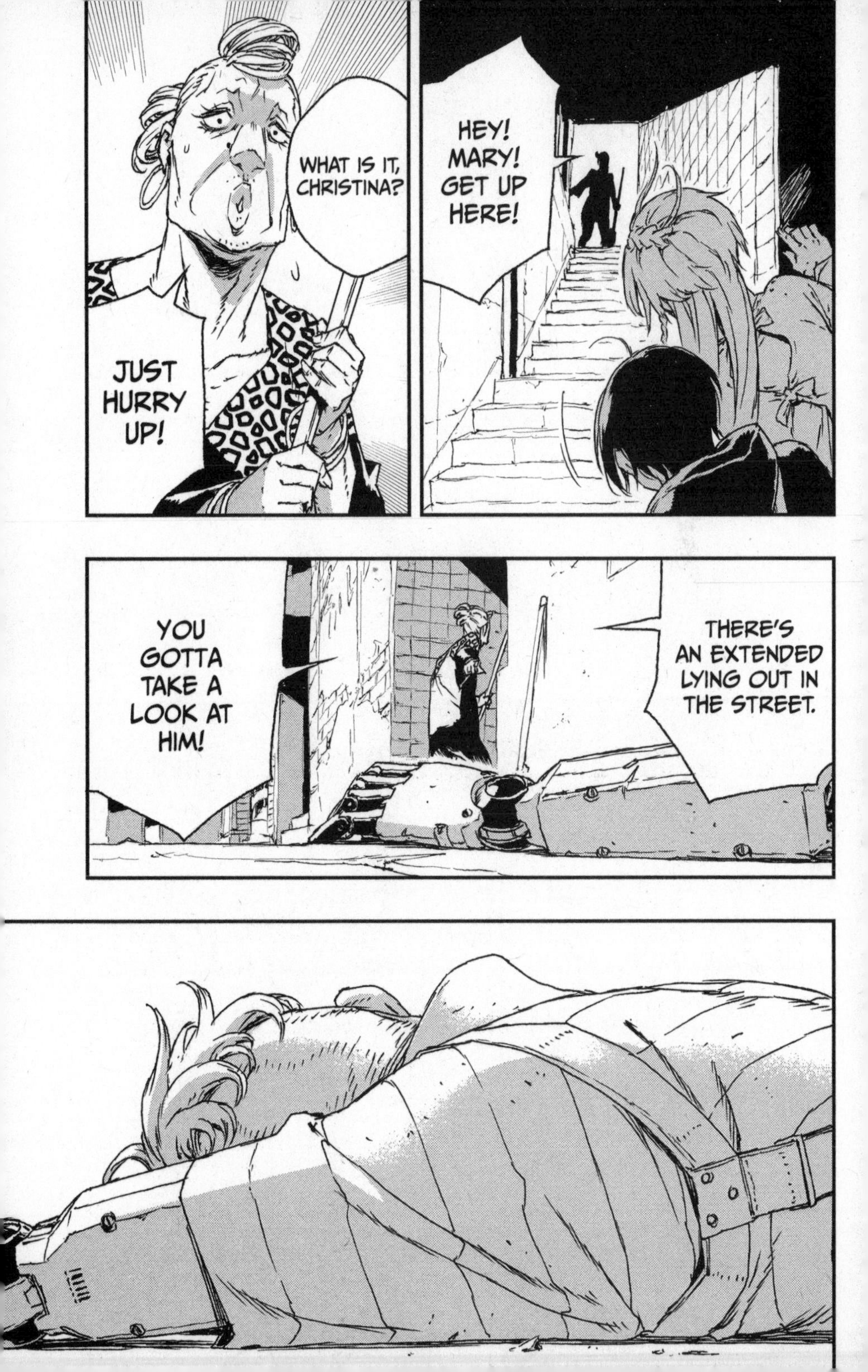
HEY! MARY! GET UP HERE!
WHAT IS IT, CHRISTINA?
JUST HURRY UP!
THERE'S AN EXTENDED LYING OUT IN THE STREET.
YOU GOTTA TAKE A LOOK AT HIM!

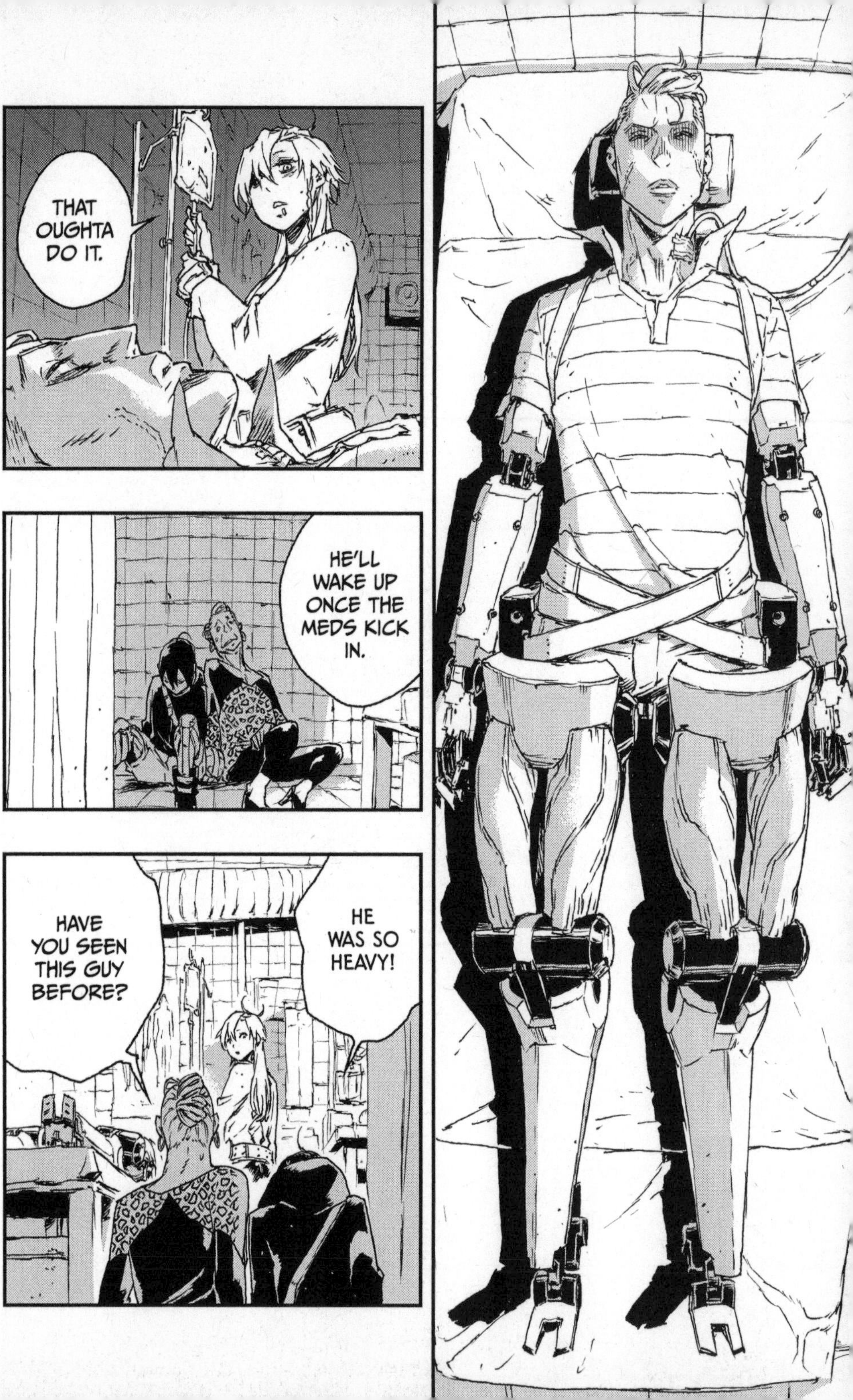
THAT OUGHTA DO IT.
HE'LL WAKE UP ONCE THE MEDS KICK IN.
HE WAS SO HEAVY!
HAVE YOU SEEN THIS GUY BEFORE?

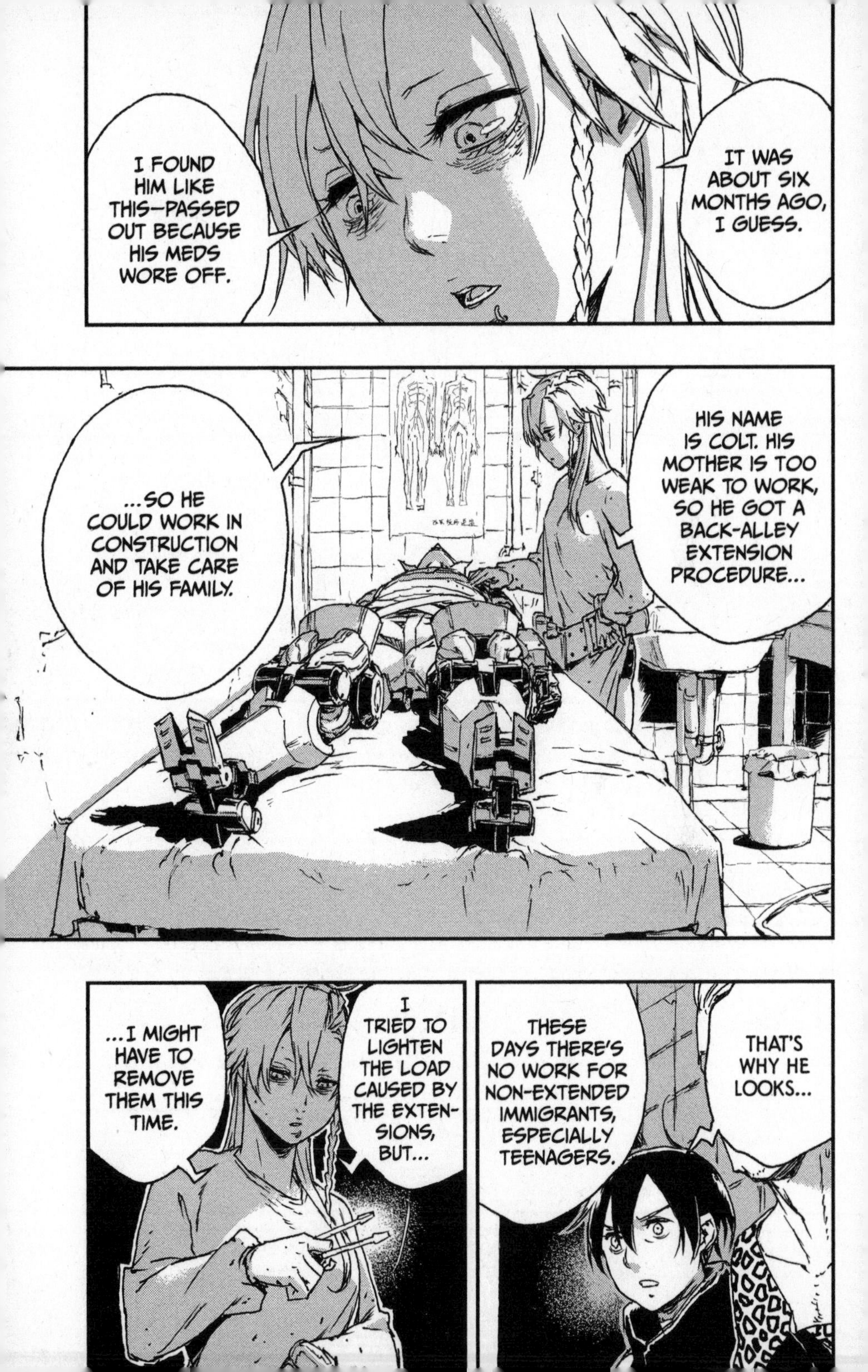
IT WAS ABOUT SIX MONTHS AGO, I GUESS.
I FOUND HIM LIKE THIS—PASSED OUT BECAUSE HIS MEDS WORE OFF.
HIS NAME IS COLT. HIS MOTHER IS TOO WEAK TO WORK, SO HE GOT A BACK-ALLEY EXTENSION PROCEDURE...
...SO HE COULD WORK IN CONSTRUCTION AND TAKE CARE OF HIS FAMILY.
THAT'S WHY HE LOOKS...
THESE DAYS THERE'S NO WORK FOR NON-EXTENDED IMMIGRANTS, ESPECIALLY TEENAGERS.
I TRIED TO LIGHTEN THE LOAD CAUSED BY THE EXTEN-SIONS, BUT...
...I MIGHT HAVE TO REMOVE THEM THIS TIME.

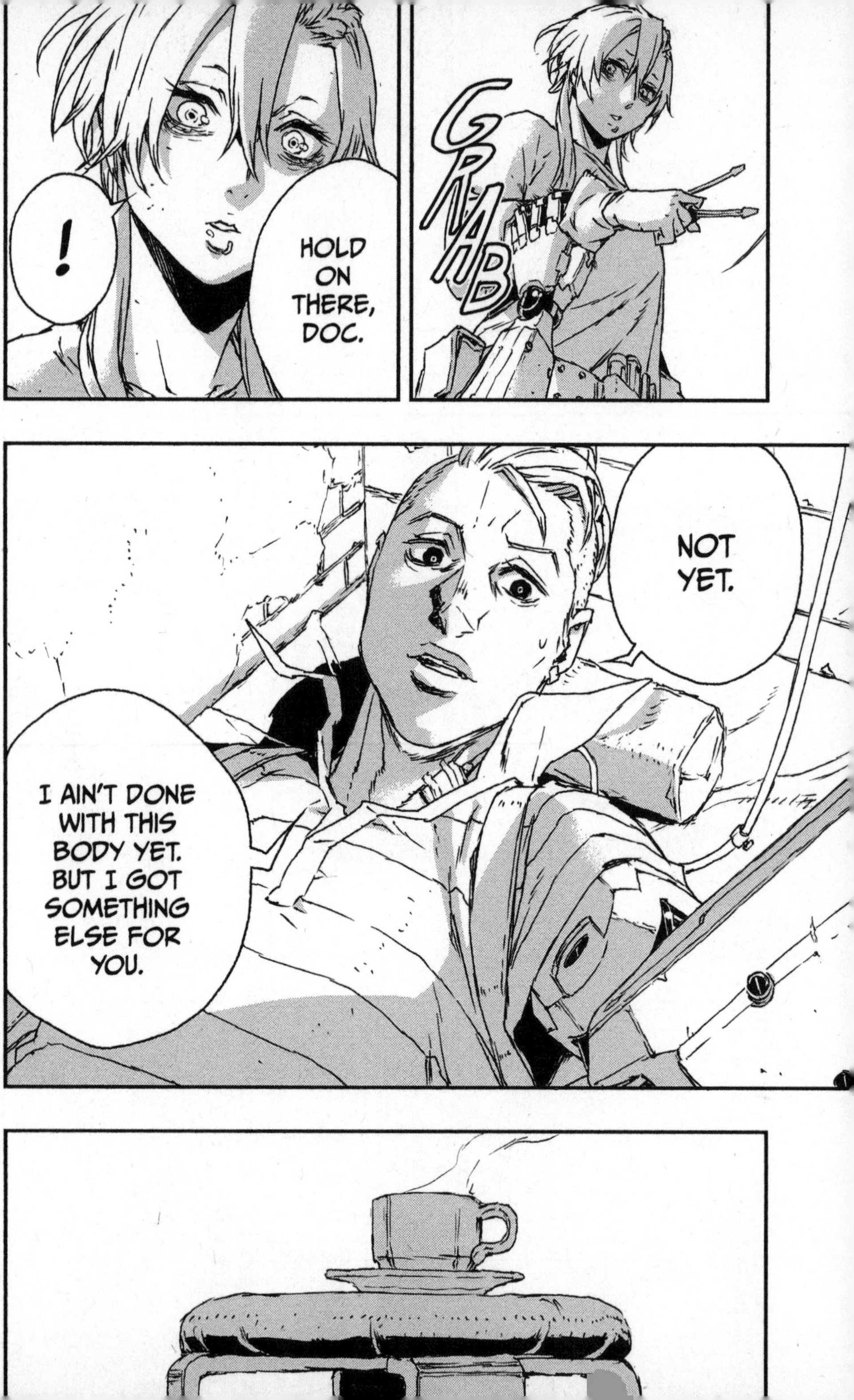
GRAB
HOLD ON THERE, DOC.
!
NOT YET.
I AIN'T DONE WITH THIS BODY YET. BUT I GOT SOMETHING ELSE FOR YOU.

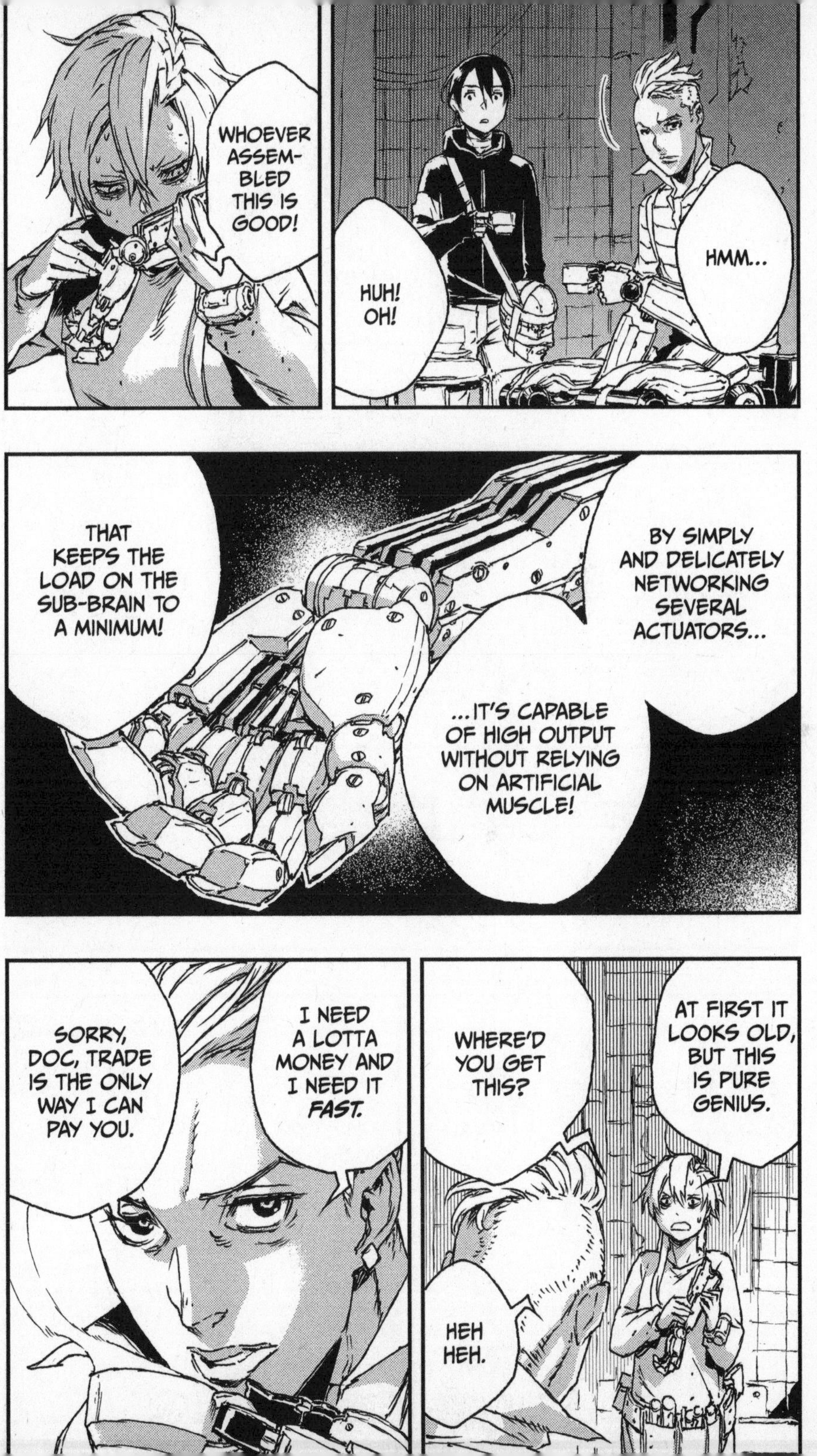
HMM...
HUH! OH!
WHOEVER ASSEM-BLED THIS IS GOOD!
BY SIMPLY AND DELICATELY NETWORKING SEVERAL ACTUATORS...
...IT'S CAPABLE OF HIGH OUTPUT WITHOUT RELYING ON ARTIFICIAL MUSCLE!
THAT KEEPS THE LOAD ON THE SUB-BRAIN TO A MINIMUM!
AT FIRST IT LOOKS OLD, BUT THIS IS PURE GENIUS.
WHERE'D YOU GET THIS?
HEH HEH.
I NEED A LOTTA MONEY AND I NEED IT *FAST.*
SORRY, DOC, TRADE IS THE ONLY WAY I CAN PAY YOU.

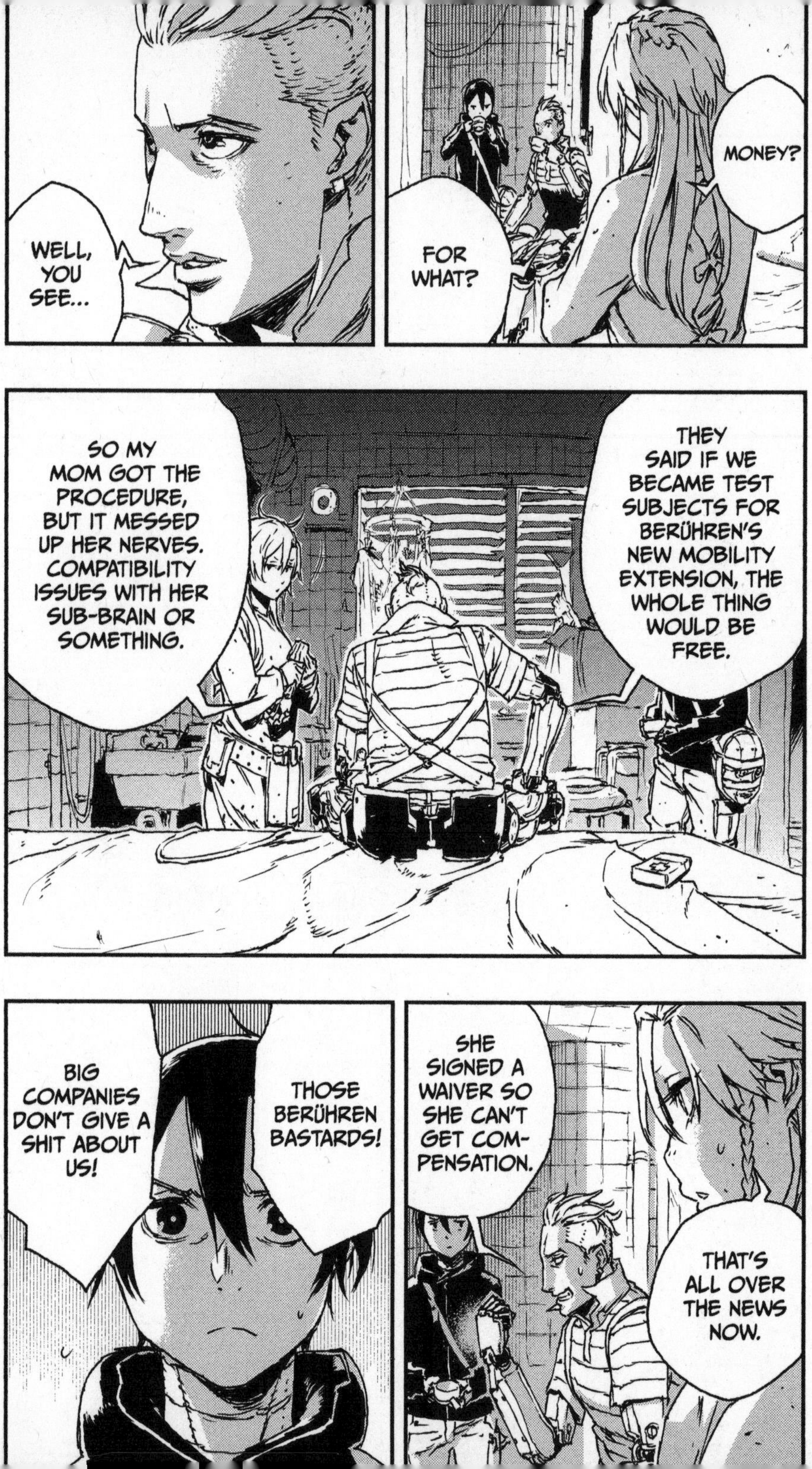
MONEY?
FOR WHAT?
WELL, YOU SEE...
THEY SAID IF WE BECAME TEST SUBJECTS FOR BERÜHREN'S NEW MOBILITY EXTENSION, THE WHOLE THING WOULD BE FREE.
SO MY MOM GOT THE PROCEDURE, BUT IT MESSED UP HER NERVES. COMPATIBILITY ISSUES WITH HER SUB-BRAIN OR SOMETHING.
SHE SIGNED A WAIVER SO SHE CAN'T GET COMPENSATION.
THAT'S ALL OVER THE NEWS NOW.
THOSE BERÜHREN BASTARDS!
BIG COMPANIES DON'T GIVE A SHIT ABOUT US!

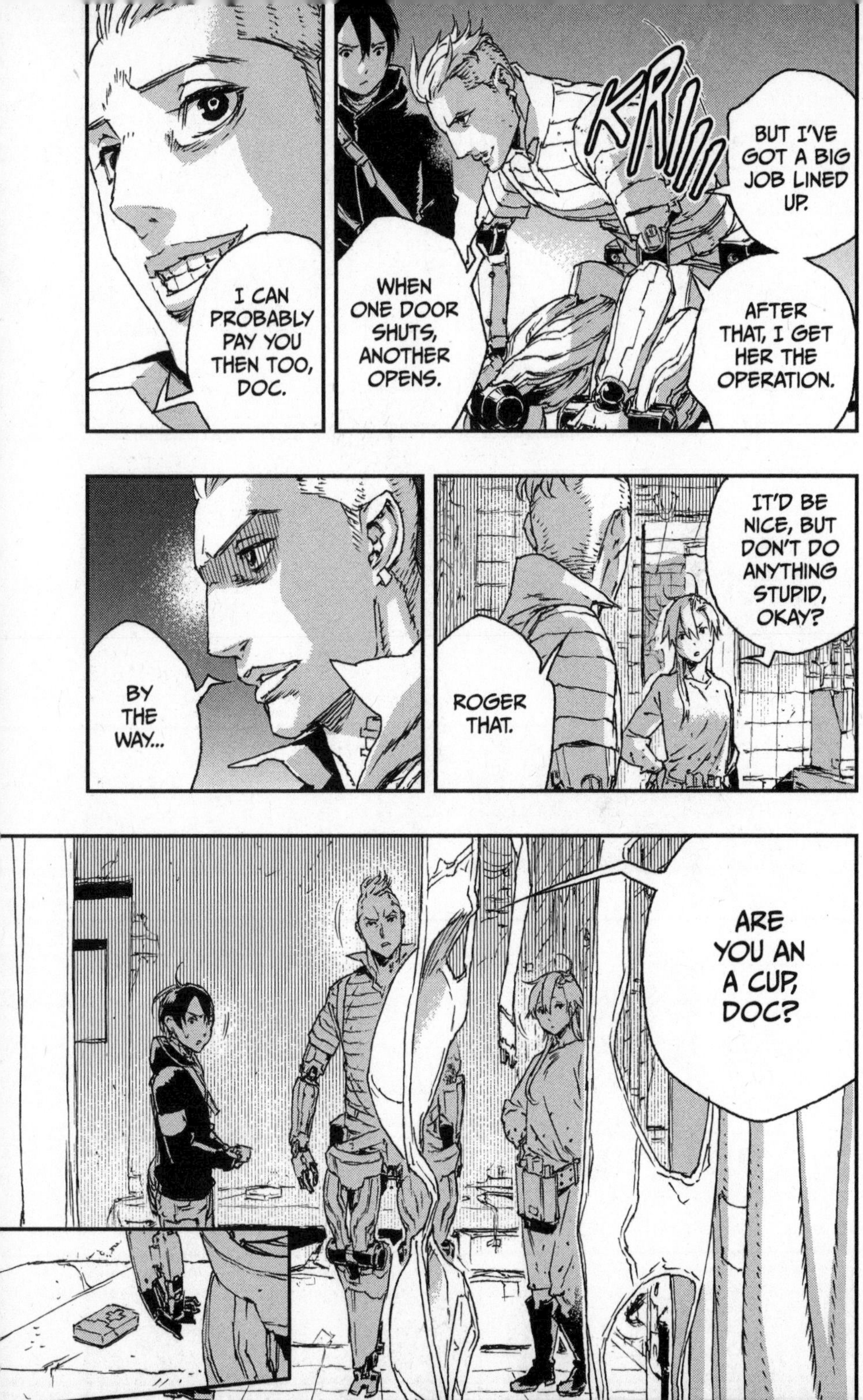
BUT I'VE GOT A BIG JOB LINED UP.
KRIII
AFTER THAT, I GET HER THE OPERATION.
WHEN ONE DOOR SHUTS, ANOTHER OPENS.
I CAN PROBABLY PAY YOU THEN TOO, DOC.
IT'D BE NICE, BUT DON'T DO ANYTHING STUPID, OKAY?
ROGER THAT.
BY THE WAY...
ARE YOU AN A CUP, DOC?

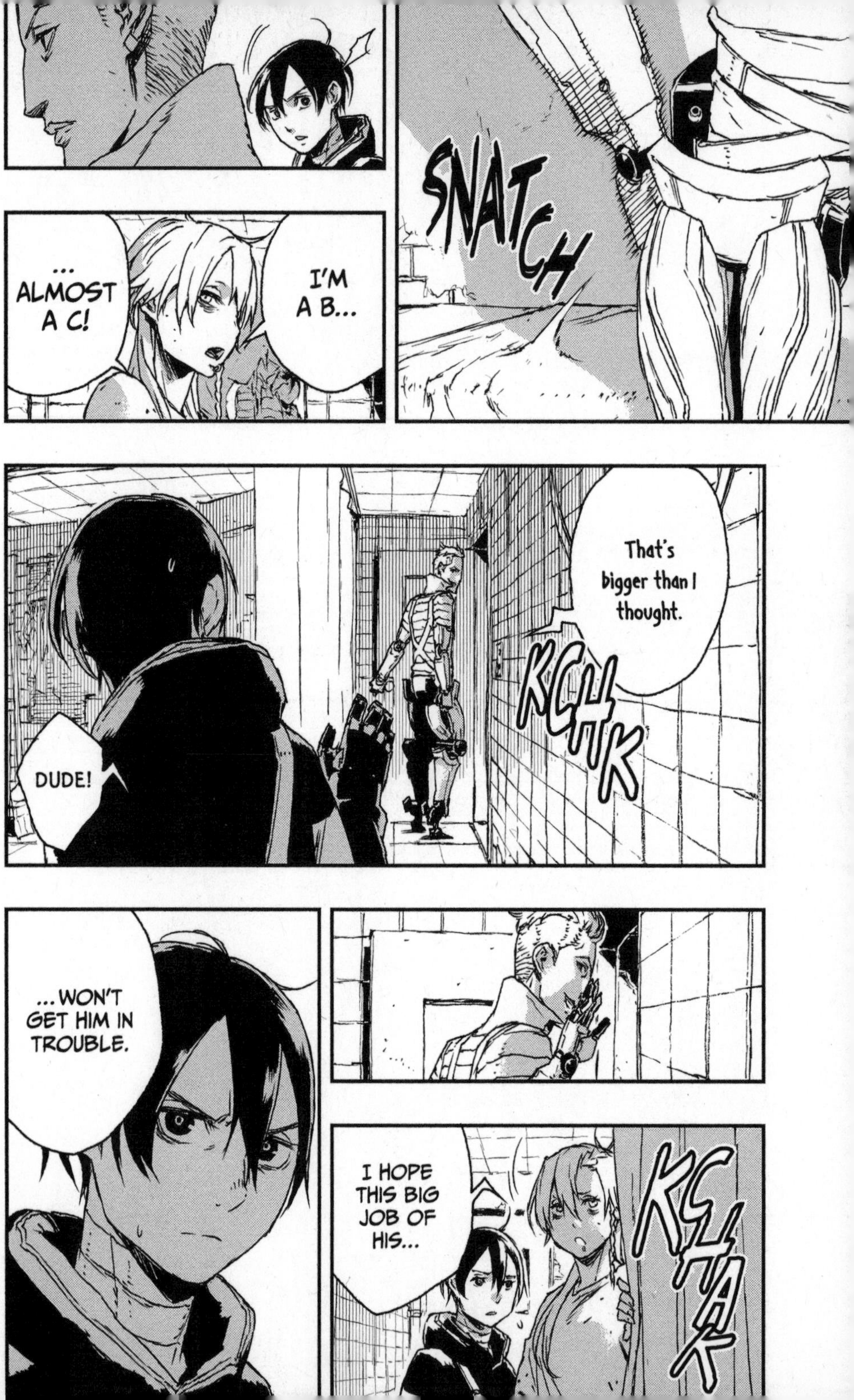
SNATCH
I'M A B...
... ALMOST A C!
That's bigger than I thought.
KCHK
DUDE!
KSHAK
I HOPE THIS BIG JOB OF HIS...
...WON'T GET HIM IN TROUBLE.

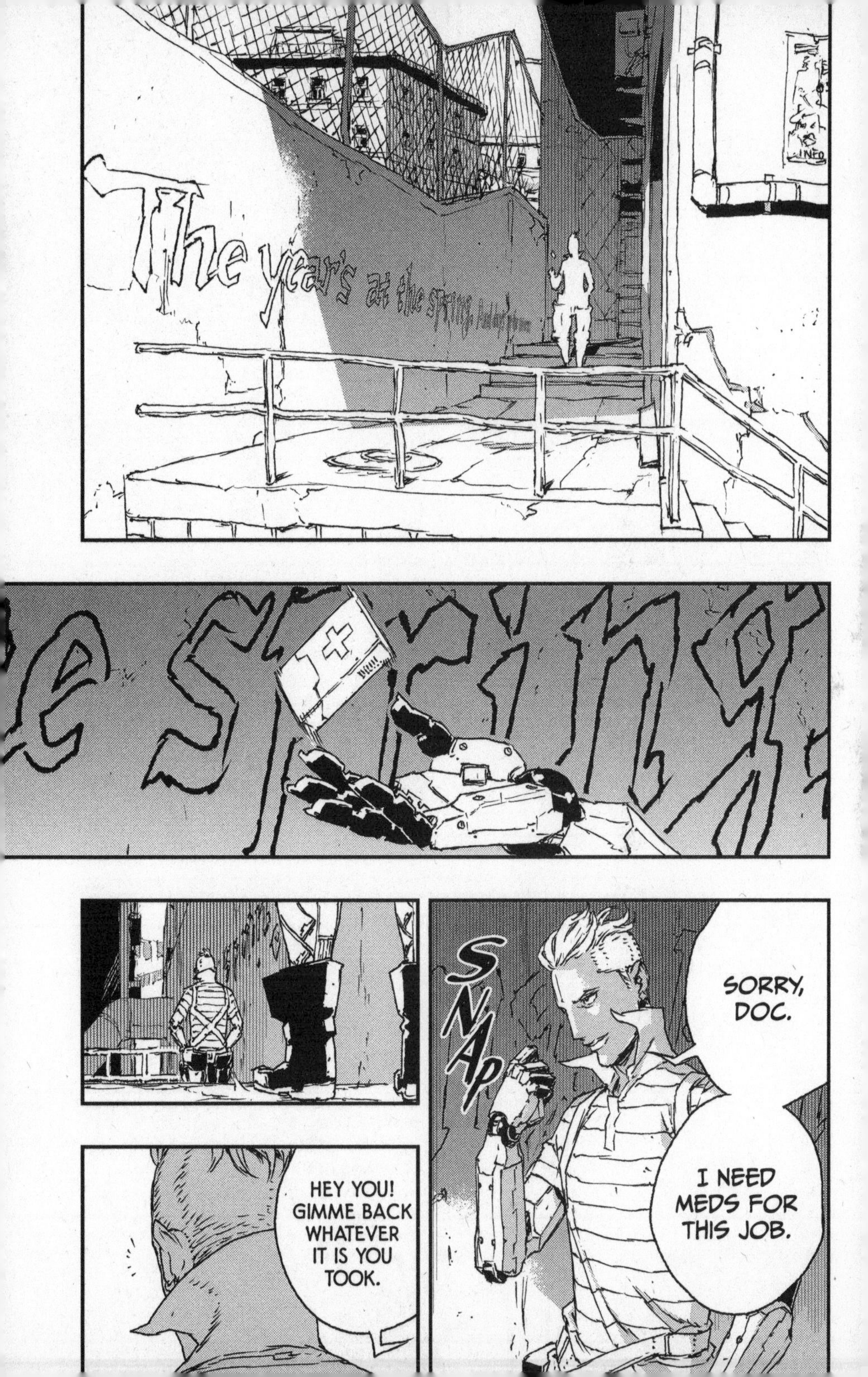
The year's at the spring
SNAP
SORRY, DOC.
I NEED MEDS FOR THIS JOB.
HEY YOU! GIMME BACK WHATEVER IT IS YOU TOOK.

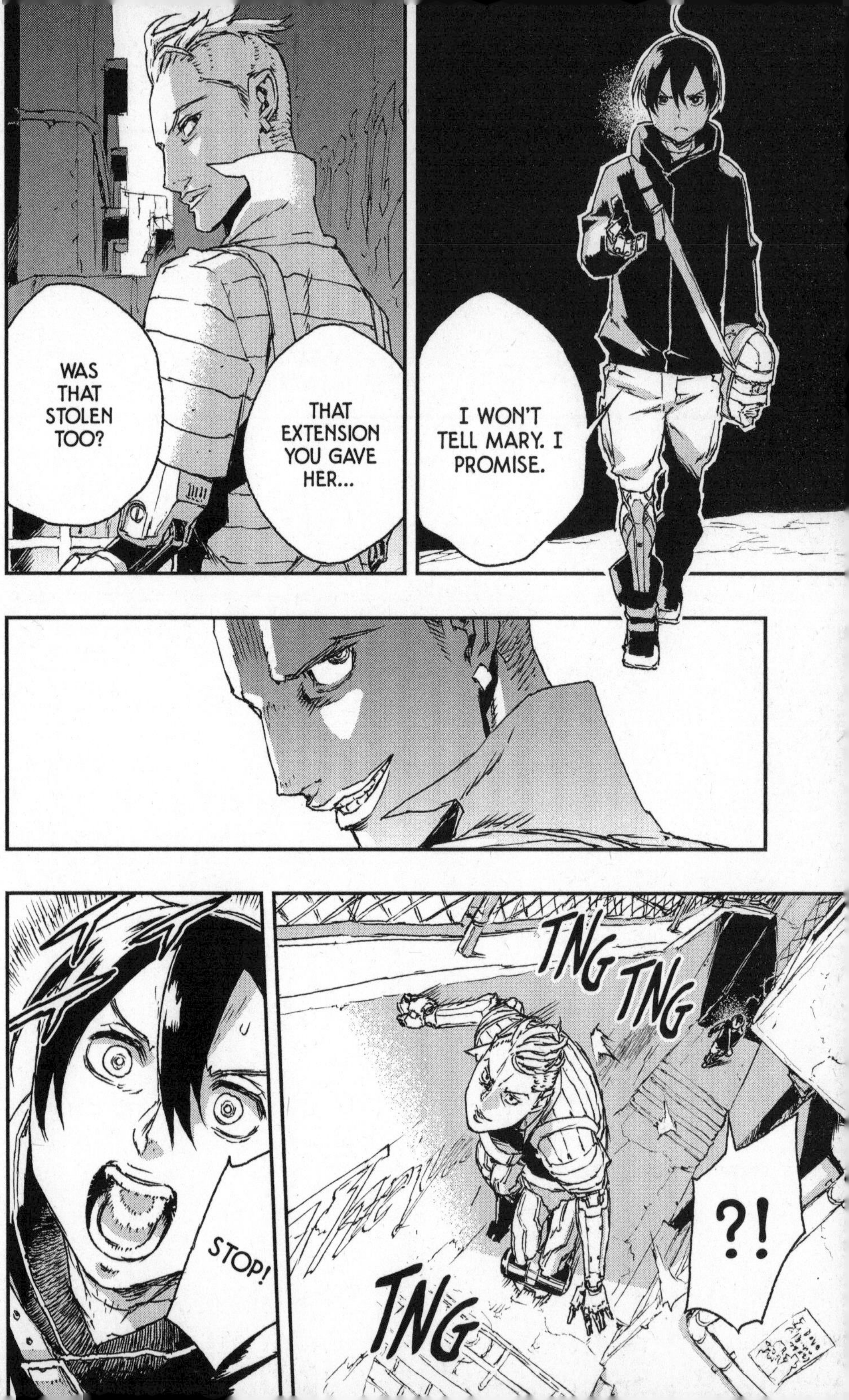
I WON'T TELL MARY. I PROMISE.
THAT EXTENSION YOU GAVE HER...
WAS THAT STOLEN TOO?
TNG TNG
?!
TNG
STOP!

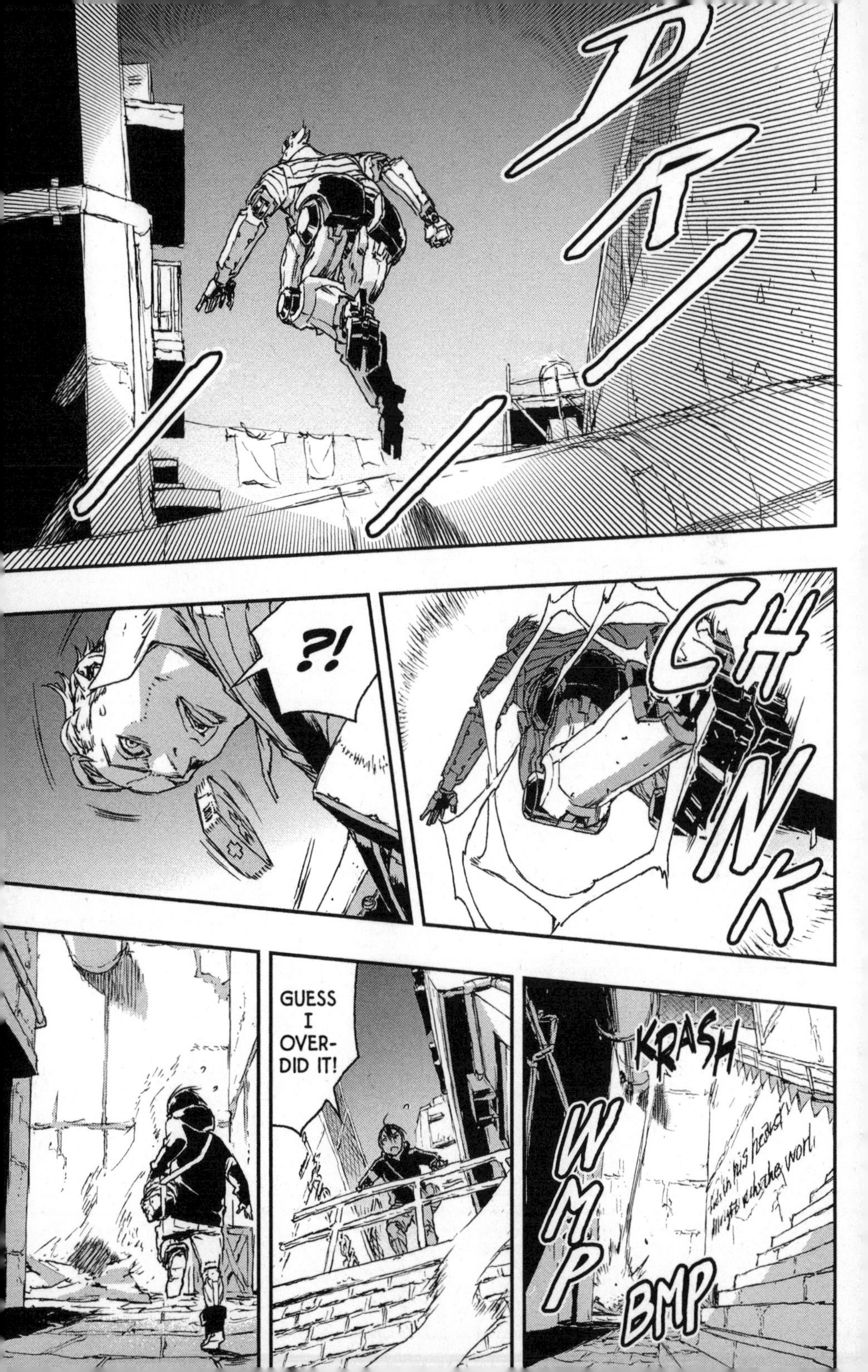
CHNK
?!
KRASH
WMP
BMP
GUESS I OVER-DID IT!

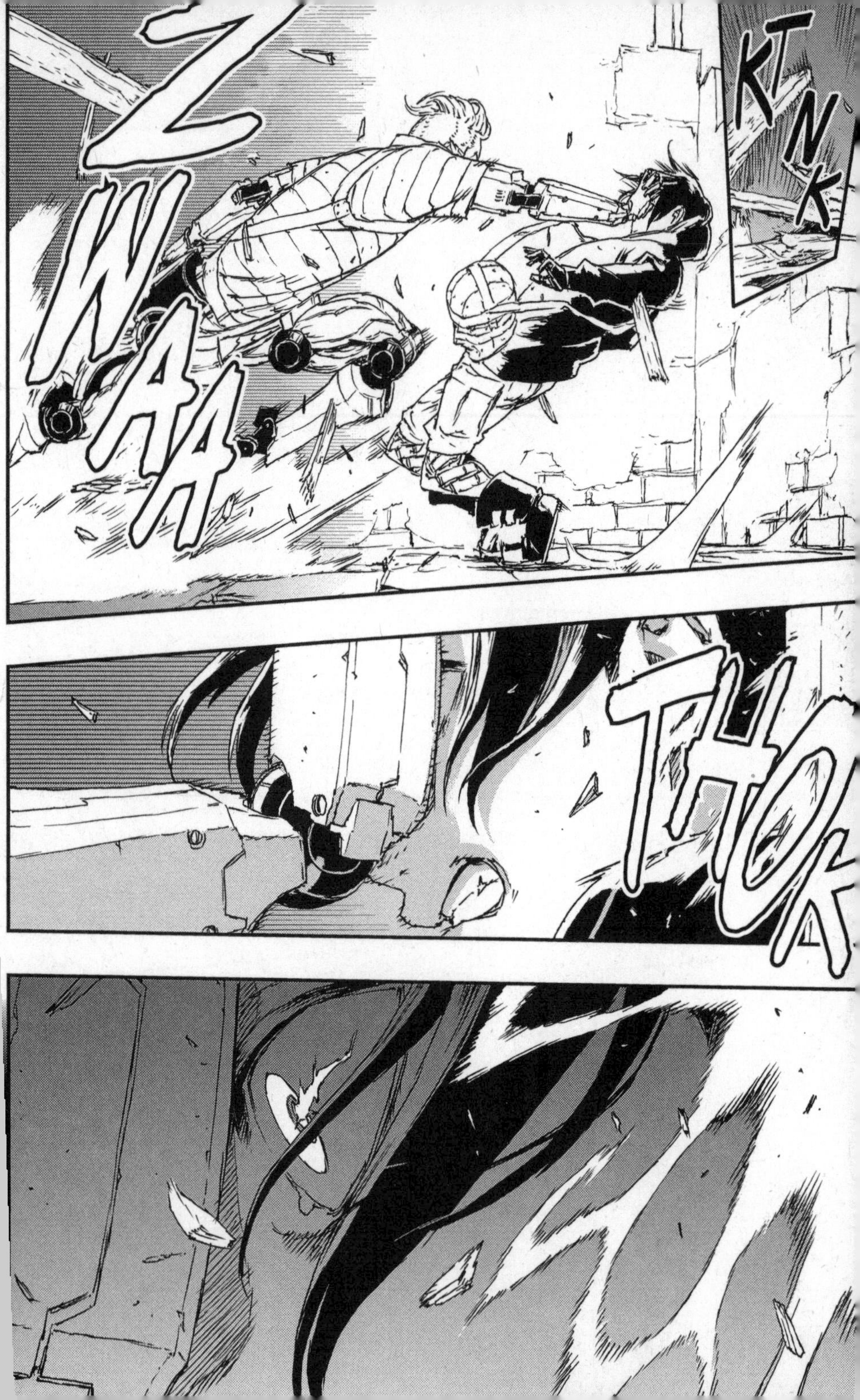
KTNK
ZWAA
THOK

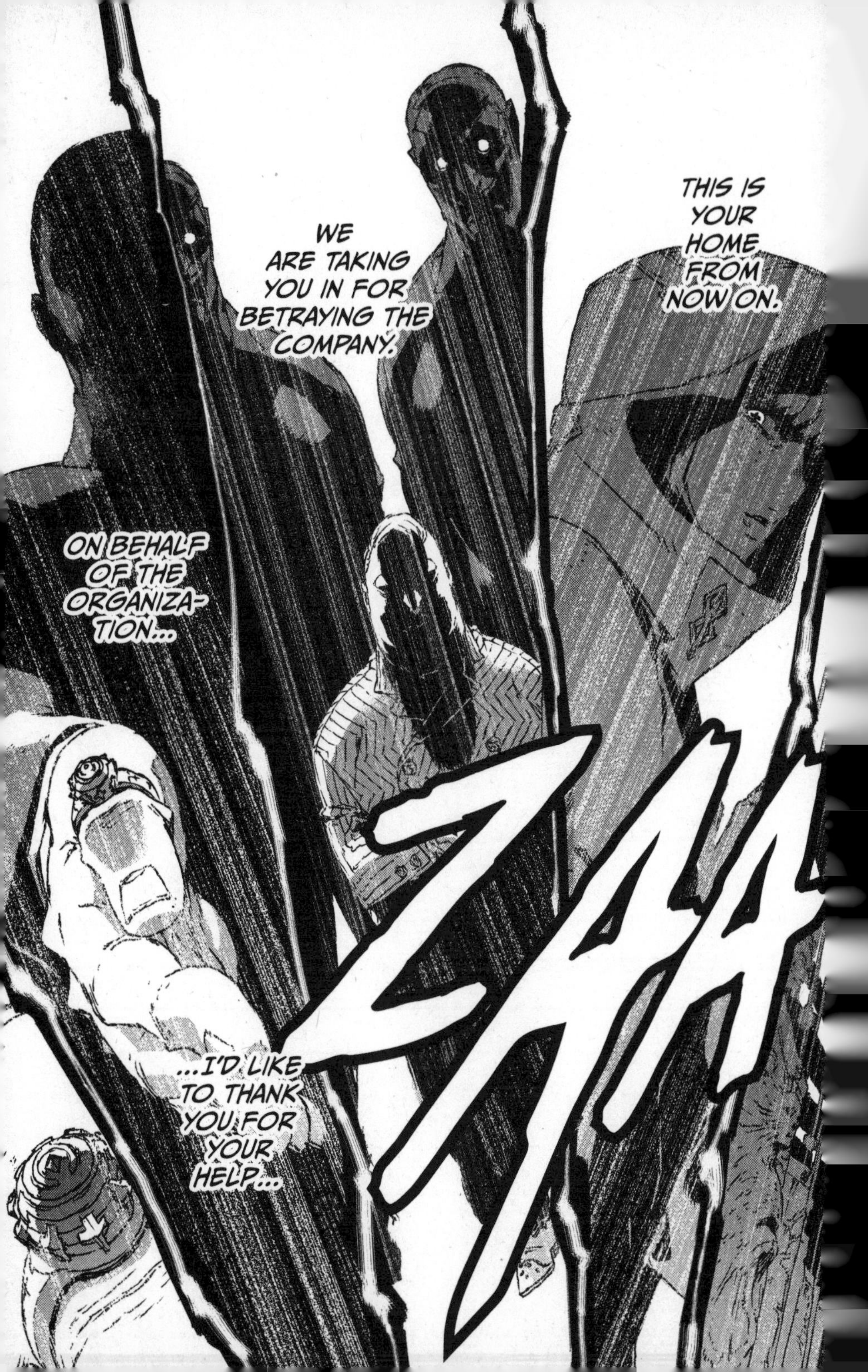
THIS IS YOUR HOME FROM NOW ON.
WE ARE TAKING YOU IN FOR BETRAYING THE COMPANY.
ON BEHALF OF THE ORGANIZA-TION...
...I'D LIKE TO THANK YOU FOR YOUR HELP...
ZAA

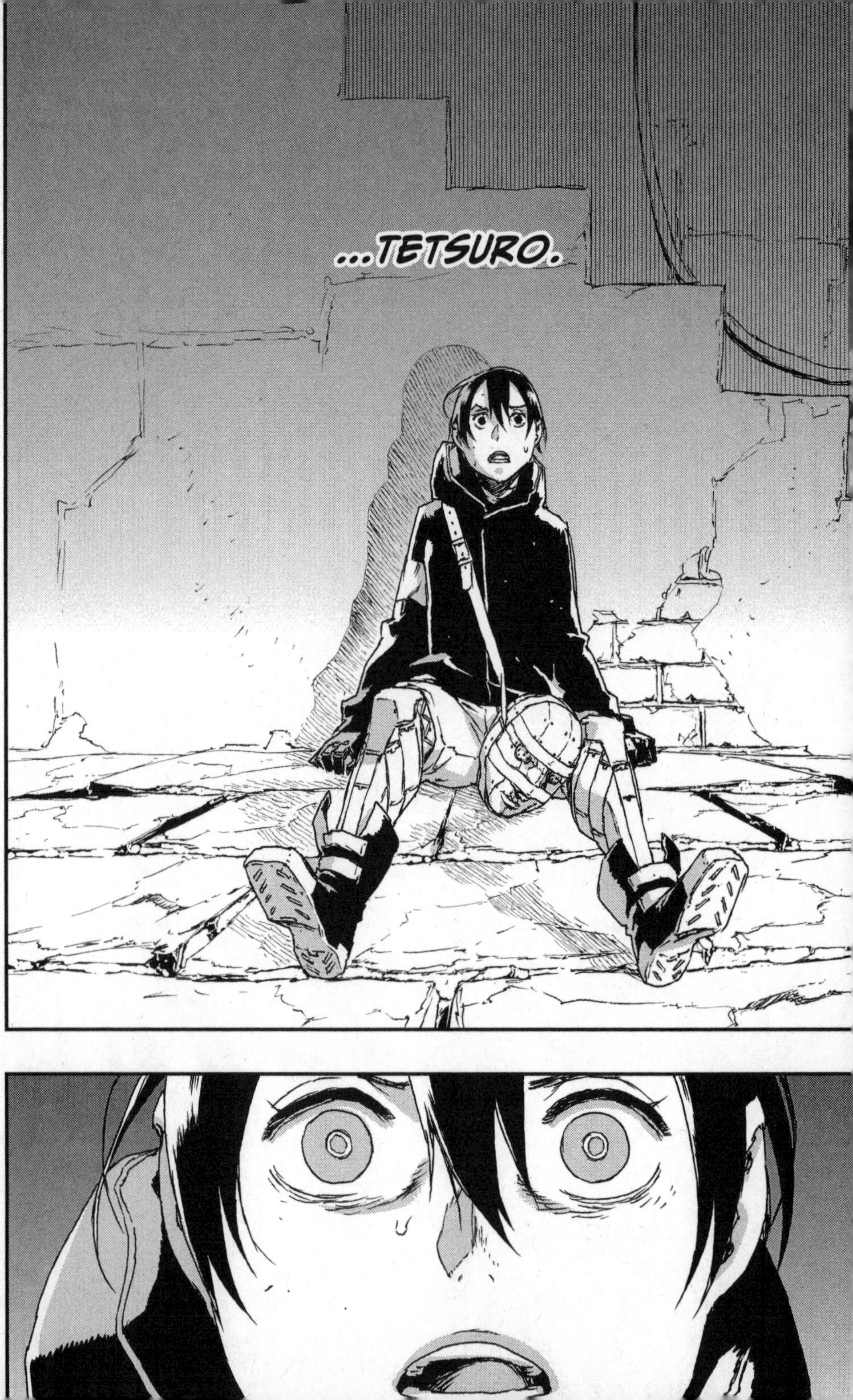
...TETSURO.

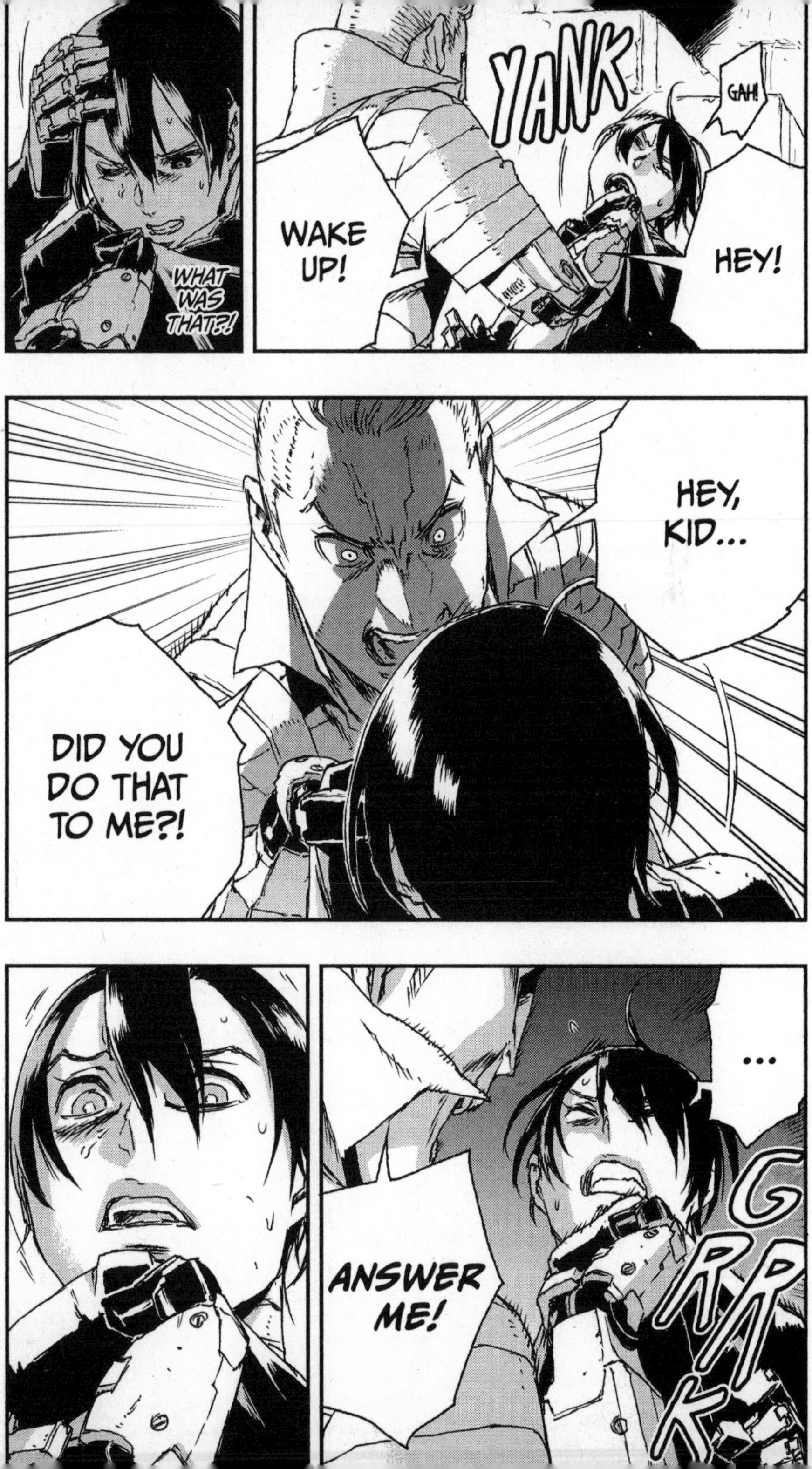
GAH!
YANK
HEY!
WAKE UP!
WHAT WAS THAT?!
HEY, KID...
DID YOU DO THAT TO ME?!
...
GRRK
ANSWER ME!

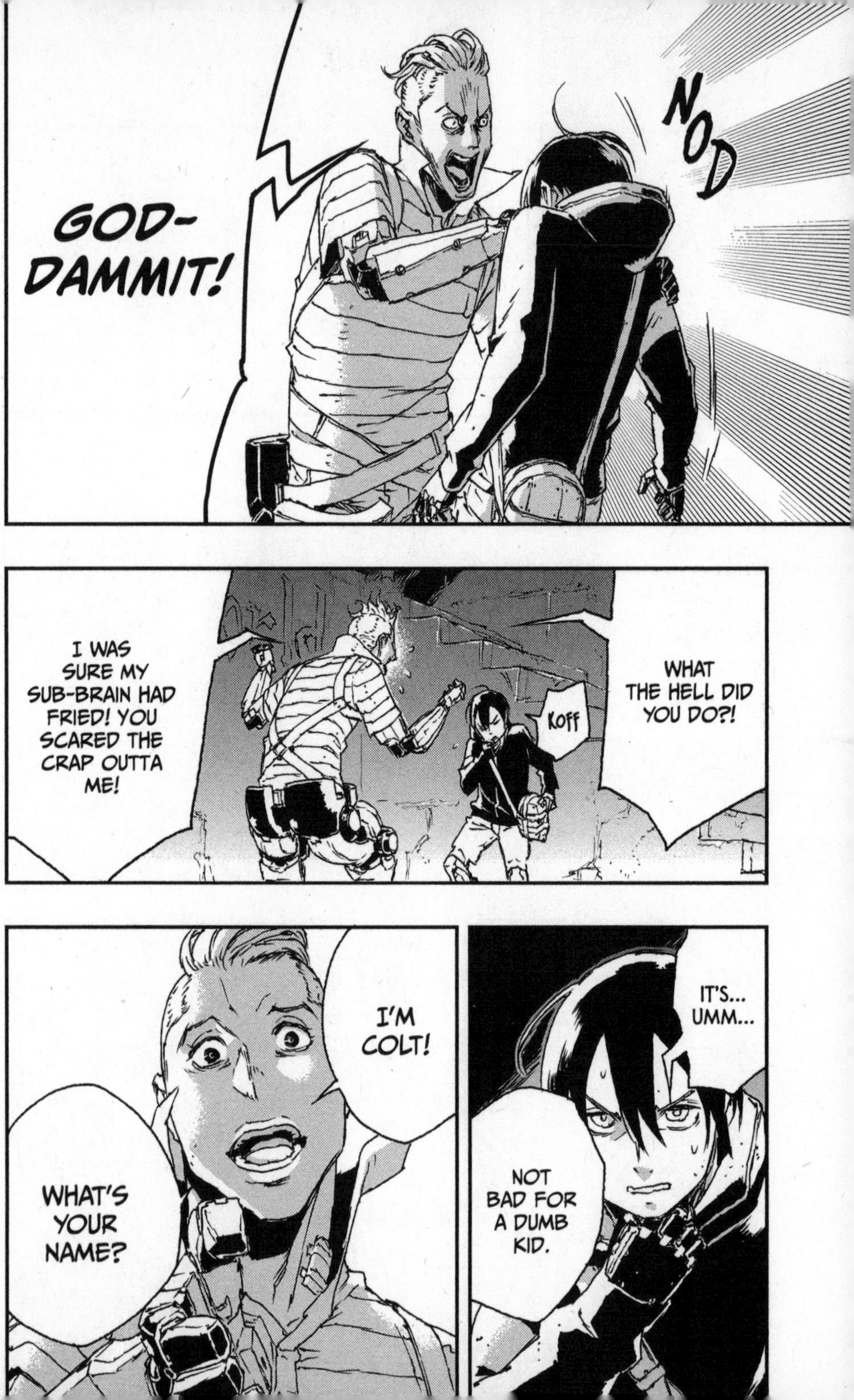
NOD
GOD-DAMMIT!
WHAT THE HELL DID YOU DO?!
KOFF
I WAS SURE MY SUB-BRAIN HAD FRIED! YOU SCARED THE CRAP OUTTA ME!
IT'S... UMM...
NOT BAD FOR A DUMB KID.
I'M COLT!
WHAT'S YOUR NAME?

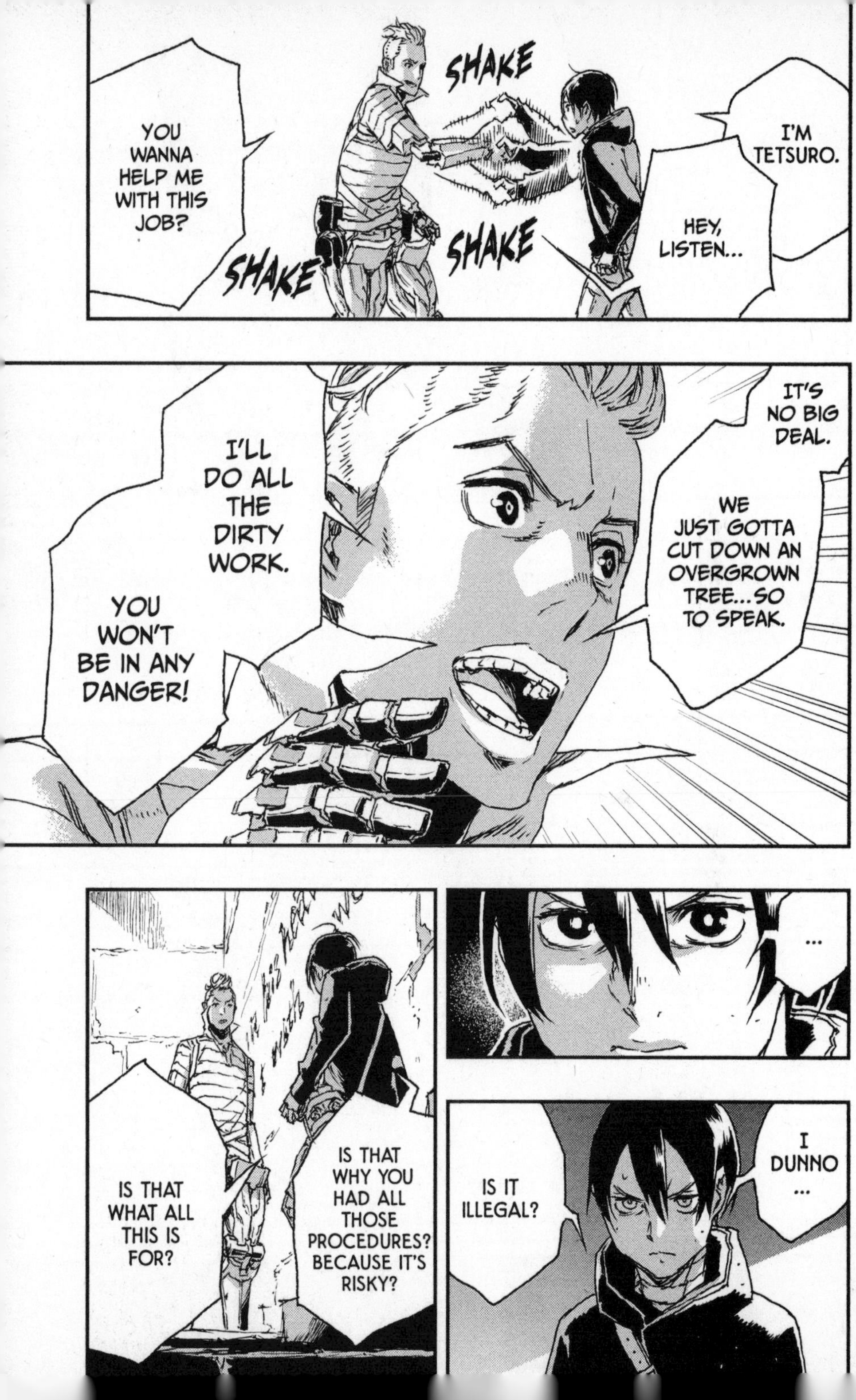
I'M TETSURO.
HEY, LISTEN...
SHAKE
SHAKE
YOU WANNA HELP ME WITH THIS JOB?
SHAKE
IT'S NO BIG DEAL.
WE JUST GOTTA CUT DOWN AN OVERGROWN TREE...SO TO SPEAK.
I'LL DO ALL THE DIRTY WORK.
YOU WON'T BE IN ANY DANGER!
...
I DUNNO ...
IS IT ILLEGAL?
IS THAT WHY YOU HAD ALL THOSE PROCEDURES? BECAUSE IT'S RISKY?
IS THAT WHAT ALL THIS IS FOR?

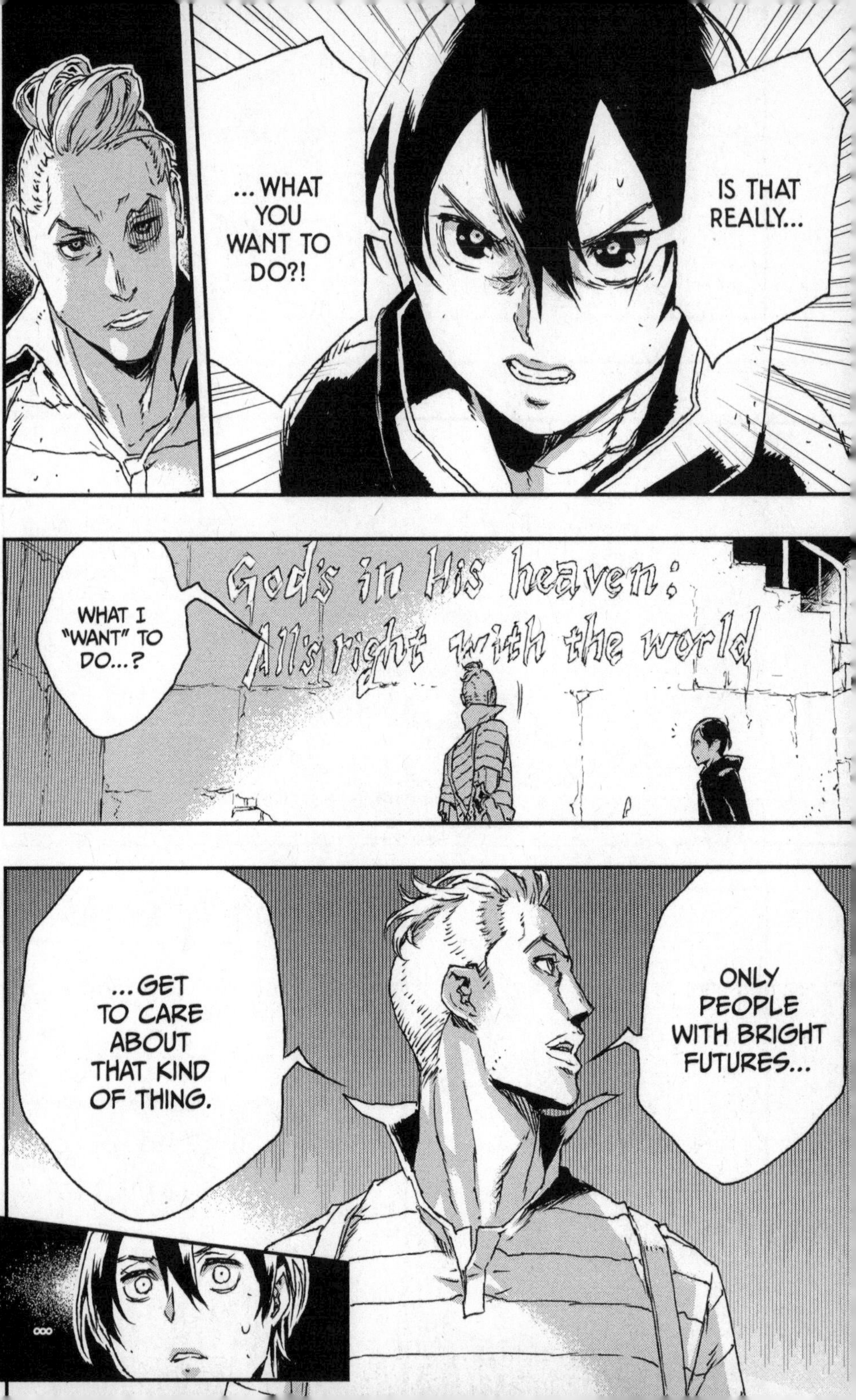
IS THAT REALLY...
...WHAT YOU WANT TO DO?!
God's in His heaven: All's right with the world
WHAT I "WANT" TO DO...?
ONLY PEOPLE WITH BRIGHT FUTURES...
...GET TO CARE ABOUT THAT KIND OF THING.

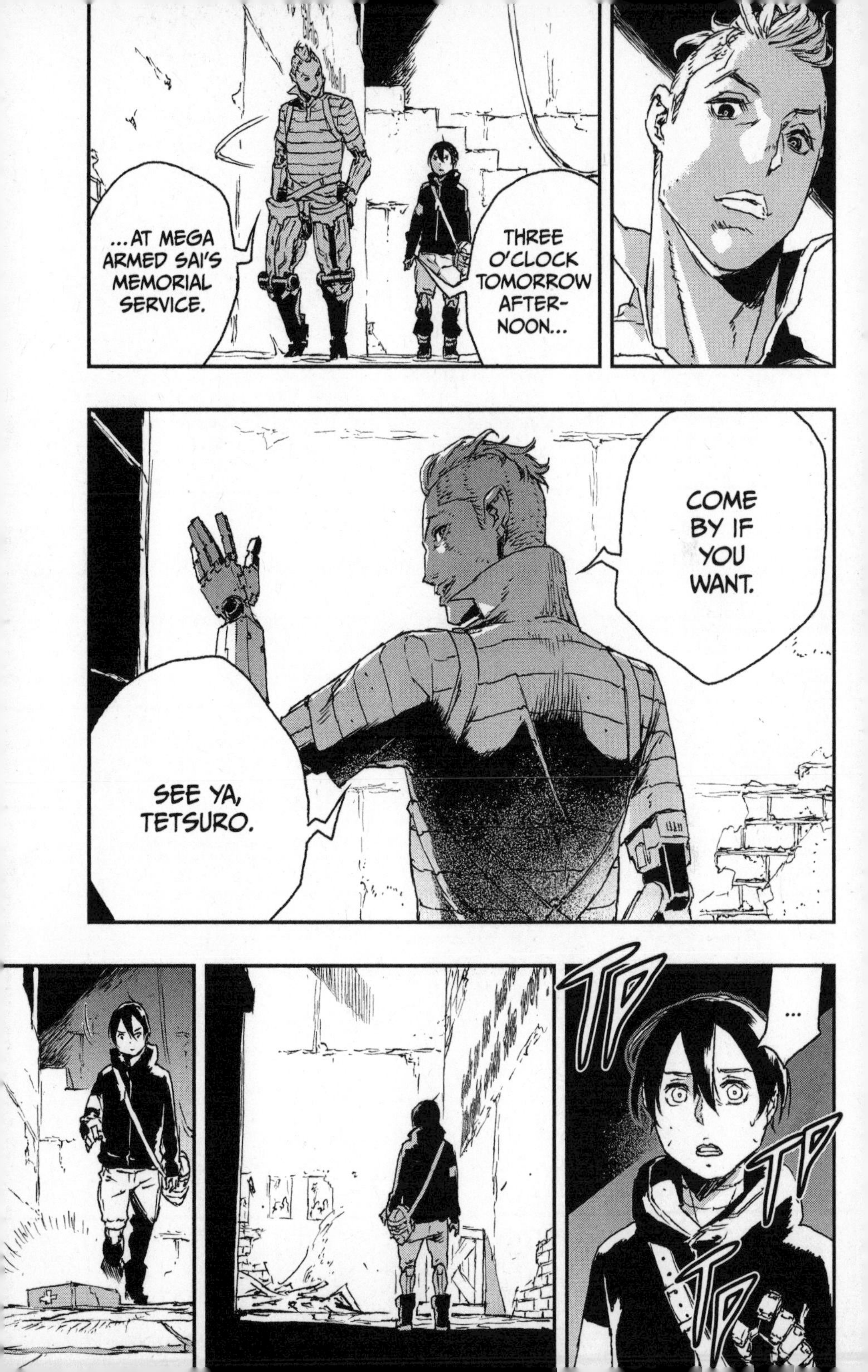
THREE O'CLOCK TOMORROW AFTERNOON...
...AT MEGA ARMED SAI'S MEMORIAL SERVICE.
COME BY IF YOU WANT.
SEE YA, TETSURO.
TP
...
TP
TP
TP

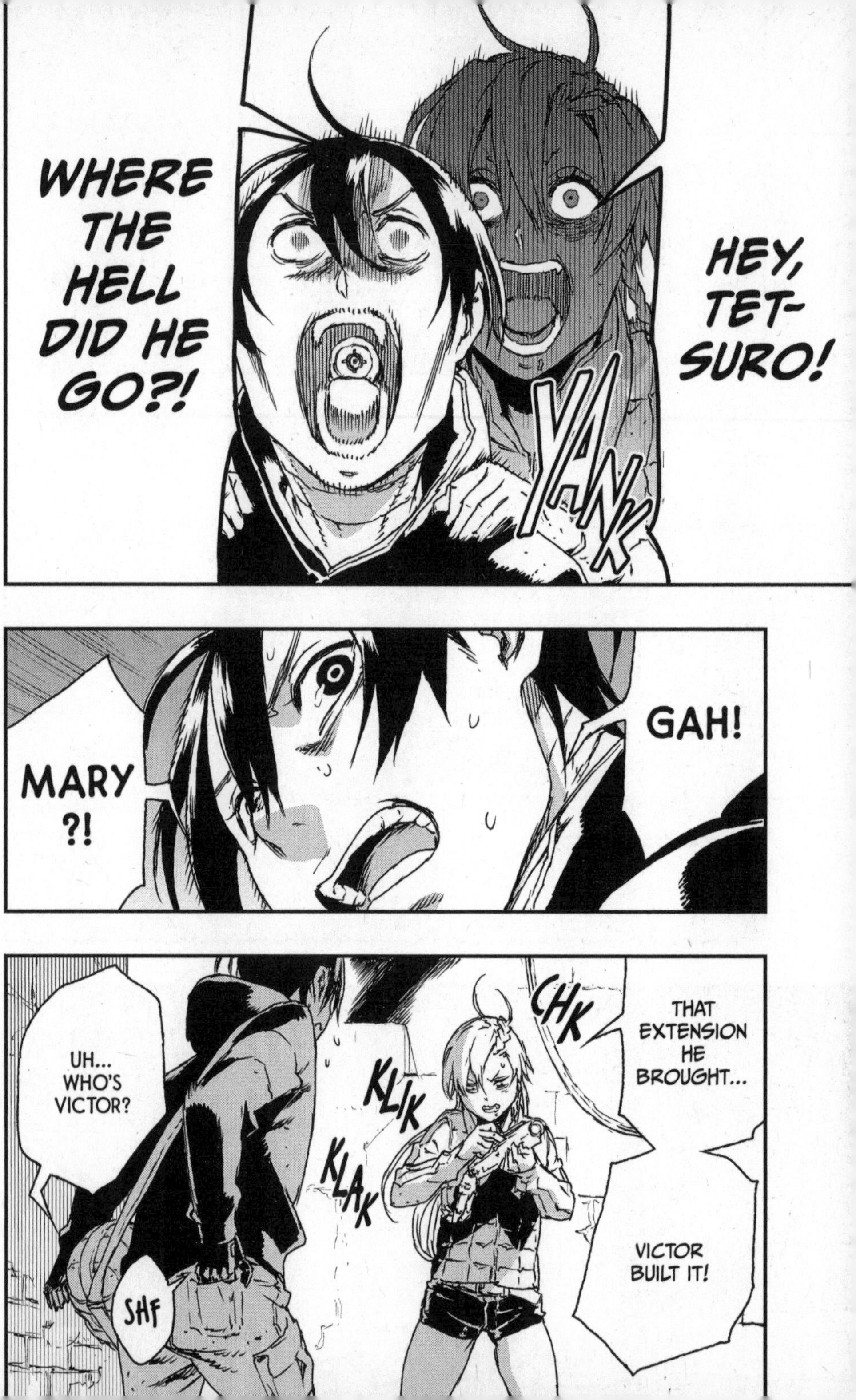
HEY, TET-SURO!
YANK
WHERE THE HELL DID HE GO?!
GAH!
MARY ?!
CHK
THAT EXTENSION HE BROUGHT...
KLIK
KLAK
VICTOR BUILT IT!
UH... WHO'S VICTOR?
SHF

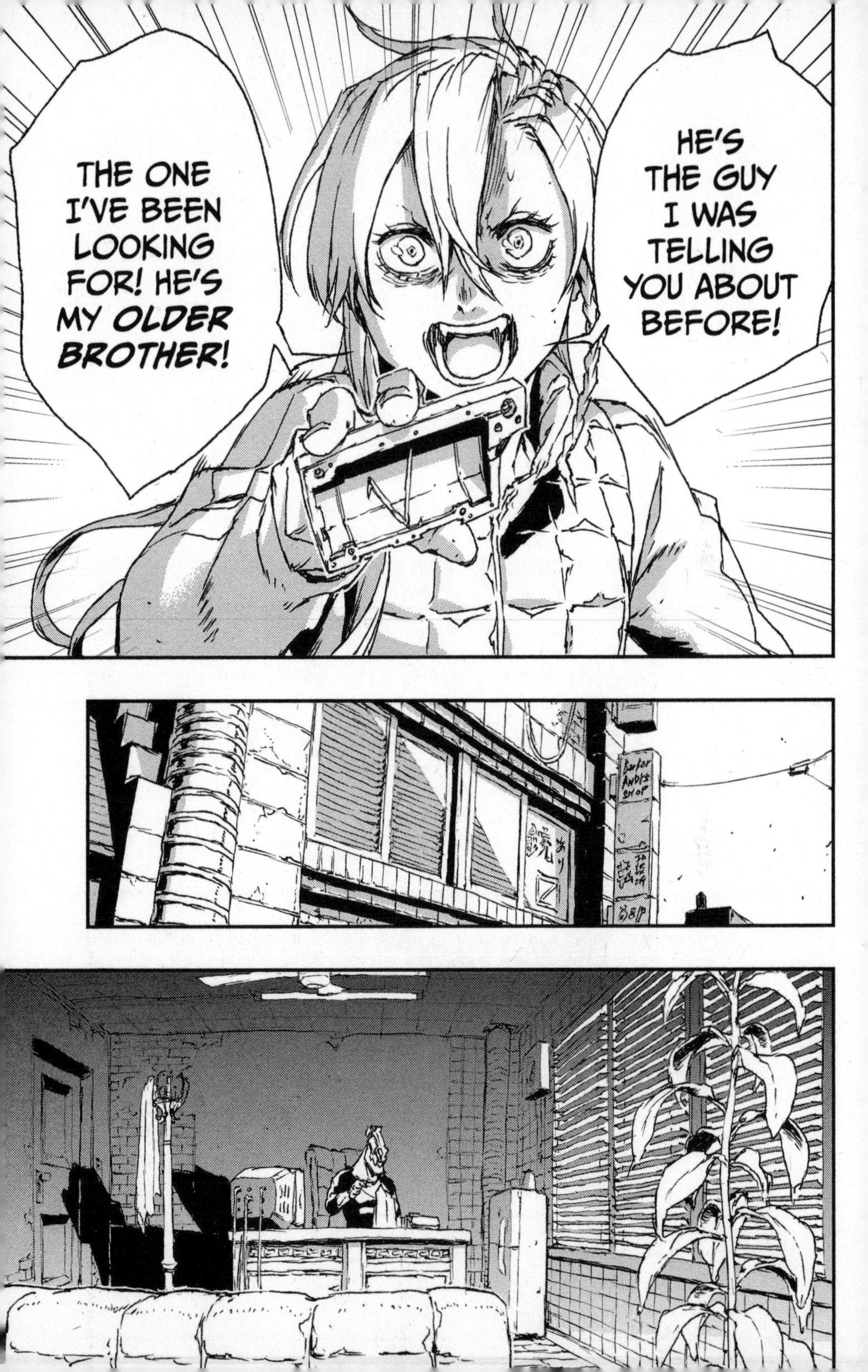
HE'S THE GUY I WAS TELLING YOU ABOUT BEFORE!
THE ONE I'VE BEEN LOOKING FOR! HE'S MY *OLDER BROTHER!*

DAMMIT, MARY!

SHE TOOK MOST OF THE REWARD OLIVIA PAID ME.

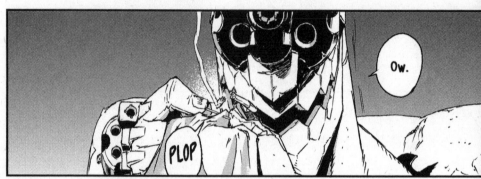

OW.

PLOP

KRIII

...

TOK TOK

THAT'S HOT!

YOUR OFFICE IS ALWAYS SO WELL VENTILATED.

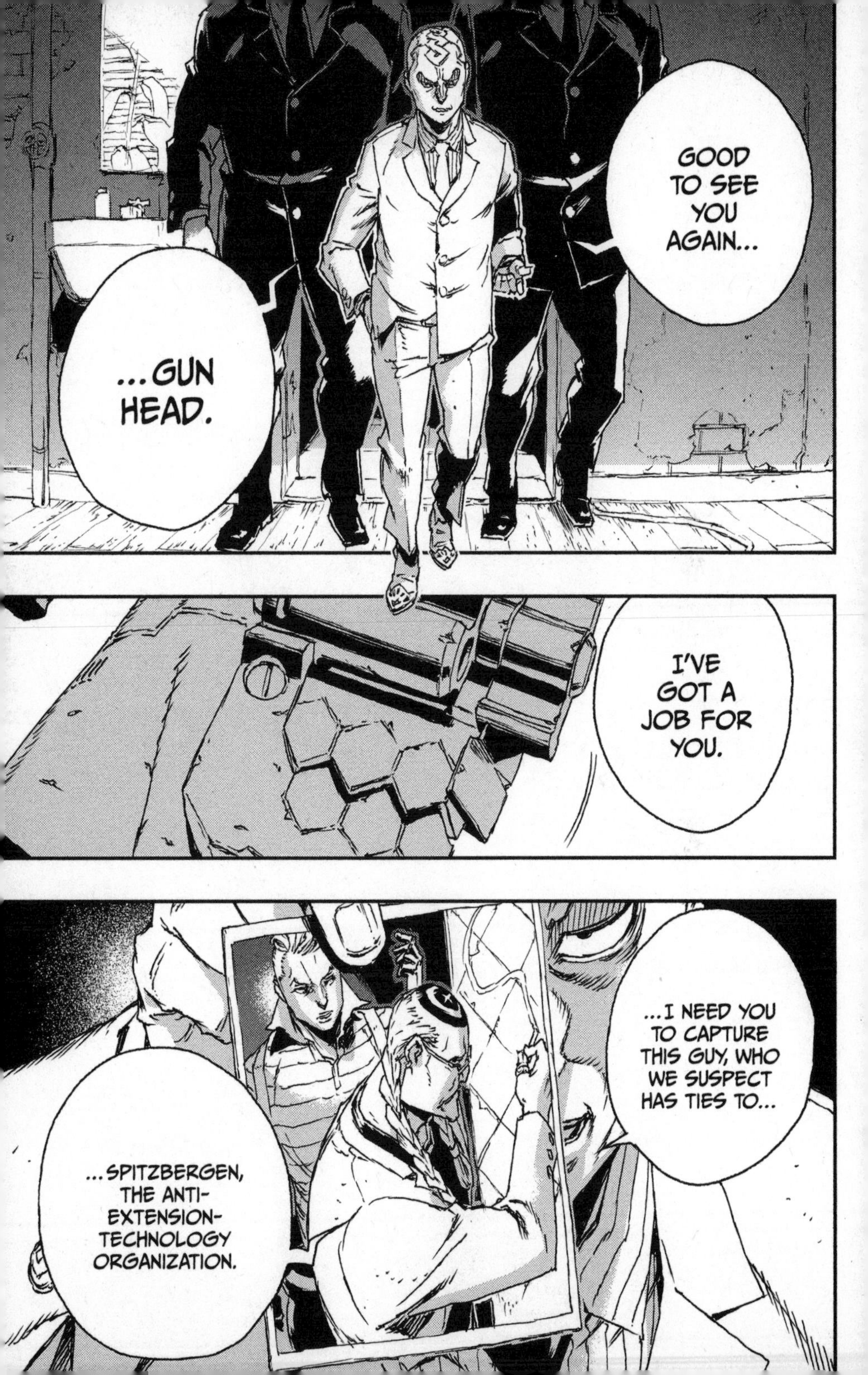
GOOD TO SEE YOU AGAIN...
...GUN HEAD.
I'VE GOT A JOB FOR YOU.
...I NEED YOU TO CAPTURE THIS GUY, WHO WE SUSPECT HAS TIES TO...
...SPITZBERGEN, THE ANTI-EXTENSION-TECHNOLOGY ORGANIZATION.

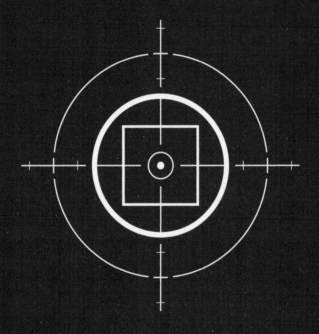

NO
GUNS
LIFE

Chapter 17
Shadow

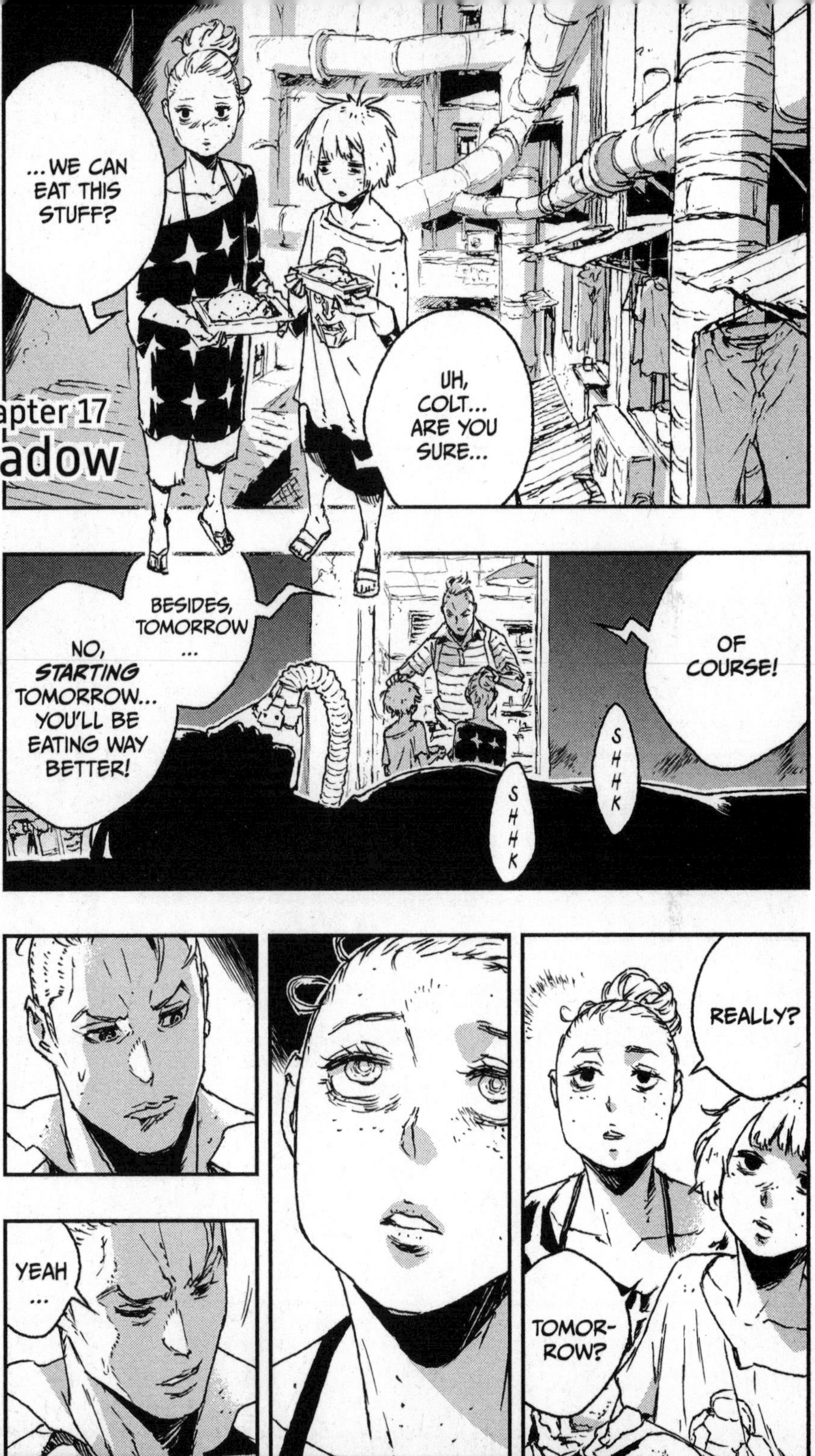
...WE CAN EAT THIS STUFF?
UH, COLT... ARE YOU SURE...
OF COURSE!
SHHK
SHHK
BESIDES, TOMORROW ...
NO, *STARTING* TOMORROW... YOU'LL BE EATING WAY BETTER!
REALLY?
TOMOR-ROW?
YEAH ...

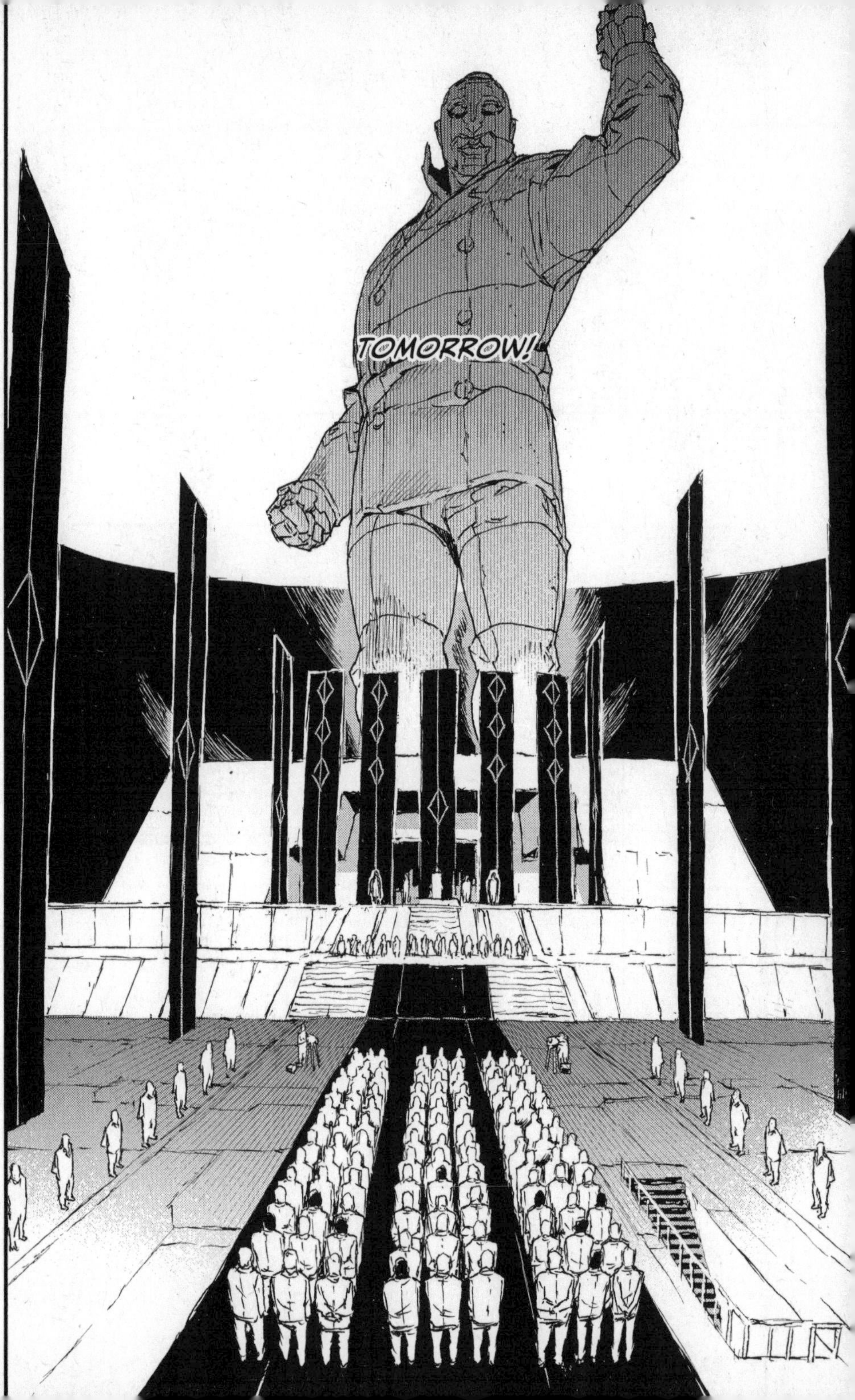
TOMORROW!

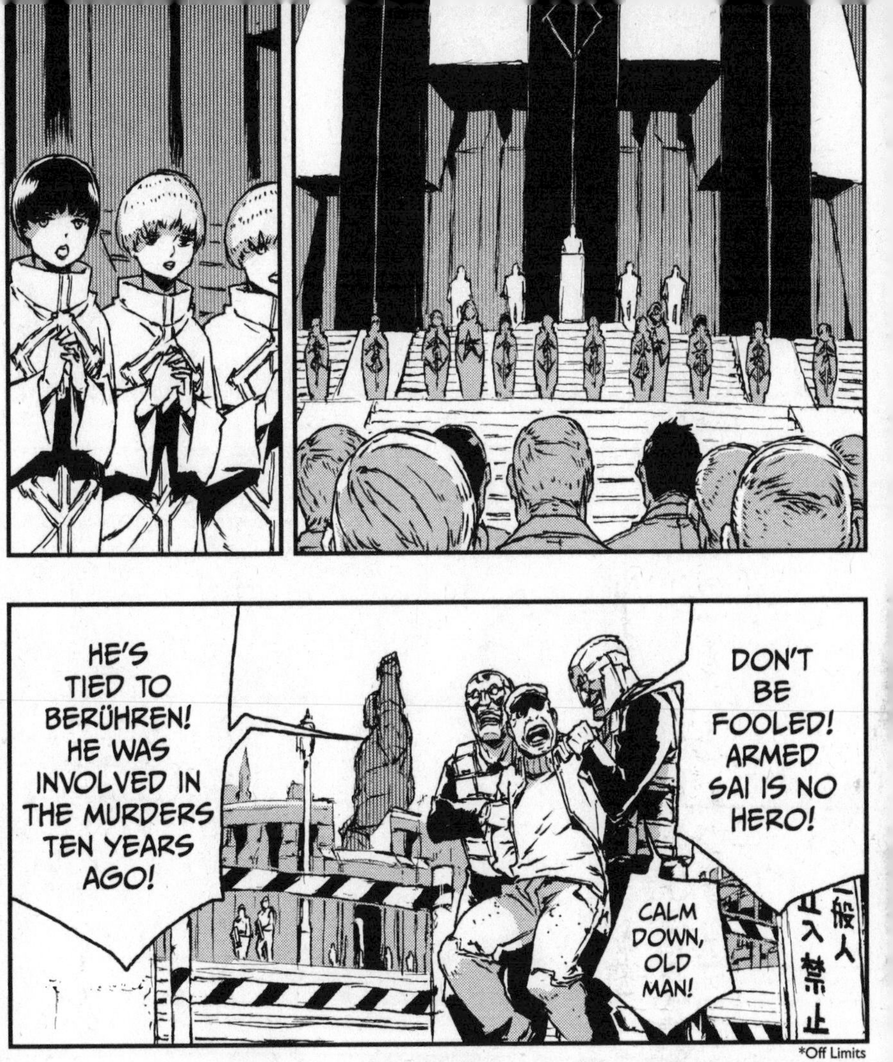
DON'T BE FOOLED! ARMED SAI IS NO HERO!
一般人立入禁止
CALM DOWN, OLD MAN!
HE'S TIED TO BERÜHREN! HE WAS INVOLVED IN THE MURDERS TEN YEARS AGO!
*Off Limits

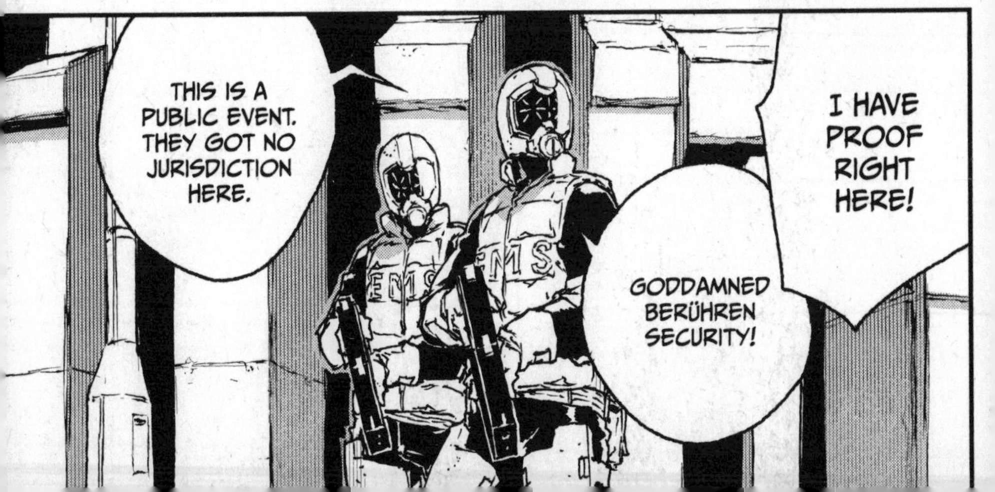
I HAVE PROOF RIGHT HERE!
GODDAMNED BERÜHREN SECURITY!
THIS IS A PUBLIC EVENT. THEY GOT NO JURISDICTION HERE.
EMS
EMS

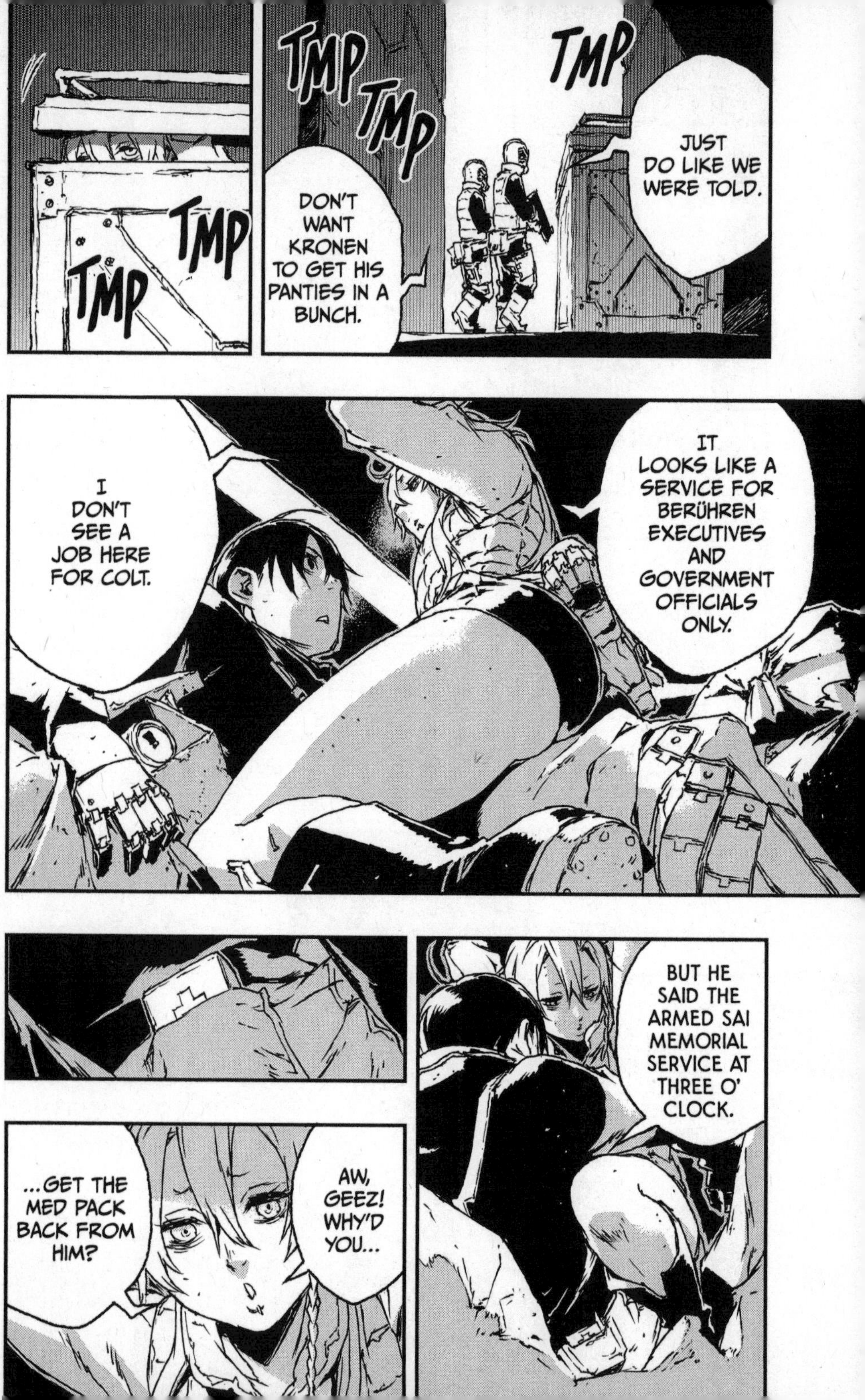
TMP
JUST DO LIKE WE WERE TOLD.
TMP TMP
DON'T WANT KRONEN TO GET HIS PANTIES IN A BUNCH.
TMP
TMP
IT LOOKS LIKE A SERVICE FOR BERÜHREN EXECUTIVES AND GOVERNMENT OFFICIALS ONLY.
I DON'T SEE A JOB HERE FOR COLT.
BUT HE SAID THE ARMED SAI MEMORIAL SERVICE AT THREE O' CLOCK.
AW, GEEZ! WHY'D YOU...
...GET THE MED PACK BACK FROM HIM?

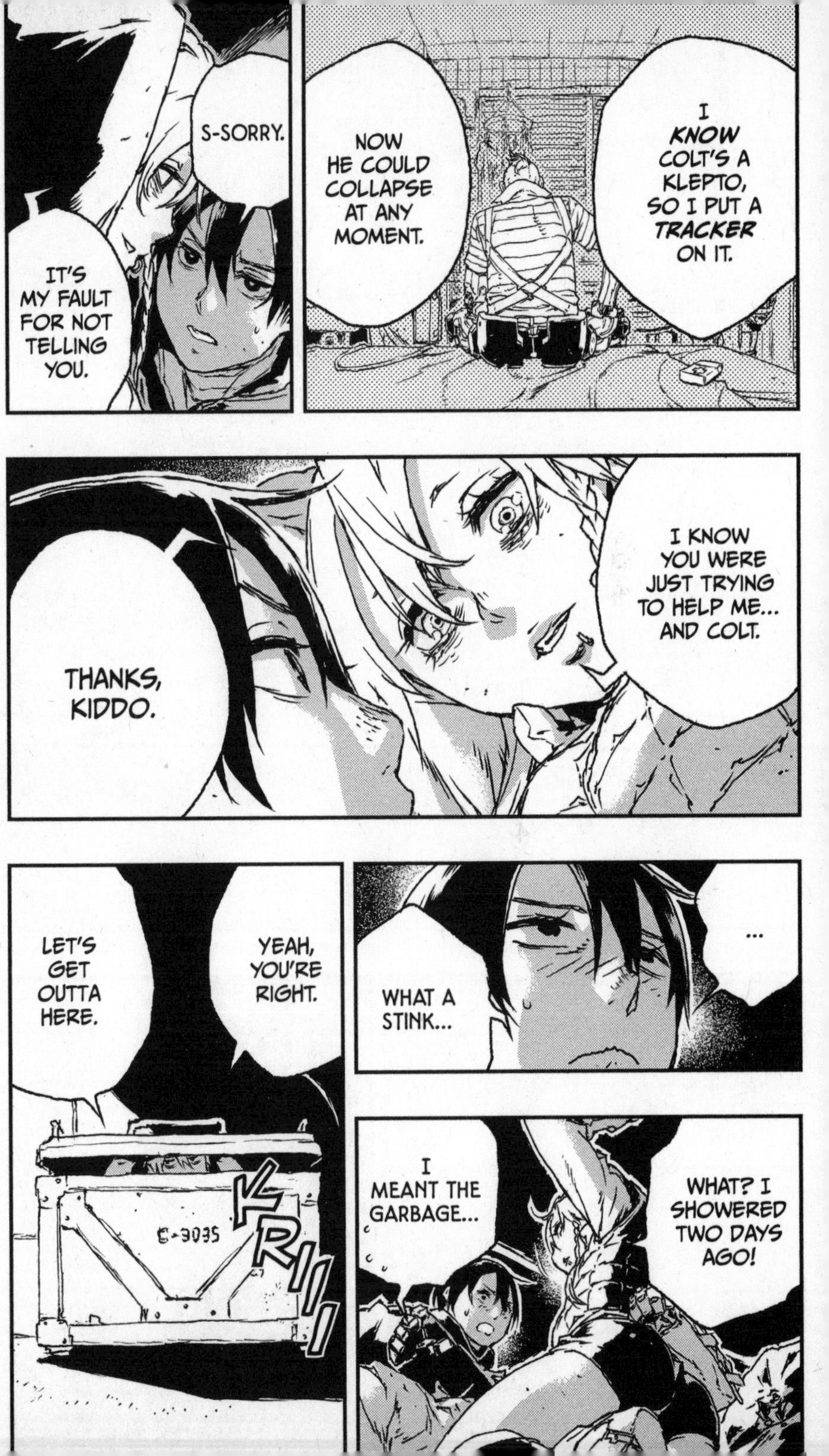
I KNOW COLT'S A KLEPTO, SO I PUT A TRACKER ON IT.
NOW HE COULD COLLAPSE AT ANY MOMENT.
S-SORRY.
IT'S MY FAULT FOR NOT TELLING YOU.
I KNOW YOU WERE JUST TRYING TO HELP ME... AND COLT.
THANKS, KIDDO.
...
WHAT A STINK...
WHAT? I SHOWERED TWO DAYS AGO!
I MEANT THE GARBAGE...
YEAH, YOU'RE RIGHT.
LET'S GET OUTTA HERE.
KRIII

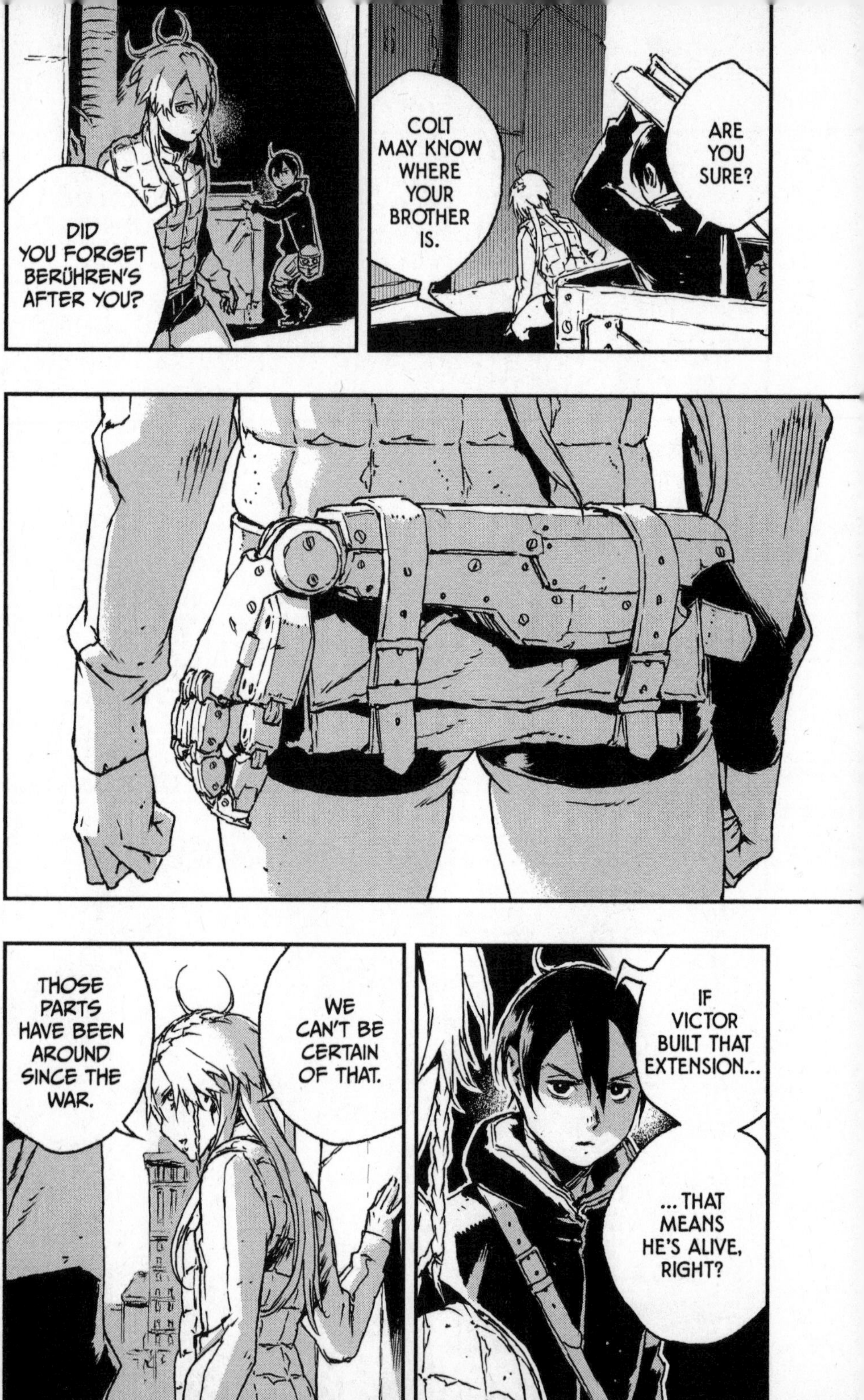
ARE YOU SURE?
COLT MAY KNOW WHERE YOUR BROTHER IS.
DID YOU FORGET BERÜHREN'S AFTER YOU?
IF VICTOR BUILT THAT EXTENSION...
... THAT MEANS HE'S ALIVE, RIGHT?
WE CAN'T BE CERTAIN OF THAT.
THOSE PARTS HAVE BEEN AROUND SINCE THE WAR.

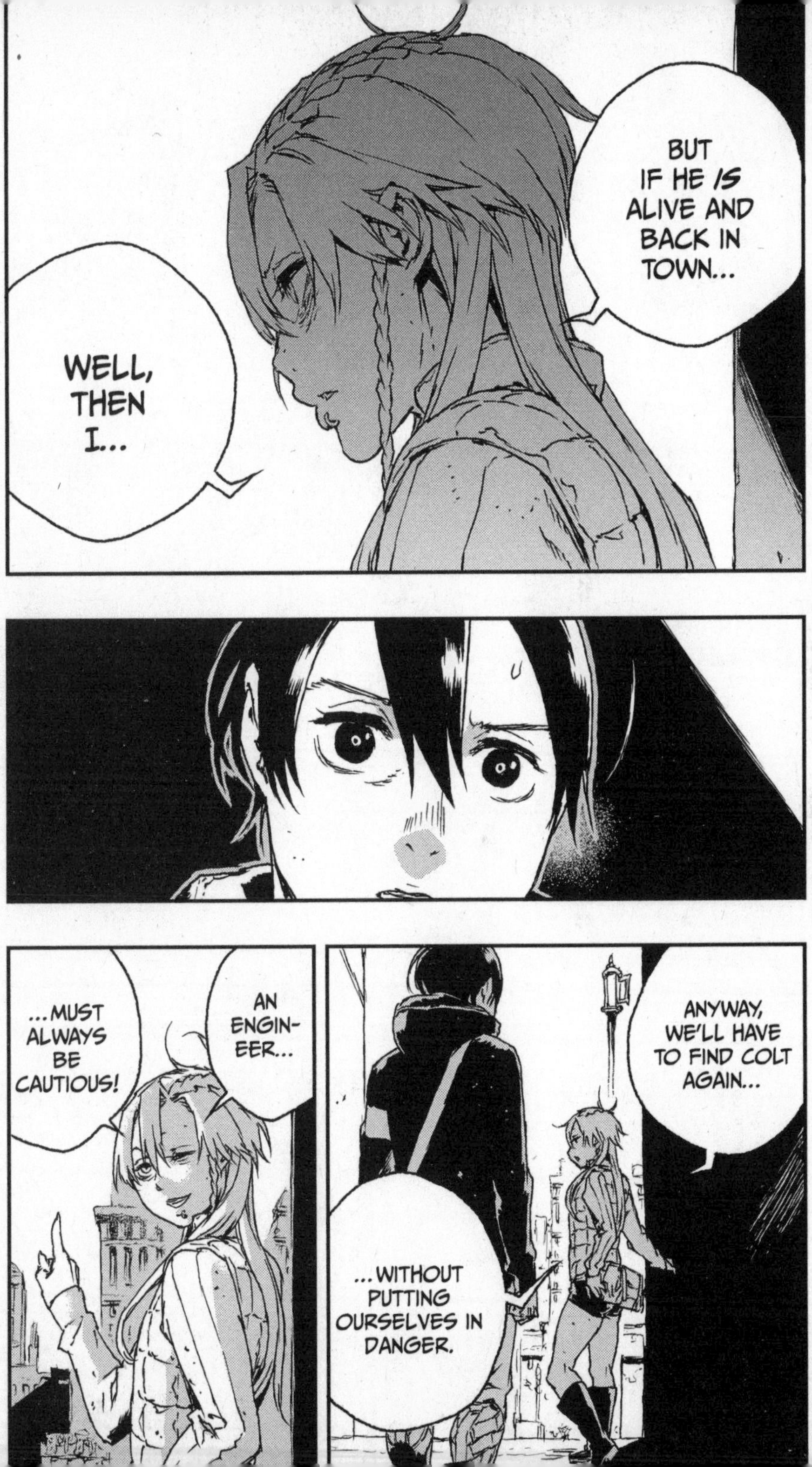
BUT IF HE *IS* ALIVE AND BACK IN TOWN...
WELL, THEN I...
ANYWAY, WE'LL HAVE TO FIND COLT AGAIN...
...WITHOUT PUTTING OURSELVES IN DANGER.
AN ENGIN-EER...
...MUST ALWAYS BE CAUTIOUS!

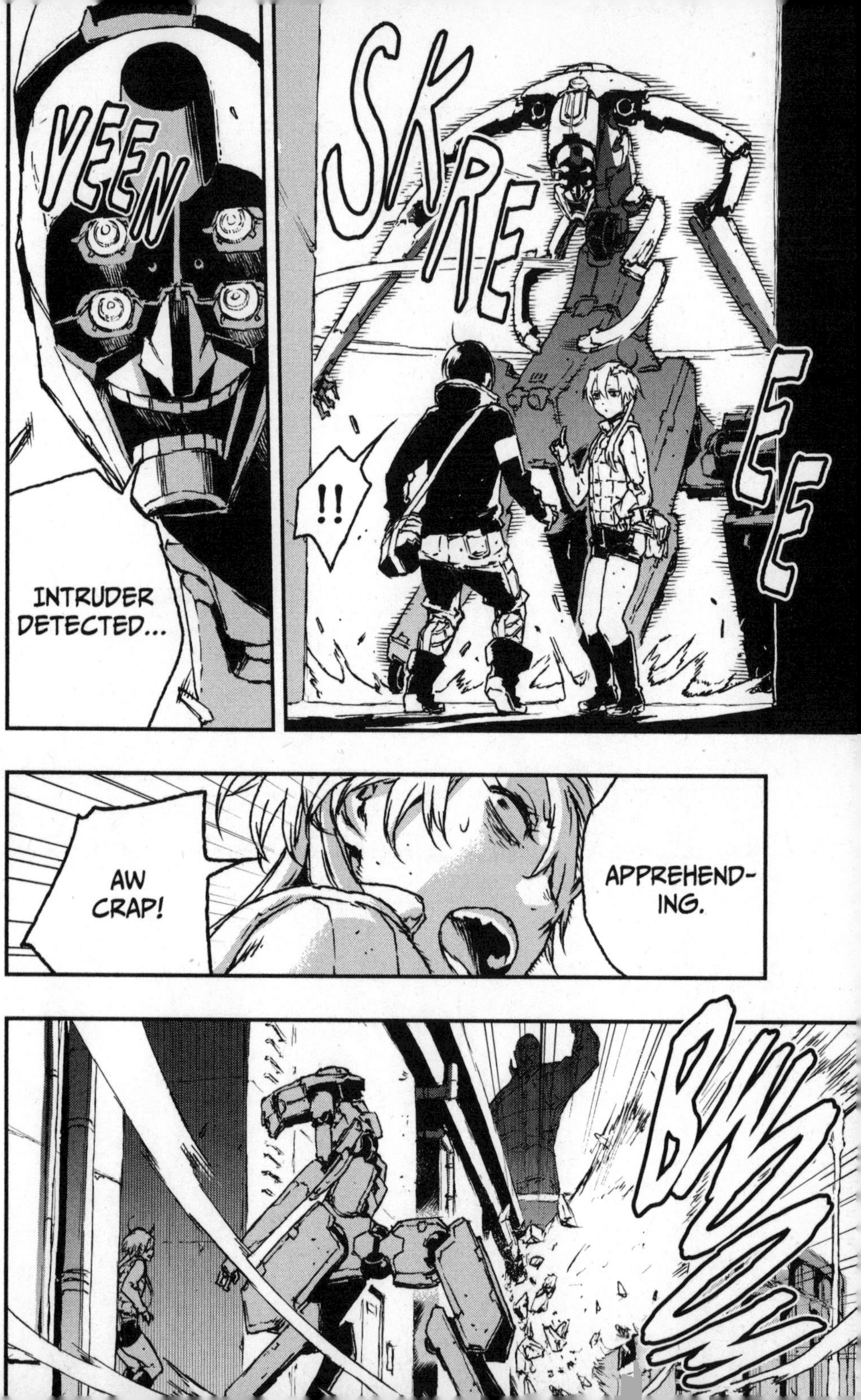
SKREEEE
!!
YEEN
INTRUDER DETECTED...
APPREHEND-ING.
AW CRAP!

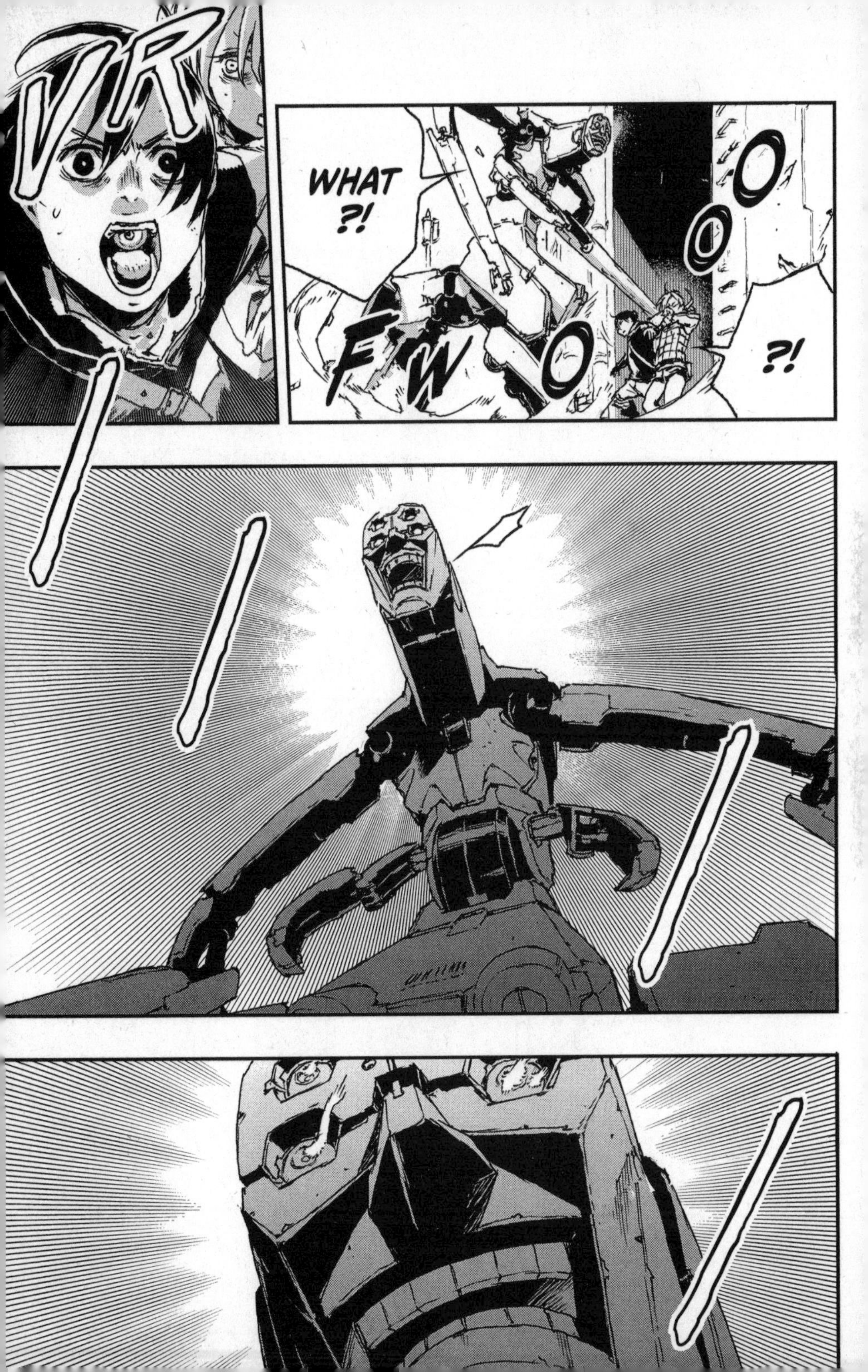
WHAT ?!
FWOOO
?!
VR

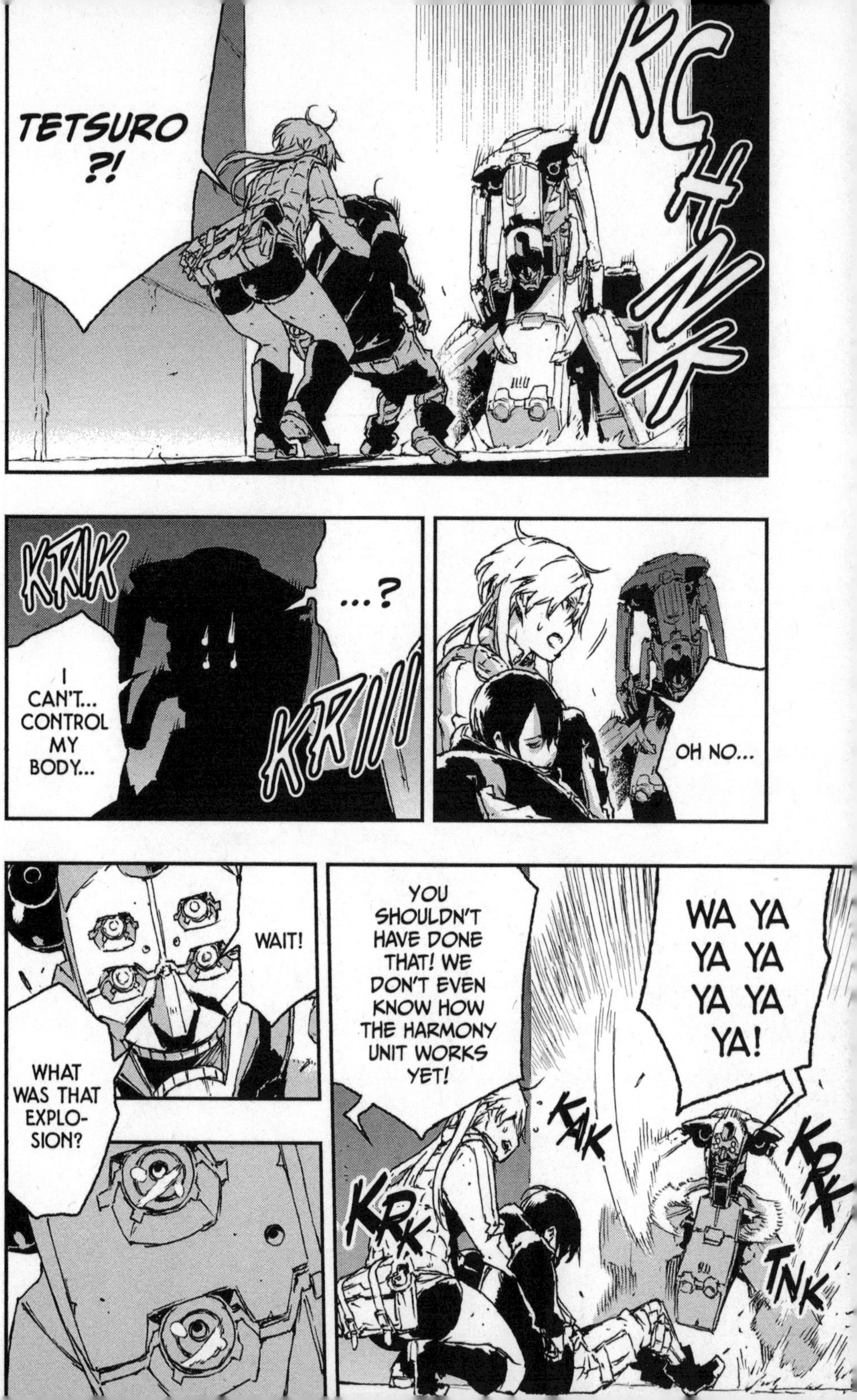
KCHNK
TETSURO ?!
OH NO...
...?
KRIK
I CAN'T... CONTROL MY BODY...
KRIII
WA YA YA YA YA YA YA!
YOU SHOULDN'T HAVE DONE THAT! WE DON'T EVEN KNOW HOW THE HARMONY UNIT WORKS YET!
KAK
KRK
TNK
KRK
WAIT!
WHAT WAS THAT EXPLOSION?

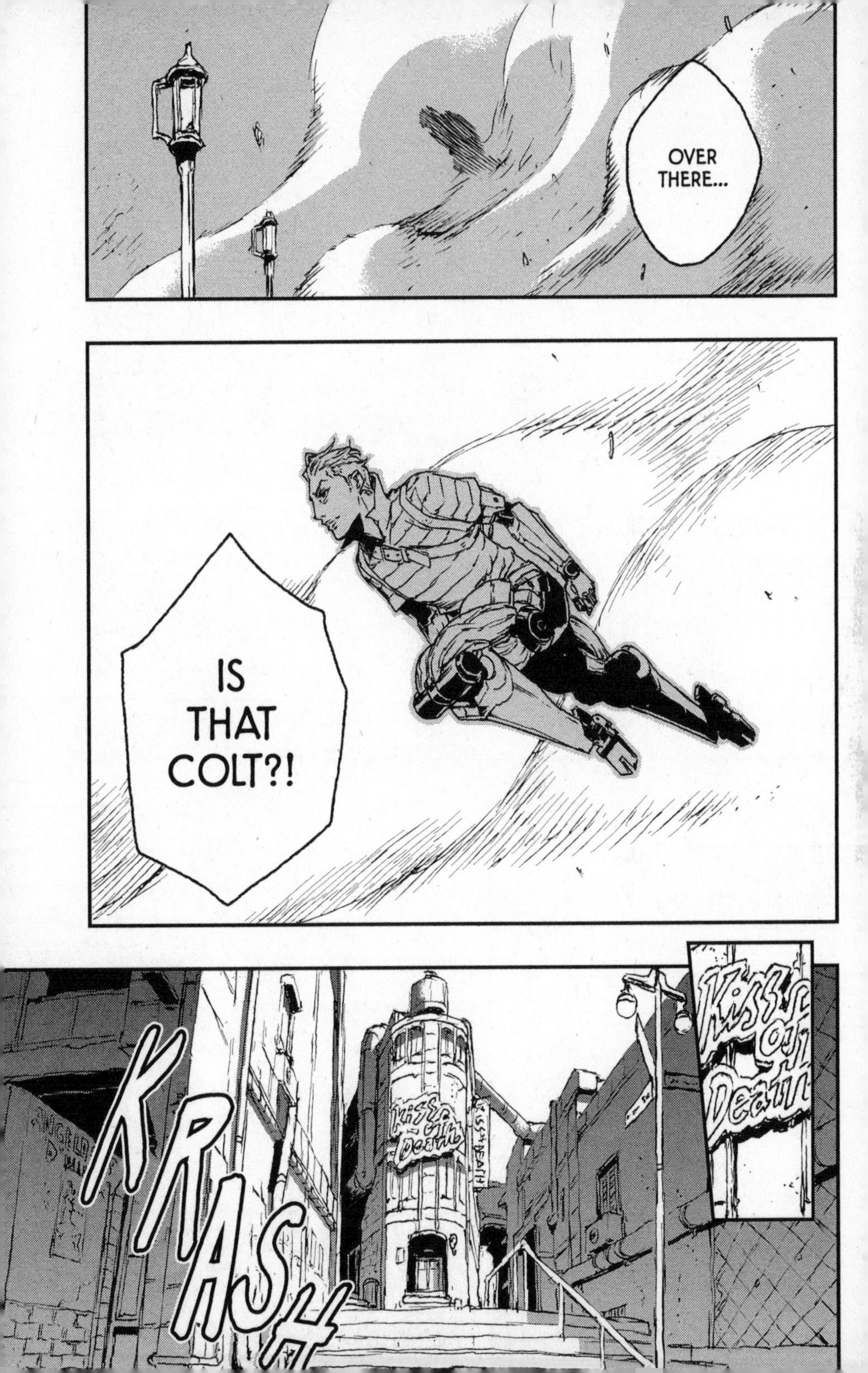
OVER THERE...
IS THAT COLT?!
Kiss of Death
KRASH

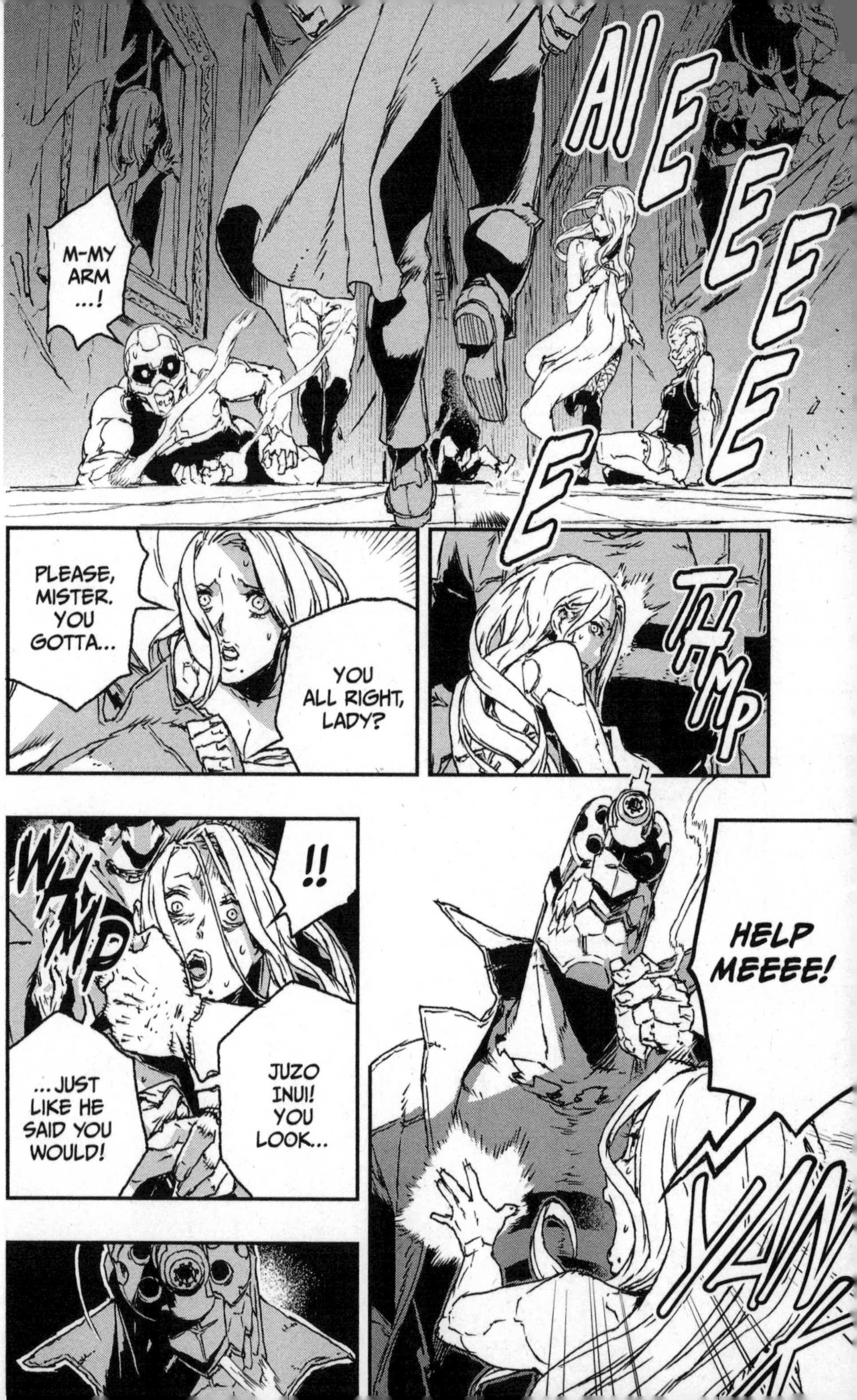
AIEEEEEE
M-MY ARM ...!
THUMP
YOU ALL RIGHT, LADY?
PLEASE, MISTER. YOU GOTTA...
HELP MEEEEE!
YANK
!!
WHUMP
JUZO INUI! YOU LOOK...
...JUST LIKE HE SAID YOU WOULD!

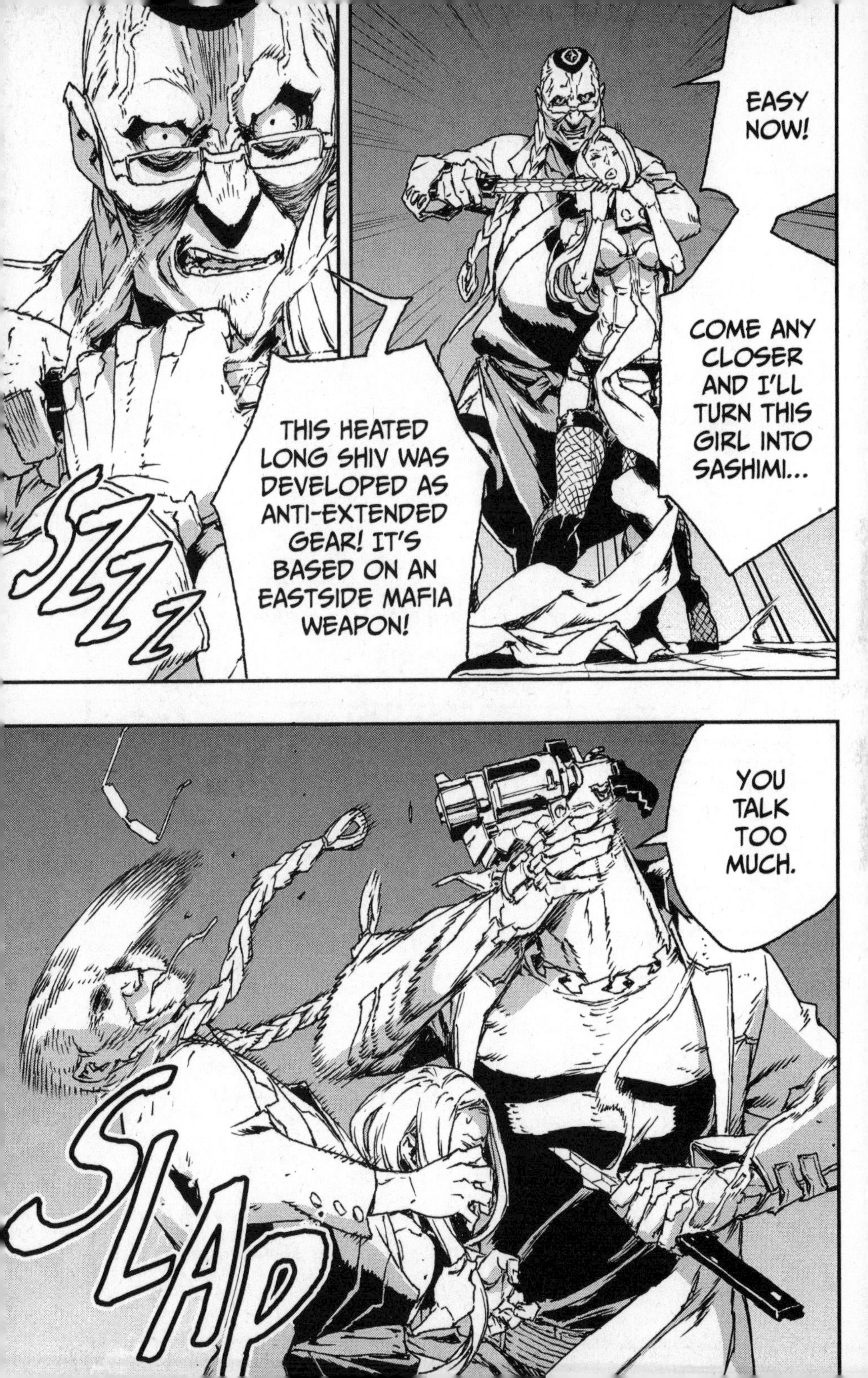
EASY NOW!
COME ANY CLOSER AND I'LL TURN THIS GIRL INTO SASHIMI...
THIS HEATED LONG SHIV WAS DEVELOPED AS ANTI-EXTENDED GEAR! IT'S BASED ON AN EASTSIDE MAFIA WEAPON!
SZZZ
YOU TALK TOO MUCH.
SLAP

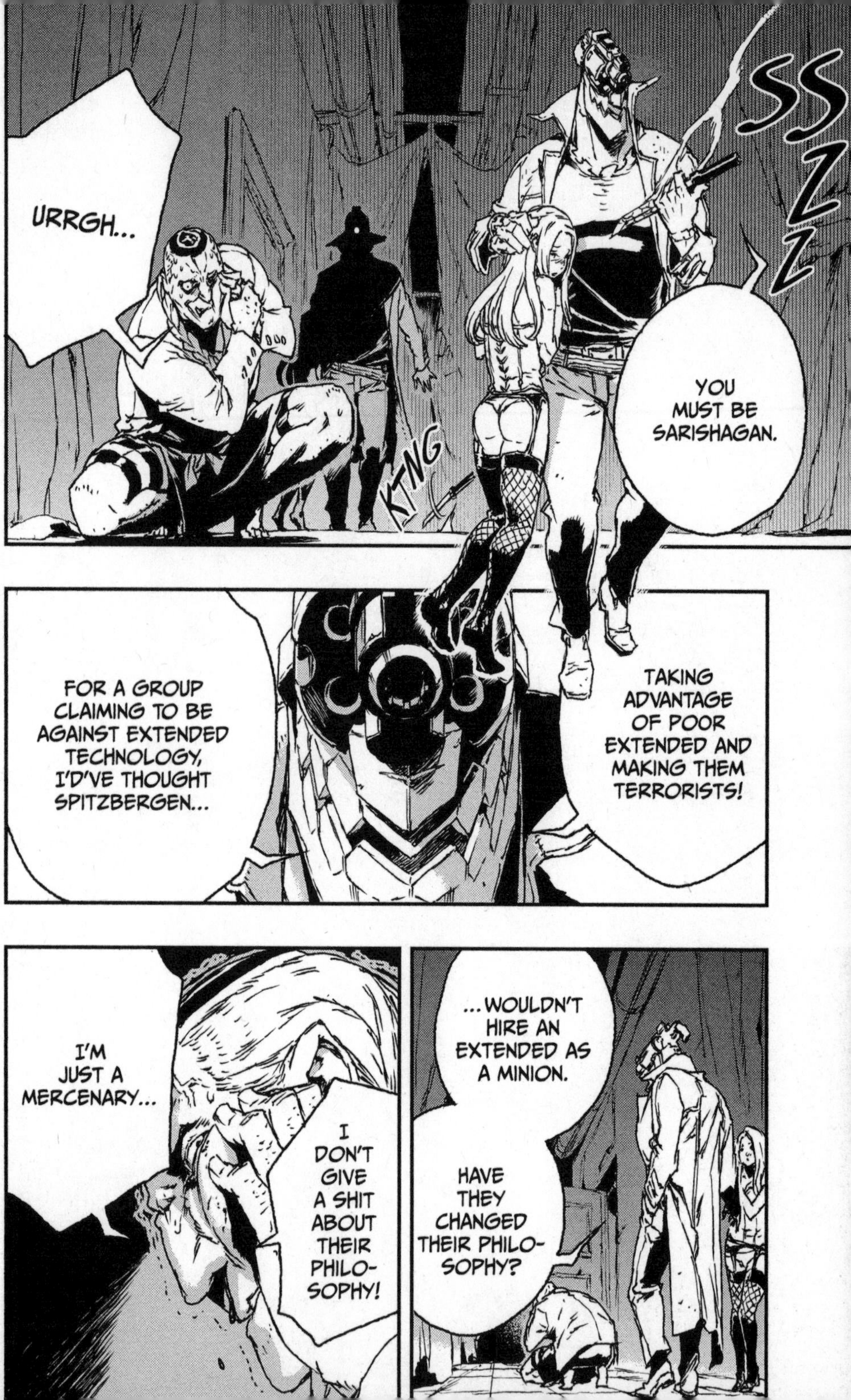
SSZZZ
YOU MUST BE SARISHAGAN.
K-TNG
URRGH...
TAKING ADVANTAGE OF POOR EXTENDED AND MAKING THEM TERRORISTS!
FOR A GROUP CLAIMING TO BE AGAINST EXTENDED TECHNOLOGY, I'D'VE THOUGHT SPITZBERGEN...
...WOULDN'T HIRE AN EXTENDED AS A MINION.
HAVE THEY CHANGED THEIR PHILO-SOPHY?
I'M JUST A MERCENARY...
I DON'T GIVE A SHIT ABOUT THEIR PHILO-SOPHY!

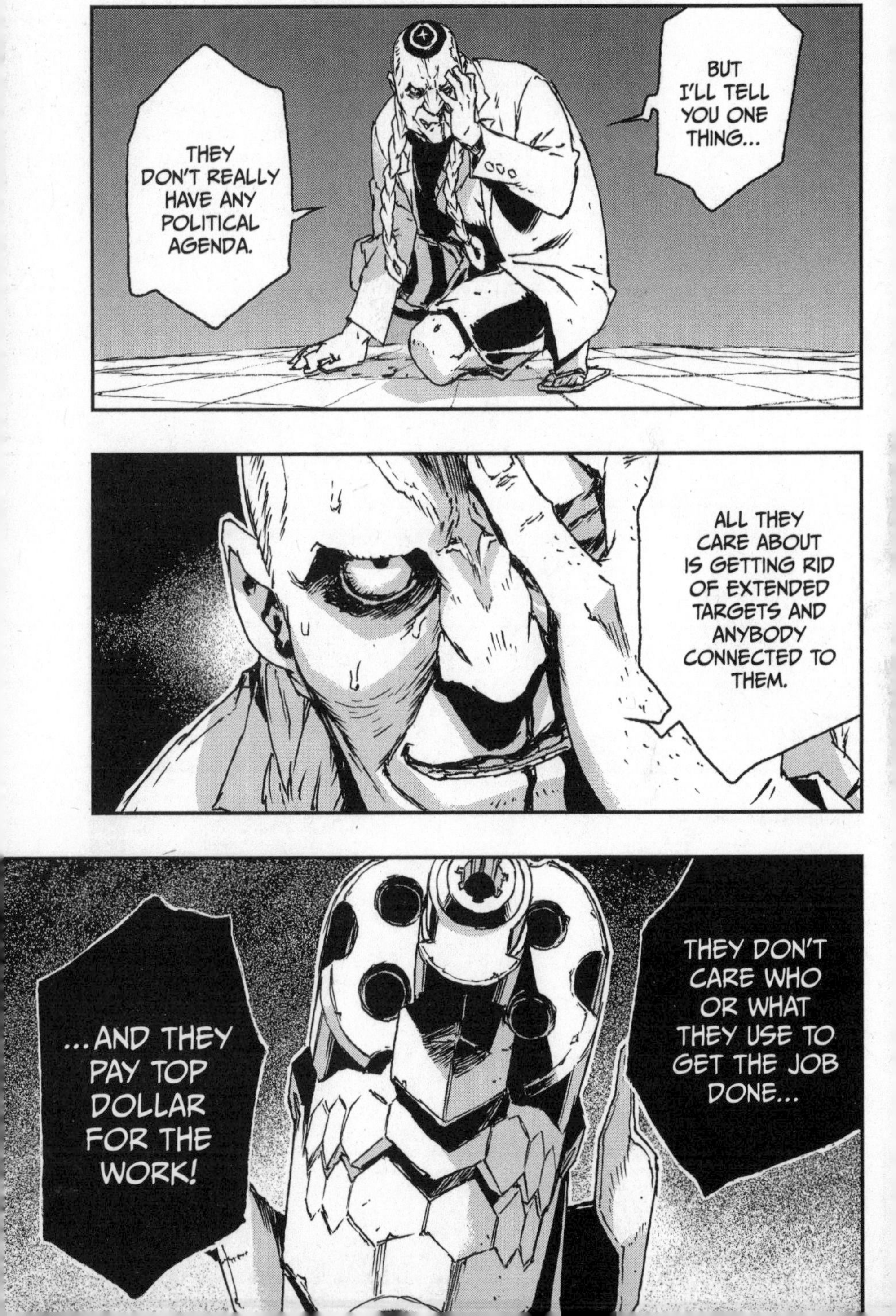
BUT I'LL TELL YOU ONE THING...
THEY DON'T REALLY HAVE ANY POLITICAL AGENDA.
ALL THEY CARE ABOUT IS GETTING RID OF EXTENDED TARGETS AND ANYBODY CONNECTED TO THEM.
THEY DON'T CARE WHO OR WHAT THEY USE TO GET THE JOB DONE...
...AND THEY PAY TOP DOLLAR FOR THE WORK!

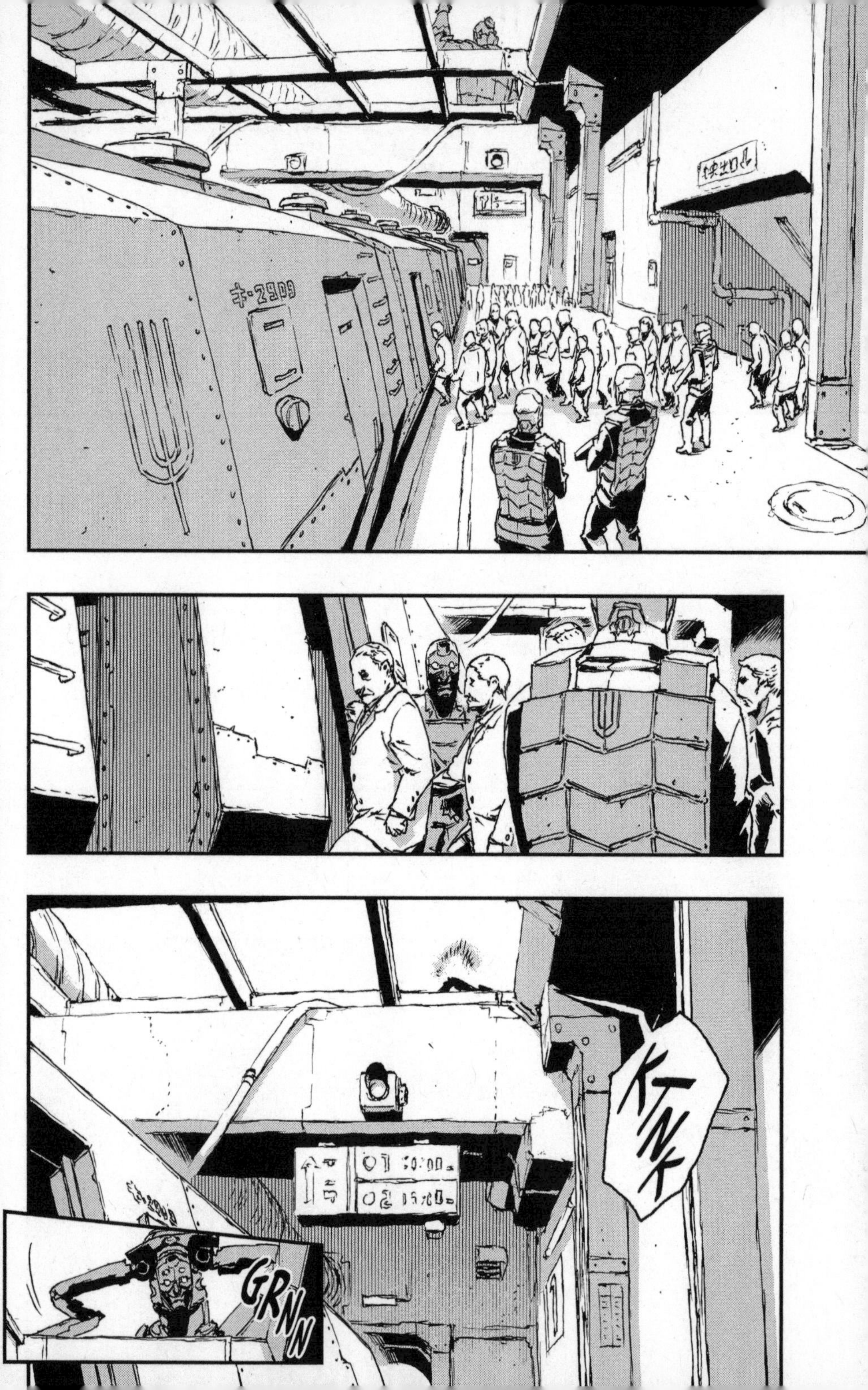
KTINK
GRNN

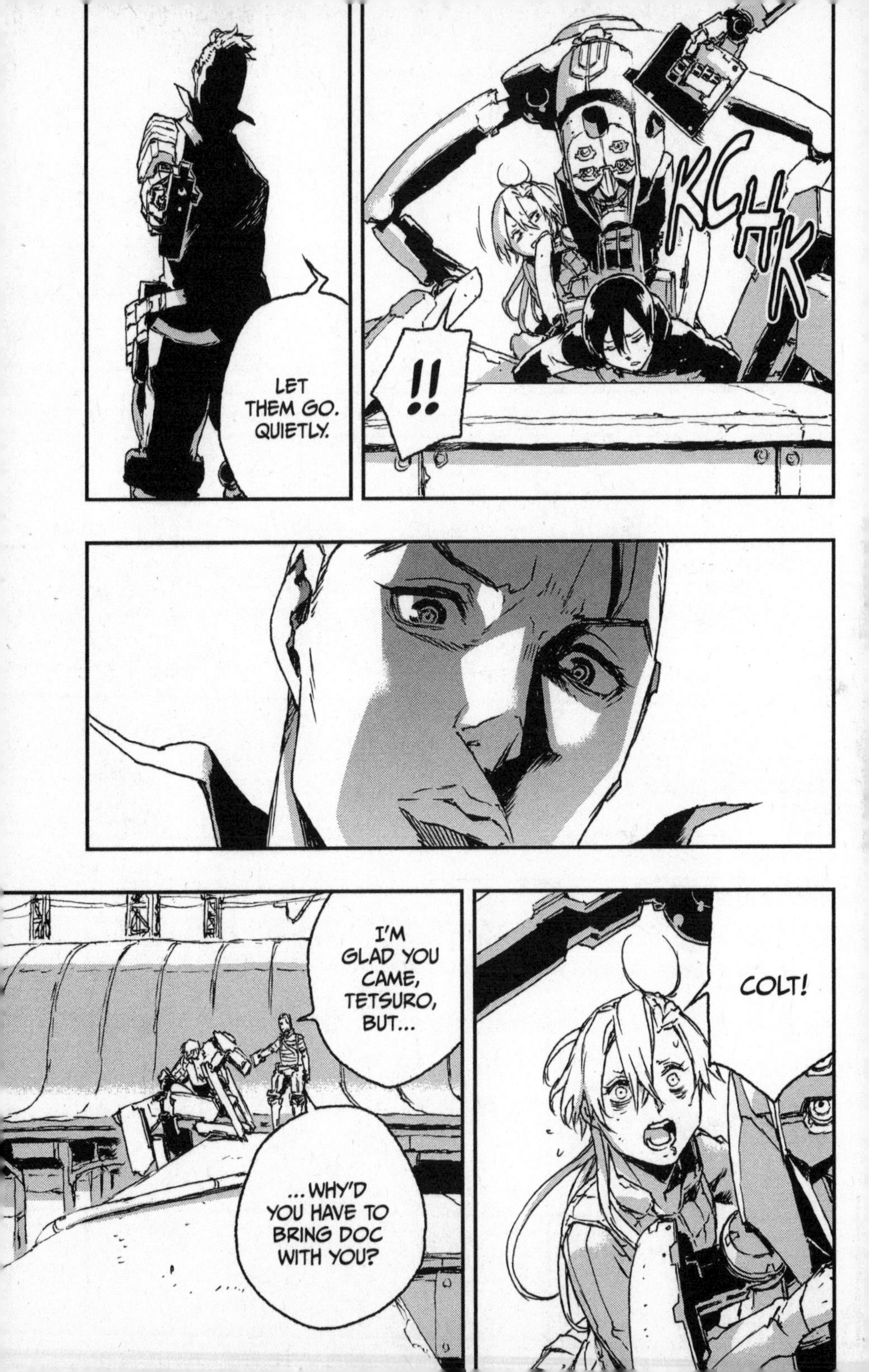
KCHK
!!
LET THEM GO. QUIETLY.
COLT!
I'M GLAD YOU CAME, TETSURO, BUT...
...WHY'D YOU HAVE TO BRING DOC WITH YOU?

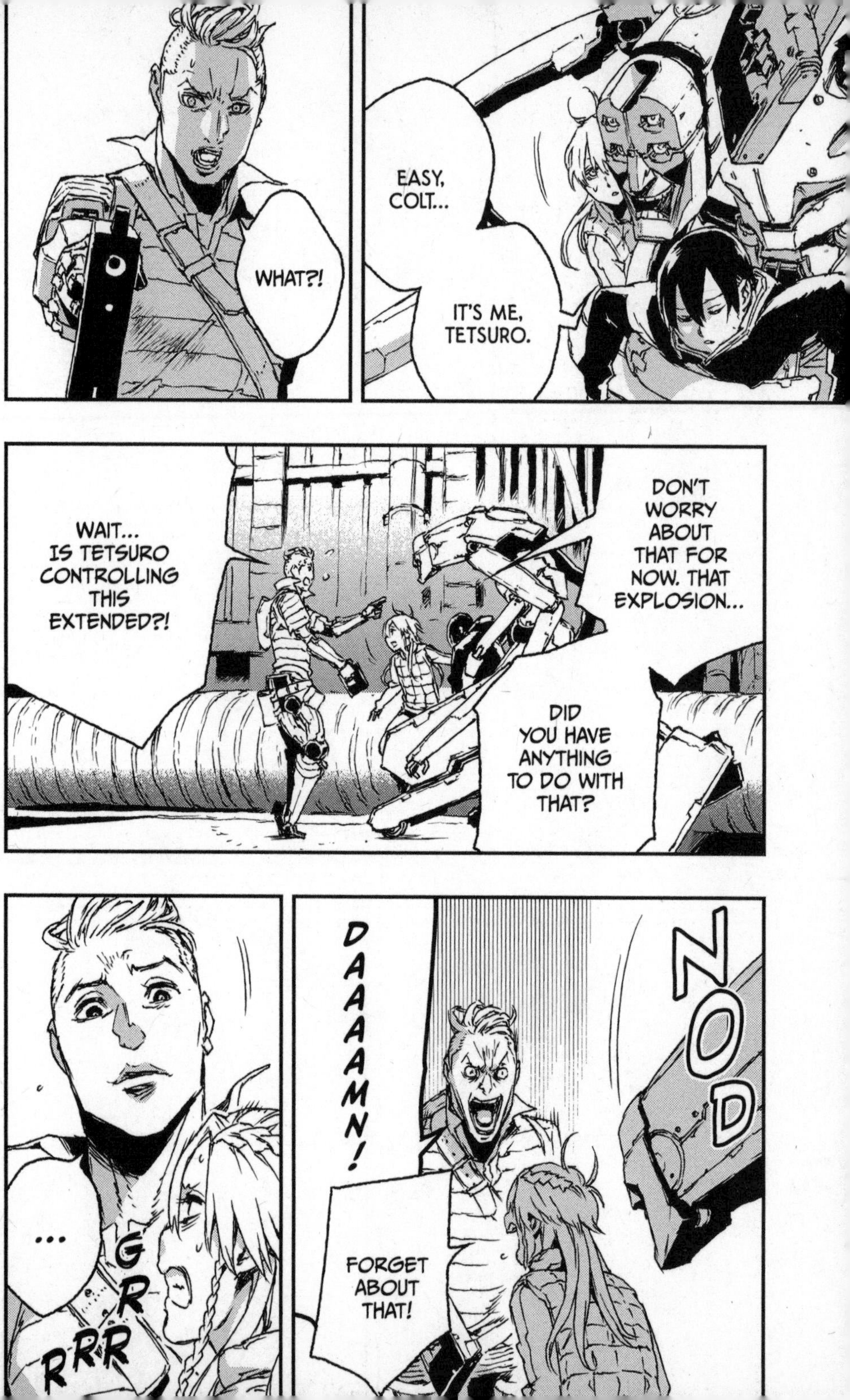
EASY, COLT...
IT'S ME, TETSURO.
WHAT?!
WAIT... IS TETSURO CONTROLLING THIS EXTENDED?!
DON'T WORRY ABOUT THAT FOR NOW. THAT EXPLOSION...
DID YOU HAVE ANYTHING TO DO WITH THAT?
ZOOD
DAAAAAMN!
FORGET ABOUT THAT!
...
GRRRRR

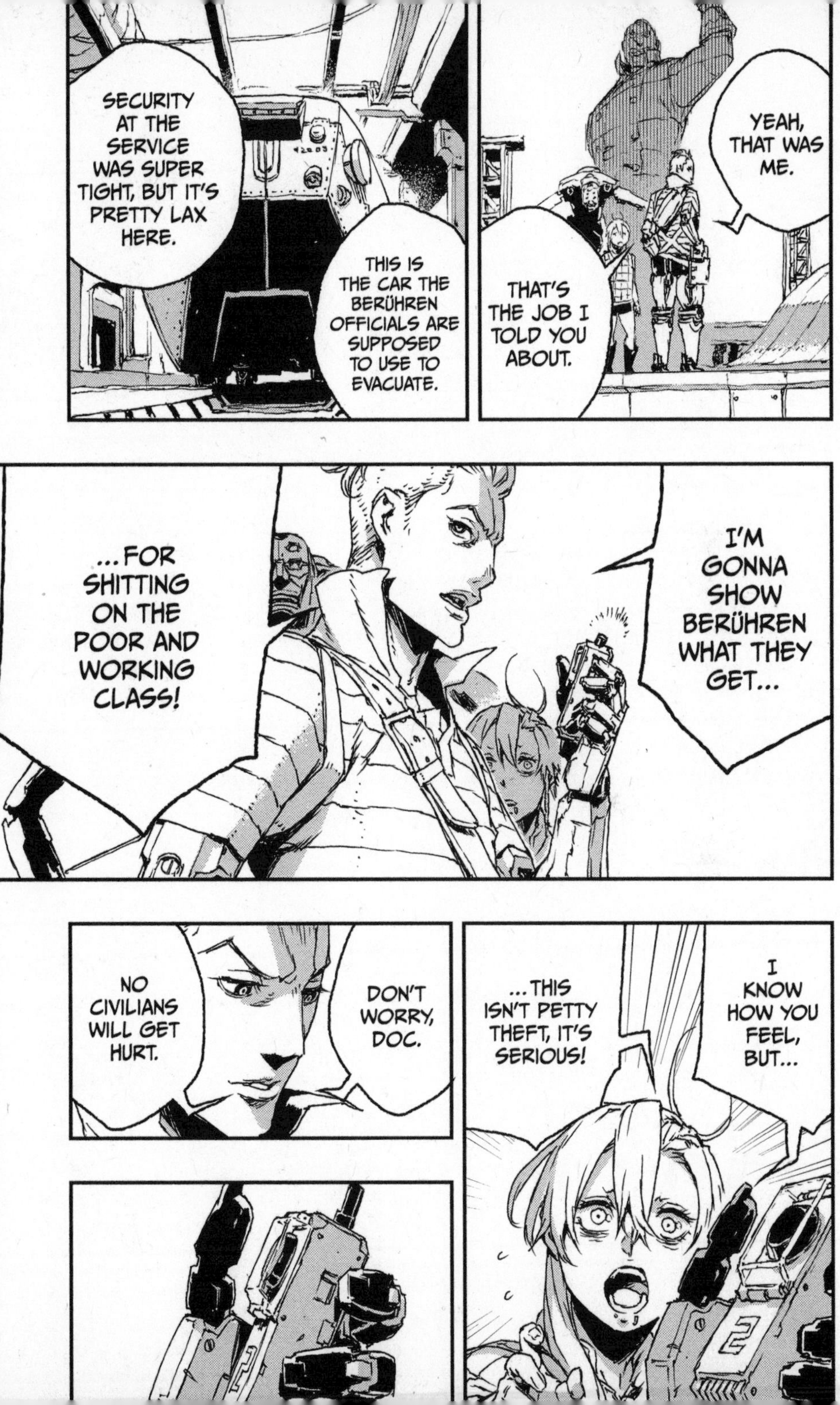
YEAH, THAT WAS ME.
THAT'S THE JOB I TOLD YOU ABOUT.
SECURITY AT THE SERVICE WAS SUPER TIGHT, BUT IT'S PRETTY LAX HERE.
THIS IS THE CAR THE BERÜHREN OFFICIALS ARE SUPPOSED TO USE TO EVACUATE.
I'M GONNA SHOW BERÜHREN WHAT THEY GET...
...FOR SHITTING ON THE POOR AND WORKING CLASS!
I KNOW HOW YOU FEEL, BUT...
...THIS ISN'T PETTY THEFT, IT'S SERIOUS!
DON'T WORRY, DOC.
NO CIVILIANS WILL GET HURT.

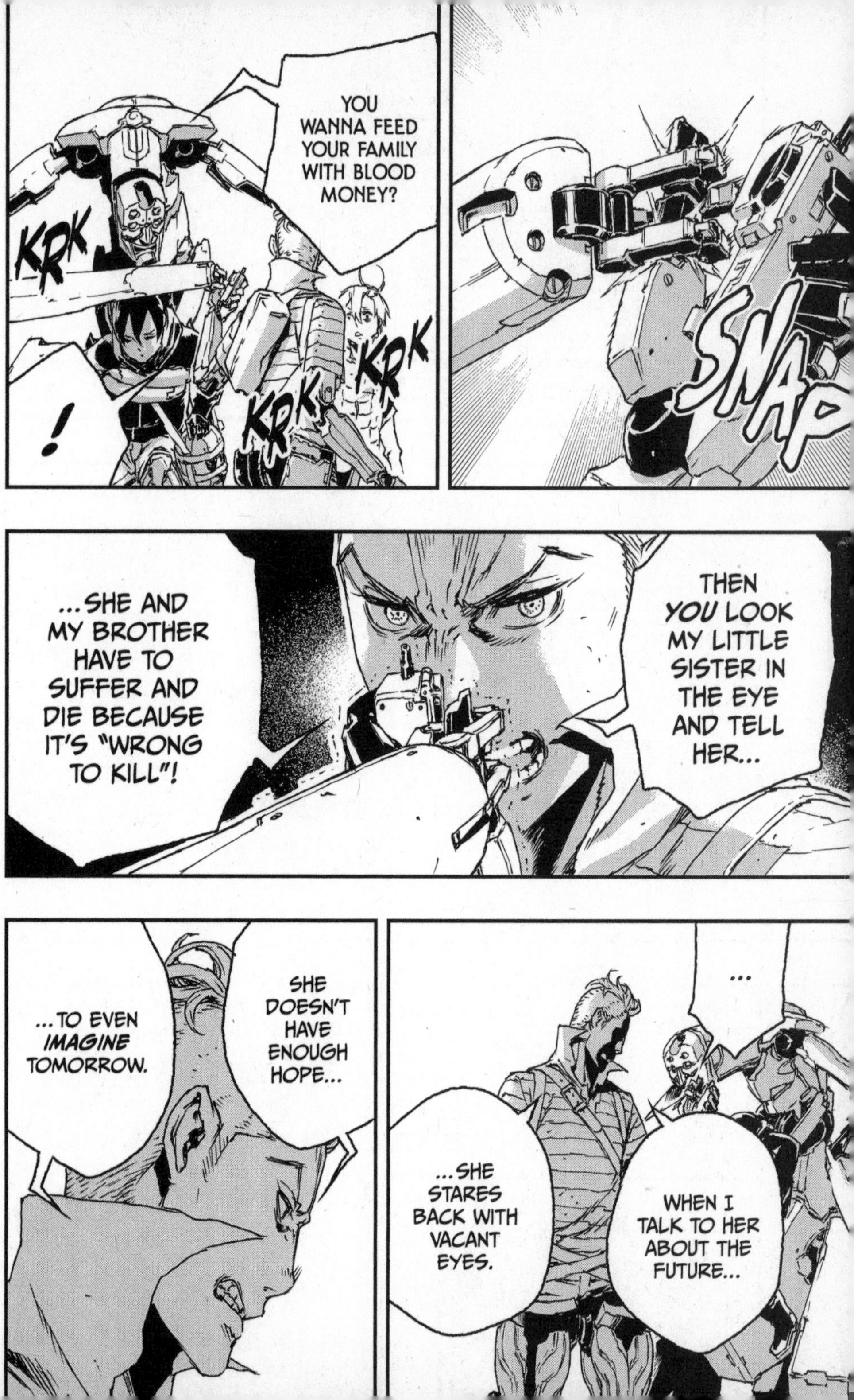
SNAP
YOU WANNA FEED YOUR FAMILY WITH BLOOD MONEY?
KRK
KRK
KRK
!
THEN *YOU* LOOK MY LITTLE SISTER IN THE EYE AND TELL HER...
...SHE AND MY BROTHER HAVE TO SUFFER AND DIE BECAUSE IT'S "WRONG TO KILL"!
...
WHEN I TALK TO HER ABOUT THE FUTURE...
...SHE STARES BACK WITH VACANT EYES.
SHE DOESN'T HAVE ENOUGH HOPE...
...TO EVEN *IMAGINE* TOMORROW.

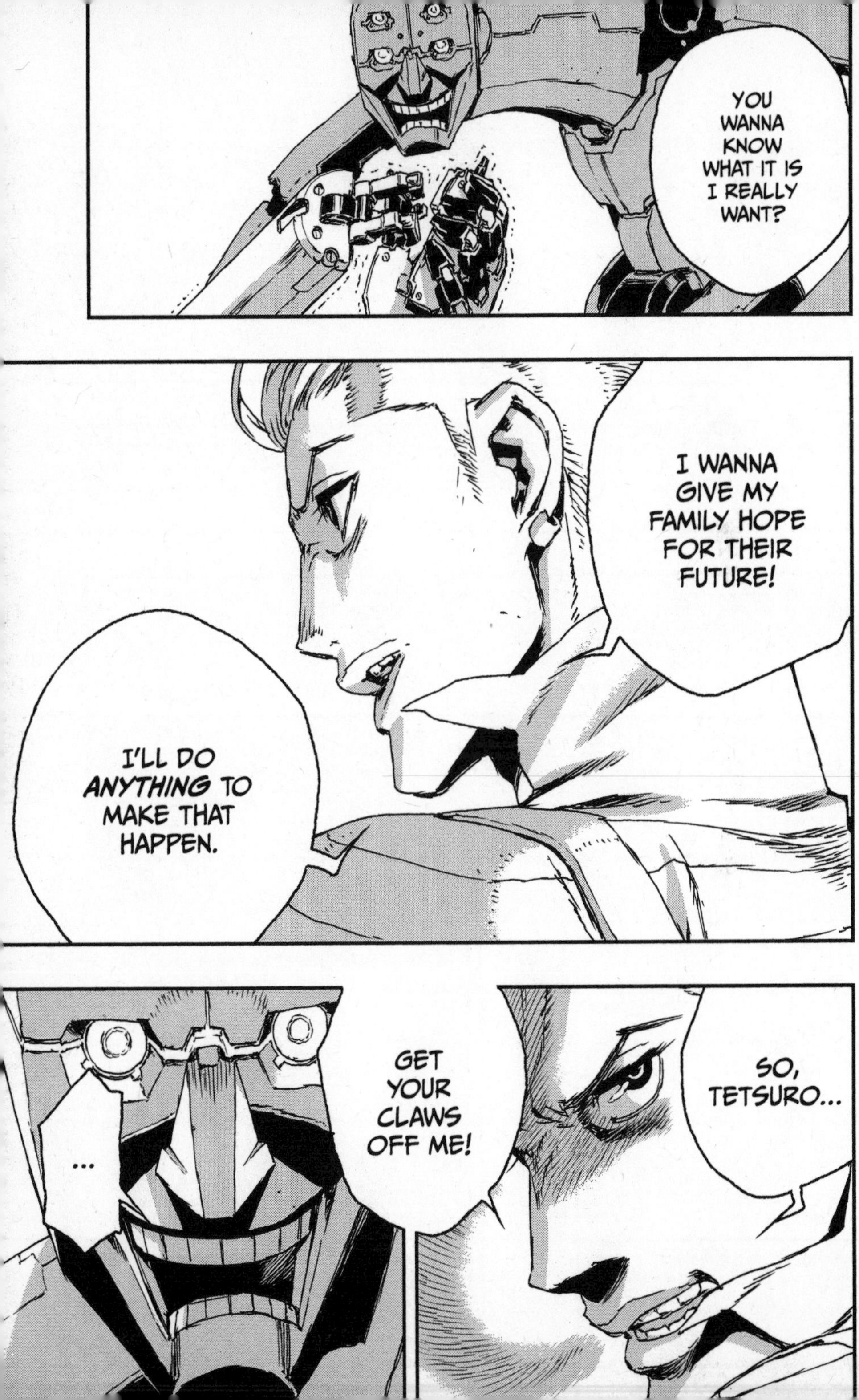
YOU WANNA KNOW WHAT IT IS I REALLY WANT?
I WANNA GIVE MY FAMILY HOPE FOR THEIR FUTURE!
I'LL DO *ANYTHING* TO MAKE THAT HAPPEN.
SO, TETSURO...
GET YOUR CLAWS OFF ME!
...

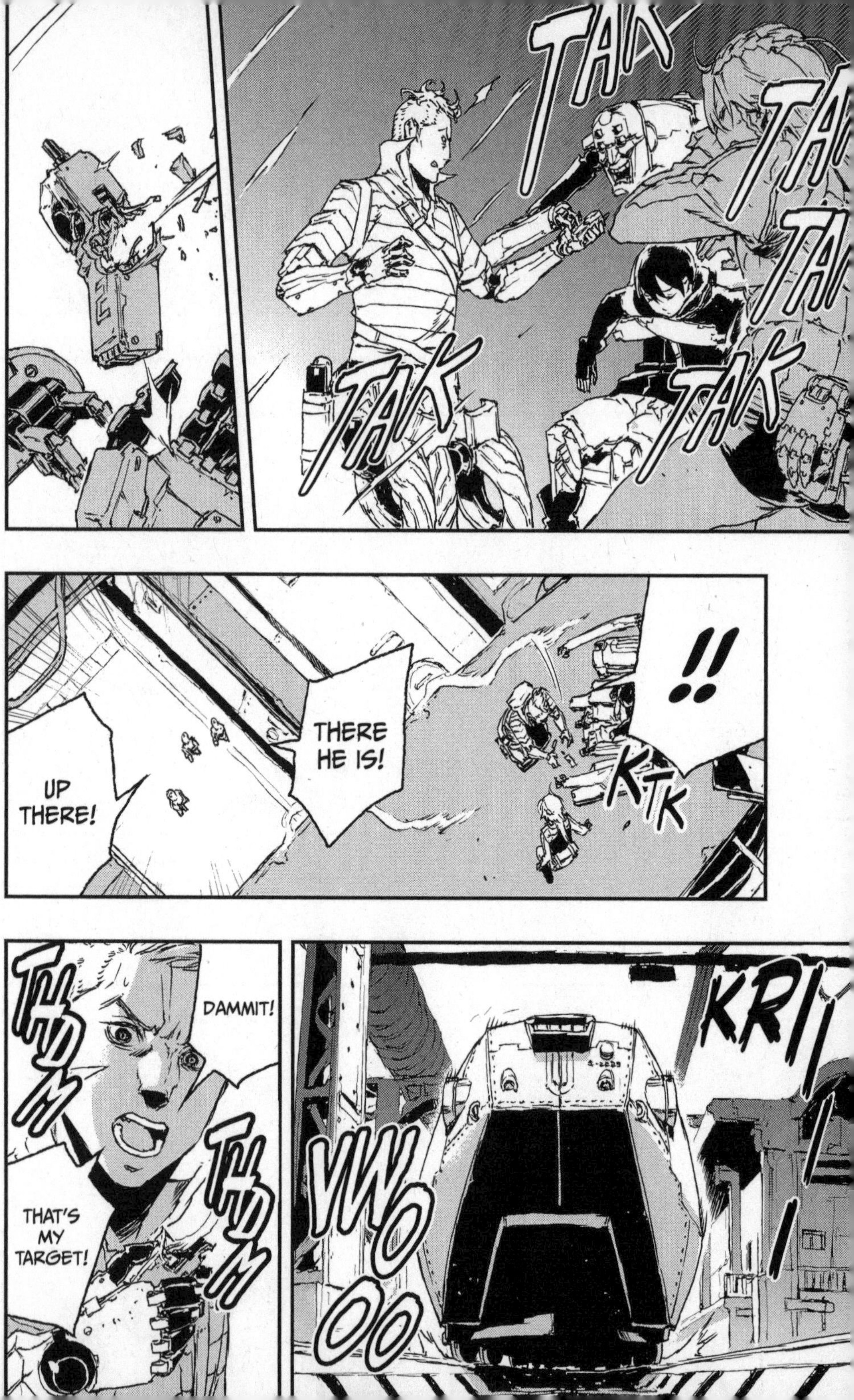
TAK
TAK
TAK
!!
KTK
THERE HE IS!
UP THERE!
KRIIII
VWOOO
THOM
DAMMIT!
THOM
THAT'S MY TARGET!

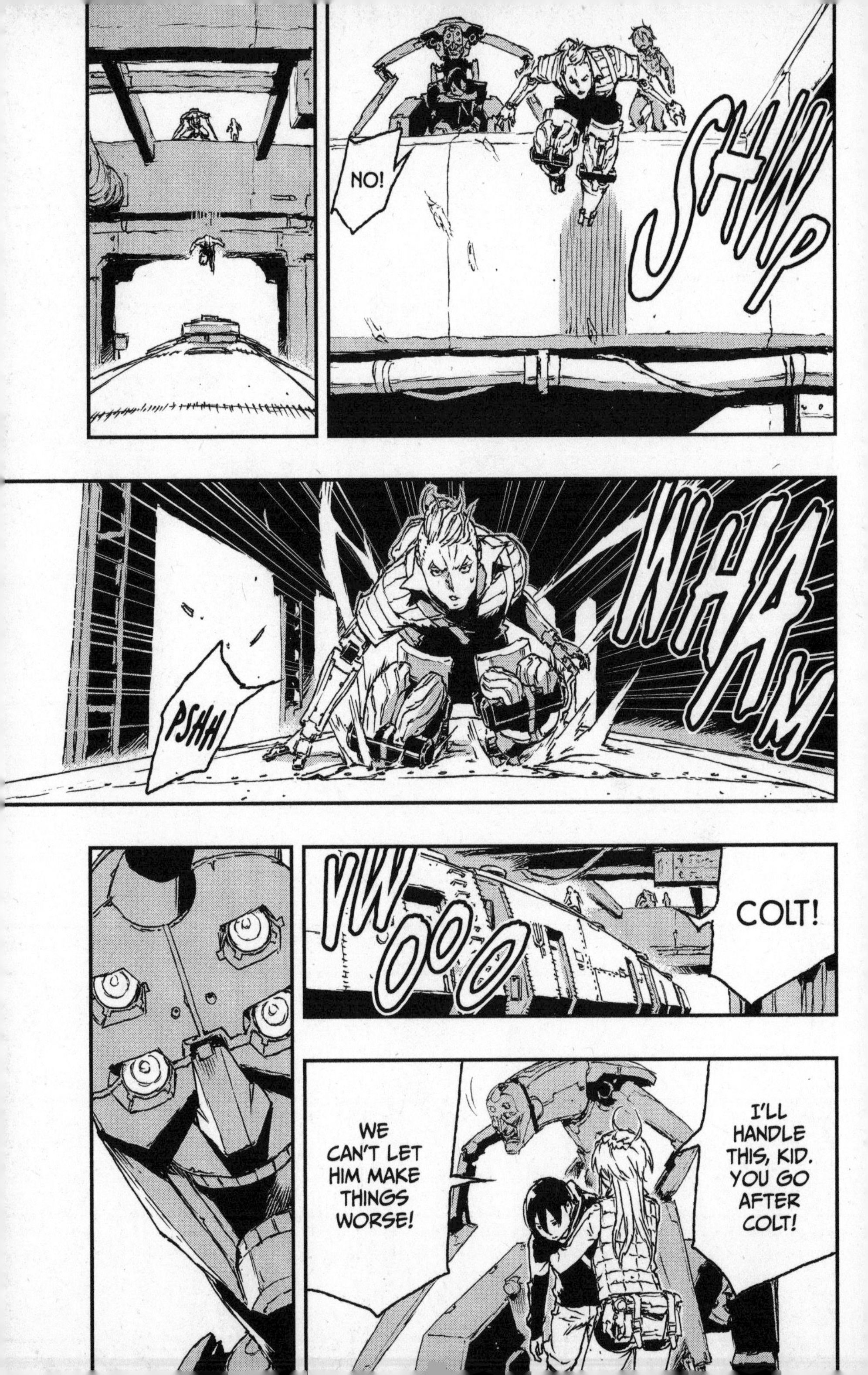

NO!
SHWP
WHAM
PSHH
COLT!
VWOOO
I'LL HANDLE THIS, KID. YOU GO AFTER COLT!
WE CAN'T LET HIM MAKE THINGS WORSE!

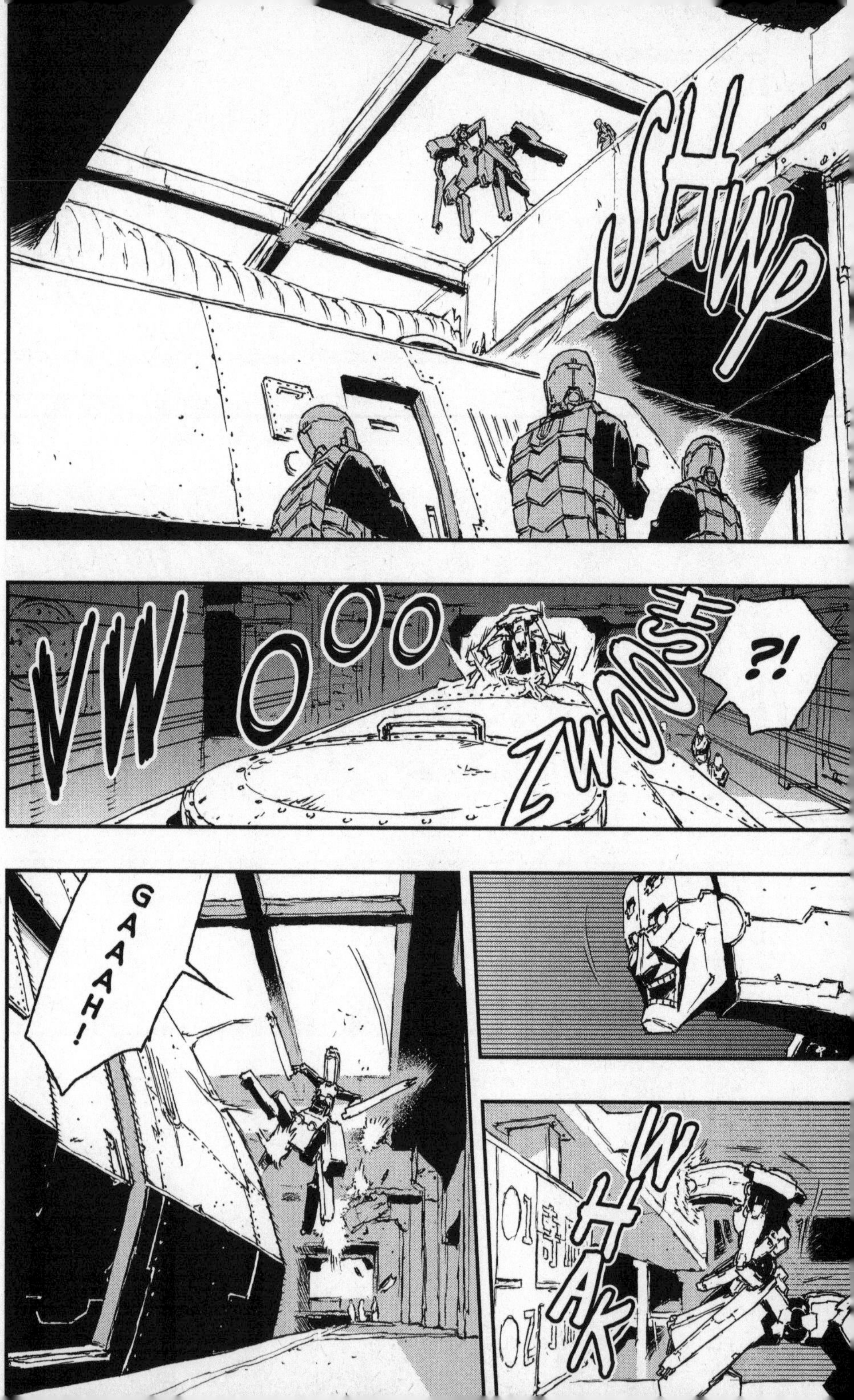
SHWP
?!
ZWOOSH
VWOOOO
WHAK
GAAAH!

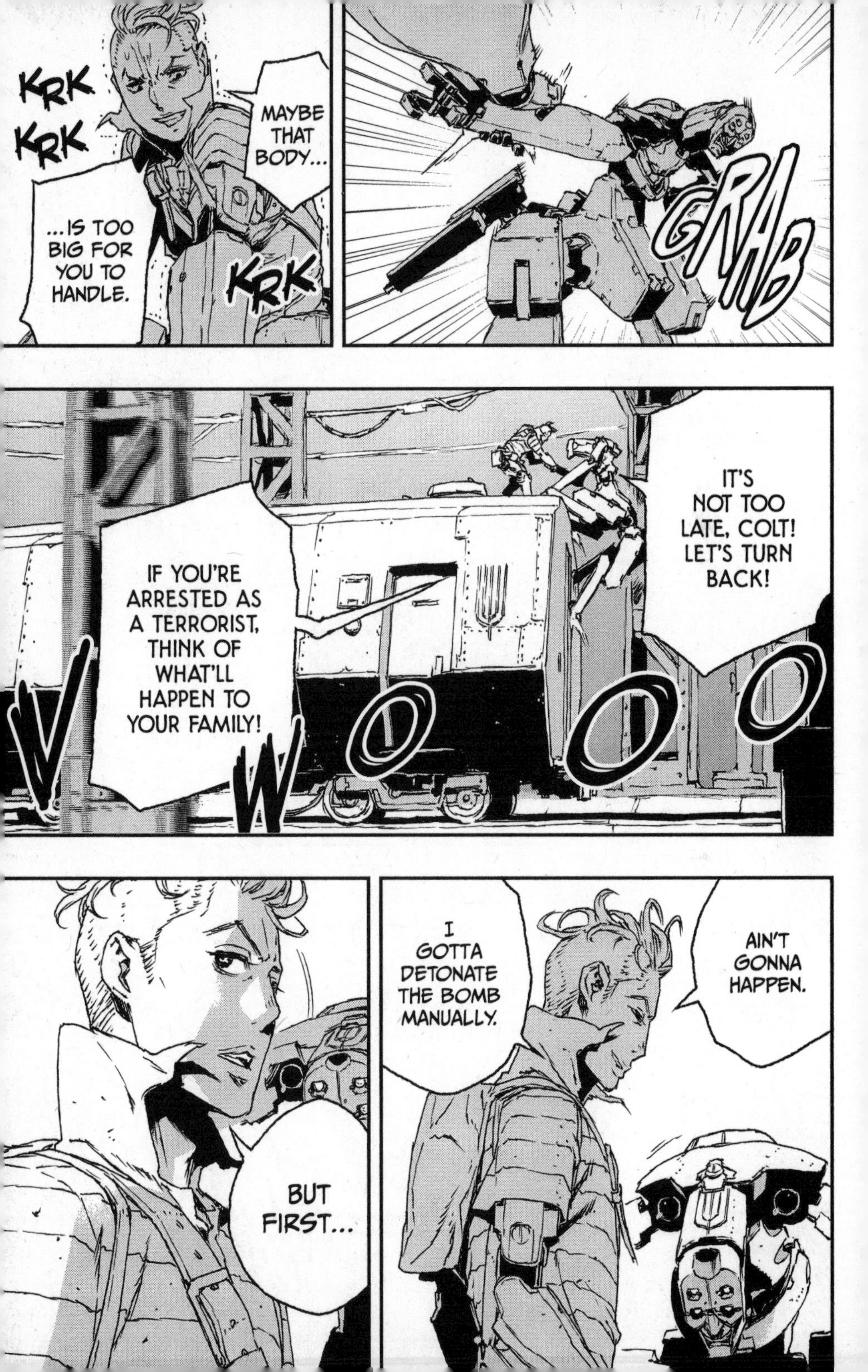
GRAB
MAYBE THAT BODY...
KRK
KRK
...IS TOO BIG FOR YOU TO HANDLE.
KRK
IT'S NOT TOO LATE, COLT! LET'S TURN BACK!
VWOOO
IF YOU'RE ARRESTED AS A TERRORIST, THINK OF WHAT'LL HAPPEN TO YOUR FAMILY!
AIN'T GONNA HAPPEN.
I GOTTA DETONATE THE BOMB MANUALLY.
BUT FIRST...

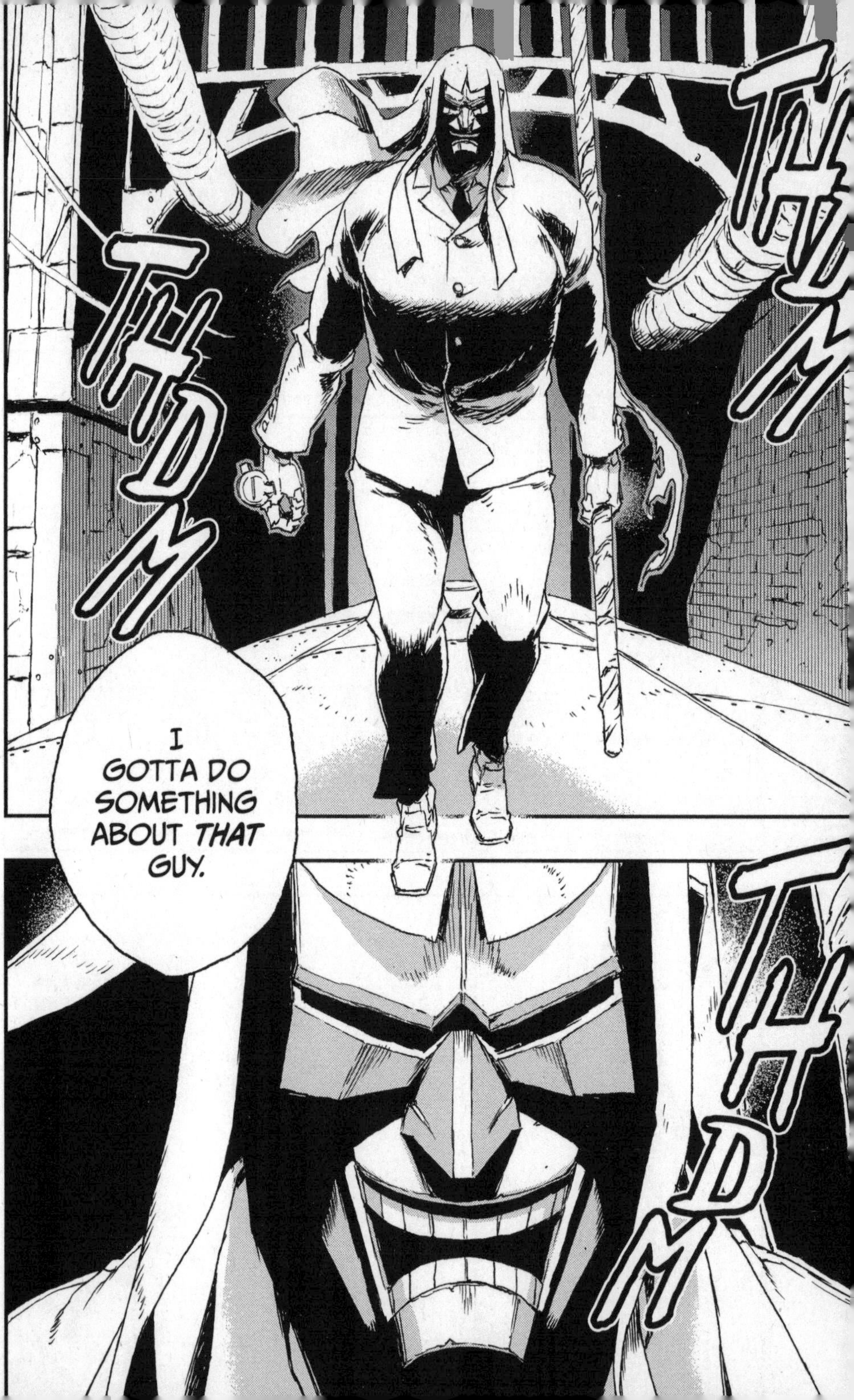
THDM
THDM
I GOTTA DO SOMETHING ABOUT *THAT* GUY.
THDM

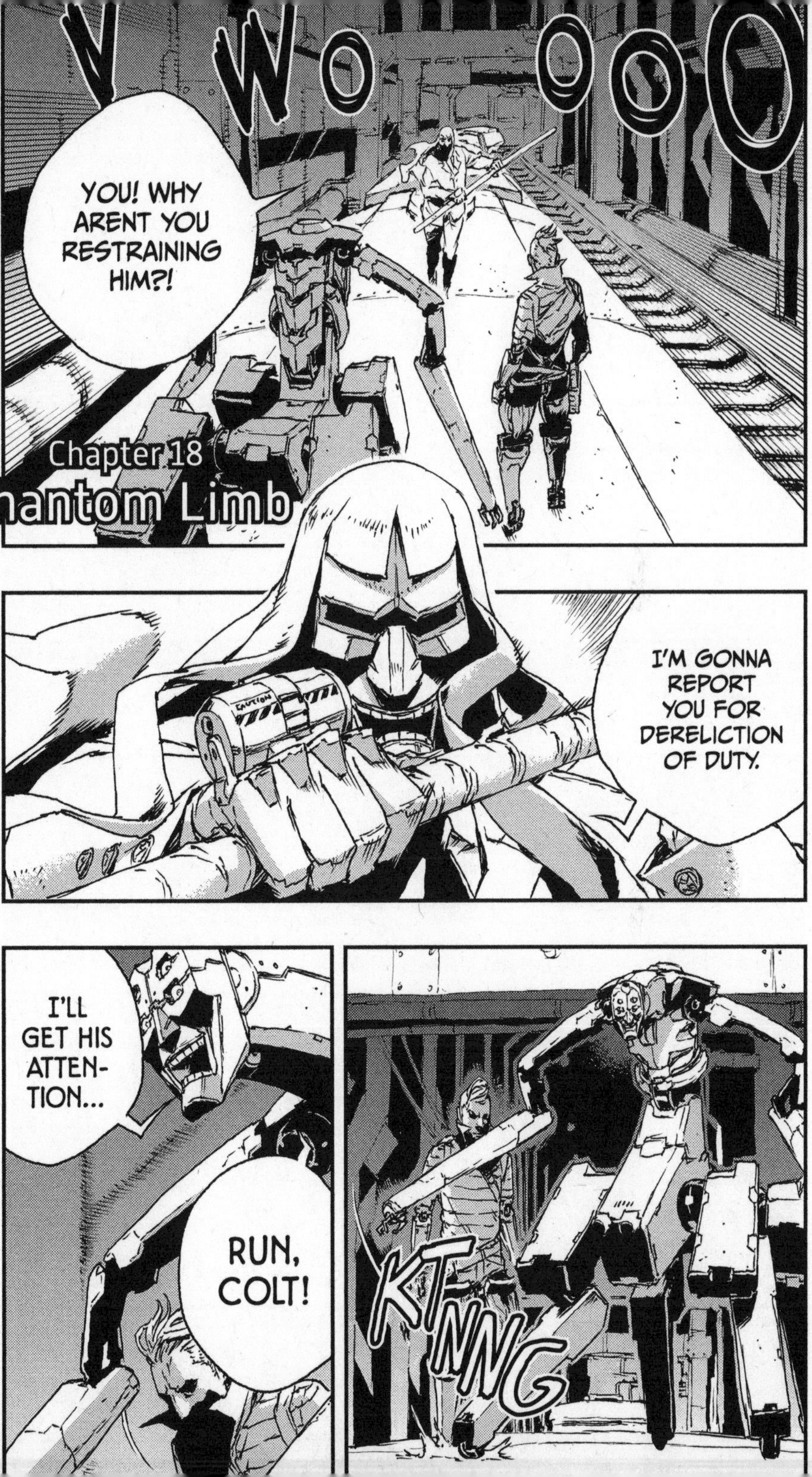
VWOOOOO
YOU! WHY ARENT YOU RESTRAINING HIM?!
Chapter 18
Phantom Limb
I'M GONNA REPORT YOU FOR DERELICTION OF DUTY.
KTNNG
I'LL GET HIS ATTEN-TION...
RUN, COLT!

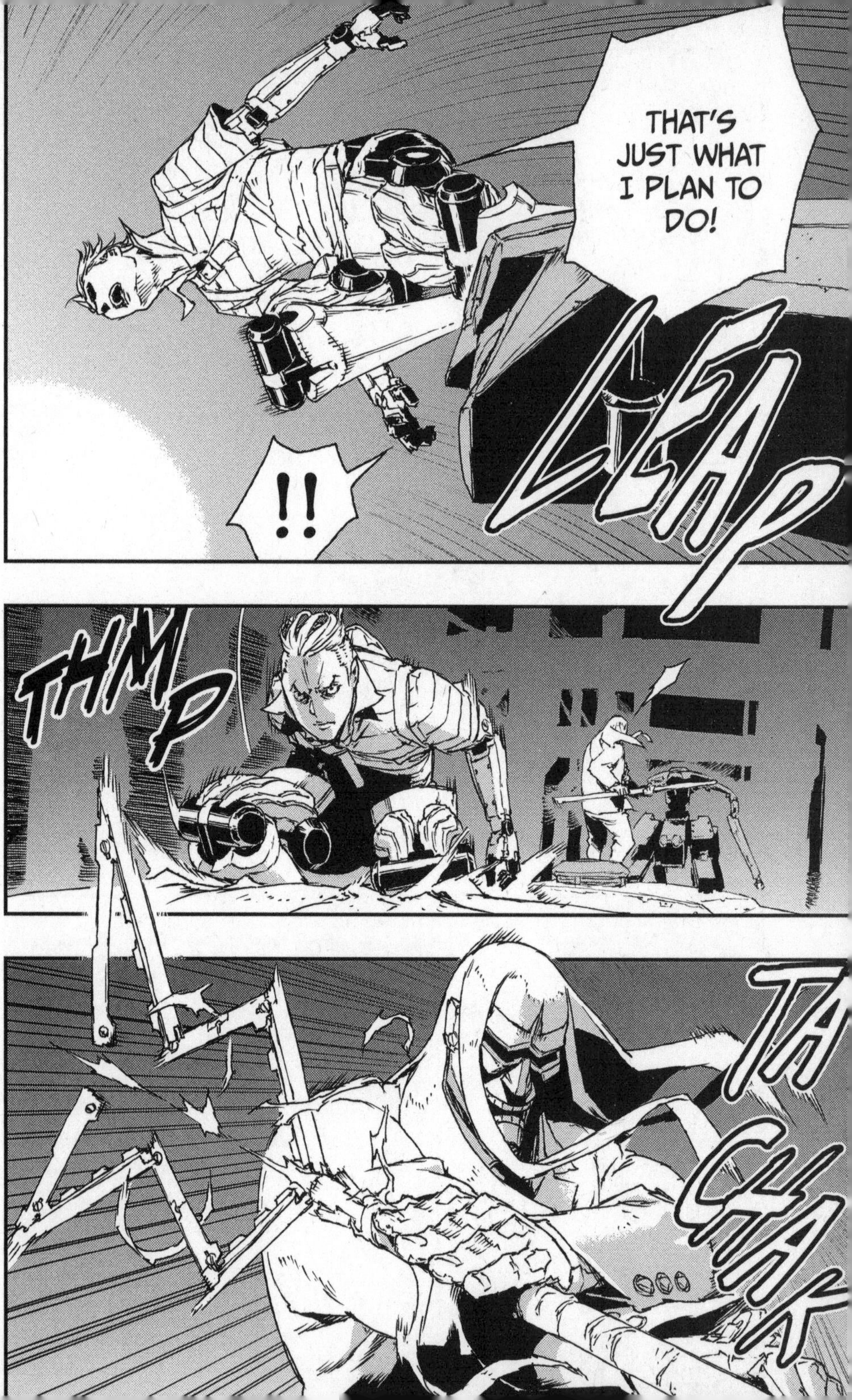
THAT'S JUST WHAT I PLAN TO DO!
!!
LEAP
THMP
TA CHAK

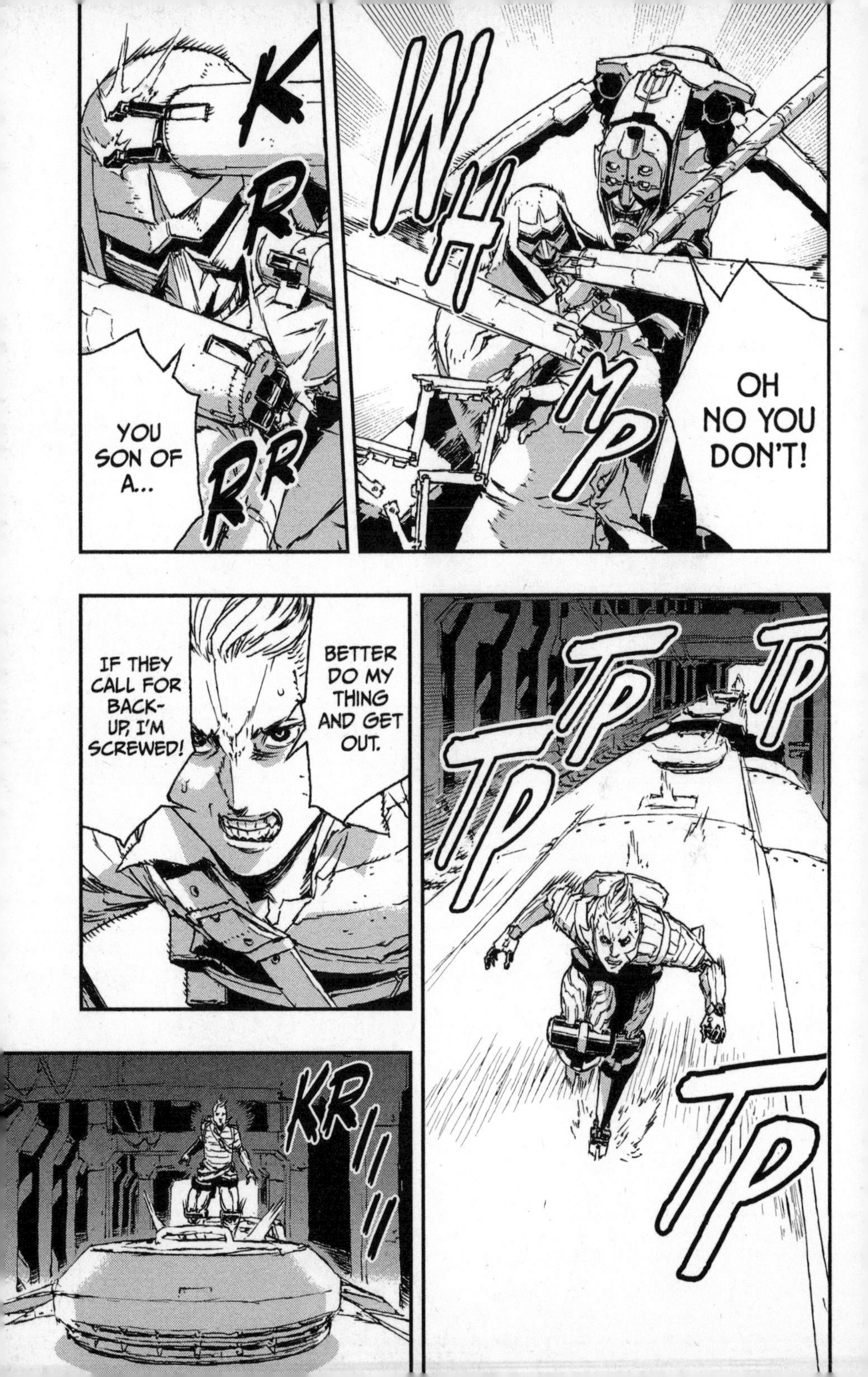
WHMP
OH NO YOU DON'T!
KRRR
YOU SON OF A...
TP TP TP TP TP
BETTER DO MY THING AND GET OUT.
IF THEY CALL FOR BACK-UP, I'M SCREWED!
KRIII

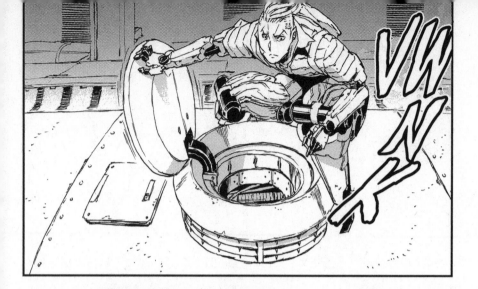

VWNK

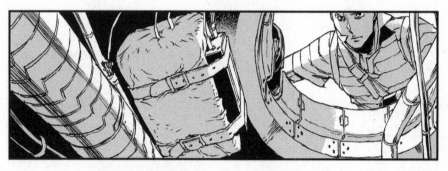

I'D BETTER GO BACK FOR TETSURO!

ALL RIGHT...

00:30

P/P
P/P
P/P

CHOK

02:58

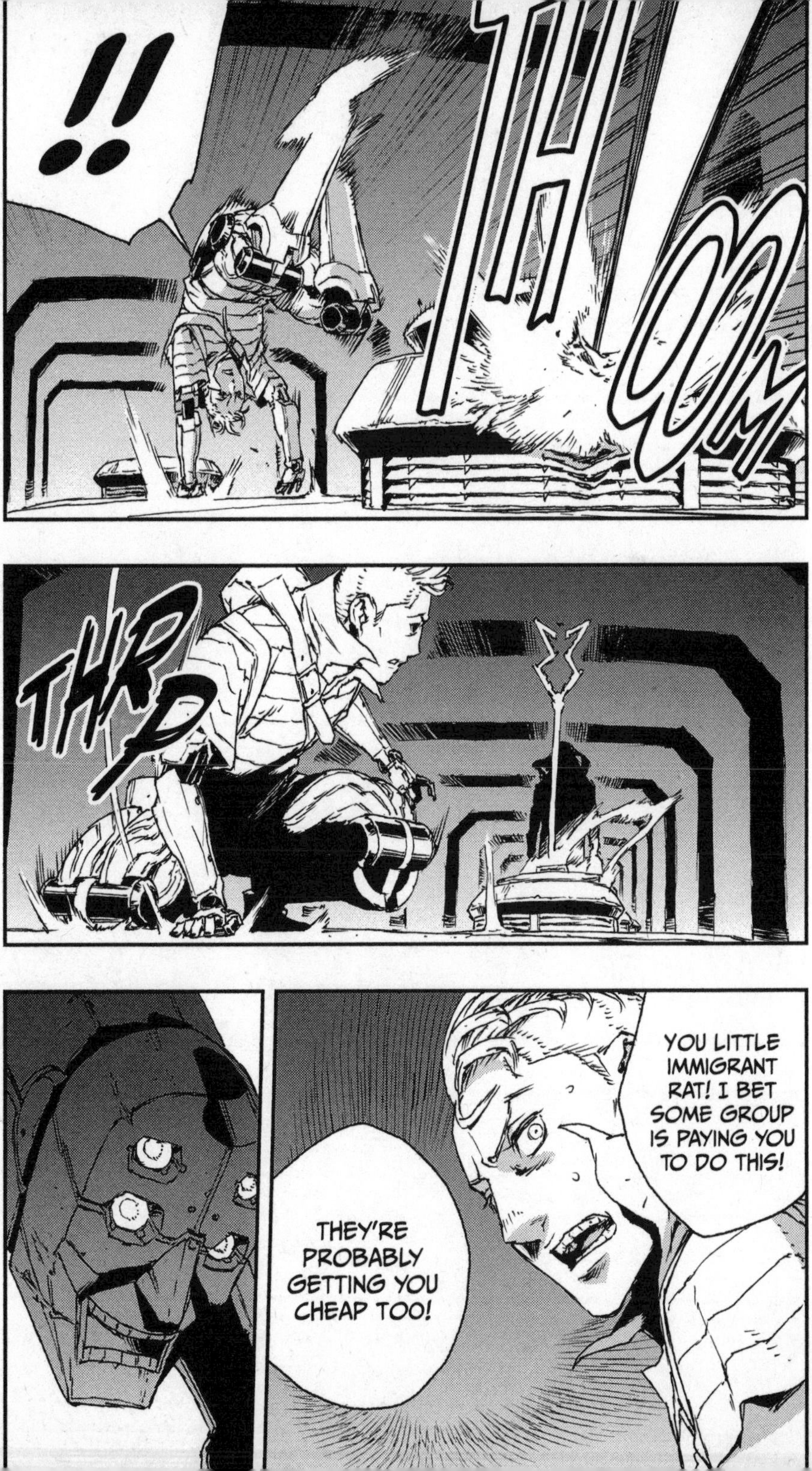
THOOM
!!
THRD
YOU LITTLE IMMIGRANT RAT! I BET SOME GROUP IS PAYING YOU TO DO THIS!
THEY'RE PROBABLY GETTING YOU CHEAP TOO!

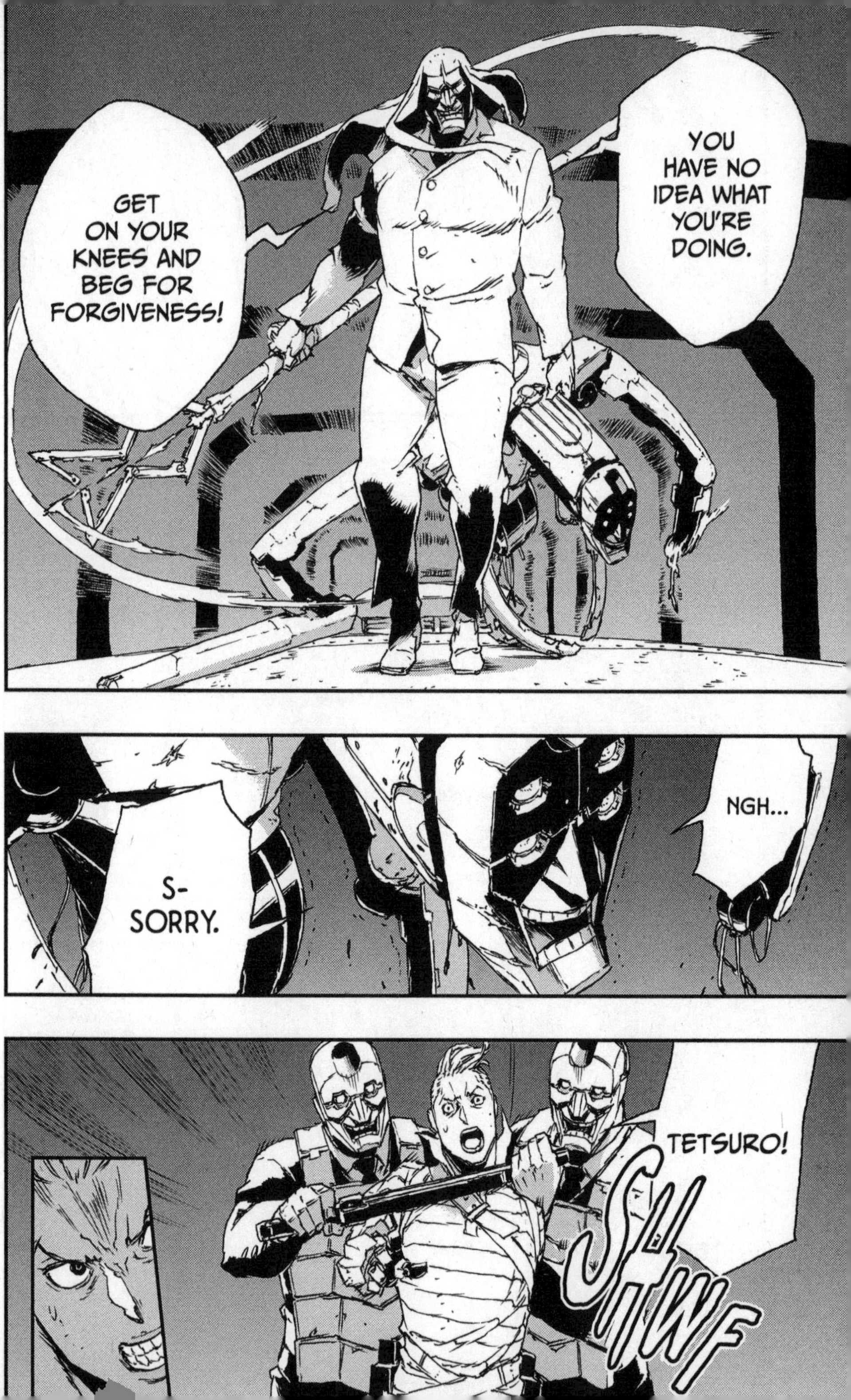
YOU HAVE NO IDEA WHAT YOU'RE DOING.
GET ON YOUR KNEES AND BEG FOR FORGIVENESS!
NGH...
S- SORRY.
TETSURO!
SHWF

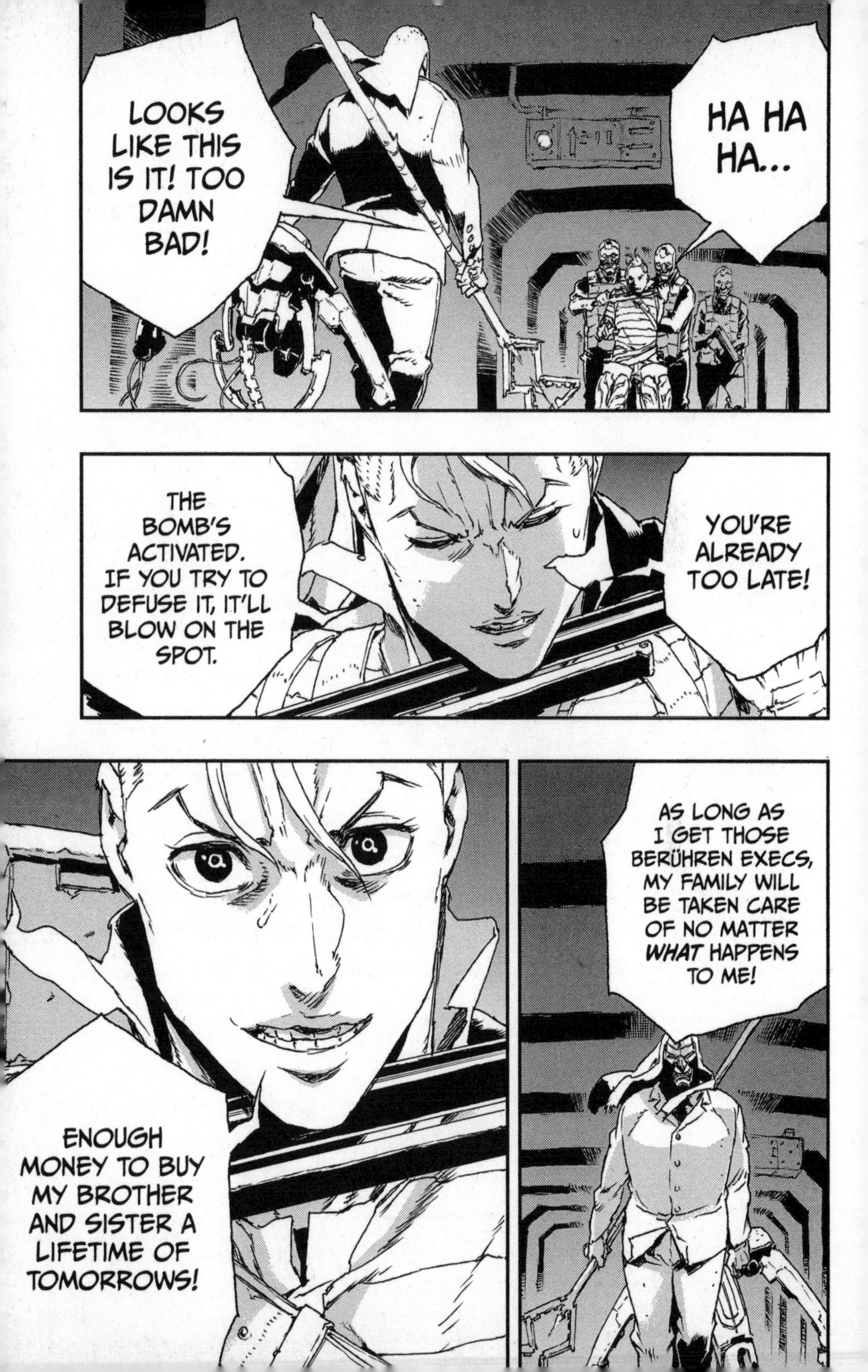
HA HA HA...
LOOKS LIKE THIS IS IT! TOO DAMN BAD!
YOU'RE ALREADY TOO LATE!
THE BOMB'S ACTIVATED. IF YOU TRY TO DEFUSE IT, IT'LL BLOW ON THE SPOT.
AS LONG AS I GET THOSE BERÜHREN EXECS, MY FAMILY WILL BE TAKEN CARE OF NO MATTER *WHAT* HAPPENS TO ME!
ENOUGH MONEY TO BUY MY BROTHER AND SISTER A LIFETIME OF TOMORROWS!

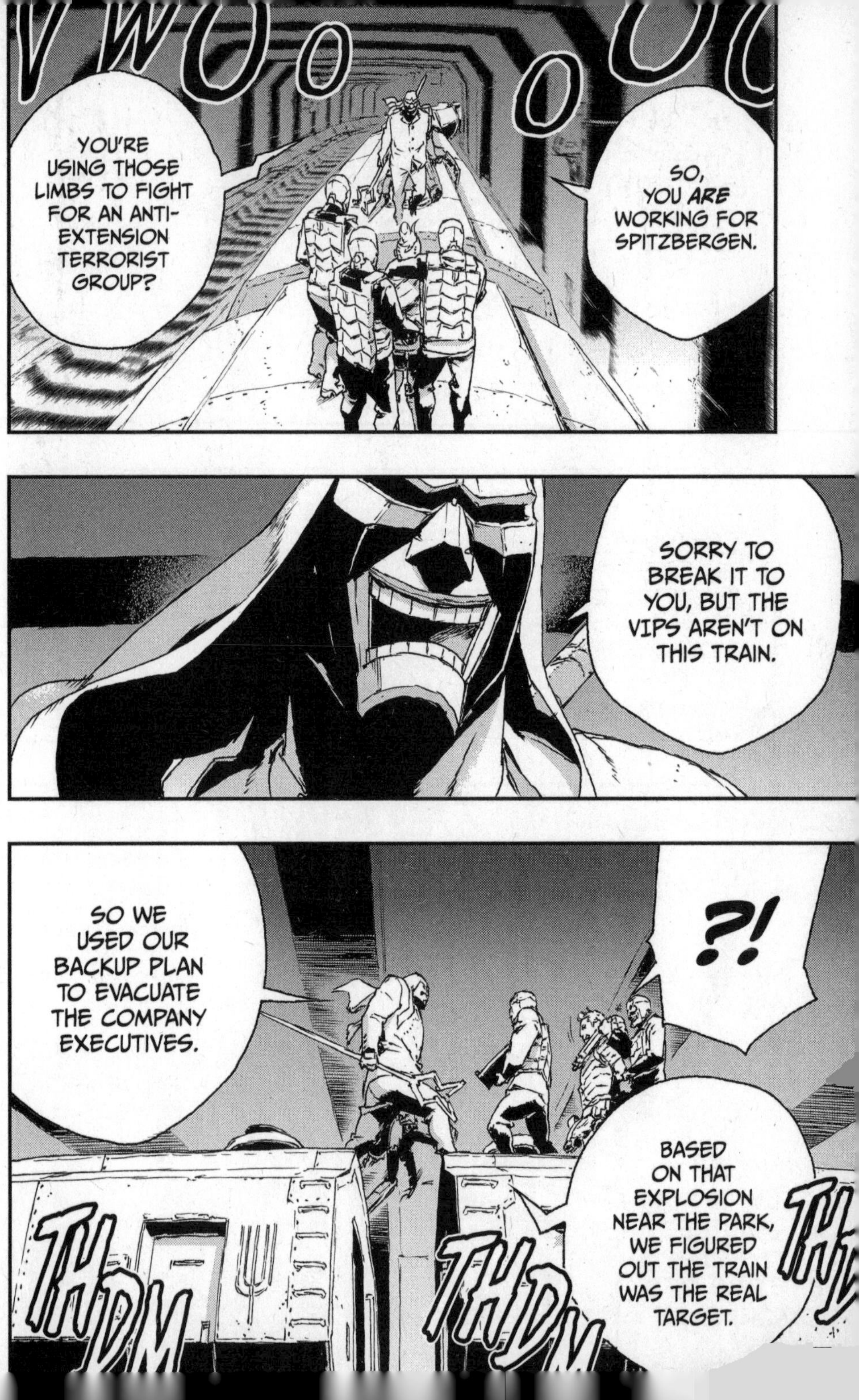
VWOOOOOO
SO, YOU ARE WORKING FOR SPITZBERGEN.
YOU'RE USING THOSE LIMBS TO FIGHT FOR AN ANTI-EXTENSION TERRORIST GROUP?
SORRY TO BREAK IT TO YOU, BUT THE VIPS AREN'T ON THIS TRAIN.
?!
SO WE USED OUR BACKUP PLAN TO EVACUATE THE COMPANY EXECUTIVES.
BASED ON THAT EXPLOSION NEAR THE PARK, WE FIGURED OUT THE TRAIN WAS THE REAL TARGET.
THDM
THDM
THDM

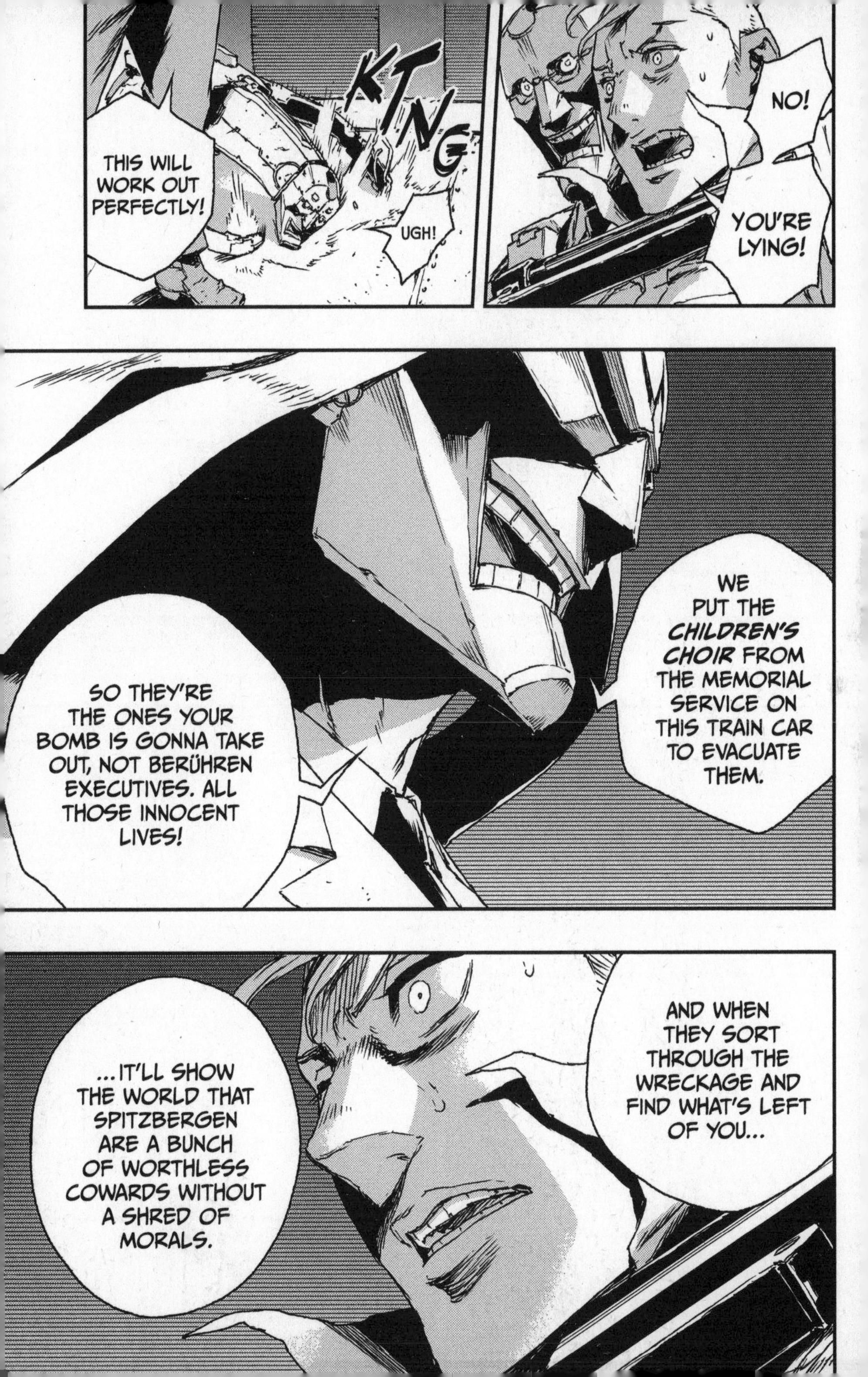
NO!
YOU'RE LYING!
KTING
THIS WILL WORK OUT PERFECTLY!
UGH!
WE PUT THE *CHILDREN'S CHOIR* FROM THE MEMORIAL SERVICE ON THIS TRAIN CAR TO EVACUATE THEM.
SO THEY'RE THE ONES YOUR BOMB IS GONNA TAKE OUT, NOT BERÜHREN EXECUTIVES. ALL THOSE INNOCENT LIVES!
AND WHEN THEY SORT THROUGH THE WRECKAGE AND FIND WHAT'S LEFT OF YOU...
...IT'LL SHOW THE WORLD THAT SPITZBERGEN ARE A BUNCH OF WORTHLESS COWARDS WITHOUT A SHRED OF MORALS.

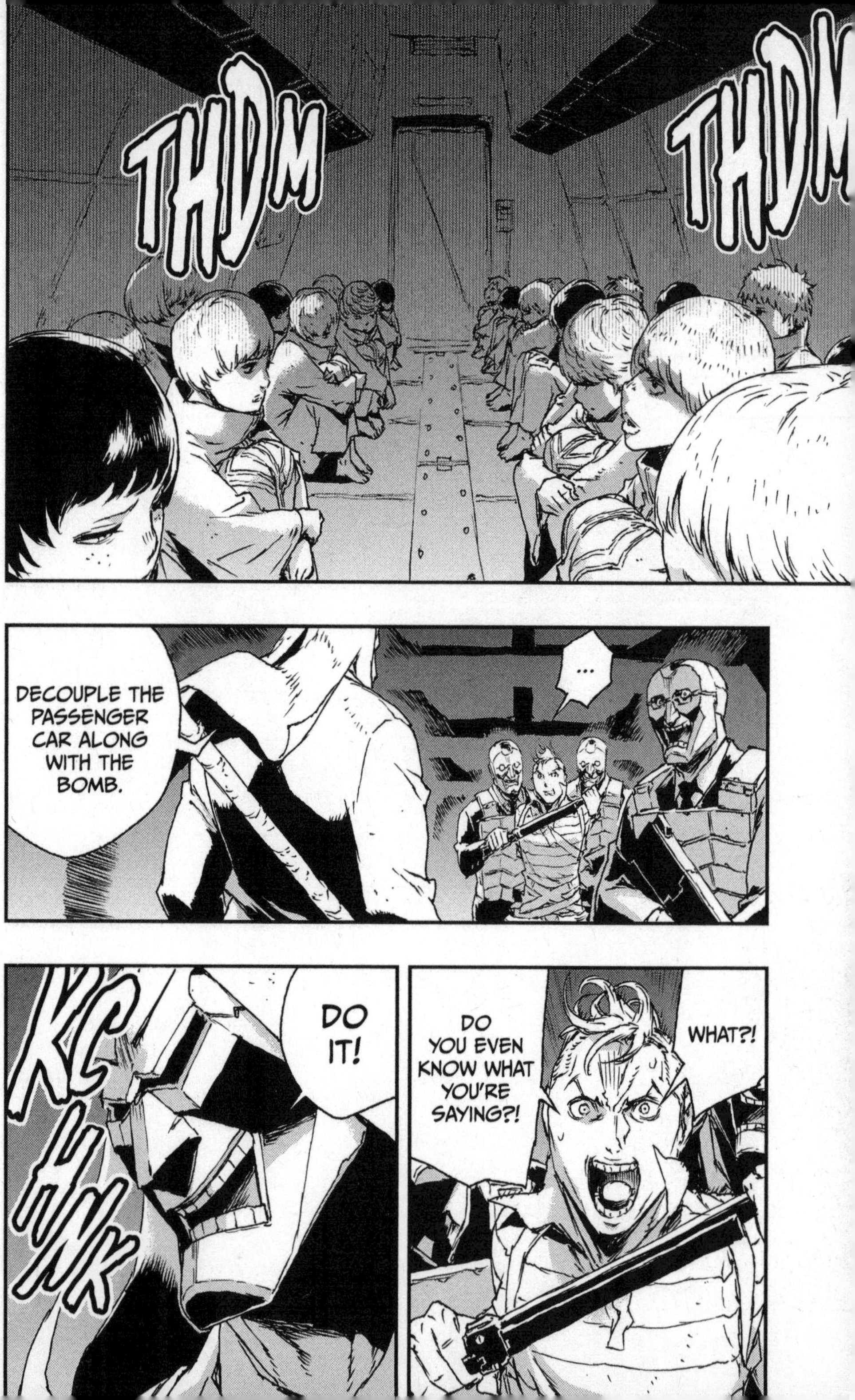
THDM
THDM
...
DECOUPLE THE PASSENGER CAR ALONG WITH THE BOMB.
WHAT?!
DO YOU EVEN KNOW WHAT YOU'RE SAYING?!
DO IT!
KCHUNK

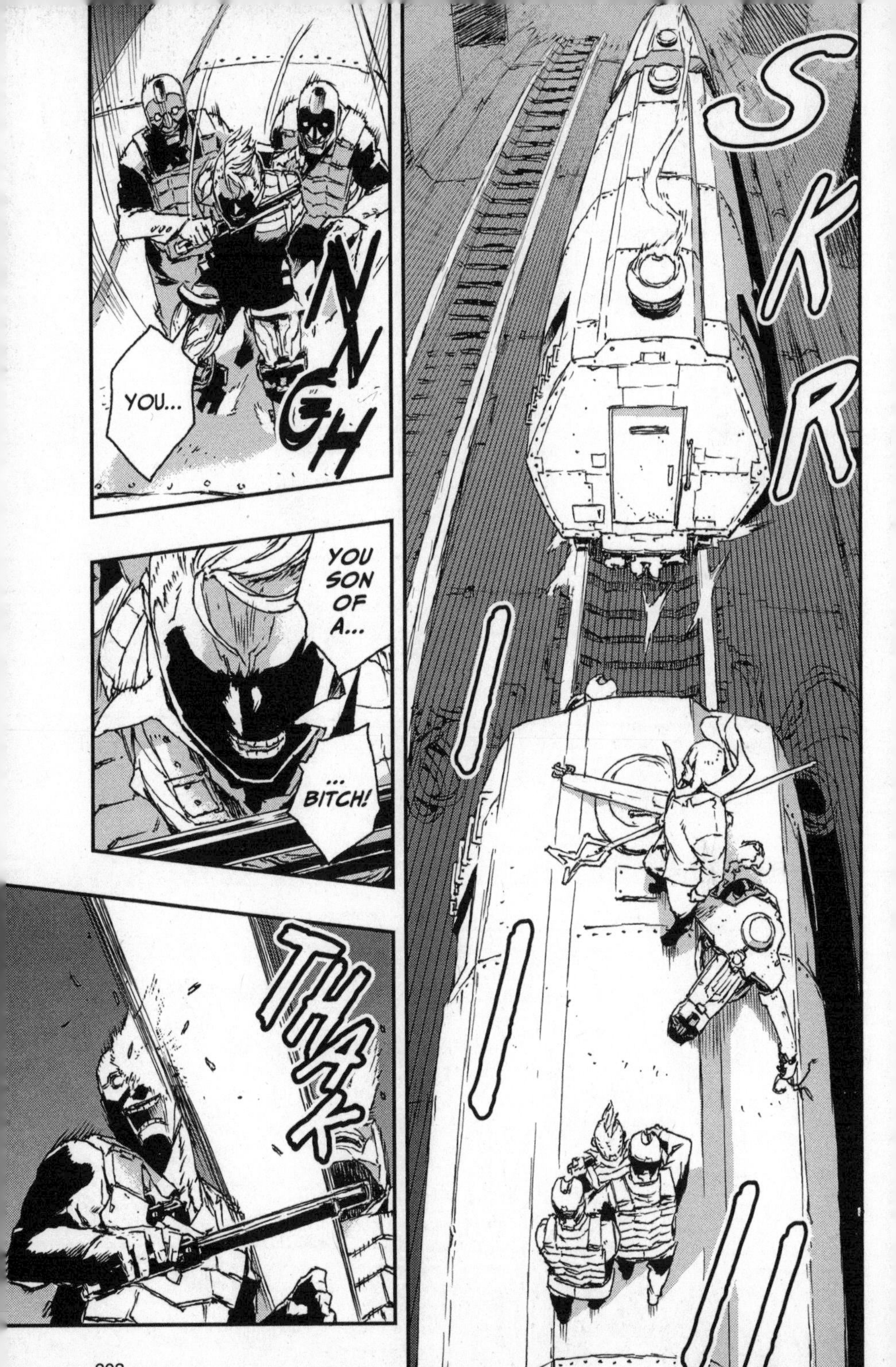
SKR
NNGH
YOU...
YOU SON OF A...
...BITCH!
THAK

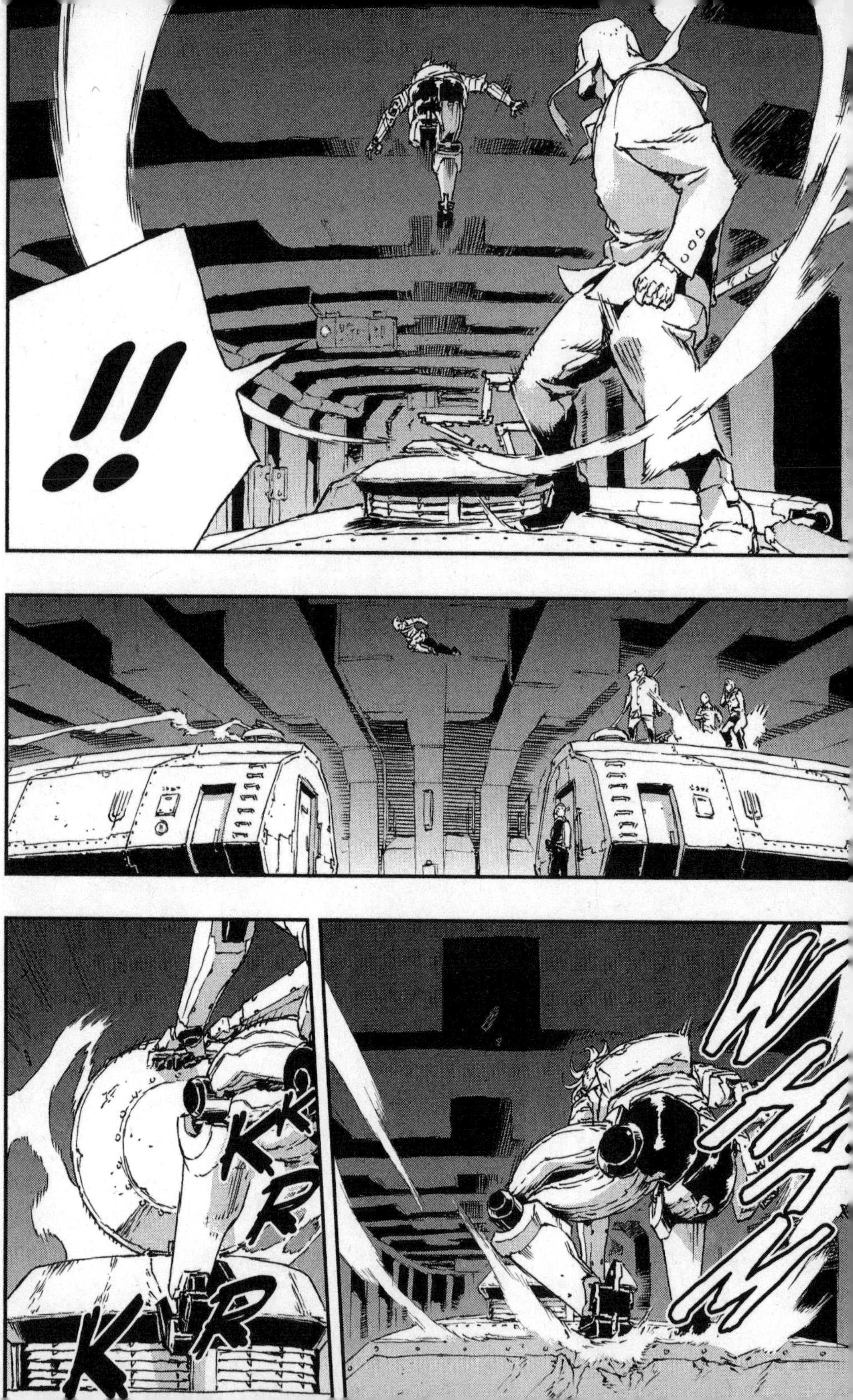
!!
WHAM
KKR
KR

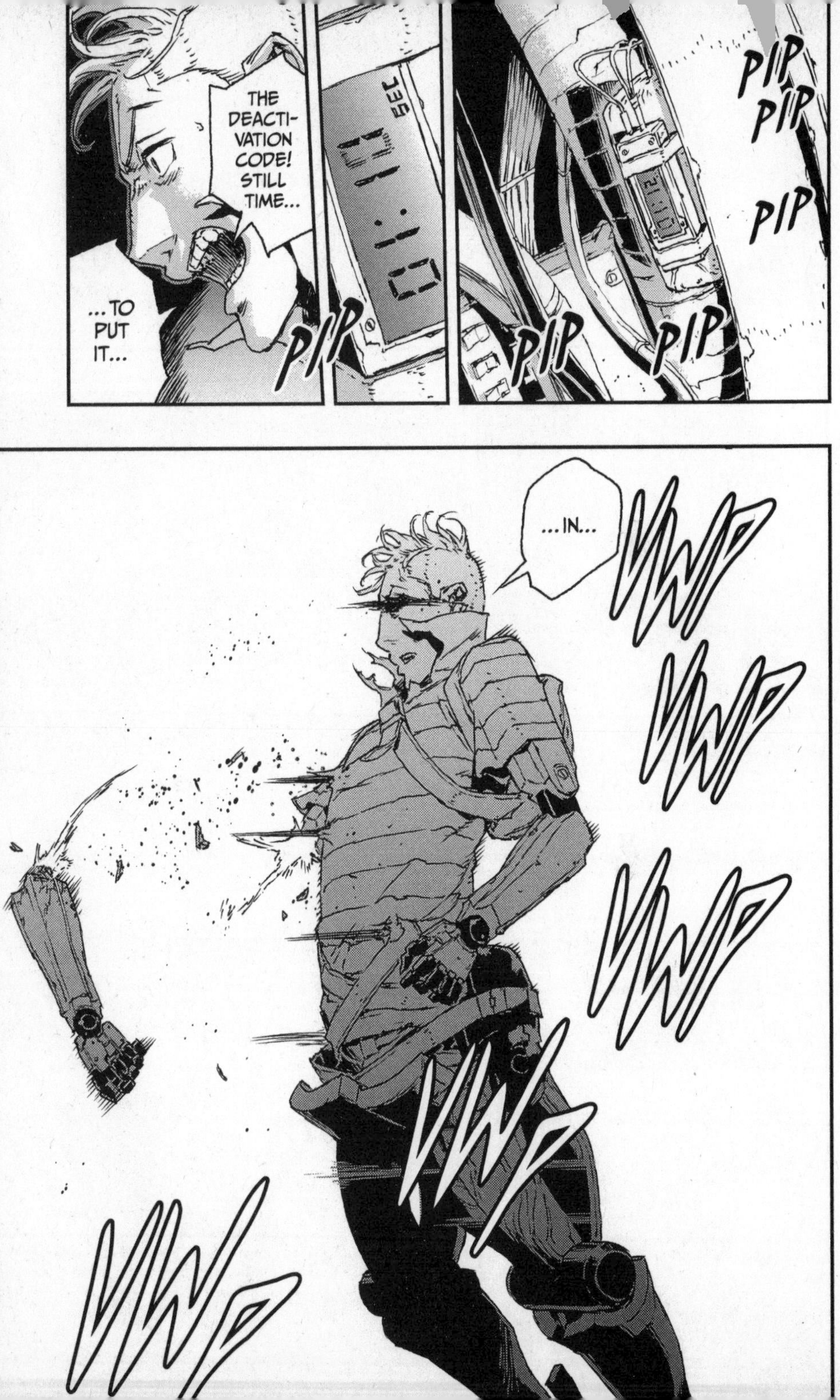
PIP
PIP
PIP
PIP
PIP
PIP
THE DEACTI-VATION CODE! STILL TIME...
...TO PUT IT...
...IN...

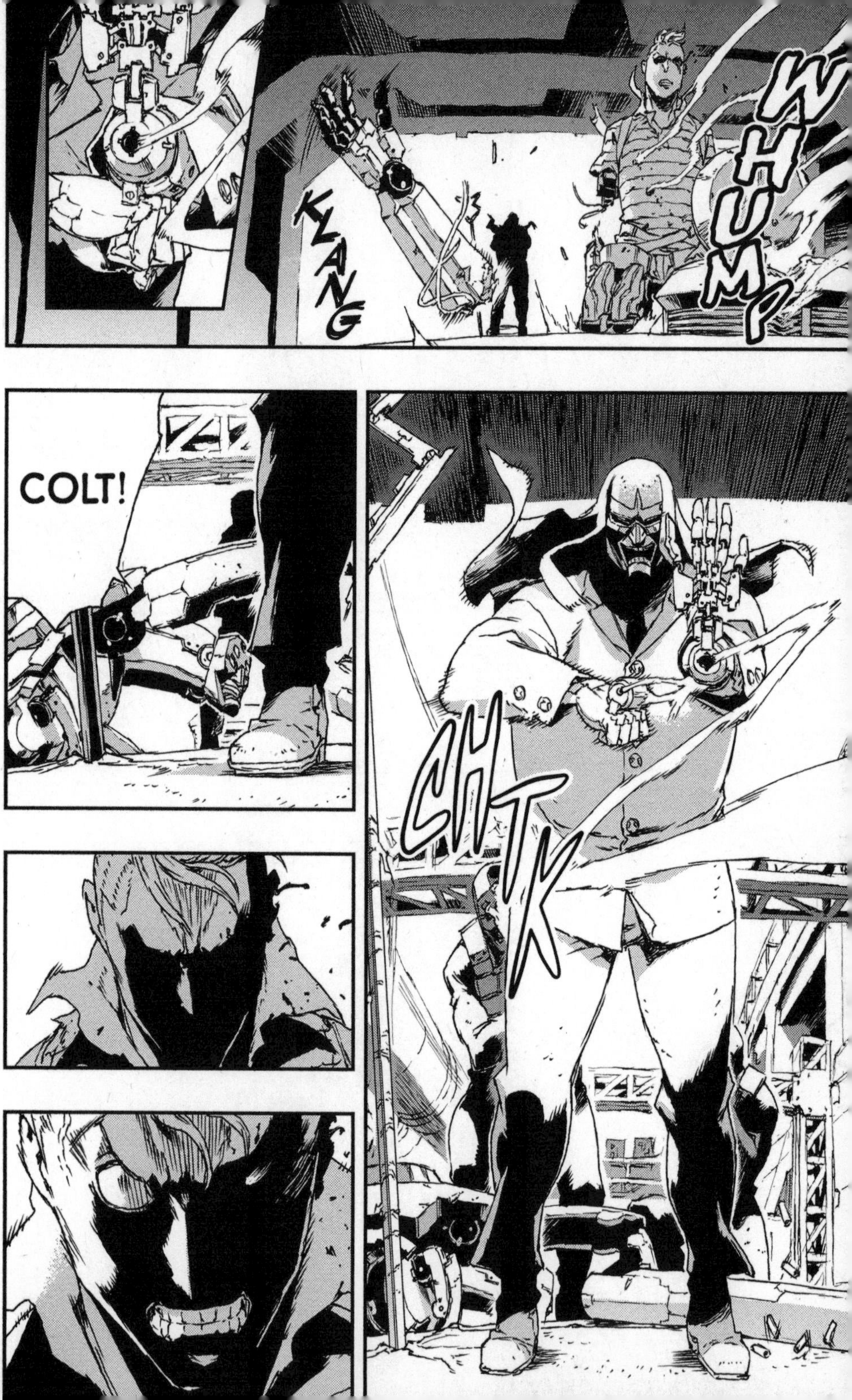
WHUMP
KLANG
CHTK
COLT!

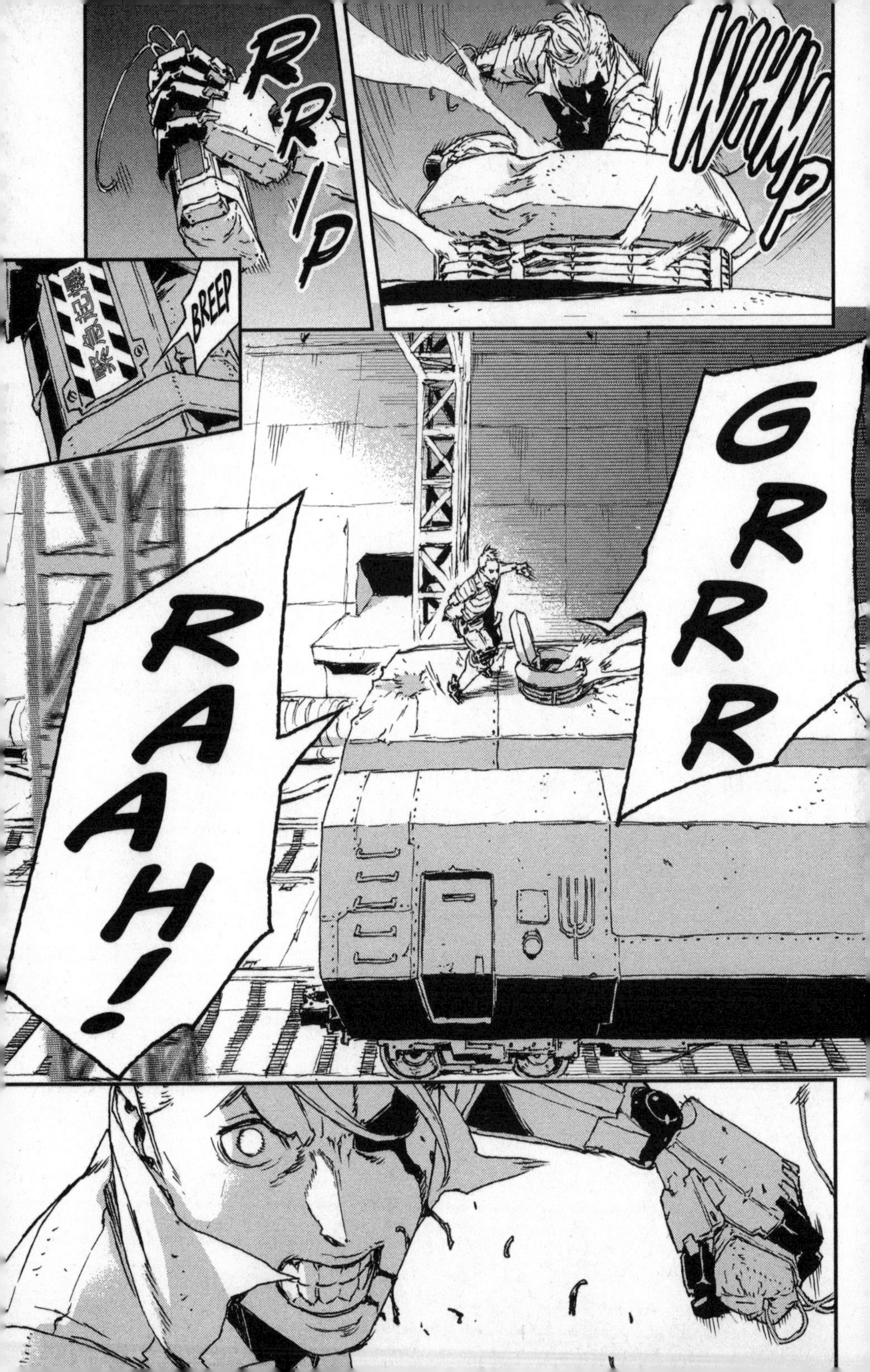
WHUMP
RRRIP
GRRRR
BREEP
RAAH!

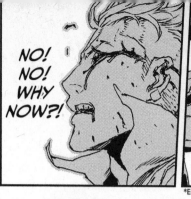

緊急起動
NO! NO! WHY NOW?!
MY MEDS HAVE WORN OFF!
*Emergency Activation

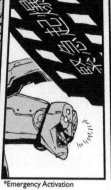

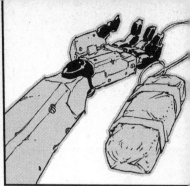

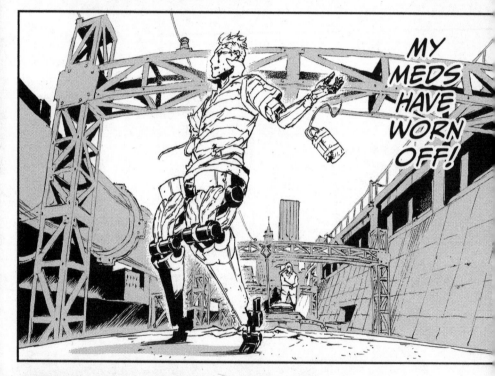

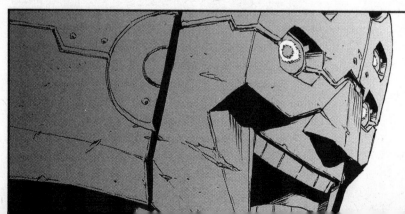

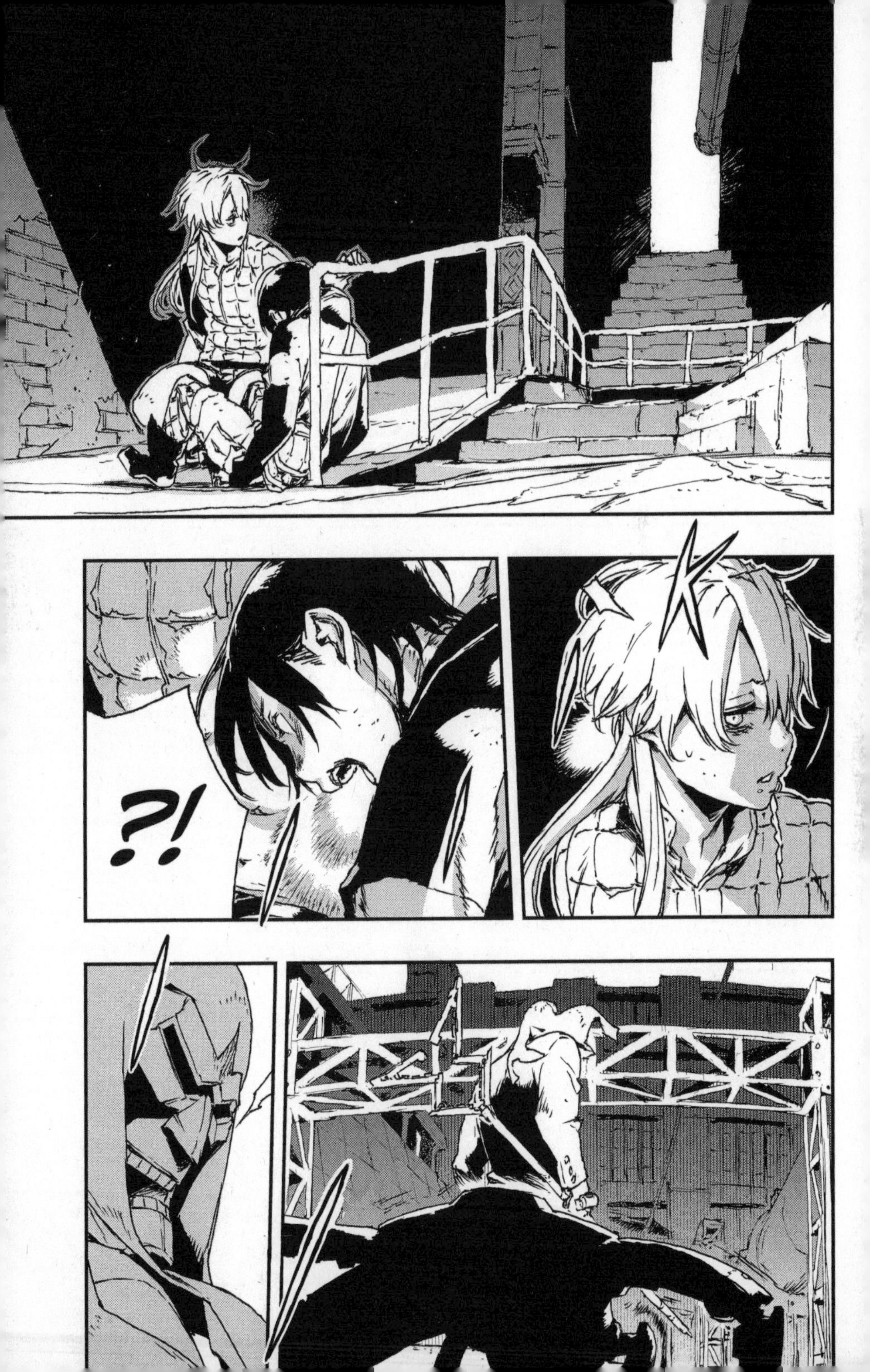
?!

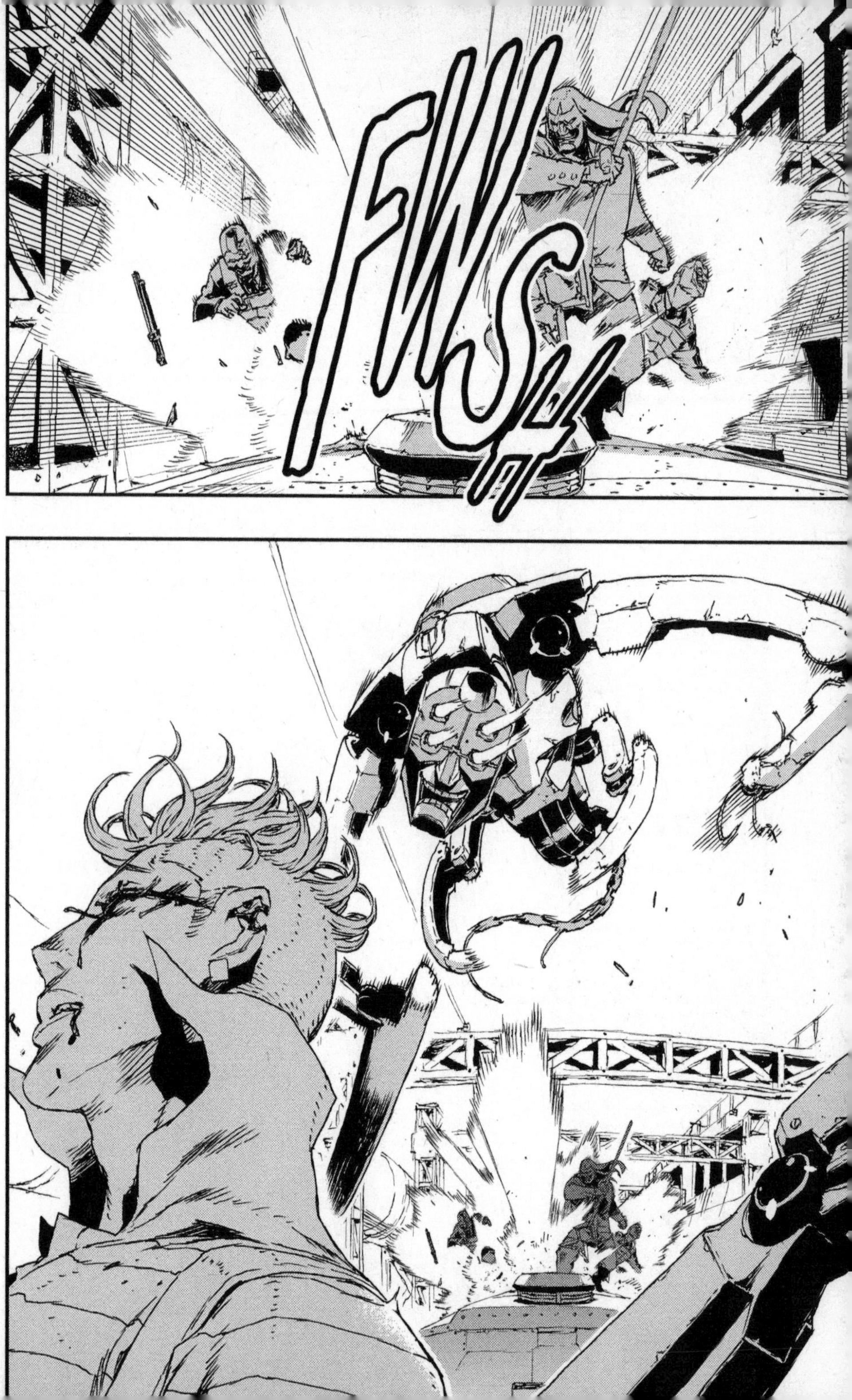
FWSH

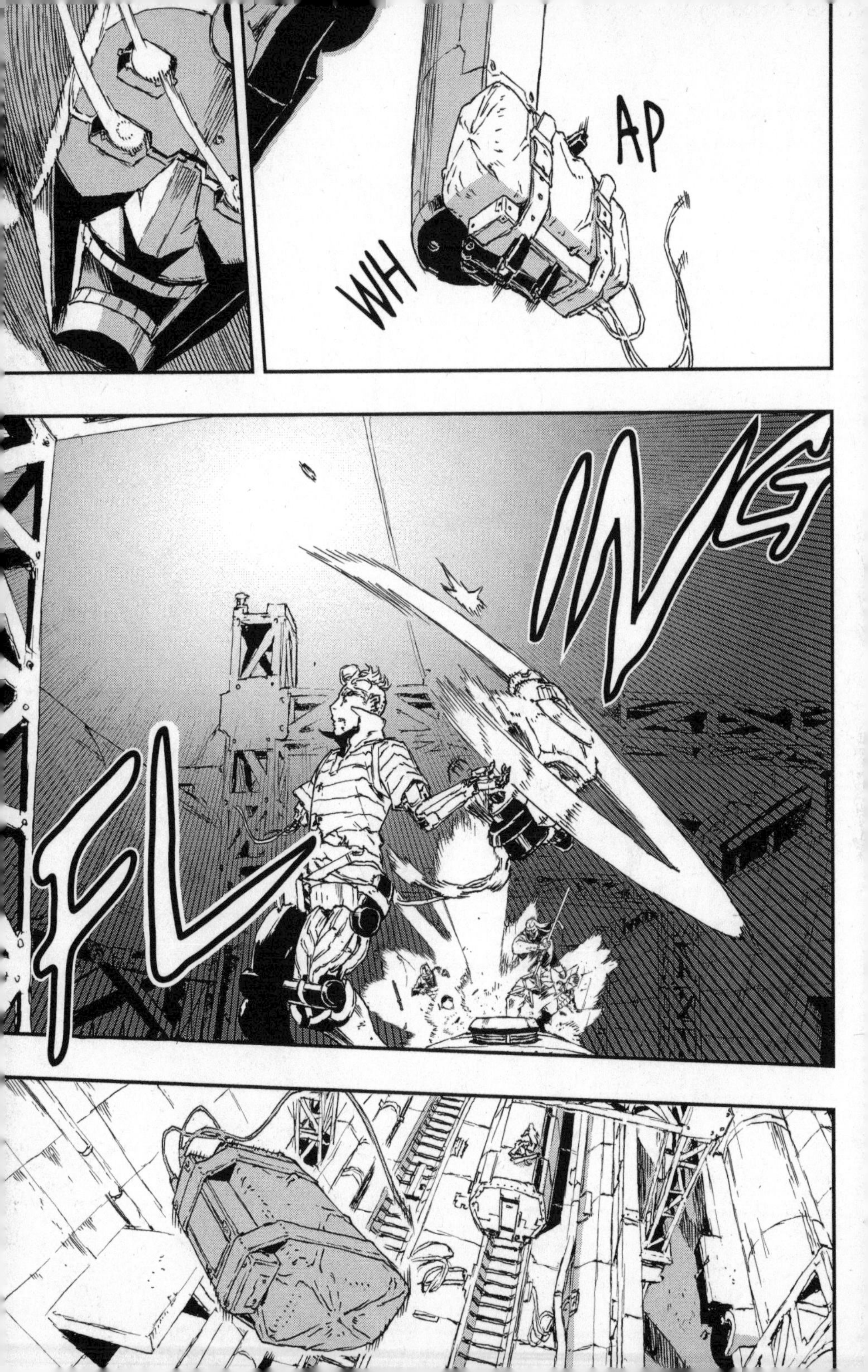
WH
AP
FL
ING

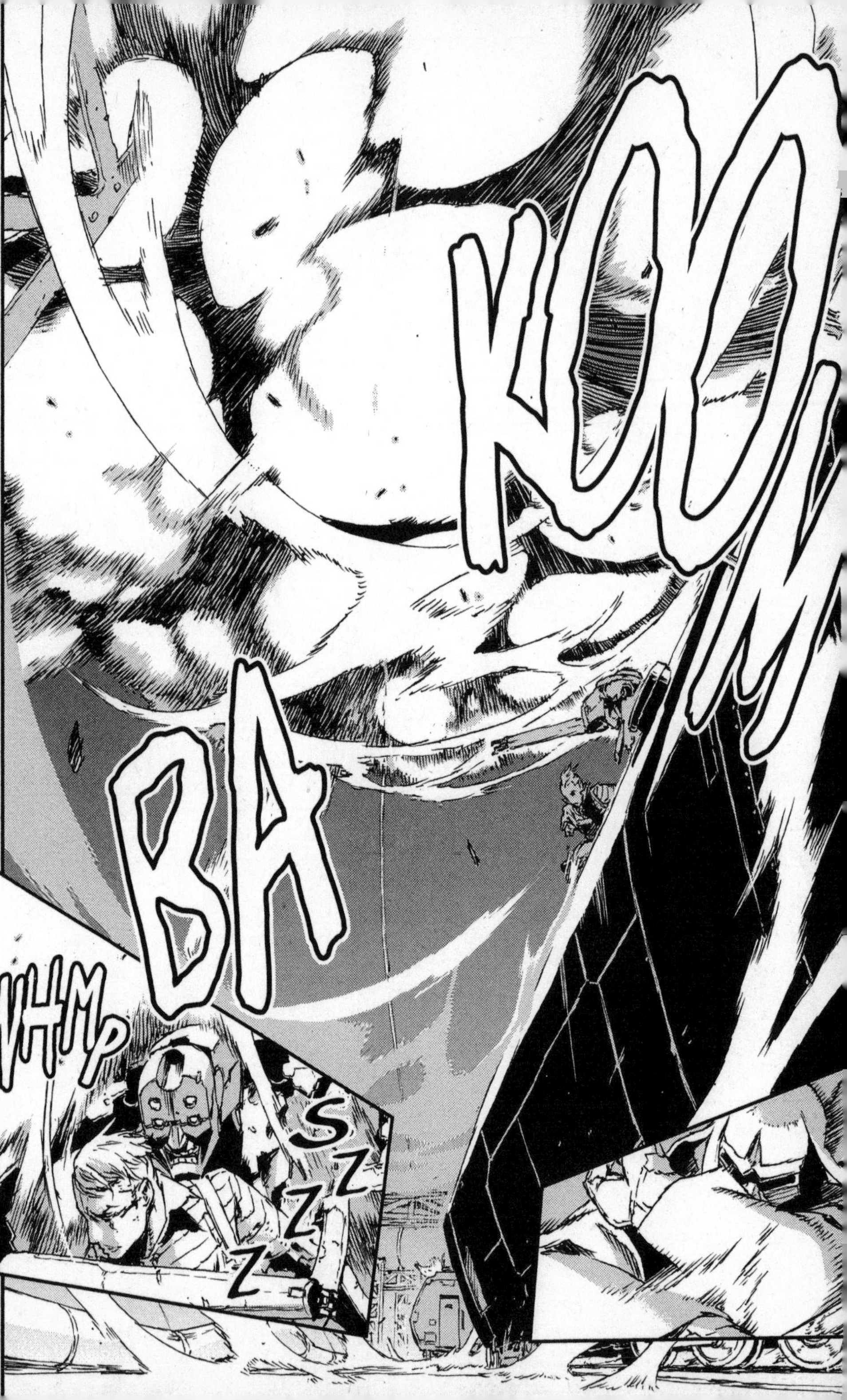
BA KOOM
WHMP
SZZZZ

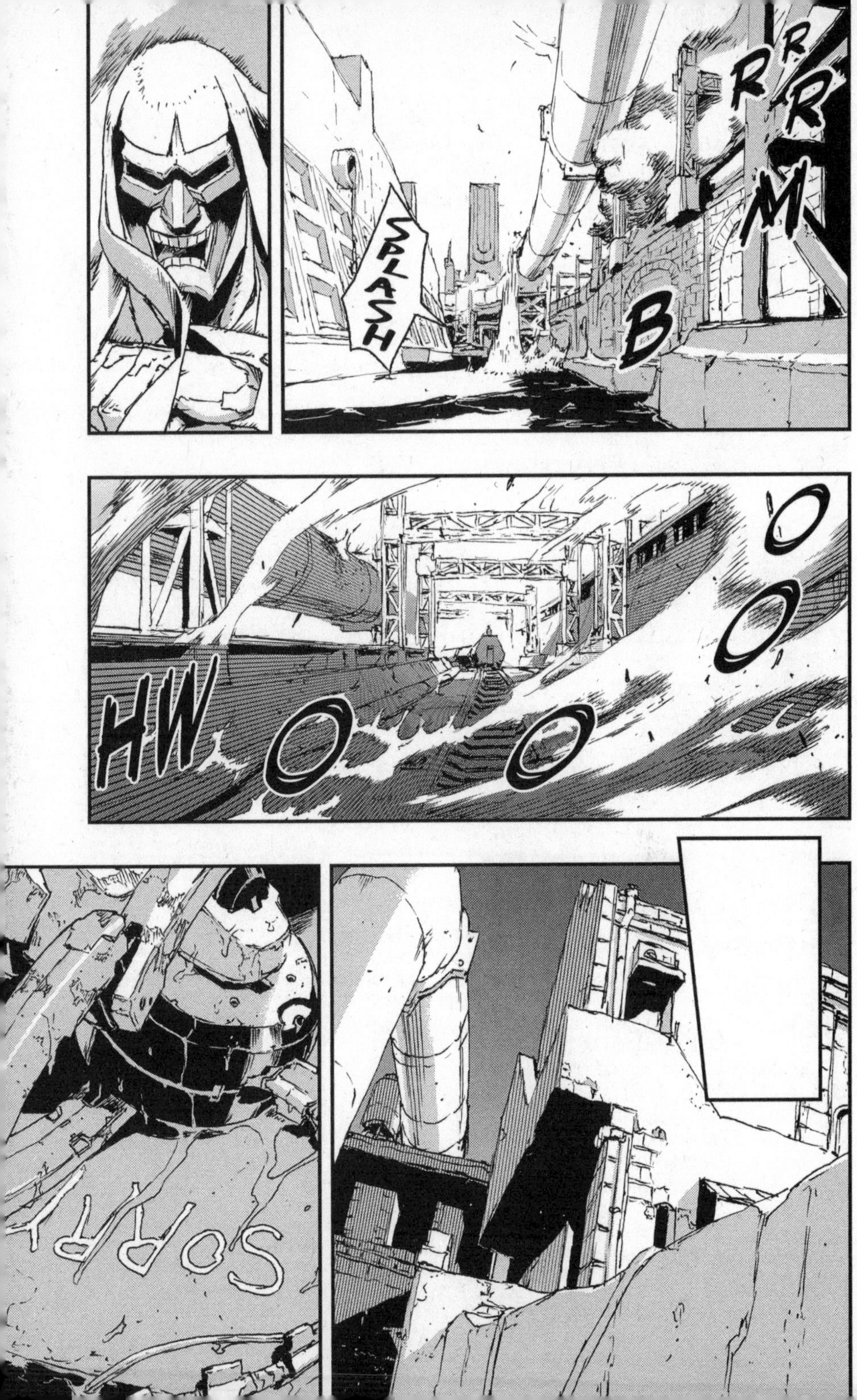
RRRMB
SPLASH
HWOOOO
SORRY

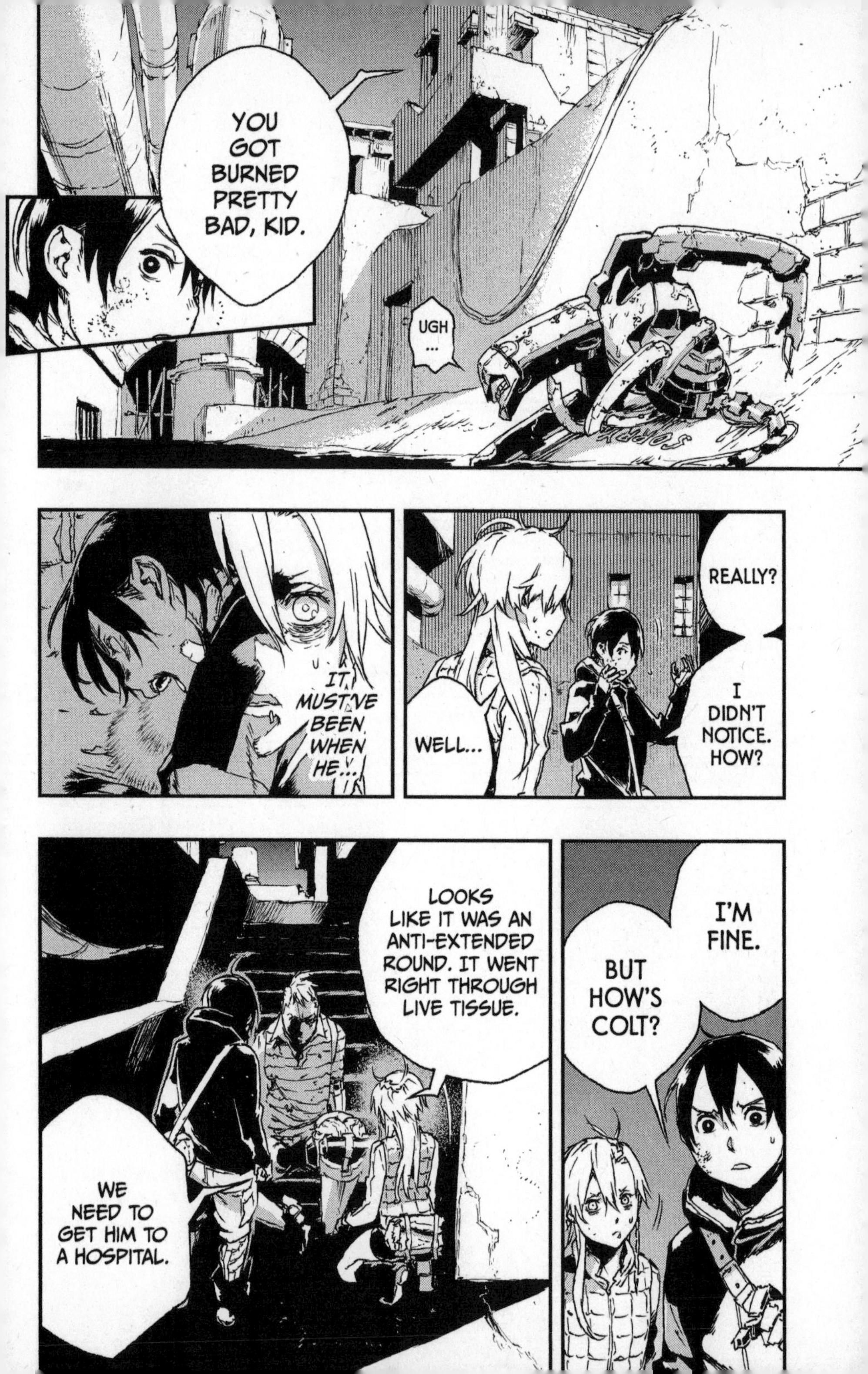
YOU GOT BURNED PRETTY BAD, KID.
UGH...
REALLY?
I DIDN'T NOTICE. HOW?
WELL...
IT MUST'VE BEEN WHEN HE...
I'M FINE.
BUT HOW'S COLT?
LOOKS LIKE IT WAS AN ANTI-EXTENDED ROUND. IT WENT RIGHT THROUGH LIVE TISSUE.
WE NEED TO GET HIM TO A HOSPITAL.

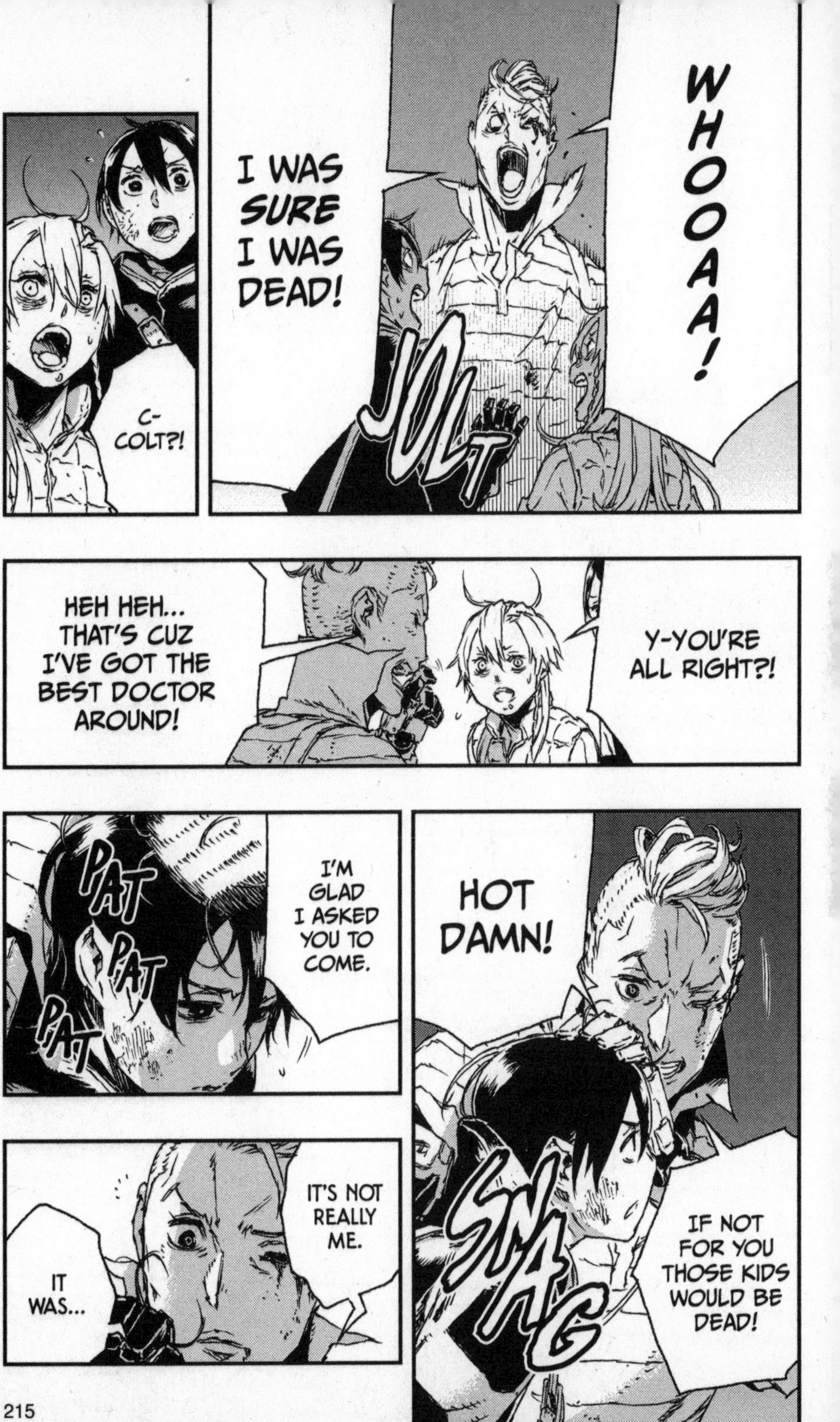
WHOOAAA!
I WAS SURE I WAS DEAD!
JOLT
C-COLT?!
Y-YOU'RE ALL RIGHT?!
HEH HEH... THAT'S CUZ I'VE GOT THE BEST DOCTOR AROUND!
HOT DAMN!
IF NOT FOR YOU THOSE KIDS WOULD BE DEAD!
SMAG
I'M GLAD I ASKED YOU TO COME.
PAT PAT PAT
IT'S NOT REALLY ME.
IT WAS...

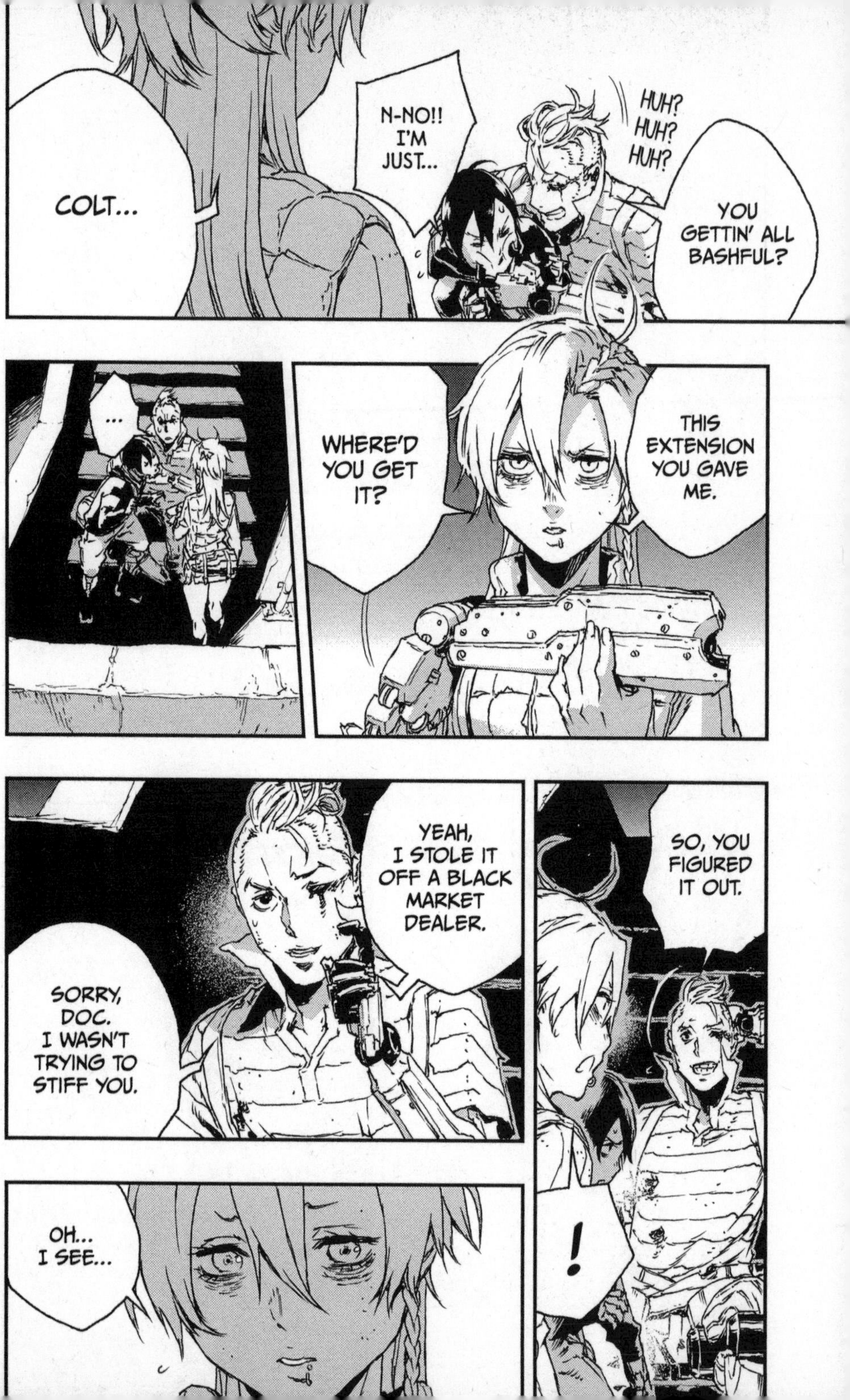
HUH? HUH? HUH?
YOU GETTIN' ALL BASHFUL?
N-NO!! I'M JUST...
COLT...
THIS EXTENSION YOU GAVE ME.
WHERE'D YOU GET IT?
...
SO, YOU FIGURED IT OUT.
!
YEAH, I STOLE IT OFF A BLACK MARKET DEALER.
SORRY, DOC. I WASN'T TRYING TO STIFF YOU.
OH... I SEE...

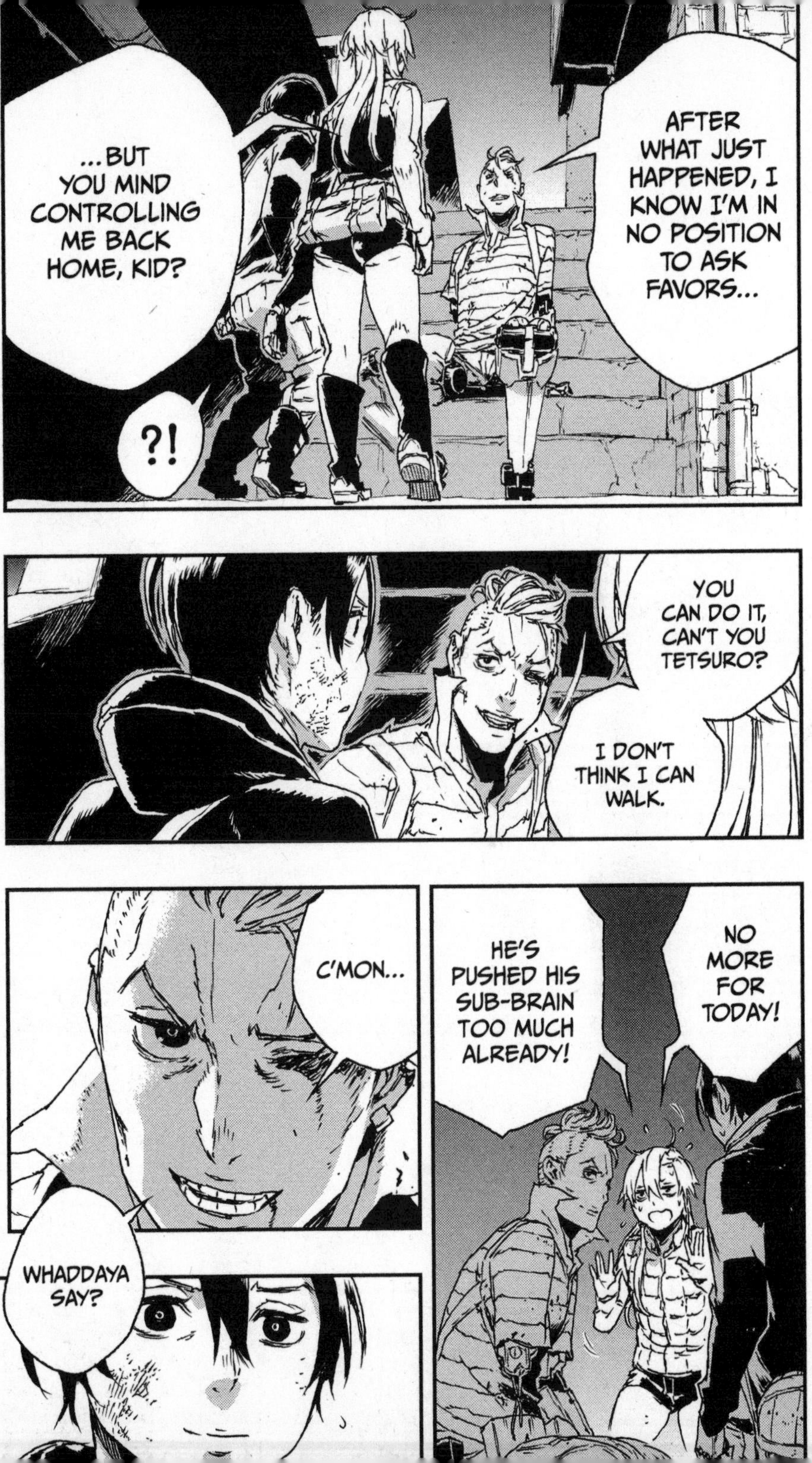
AFTER WHAT JUST HAPPENED, I KNOW I'M IN NO POSITION TO ASK FAVORS...
...BUT YOU MIND CONTROLLING ME BACK HOME, KID?
?!
YOU CAN DO IT, CAN'T YOU TETSURO?
I DON'T THINK I CAN WALK.
NO MORE FOR TODAY!
HE'S PUSHED HIS SUB-BRAIN TOO MUCH ALREADY!
C'MON...
WHADDAYA SAY?

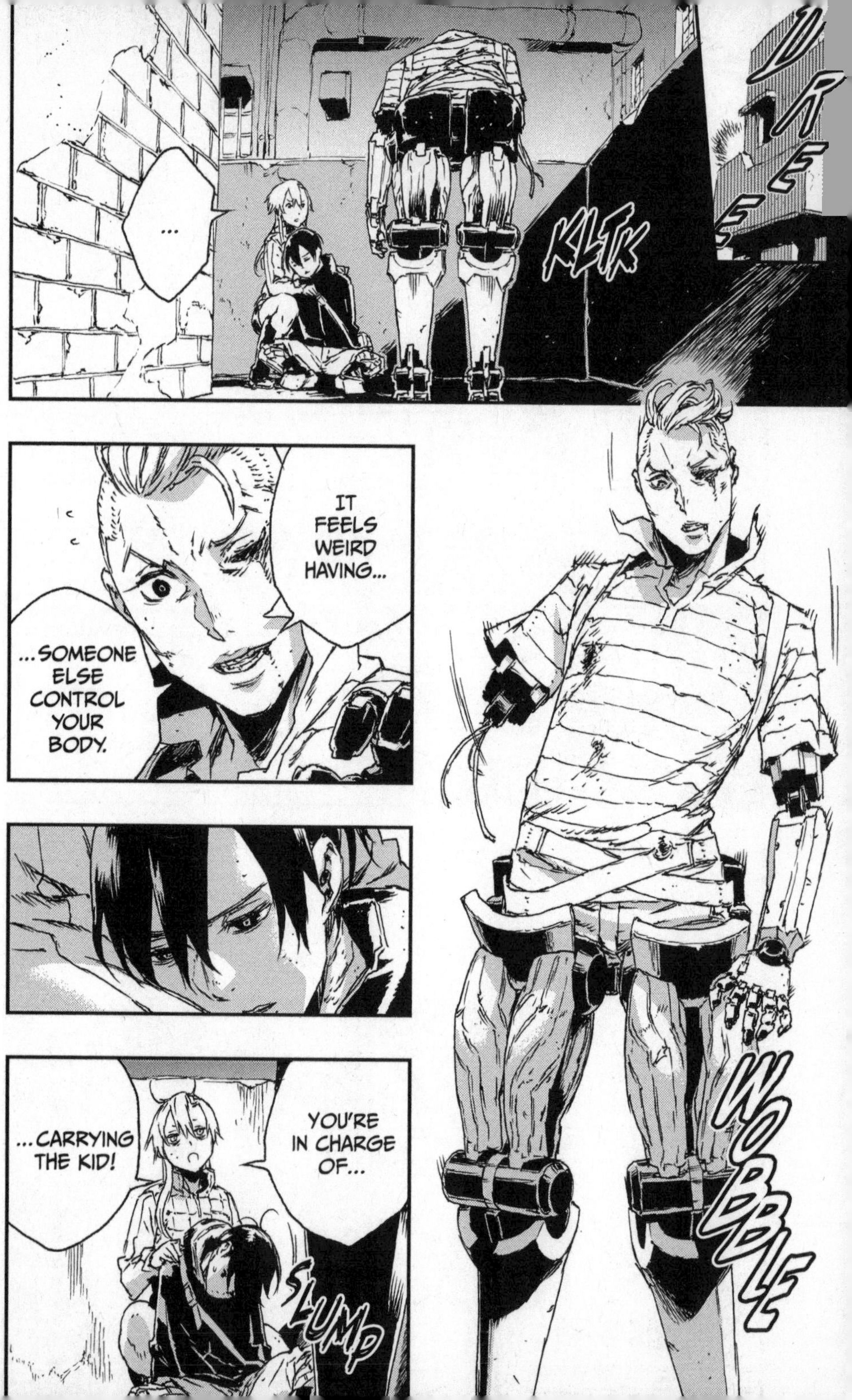
DREEEE
KLTK
...
WOBBLE
IT FEELS WEIRD HAVING...
...SOMEONE ELSE CONTROL YOUR BODY.
YOU'RE IN CHARGE OF...
...CARRYING THE KID!
SLUMP

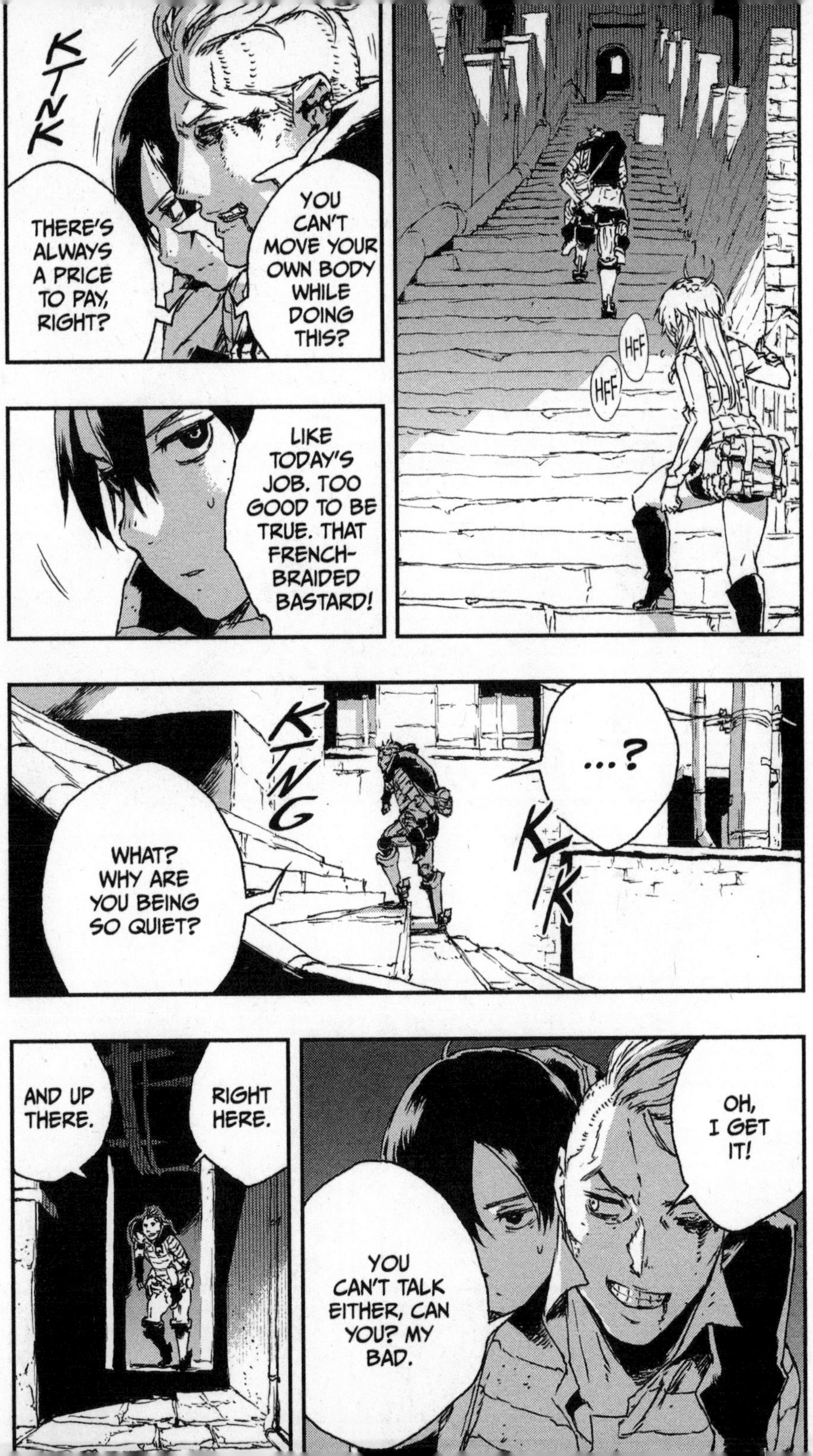
HFF
HFF
YOU CAN'T MOVE YOUR OWN BODY WHILE DOING THIS?
THERE'S ALWAYS A PRICE TO PAY, RIGHT?
KTNK
LIKE TODAY'S JOB. TOO GOOD TO BE TRUE. THAT FRENCH-BRAIDED BASTARD!
...?
KTNG
KTNK
WHAT? WHY ARE YOU BEING SO QUIET?
OH, I GET IT!
YOU CAN'T TALK EITHER, CAN YOU? MY BAD.
RIGHT HERE.
AND UP THERE.

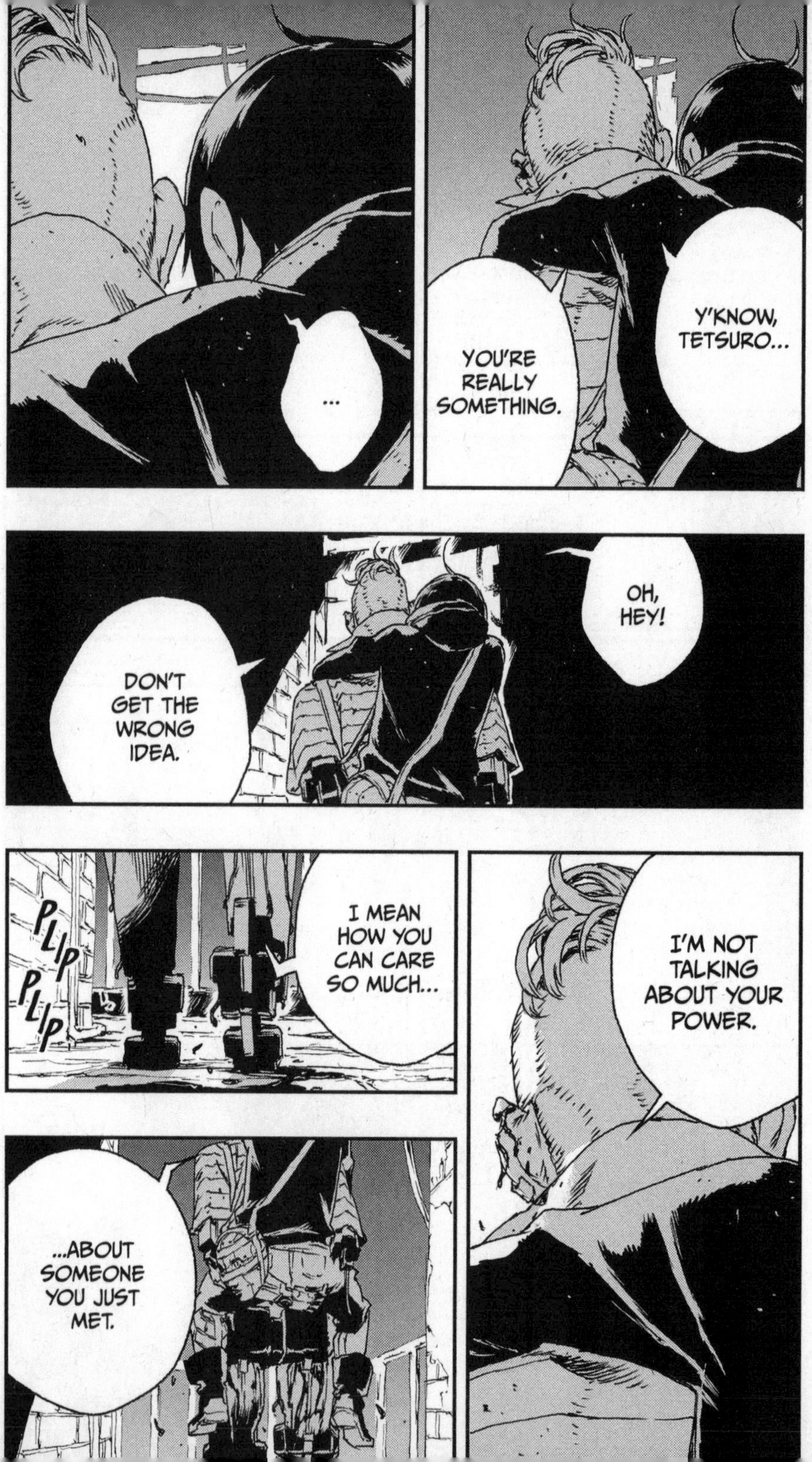
Y'KNOW, TETSURO...
YOU'RE REALLY SOMETHING.
...
OH, HEY!
DON'T GET THE WRONG IDEA.
I'M NOT TALKING ABOUT YOUR POWER.
I MEAN HOW YOU CAN CARE SO MUCH...
PLIP PLIP
...ABOUT SOMEONE YOU JUST MET.

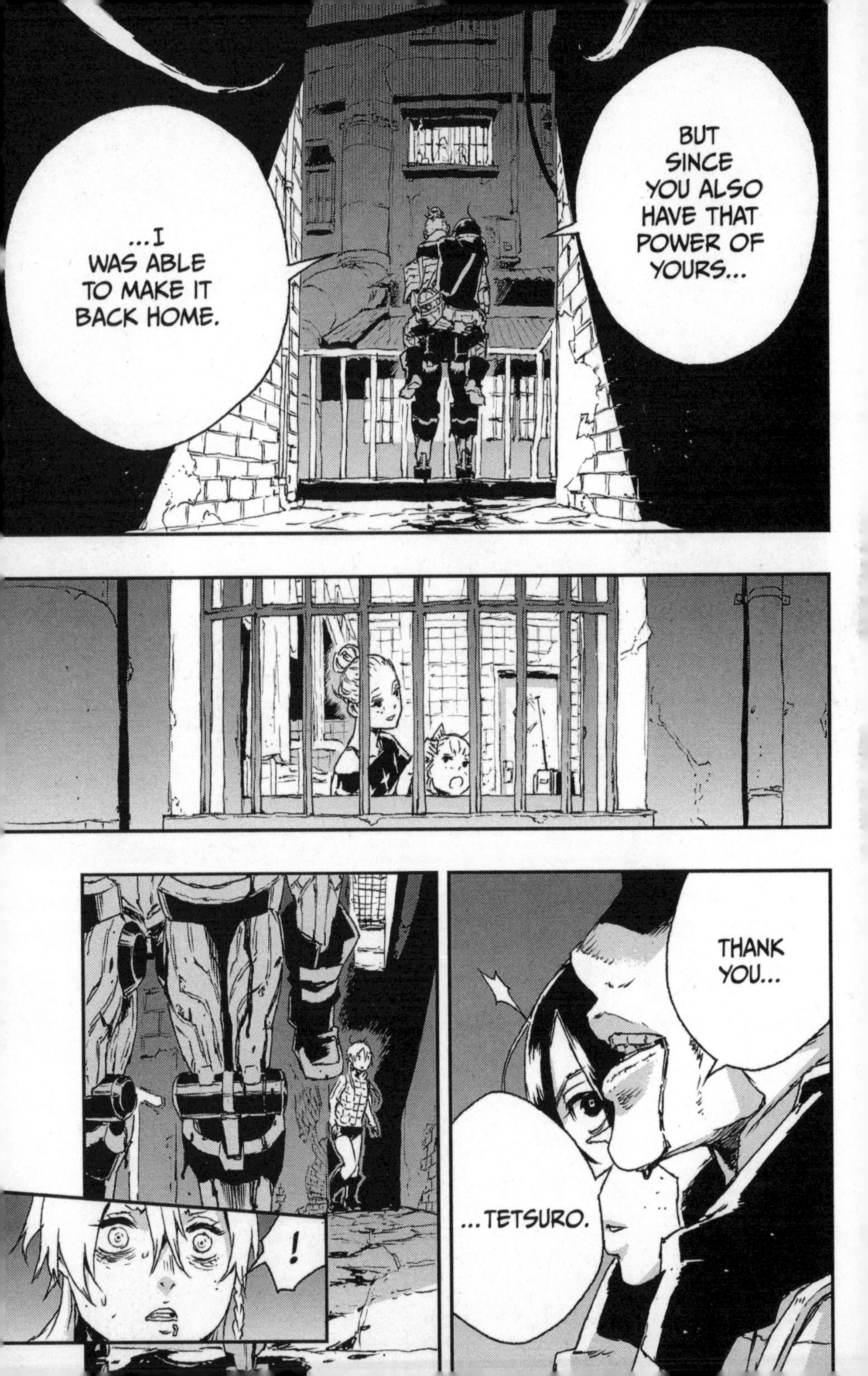
BUT SINCE YOU ALSO HAVE THAT POWER OF YOURS...
...I WAS ABLE TO MAKE IT BACK HOME.
THANK YOU...
...TETSURO.
!

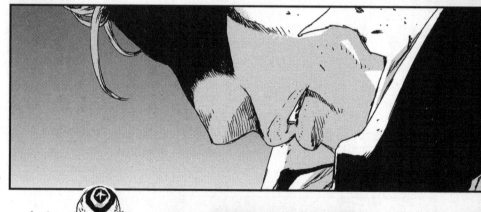

THE ATTACK
ON BERÜHREN'S
PRIVATE TRAIN WAS
A COMPLETE BUST,
SARISHAGAN.

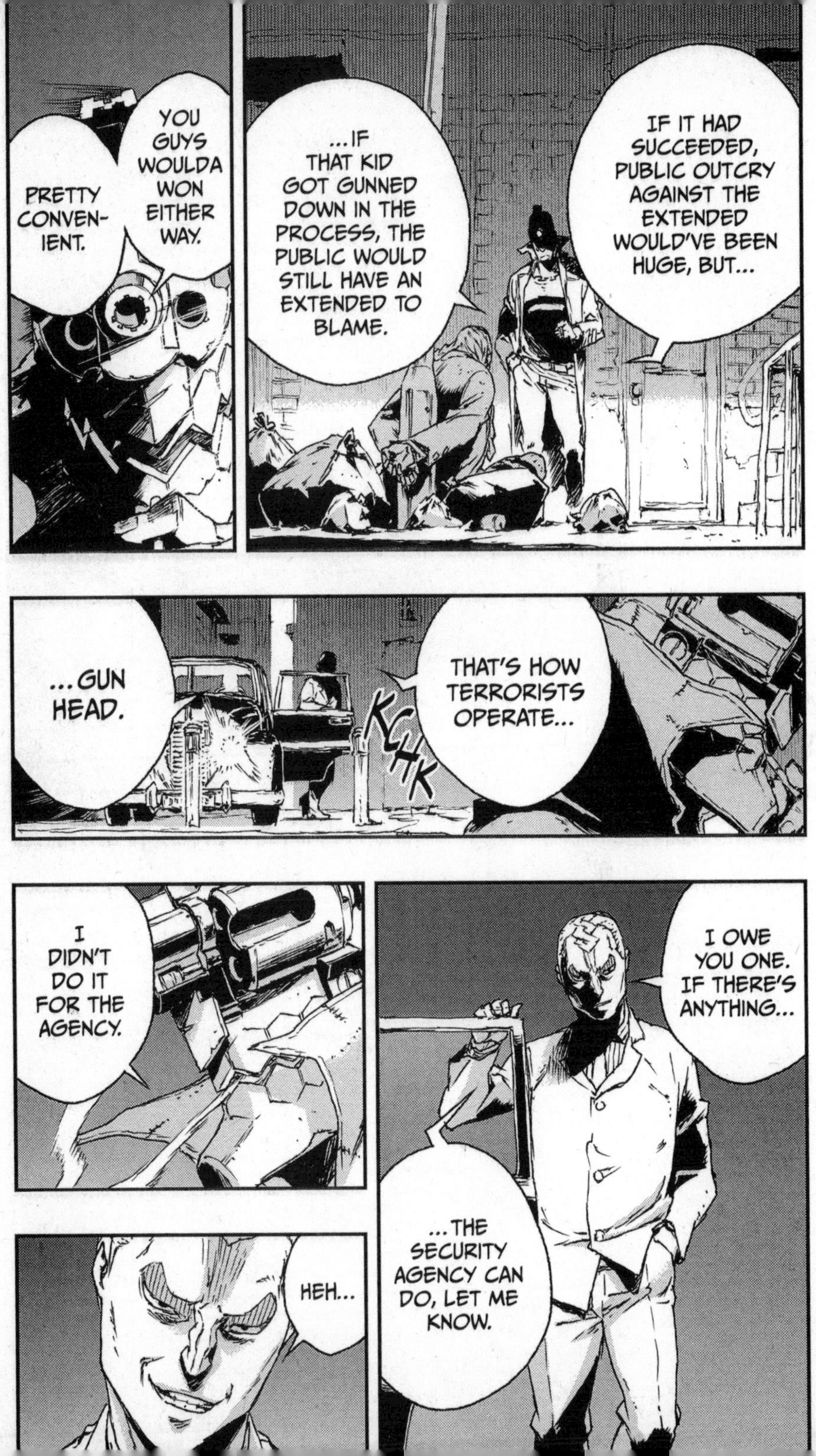
IF IT HAD SUCCEEDED, PUBLIC OUTCRY AGAINST THE EXTENDED WOULD'VE BEEN HUGE, BUT...
...IF THAT KID GOT GUNNED DOWN IN THE PROCESS, THE PUBLIC WOULD STILL HAVE AN EXTENDED TO BLAME.
YOU GUYS WOULDA WON EITHER WAY.
PRETTY CONVEN-IENT.
THAT'S HOW TERRORISTS OPERATE...
KCHK
...GUN HEAD.
I OWE YOU ONE. IF THERE'S ANYTHING...
...THE SECURITY AGENCY CAN DO, LET ME KNOW.
I DIDN'T DO IT FOR THE AGENCY.
HEH...

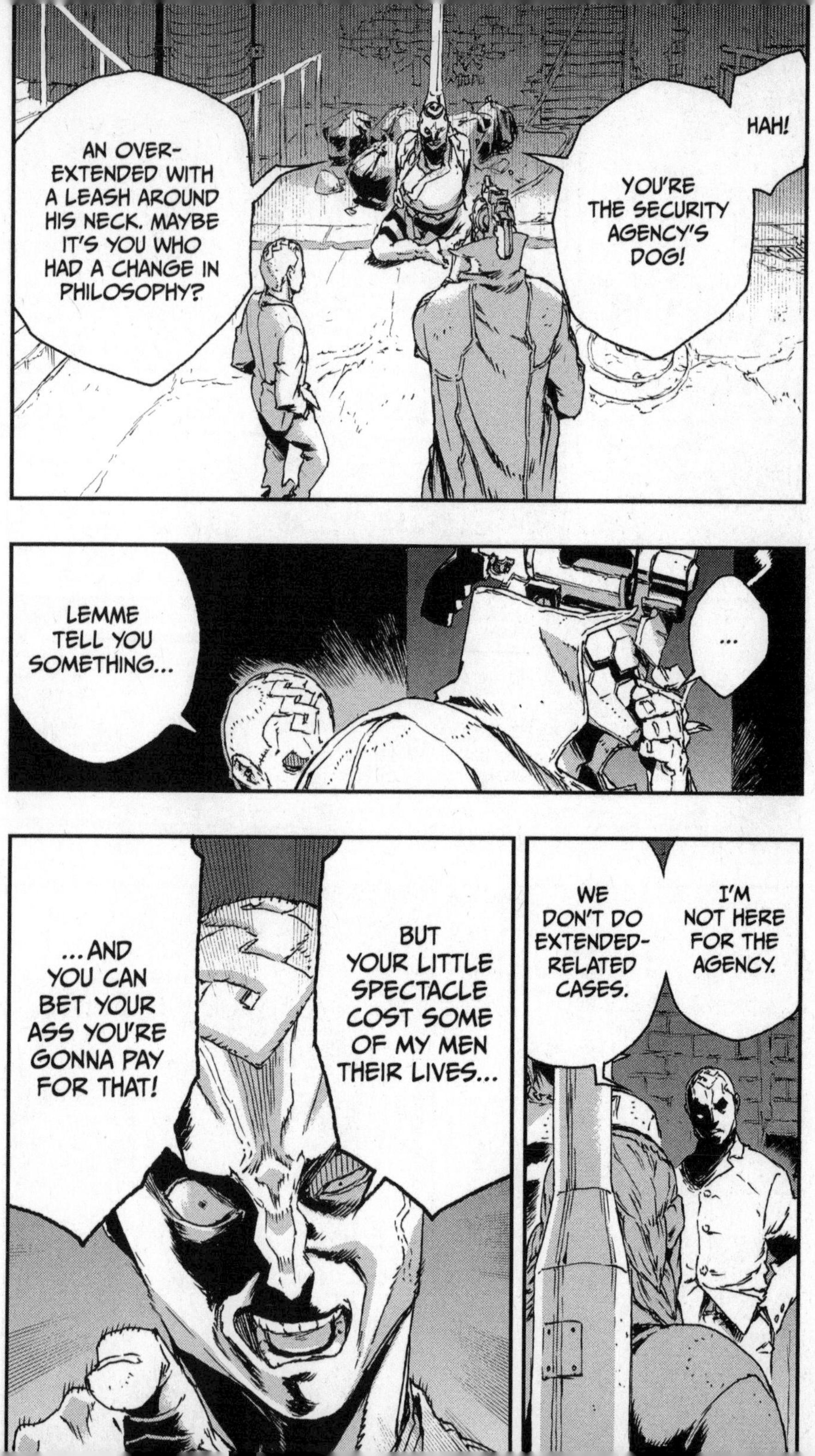
HAH!
YOU'RE THE SECURITY AGENCY'S DOG!
AN OVER-EXTENDED WITH A LEASH AROUND HIS NECK. MAYBE IT'S YOU WHO HAD A CHANGE IN PHILOSOPHY?
...
LEMME TELL YOU SOMETHING...
I'M NOT HERE FOR THE AGENCY.
WE DON'T DO EXTENDED-RELATED CASES.
BUT YOUR LITTLE SPECTACLE COST SOME OF MY MEN THEIR LIVES...
...AND YOU CAN BET YOUR ASS YOU'RE GONNA PAY FOR THAT!

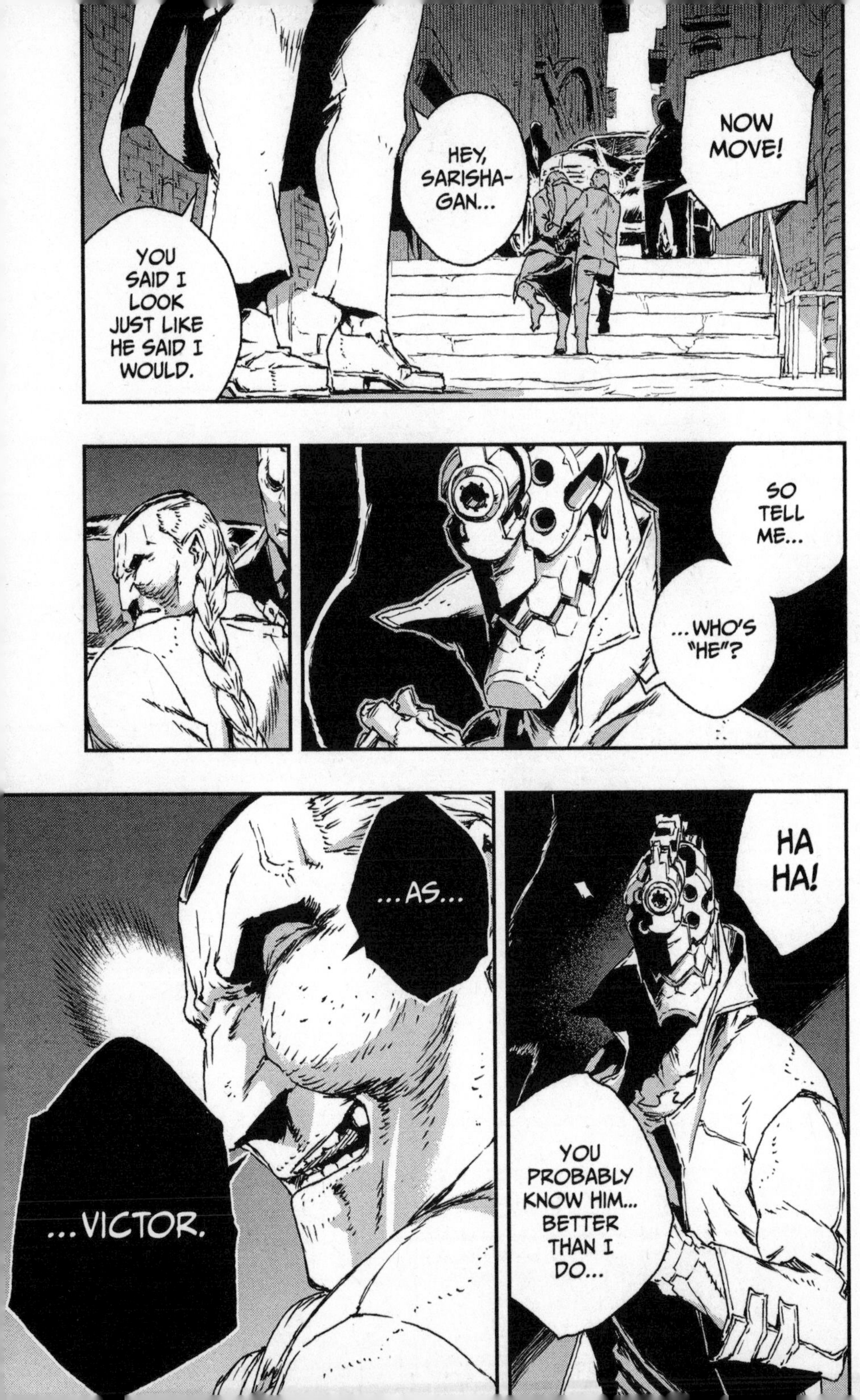
NOW MOVE!
HEY, SARISHA-GAN...
YOU SAID I LOOK JUST LIKE HE SAID I WOULD.
SO TELL ME...
...WHO'S "HE"?
HA HA!
YOU PROBABLY KNOW HIM... BETTER THAN I DO...
...AS...
...VICTOR.

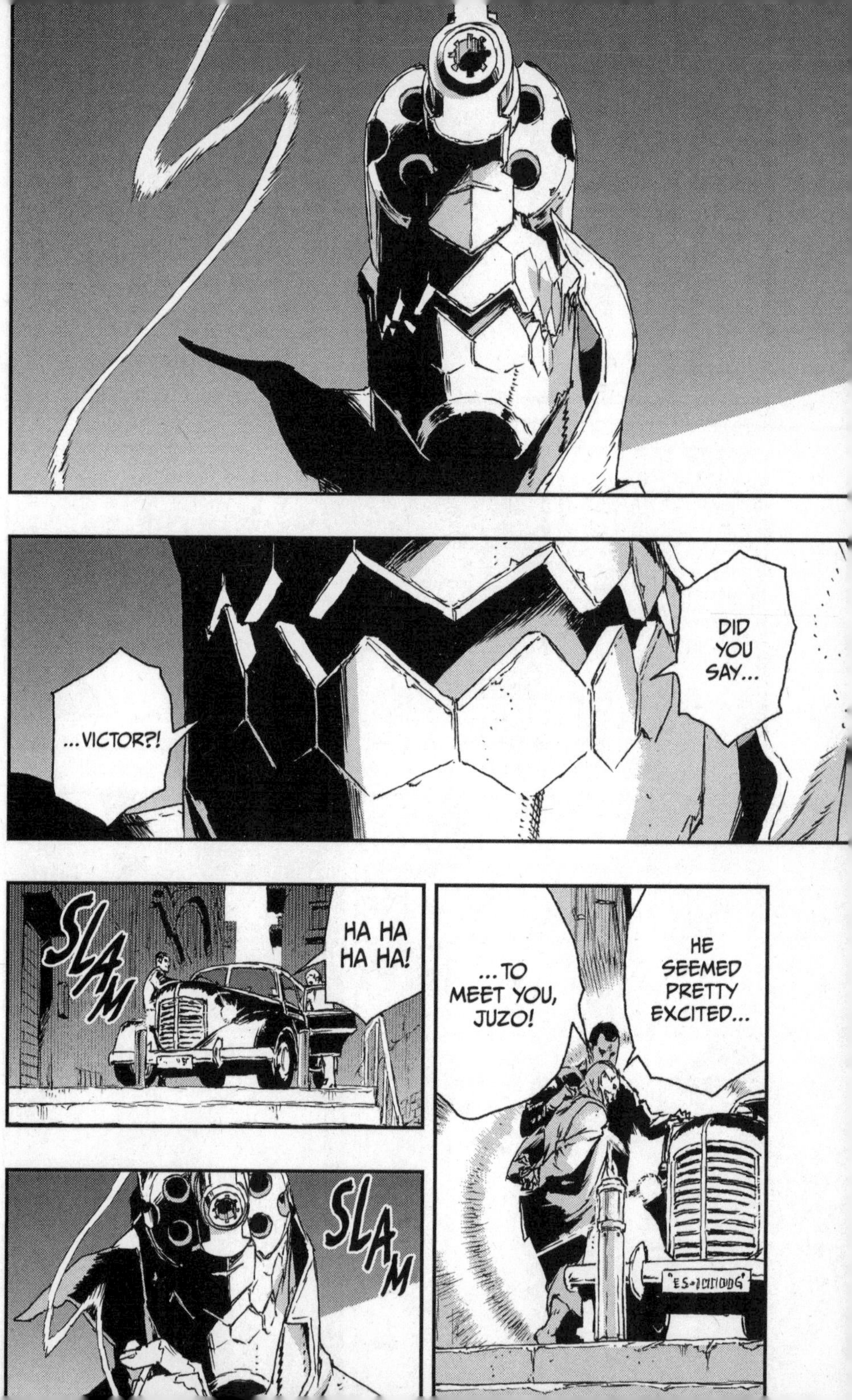
DID YOU SAY...
...VICTOR?!
HE SEEMED PRETTY EXCITED...
...TO MEET YOU, JUZO!
SLAM
HA HA HA HA!
SLAM

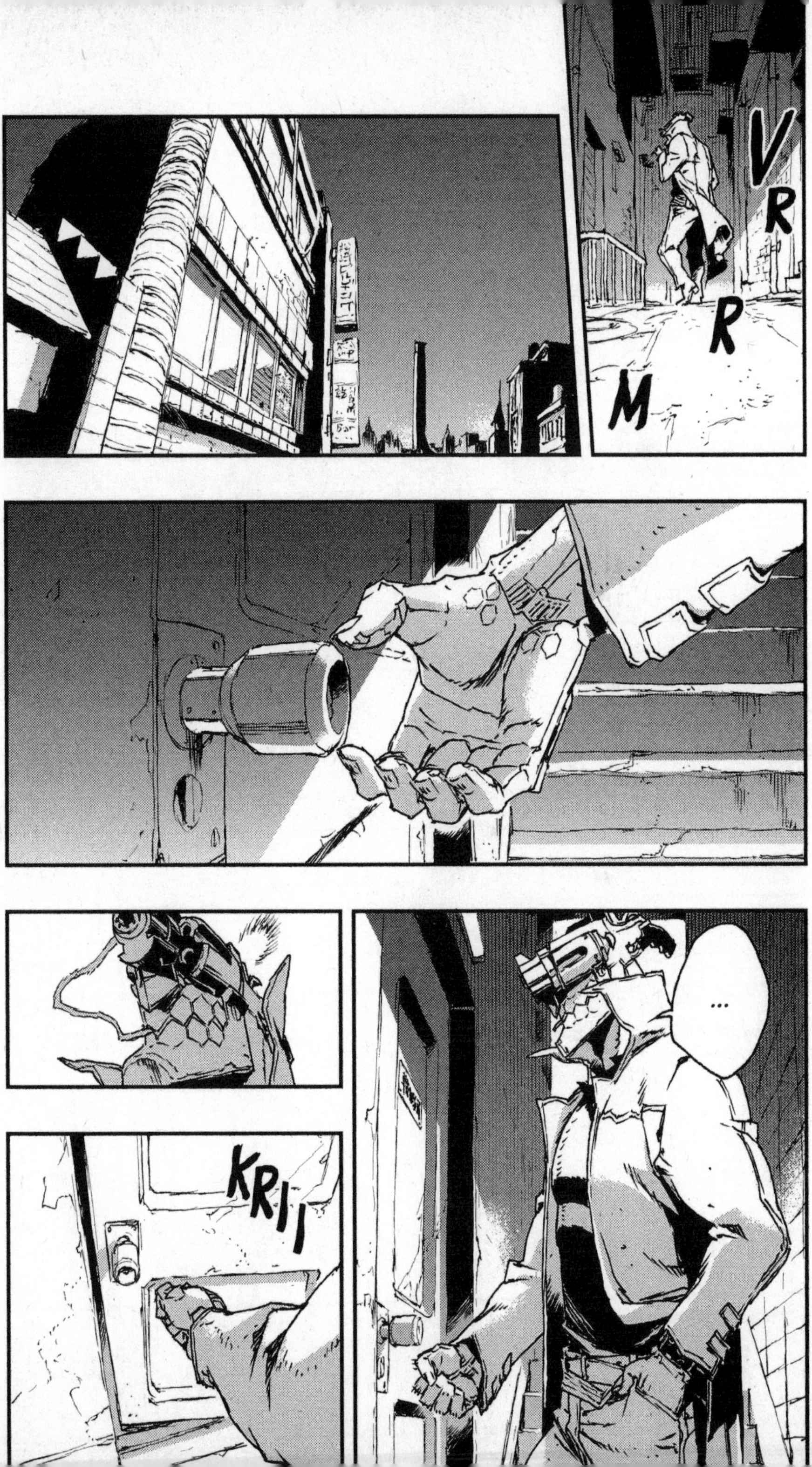
VRRM
...
KRII

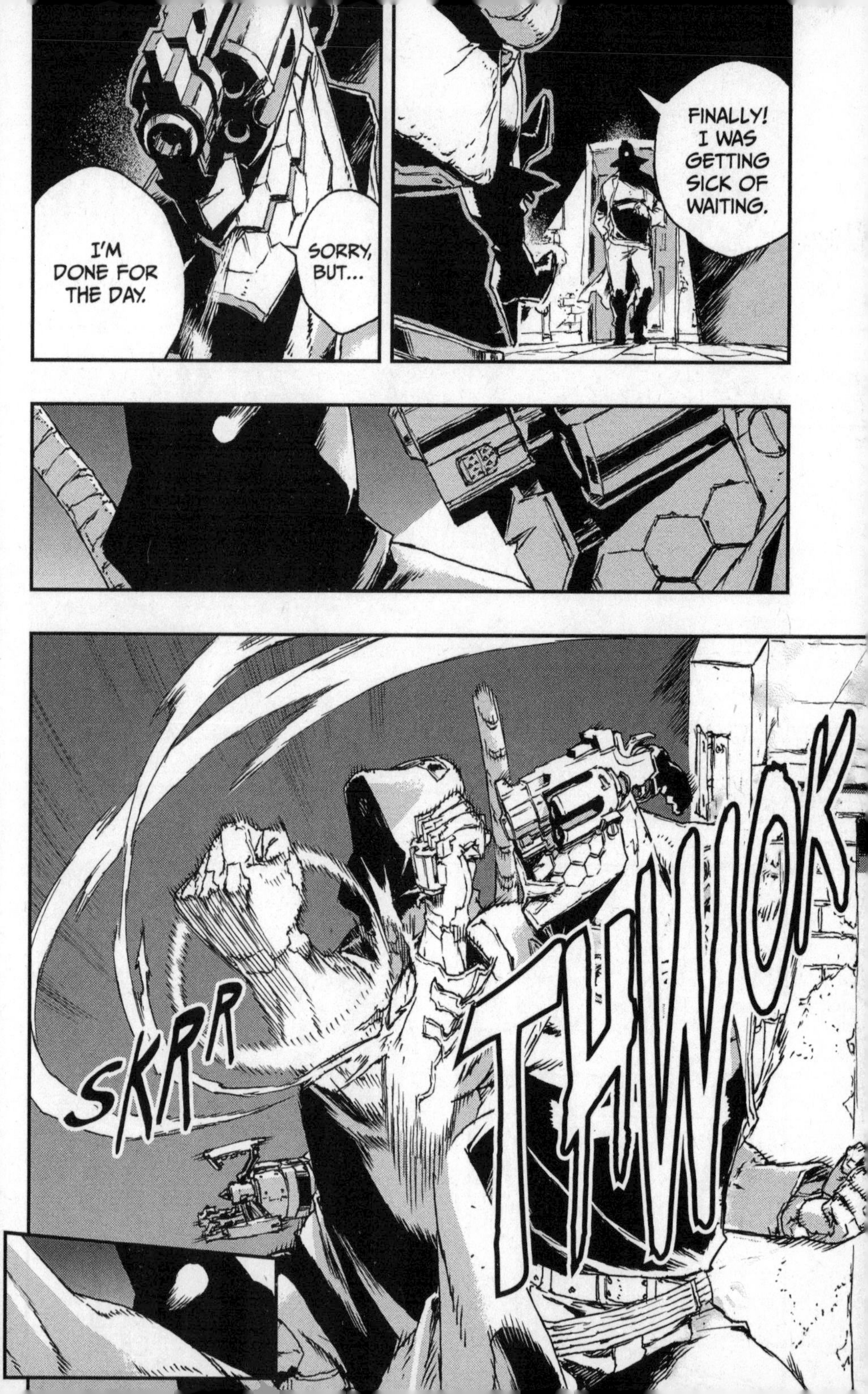
FINALLY! I WAS GETTING SICK OF WAITING.
SORRY, BUT...
I'M DONE FOR THE DAY.
THWOK
SKRR

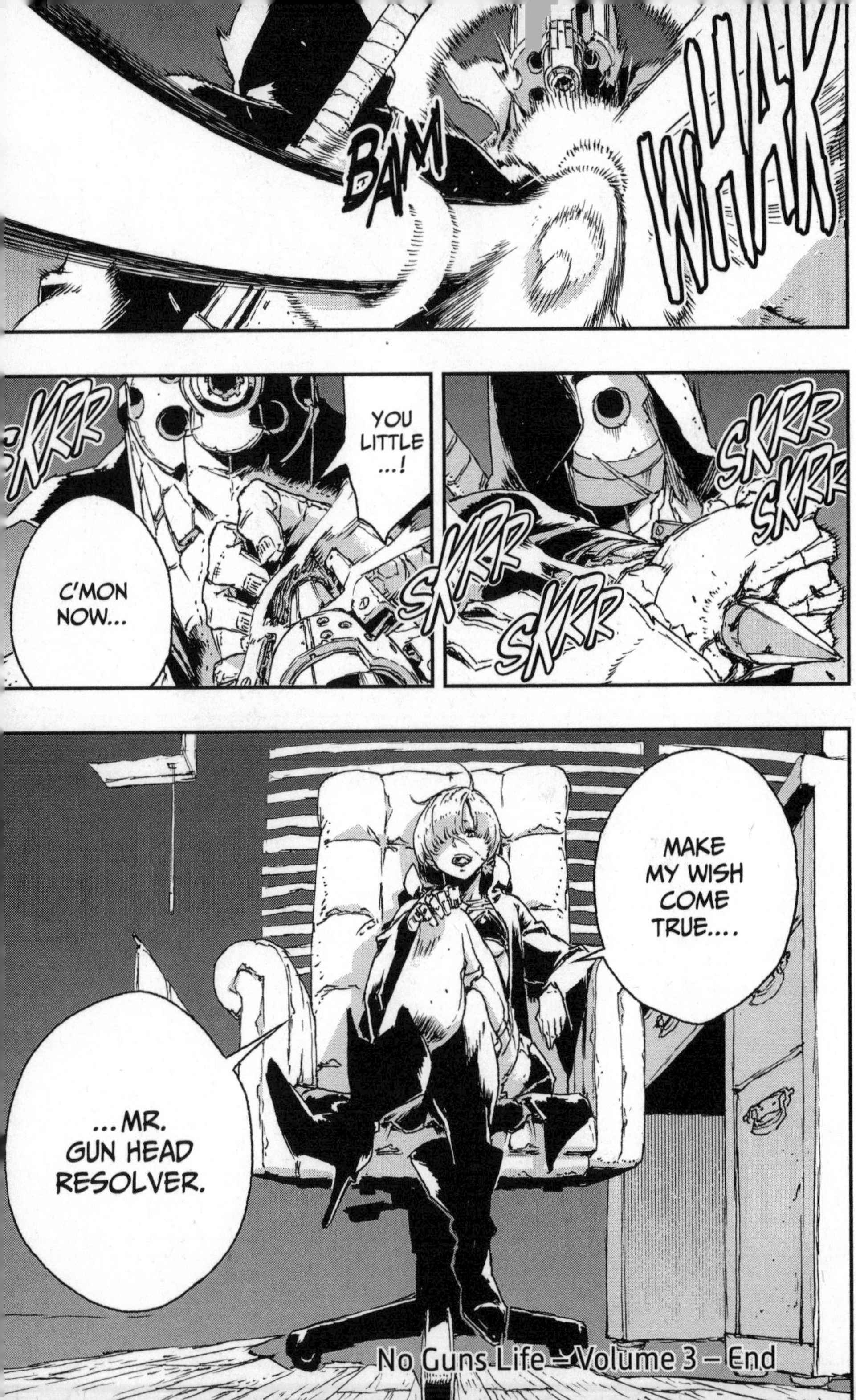
WHAK
BAM
SKRR
SKRR
SKRR
SKRR
YOU LITTLE ...!
SKRR
C'MON NOW...
MAKE MY WISH COME TRUE....
...MR. GUN HEAD RESOLVER.
No Guns Life – Volume 3 – End

No Guns Life

3

STORY AND ART BY
TASUKU KARASUMA

VIZ SIGNATURE EDITION

TRANSLATION **Joe Yamazaki**
ENGLISH ADAPTATION **Stan!**
TOUCH-UP ART & LETTERING **Evan Waldinger**
DESIGN **Shawn Carrico**
EDITOR **Mike Montesa**

NO・GUNS・LIFE © 2014 by Tasuku Karasuma
All rights reserved.
First published in Japan in 2014 by SHUEISHA Inc., Tokyo.
English translation rights arranged by SHUEISHA Inc.

The stories, characters and incidents mentioned
in this publication are entirely fictional.

No portion of this book may be reproduced or
transmitted in any form or by any means without
written permission from the copyright holders.

Printed in the U.S.A.

Published by VIZ Media, LLC
P.O. Box 77010
San Francisco, CA 94107

10 9 8 7 6 5 4 3 2 1
First printing, January 2020

PARENTAL ADVISORY
NO GUNS LIFE is rated T+ for Older Teen
and is recommended for ages 16 and
up. This volume contains violence, strong
language and adult themes.

YOU'RE
READING THE
WRONG WAY.

NO GUNS LIFE is printed from right to left in the original Japanese format in order to present the art as it was meant to be seen.